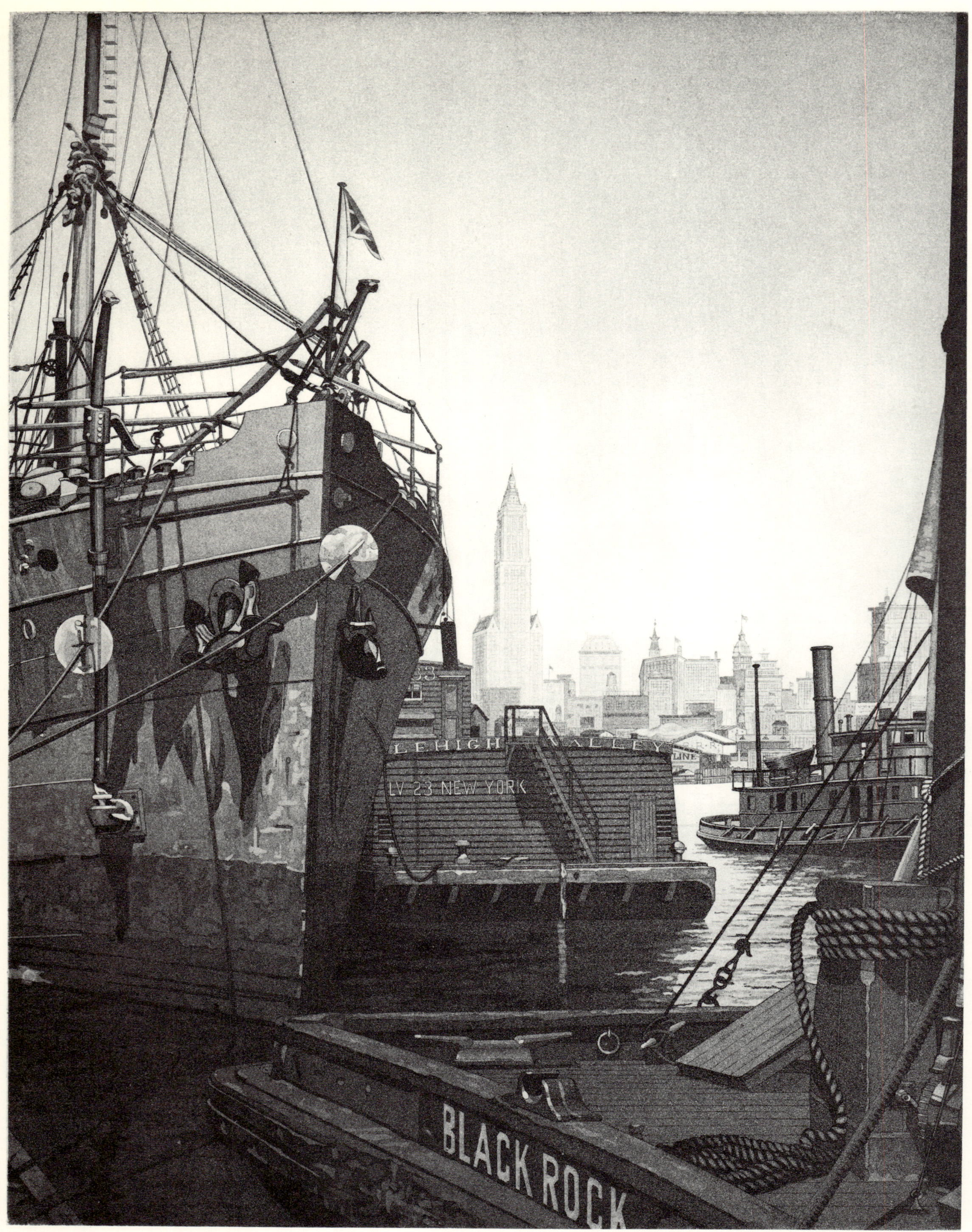
LEHIGH VALLEY
LV 23 NEW YORK
BLACK ROCK

GREAT AMERICAN PRINTS 1900-1950

138 LITHOGRAPHS, ETCHINGS AND WOODCUTS

June and Norman Kraeft

DOVER PUBLICATIONS, INC.
NEW YORK

Published in Canada by General Publishing Company, Ltd.,
30 Lesmill Road, Don Mills, Toronto, Ontario.
Published in the United Kingdom by Constable and Company,
Ltd., 10 Orange Street, London WC2H 7EG.

Great American Prints, 1900–1950: 138 Lithographs, Etchings and Woodcuts is a new work, first published by
Dover Publications, Inc., in 1984.

Manufactured in the United States of America
Dover Publications, Inc., 31 East 2nd Street,
Mineola, N.Y. 11501

Library of Congress Cataloging in Publication Data

Kraeft, June.
Great American prints, 1900–1950.

1. Prints, American. 2. Prints—20th century—
United States. 3. Printmakers—United States—Biography.
I. Kraeft, Norman. II. Title.
NE508.K7 1984 769.973 83-20580
ISBN 0-486-24661-2

ACKNOWLEDGMENTS

The print world is a wonderful field in which to work; so many of the people one encounters are warm, kind, enthusiastic and helpful. Such are the artists and members of their families, the curators, collectors and others listed in the paragraphs below, each of whom has generously cooperated with us in the preparation of this book. To each and every one a heartfelt thank-you.

We are pleased that all but six of the 138 illustrations in this book were made directly from original prints. The Butler Institute of American Art, Youngstown, Ohio, kindly lent the following original prints from their collection for reproduction: No. 46, *Still Life*, by Philip Evergood (gift of Carl L. Dennison); No. 78, *Circus Performer Balanced on a Ball*, by Yasuo Kuniyoshi (gift of Mrs. Edith Halpert); No. 79, *Girl Dressing*, by Yasuo Kuniyoshi; Nos. 96 and 97, *Gaiety Burlesk* and *2nd Avenue El*, by Reginald Marsh (gift of Louis Held).

The following original prints from their John Taylor Arms Collection were generously lent us for reproduction by the College of Wooster Art Museum, Wooster, Ohio: No. 4, *Self Portrait at 55 East Division Street*, by Ivan Albright; No. 53, *Where Next?*, by Douglas Gorsline; No. 58, *Mirror of the Goddess*, by Ernest Haskell; No. 61, *Virginia and a New York Winter Window*, by Childe Hassam; No. 81, *Three Kids and a Horse*, by Paul Landacre; and No. 135, *Abbot of Grottaferrata*, by Franklin T. Wood.

We are in the debt of the individuals who lent us the following originals from their own collections: No. 40, *Bourbon Street—New Orleans*, by Caroline Durieux, lent by Earl Retif; No. 41, *City Lights*, by Fritz Eichenberg, lent by the artist; No. 47, *Dawn in the Assembly*, by Don Freeman, lent by David Prosser, Jr.; No. 90, *Relics*, by Martin Lewis, lent by Mrs. Patricia Lewis; No. 93, *Traffic*, by Louis Lozowick, lent by Mrs. Louis Lozowick; No. 99, *Arrangement—New York*, by Jan Matulka, lent by John Axelrod. The balance of the original prints lent for reproduction in this book were provided by the authors.

We are grateful to The Cleveland Museum of Art for providing us with excellent photographs of the following prints in its collection: No. 43, *Queer Fish*, by Mabel Dwight (Mr. and Mrs. Lewis B. Williams Collection); No. 119, *Industrial Series No. 1*, by Charles Sheeler (gift of Mrs. Malcolm L. McBride). Similar thanks to The Art Institute of Chicago for Nos. 68 and 69, *The Lonely House* and *Night on the El Train*, by Edward Hopper; Nos. 94 and 95, *L'Opéra, Paris* and *Woolworth Building (The Dance)*, by John Marin (Alfred Stieglitz Collection).

Many artist-printmakers were helpful to us as this volume moved closer to reality. Among them: Aaron Bohrod, Paul Cadmus, Howard Cook, John Rogers Cox, Caroline Durieux, Clement Haupers, Irwin D. Hoffman, Gene Kloss, Armin Landeck, Roi Partridge, Doel Reed and James Swann.

We wish to extend our appreciation also to members of the families of artists, including Nicolai Cikovsky, Jr.; Mrs. Sally Kent Gorton, widow of Rockwell Kent; Mrs. Lawrence Kupferman; Ms. Tatiana Ruzicka, daughter of the late Rudolph Ruzicka; Mrs. Stow Wengenroth; and Mrs. John Winkler.

Museum officials and print curators have assisted us in many ways, too, and we sincerely thank Harold Joachim, Esther Sparks and Anselmo Carini of The Art Institute of Chicago; Sinclair Hitchings and Paul Swenson of the Boston Public Library; Clyde Singer of the Butler Institute of American Art; Louise Richards and Jane Glaubinger of The Cleveland Museum of Art; Karen Beall, formerly of the Library of Congress; Ira Bartfield of the National Gallery of Art, Washington, D.C.; Robert Rainwater of the New York Public Library; Mary Suzor of the Museum of Fine Arts, Springfield, Massachusetts; Clinton Adams of Tamarind Institute and the University of New Mexico Art Museum; and Karen Smith Shafts of the College of Wooster (Ohio) Art Museum.

Other individuals have been most helpful, too. Here are some of them, listed with the name of the artist on whom they shed new light for us: Ben Bassham (Robert Riggs); Marge and Julius Cohn (Grace Albee); David Finkbeiner (Charles Locke); Antoinette Kraushaar and Carole M. Pesner of Kraushaar Galleries (Peggy Bacon); Richard J. Miller (Lester G. Hornby); Dr. S. William Pelletier (John Taylor Arms); and Mrs. Gertrude Dennis of Weyhe Gallery (Mahonri Young).

Our publishers, Blanche and Hayward Cirker, and our editors, James Spero, Clarence Strowbridge and Stanley Appelbaum, took a lively, continuing and knowledgeable interest in our book, serving in many ways that exceeded the call of duty.

On the home front, Brian Hayes, our dependable Man Friday, did so many things for us as we plowed ahead through the book that he has almost become our Everyman Everyday. Finally, Prints, our German-shepherd puppy, while not exactly long-suffering during the writing, can now get back to more of those long, bounding excursions across the pasture that he loves.

CONTENTS

LIST OF PRINTS

A TRIUMPHANT REALISM IN PRINTS

Taken as a whole, American printmaking during the first half of the twentieth century was as rich, varied and accomplished as that of any country in any period in the history of the art. American printmakers of the period developed a multitude of art movements, but the dominant voice was a vibrant, triumphant realism that grew out of—and advanced—the realist tradition that had been at the core of American art from its beginnings. Our book focuses on the blossoming of this realism throughout the period 1900–50, but it does not include in its scope contemporary modernist movements which, for the most part, grew out of developments in European art and which have been the subject of other books.[1]

The period under discussion has already produced its giants, in the world view. George Bellows, Childe Hassam, Edward Hopper, John Marin, Charles Sheeler and John Sloan have deservedly achieved international renown; at least a dozen of their contemporaries are breathing at their heels.

In sheer number of artists, this remarkable period is staggering. The Library of Congress records more than 1,000 American printmakers whose major work was done between 1900 and 1950,[2] and prints by most of these artists are of considerably more than passing interest.

We believe that the 138 prints by 109 artists in this book give a true picture, a fair cross-section, a glimpse at the greatness achieved in this period. Our challenge was not to find 138 fine prints to represent the era; our problem was to edit the list of eligibles down to 138—538 would have been easier.

Why 1900 to 1950? These dates encompass the rise and full flowering of realist printmaking here in America and the beginnings of its temporary demise. Etching, lithography and the woodblock print all leaped to life here in America in fresh ways, as if the turn of the new century had given the stone, the copper plate and the boxwood block a new lease on life. A lively time it was as, for example, when John Sloan began his *New York City Life* series of etchings in 1905, depicting this life with a realism previously unknown in American graphic art—so much so that when "at the invitation of Charles Mielatz, in March, 1906, he [Sloan] sent the set of ten [etchings] to the American Water Color Society exhibition in New York, four of them were promptly rejected for being 'vulgar' and 'indecent.' "[3] Today, of course, all ten are classics.

In lithography it was Joseph Pennell who broke the ice. In 1904 he created 18 stunning lithographs of New York skyscrapers done with an exuberance and excitement new to American printmaking. Albert Sterner was another key figure who pioneered lithography as a fine art in the earliest years of this century.

In America the opening of the century also heralded a new era for the oldest of the print media—the woodcut. Prior to 1900 the woodblock print was utilized in this country largely for book and magazine illustration. Arthur Allen Lewis (in 1903) and Rudolph Ruzicka (about 1906) pioneered the woodcut as an art form independent of illustration.

Eugene Speicher put his finger on the pulse of the new realism in art when he wrote, "The lithographs and drawings of George Bellows are the glowing manifestations of a nature that was filled with a fierce passion for life. His enthusiasms were peculiarly American, and were charged with vitality, fresh air and frankness."[4] The same words could have been written of John Sloan, Reginald Marsh and many of the other realist American printmakers who followed these leaders.

Before we proceed, we should define what we mean by "realism" in prints. Webster defines realism in art and literature as "the attempted picturing of people and things as they really are." The *Random House Dictionary* agrees, describing realism in the fine arts as "treatment of forms, colors, space, etc., in such a manner as to emphasize their correspondence to actuality or to ordinary visual experience." The printmakers in this book are realists in these terms but, as artists, they add a dimension to their realism that gives added force to their creations. While picturing "things and people as they really are," they do so through the alchemy of their own vision and perception, abstracting what is significant to them and, through their technical skills, making simple, realistic scenes express all the beauty and power they feel in what they see before them. That is the magic of these printmakers: Finding no need to leave the real world for abstract realms, they reach into the highest, most exhilarating skies with both feet firmly planted on the ground.

ORGANIZING TWENTIETH-CENTURY AMERICAN REALIST PRINTS

Viewed historically, the realist tradition in American printmaking from 1900 to 1950 divides itself into six categories or movements, although not one of the artists represented in this book pledged allegiance to, or took membership in, any of these groups. Artists create art. Usually, they lend the lion's share of their energies to creating art rather than to organizing and working in groups, though they do that too. Historians find it useful to categorize. The work of many of these artists falls into two or more of the six above-mentioned categories, but the major thrust of the work of each usually places them easily into one group. The categories are: American Scene—Urban; American Scene—Rural and Small Town; "The People, Yes"; Satire and Caricature; Architectural Prints; Universal and Symbolic Themes.

The first two categories, identifying prints of the American Scene, represent more artists, more prints and more artistic activity than the other four groups combined. "American Scene" describes what this movement was all about. In the first years of the twentieth century, American artists looked about them and found in their own neighborhoods and environments a mother lode of esthetic riches none before them had discovered. As Christopher Columbus to their muse, they found a New World across the street, on the roof of the building in which they lived, in a dimly lit alley, a dingy hotel room, a crowded beach, a burlesque house. They looked hard and found simple but marvelous wonders in New England towns, in frontier villages, in Charleston, New Orleans, Chicago, Taos, New York and at points west, south and north from there. The mountains and valleys, wilderness and cotton plantations, farmland and desert, endless vistas and corner stores—all of the American Scene—turned into a promised land of inspiration for these artists and breathed fresh air through their esthetic impulses. The heart and soul of a barn, a movie marquee, a fishing shack or a taxicab glowed as it passed through the eye, mind, heart and then the hand of the artist who seemed literally to tremble in the exultation of discovery, finding in a familiar scene a new and exciting essence. These artists then applied their printmaking skills to these scenes, attaining uncommonly rich artistic achievements in deceptively simple pictures.

We selected each of the 138 prints in this volume not because it exemplifies something important about one of the movements dominating the era but simply because in the treasure chest of available choices it rose above its fellows as a superb work of art. We made no attempt to equalize by numbers the prints representing any particular category or movement. Our process told us what is becoming increasingly clear about this period of printmaking: American Scene was the name of the game from the earliest years of this century, even though the term was not applied to the printmaking art until sometime in the 1920s. More than 100 of the prints pictured here are accurately described as American Scene, and many of the others could also be placed in this category, even though stronger elements of their composition suggest that they belonged elsewhere.

The traditional histories of American realist prints from the first half of the twentieth century name and describe movements or schools of printmaking that arose during this period. Prominent among these were the Ashcan School (The Eight), the 14th Street School, The Ten (Impressionists), the Federal Art Projects (WPA) and the Regionalists. The reader may well ask why we do not use these categories, since they are established entities. The reasons are many. In the first place, a number of important figures (and lesser ones too) were not affiliated with any of these groups: Bellows, Hopper, Martin Lewis, to name a few. Second, in some cases only a few members of a group made prints. Of the Ashcan School, for example, only John Sloan and Arthur B. Davies made any important body of prints. Of The Ten, prints were created only by Childe Hassam, John Henry Twachtman and Julian Alden Weir. Third, the stormy history of Regionalism and its identity problems caused by American Scene art, a broader movement contemporaneous with Regionalism, suggest a blending of these two, for historical purposes. Fourth, the thousands of prints made by artists on the WPA projects were of so many styles and techniques that about the only thing they had in common was that they were made on the WPA.

Two other entities on the American art scene in the early years of this century have left their mark on art history: the Armory Show of 1913 and the movement spearheaded by Alfred Stieglitz. However, the Armory Show, an extravaganza that opened the doors of modern European art to American audiences, primarily featured paintings and sculpture; there were relatively few prints: representing American realist printmakers we only find prints by Frank Nankivell, John Sloan, J. Alden Weir and a monotype by Abraham Walkowitz in the catalogue raisonné. While Alfred Stieglitz was a seminal figure on many fronts in the first decades of the century, the artists and printmakers featured in his "291" and, later, An American Place galleries, were, for the most part, stylistic innovators rather than those whose work was grounded in realism.

We have concluded that any study purporting to cover American realist printmaking of the first half of the twentieth century would face insurmountable problems proceeding from a consideration of only the known movements of that period. That is why we have devised our groupings which, we believe, encompass all (or nearly all) of the realist printmaking of the era. The work of artists in all of the known groups fits appropriately, we think, into at least one of the six categories.

AMERICAN SCENE—URBAN

"Hail, Manhattan!" wrote Jerome Myers. "The Unbelievable City!" exclaimed Joseph Pennell. These are just two of the expressions of twentieth-century American artists who were awed as they experienced the life, the people, but primarily the architecture of the American Big City.

> . . . myself with a solitary crayon pencil, peering at the crowded East Side of New York City, making notes of the historical poor . . . At nightfall the surcease of a great city, the repose in the parks, or on the recreation piers, the aged gossip, the children at their endless play—a panorama which was for me unceasing in its interest, thrilling in its significance.[5]

Thus Jerome Myers tells us how he reacted to the urban American Scene.

Joseph Pennell describes how it was to come sailing into New York harbor:

> As the steamer moves up the bay, on its left the Great Goddess greets you . . . with the city beyond, finer than any in the world that ever existed . . . Piling up higher and higher right before you is New York . . . To the right, filmy and lace-like by day, are the great bridges; by night a pattern of stars that Hiroshige never knew. Golden statues are about you, triumphal arches make splendid frames for endless vistas . . . The Unbelievable City . . . the city that inspires me, that I love.[6]

Myers and Pennell (and we could have quoted many of

their fellow American artists of the early twentieth century) set the stage for the printmaking heyday that burst upon the American Scene with the turn of the century, a time of exuberant discovery of all the magic contained in the American Big City, in all its aspects. Let us look at how these printmakers treated them.

Streets and Dwellings. In the 1890s Charles Frederick William Mielatz broke new ground in American etching when he brought a fresh realism to his many prints of New York City, anticipating by a decade or more what Sloan, Bellows, Martin Lewis, Marsh and their generation achieved in prints that celebrate the exhilaration and excitement of the metropolis. Mielatz's 1892 etching *Wall Street* (No. 103) shows an architectural etcher at work, choosing a group of buildings from a vantage point that shows each one as different from each of its neighbors in shape, style, personality and etched color.

Childe Hassam's 1918 lithograph *Lafayette Street* (No. 60) catches the pulse of New York thoroughfares—rich with flags—as surely as do his etchings and paintings of similar subjects. We do not know of another artist whose lithographs differ so completely from his etchings. Hassam's etchings—literal renderings executed in strokes that dance—contrast sharply with the seemingly primitive drawing in his lithographs—line and smear that somehow coalesce in an imaginative but clarion-clear statement of his subject.

At about the same time, Lester George Hornby, a Boston artist who liked to travel, caught superbly the contagious confusion of Chicago's downtown streets in his bold but controlled etched lines in *State Street from Van Buren Street* (No. 67).

Contemporaneously, John Winkler was busy etching picturesque scenes in San Francisco. *Fisherman's Home on Telegraph Hill* (No. 133) exemplifies his free and inventive drawing style. Julius Lankes found in Washington, D.C. a subject well suited to his skills in wood engraving. In *"N" Street House, Georgetown* (No. 84), he elicits from his woodblock creamy whites and haunting blacks that blend in a richly satisfying atmospheric piece. Earl Horter caught the essence of New Orleans, its lacy grillwork, its balconied architecture, in his *Creole Quarter—New Orleans* (No. 70). Back in New York, Peggy Bacon told just how it was at *The Noon Hour* (No. 7) on East 15th Street near Irving Place and Third Avenue. Her etching needle was never busier—neither was the street, with its vegetable cart, dog-walker, street musicians, kids, brawlers, cleaning woman and the ubiquitous people looking from upstairs windows.

At the Water's Edge. The rivers and harbors and marine vistas that surround the island of Manhattan were not lost on its printmakers. In 1910 Rudolph Ruzicka, one of the earliest of the twentieth-century American woodblock artists, lent subtle brilliance to a superb composition, *East River, Winter* (No. 115). In 1921 John Taylor Arms created one of his masterpieces in aquatint, *Early Morning, North River* (No. 2), in which a configuration of ships in the foreground is boldly strengthened in the sinews of Arms's architectural skills and played off against the New York skyline in the background, done in contrasting lighter tones. The harbor at night, with a tall ship standing erect and majestic in the water, seen in the reflection of many lights along the shore, is rendered by Kerr Eby in his richly atmospheric *Harbor Lights* (No. 44). Genre American Scene, at the water's edge, was never more poignantly portrayed than in Nicolai Cikovsky's marvelous *On the East River* (No. 26), with its two men, world-weary, resting on the pier. Victoria Hutson Huntley, in what is possibly her most ambitious print, *Lower New York* (No. 71), uses the city as a proscenium for a harbor vista in which the Statue of Liberty is but one element enriching the horizon.

City People Doing Their Thing. Jerome Myers describes the action in his lithograph *An Old Doorway* (No. 104): "Children are playing school, changing places with one another as teachers, a miniature democracy of make-believe education . . ."[7] One could single out many elements that have gone into the intense realism of Edward Hopper's etching *Night on the El Train* (No. 69), but the focus, in our view, must be on the man and the woman, the twist of whose bodies reflects and symbolizes the tensions between them. John Sloan devoted much of his etching career to New York City people going about their business and pleasure. Of his 1926 *Easter Eve, Washington Square* (No. 120), Sloan wrote, "An aquatint record of an April shower, happy girls and spring flowers . . . I saw that. It happened."[8] Those last five words are the quintessence of Sloan. We also include Sloan's 1941 etching *Sunbathers on the Roof* (No. 121), one of the last of his many great etchings of New York City life. Sloan wrote of it, "This etching, done many years after most of my New York plates, is, I think, of equal merit."[9]

George Overbury ("Pop") Hart knew city people, and he drew them with a warmth and compassion seldom matched in the art of his time. His etching *Working People* (No. 57) conveys the boredom, the stultifying routines that thread their daily lives. Working people of another sort are pictured in the four lithographs comprising the series *The People Work*, mural-like pieces, each depicting a time of day, done by Benton Spruance in 1937. Our choice, *The People Work—Night* (No. 123), in a series of newsreel flashes, gives perspective and a sharp immediacy to his subject.

Kenneth Hayes Miller is best known for his etchings of women shoppers, perhaps the most famous being *Leaving the Shop* (No. 101). Other incisive prints made during the 1930s showing city people in action include Isabel Bishop's classic etching of two working girls talking things over in *The Noon Hour* (No. 14); Grant Reynard's evocation of theatergoers in all their finery seated in *The Loge* (No. 112); Minna Citron's wonderful spoof *Dress Circle—Carnegie Hall* (No. 27), in which the upper crust pose in their last-row seats while hoi polloi drape themselves on and around the floor behind. Fritz Eichenberg's *City Lights* (No. 41) captures Times Square at its most raucous. Sailors on the prowl, a mad saxophonist, mounted police trying to keep order, a newsboy hawking the headlines, and the million and one signs in lights all jell in Eichenberg's crowded but deftly organized composition.

Night Over the City. New York at night was a subject that many American printmakers of the 1920s and 1930s found irresistible. In 1928 Martin Lewis created his haunting masterpiece *Relics* (No. 90), a brilliant drypoint of a New York street corner at night, seen from a slight elevation, perhaps a second-story window. The work has a surface similarity to

Edward Hopper's 1921 etching, *Night Shadows*. The Lewis print is more realistic; Hopper's concentrates on mood.

Jefferson Market (No. 15), a 1931 lithograph by Aaron Bohrod in powerful blacks and menacing grays, pictures an el train rumbling through a lonely night over a nearly deserted street corner, against the backdrop of a tall black clock tower (a part of the Jefferson Market Courthouse in Greenwich Village). Much of the awe that Joseph Pennell felt as he gazed upon his "Unbelievable City" must have been felt also by Walter Tittle as he created his *Manhattan Minarets* (No. 126), picturing a young man (possibly the artist) sitting on a New York rooftop gazing in awe at the skyscrapers, swathed in their own light, which rise above him into the night. Ernest Fiene, most of whose graphic work consisted of lithographs, ventured occasionally into etching. His 1932 *City Lights* (No. 48), subtitled *Madison Square Park*, shows us the magic of New York buildings lit at night and seen from one of the city's delightful small parks. Urban printmakers across America also saw the bewitching tonalities across their own towns at night. An example is James Swann's etching *Night in Chicago* (No. 125), which catches the excitement of Lake Shore Drive on the near north side, looking south to the beginning of the Loop.

From the Subway to the Elevated. Below ground, at street level and above ground, New Yorkers have always been on the move. Charles Mielatz's excitingly composed 1891 etching *In the Bowery* (No. 102), teems with transportation on two levels: horse-drawn streetcars, wagons and carts on the ground; steam-powered elevated trains above. Reginald Marsh's 1929 etching *2nd Avenue El* (No. 97) takes us inside an elevated car. The scene reflects the "slice-of-life" realism made popular in the literature of the day by such novelists as Theodore Dreiser and James T. Farrell. In 1930 Louis Lozowick composed *Traffic* (No. 93), a remarkable lithograph in which vehicular movement on three levels is brilliantly meshed: automobiles at street level, and elevated trains on several planes above in an orchestration of posed motion. Also from 1930 comes Martin Lewis' extraordinary *Subway Steps* (No. 91), American realism at its finest. Lewis has selected a most unusual vantage point, the bottom of a subway stairway, as he looks up the stairs to the street, to the buildings and to the sky above. The two women and the little girl on the stairway, New Yorkers all, give the scene life.

Footlights, Backstage and the Circus Trail. Reginald Marsh never tired of depicting the burlesque house or its habitués—on both sides of the footlights. Typical is *Gaiety Burlesk* (No. 96). Of burlesque Marsh said, "The whole thing is extremely pictorial. You get a woman in the spotlight, the gilt architecture of the place, plenty of humanity. Everything is nice and intimate."[10] A casual side of the entertainment world was caught in the skillfully composed and executed *Dancers Resting* (No. 122) by Raphael Soyer. The circus, a favorite theme of many printmakers of various periods and places, also attracted Americans, who imparted to their renditions a distinct national spark and flavor. We picture two examples—Yasuo Kuniyoshi's *Circus Performer Balanced on a Ball* (No. 78) and Robert Riggs's *Elephant Act* (No. 113).

The City's Magic. Though the works about to be mentioned could have been included in one or another of the preceding subdivisions of American Scene—Urban prints, we single them out as portraying the big city in an epic, or otherwise special, manner transcending the particular realism that brings it to life. John Marin's 1913 etching *Woolworth Building (The Dance)* (No. 95) is pure exuberance. One cannot but share the exhilaration that Marin must have experienced as he looked at that structure and imagined it veering, dancing, into the sky, with even the trees joining in the movement. The flights of Marin's fancy go far, to be sure, from the realist base upon which they are built, and this etching exemplifies (though with greater imagination than in the work of many) what his contemporaries among American printmakers had in common with him: Without losing to total abstraction the particular American scene that inspired them, they did abstract what was important to them in that scene, and made it richer by investing it with their artistry.

Jan Matulka's breathtaking—and breathless—lithograph of New York buildings from about 1925, *Arrangement—New York* (No. 99), is a rhapsodic vista of a New York skyline seen from the middle of the city, where the buildings all seem related, almost ready to pose for a family portrait. Glenn O. Coleman's *Still Life* (No. 30) again pictures a rich vista of New York, but through an original device. The vista is seen in the mirror of a dresser in what must be a young man's room. New York is many things, not the least of them being elegance. And who has captured that aspect of the city more surely than Childe Hassam? *Virginia and a New York Winter Window* (No. 61) is elegance from platemark to platemark. The serene portrait of the lady, the magnificent lilies that must give her deep pleasure, the lacy curtains that do so much to establish the mood of the piece, and the New York street viewed through the window, all create a many-splendored scene.

What more fitting climax to this section than reference to a great lithograph of the Brooklyn Bridge: Stow Wengenroth's *Manhattan Gateway* of 1948 (No. 130), one of the four prints he made of this wonder of the world. It is evening, and the piece is bewitchingly illuminated. In a charge of super-realism, Stow brings us right onto the bridge and, if we were barefoot, we would surely get slivers between our toes, so real are the boards on which we are walking. Splendid lithography enhances his celebration of the structure, making the print a landmark triumph of realism in American art.

AMERICAN SCENE—RURAL AND SMALL TOWN

In the preceding section we reviewed some of the high points among the prints made by American artists of the first half of the twentieth century depicting the big-city aspect of the American Scene. The other large category of American Scene prints created in this period shows rural and small-town scenes in every part of the United States. The prints of rural scenes in particular became known as "Regionalist." "The name Regionalism," wrote Thomas Hart Benton, one of its major practitioners,

> was taken, I believe, from a group of southern writers . . . who in the late twenties called themselves "agrarians." These, turning from the over-mechanized, over-commercialized, over-cultivated life of our metropolitan centers, were seeking the sense of American life in its sectional or regional cultures. It was

applied to [Grant] Wood, [John Steuart] Curry and me with some degree of fitness but mainly, I suspect, because the fashions of the time called for classifications . . .[11]

Grant Wood, in his credo in support of Regionalism, wrote, "I believe in the regional movement in art and letters . . . but I wish to place no narrow interpretation on such regionalism. There is, or at least there need be, no geography of the art mind or of artistic talent or appreciation." In the same essay he also wrote, "a cult or a fad for Midwestern materials is just what must be avoided. Regionalism has already suffered from a kind of cultism which is essentially false."[12]

John Steuart Curry, the other member of the Regionalist Big Three, in a 1935 article on the subject, "What Should the American Artist Paint?," does not mention the word Regionalism even though he, with Benton and Wood, was front and center in the controversy swirling about this school of art. He does refer to the Regionalist concept, but in terms of American Scene: "Thousands of us are now painting what is called 'the American scene.' We are glorifying landscapes, elevated stations, subways, butcher shops, 14th Street, Mid-Western farmers, and we are one and all painting out of the fullness of our life and experiences."[13]

Benton, too, saw serious limitations to the concept of "Regionalism." He wrote, "But this Regionalism was not a clear term. Neither Wood, Curry nor I ever held ourselves, either in space or time, to any American region. . . . This was particularly true of my case. I was after a picture of America in its entirety." He concludes, ". . . we were bent on returning painting to its historic representational purpose and, further, in the interests of an American art, to making it represent matter drawn from American life and meaningful to those living that life."[14]

These quotations from the leaders of Regionalism give the essence of their beliefs. Through all of them, and through many of their other writings, runs this thread: Regionalism as such was too confining, too restrictive a concept to embrace adequately all that they and their fellow "Regionalists" were trying to do in their art. Benton again:

Wood, Curry and I thought of ourselves simply as American or Americanist painters, sectional at one moment, national and historical at others. If we dealt largely with "agrarian" subjects, it was because these were significant parts of our total American experience. Surely man and the earth were not so new to art that our returns thereto needed a special name.[15]

Curry apparently preferred the term American Scene, as do the present writers. All Regionalist prints are prints of some American Scene, and nearly all American Scene prints depict some Regionalist scene. (There are exceptions: for example, interior scenes such as Wanda Gág's *Siesta*, No. 50, or George Jo Mess's *Four O'Clock*, No. 100, could have been found in different parts of the United States.)

Therefore (and also for purposes of simplification) we are using the classification American Scene to embrace all prints in which representations of urban, rural and small-town subjects predominate.

American Scene—Rural. Many sights across America—her farms, prairies, deserts, mountains and valleys—attracted printmakers who made memorable images of them. John Edward Costigan etched *Woman, Boy, Goats* (No. 31) in a strong, mysterious setting. In her sparkling *Forgotten Things* (No. 1), Grace Albee memorializes barnyard relics. The highly dramatic *The Fertile Earth* (No. 8), exemplifies Albert Barker's original and telling lithographic style and technique. In *Wheat Shocks* (No. 34), John Rogers Cox achieves an almost surrealistic patina that forcefully brings his wheat field to life. Adolf Dehn's *Minnesota Shower* (No. 37) gives sound evidence for his reputation as landscape magician. Peter Hurd's *The Windmill Crew* (No. 72) is big, brash and set in a lonely expanse—just the way the land looks in that part of the country. Alfred Hutty brings the power of drypoint to bear on a strong rendition in *Rural South* (No. 73). We have all seen rich sunsets create effects challenging belief. Thomas Nason captured one in *Near Lyme, Sunset* (No. 107). A classic example of how printmakers of the period made art of common things is Dale Nichols' splendid *Grain Elevator* (No. 105). Levon West always graphically realized the drama in his nature scenes, as in *Blizzard Coming* (No. 132). Violently as West's drypoint blizzard blows, so is the snow peaceful and beautiful in Ronau Woiceske's etchings, from which we have chosen *Winter Interlude* (No. 134).

Charles Burchfield made only three lithographs. *Summer Benediction* (No. 17), like the others, gives a rich, imaginative flair to the realism of his subject, in this instance, trees, flowers, grass and hillock at peace. Many of George Elbert Burr's more than 300 etchings depicted the Western desert. Certainly no other single-subject artist ranged so brilliantly around the intaglio media to create such splendid effects, as in No. 18, *Superstition Mountain, Apache Trail, Arizona, Night (No. 2),* with its haunting majesty. In the first years of the twentieth century Allen Lewis—together with Rudolph Ruzicka—made the woodcut an independent work of art rather than an illustration of somebody else's work. Lewis' *Swinging the Gate* (No. 89) tells its own delightful story. Stow Wengenroth's *Untamed* (No. 131) is filled with grandeur and lighted a thousand ways, as after a storm.

With Tom Benton things were always bigger and louder and bolder than life, but so were Paul Bunyan and Rip Van Winkle and Walt Whitman and other Americans. You cannot mistake a Benton lithograph for anybody else's, nor do you have to search for his message. That may be why his art is so great. We have chosen *The Boy* (No. 12) and *Threshing* (No. 13) for inclusion here.

John Steuart Curry was a more literal artist. For years he did illustrations to support himself, but gave it up because, as an artist, he chafed at having to illustrate somebody else's work. He wanted to express himself, which he did in his paintings and prints, faithful renditions of things he found fascinating and important. His last lithograph, *Valley of the Wisconsin* (No. 33), touches the magnificent in its panoramic sweep.

The stylized realism of Grant Wood's lithographs has been accepted as a classic achievement in American printmaking in a relatively short period of time. Any of his 19 lithographs would tell the story; we think *Fertility* (No. 136) and *March* (No. 137) reflect important aspects of his signal contributions to American art.

American Scene—Small Town. America's towns and villages, as well as the farmlands, prairies and deserts that stretch out from them, have also attracted the attention of printmakers. Sometimes a print pictures a specific, known place; often the print presents a generalized scene that is repeated in or near towns across the entire U.S.A. Bolton Brown and Emil Ganso were two of the artists who spent much of their creative lives in Woodstock, New York, one of the major art colonies in this country during much of this century. Brown made a superb lithograph, *My House* (No. 16), of the place where he lived and worked (the elongated section at the rear of the house was his studio). Ganso memorialized a local sight in the rich aquatint *Meat Market—Woodstock* (No. 51). Andrew Butler shows citizens of Walpole, New Hampshire, arriving at the post office on a wintry morning in *Winter at Walpole* (No. 19), which exemplifies what one critic noted about his prints: "It is as much what he leaves out as what he puts into a picture that helps to make his work so distinctive, and the quality of his line is always a delight."[16]

Summer Shadows (No. 23) by Samuel Chamberlain shows a familiar street in Chamberlain's hometown of Marblehead, Massachusetts, rendered in the rich, textured drypoint that he made his own. Gene Kloss has found (and is still finding) endless inspiration for her glowing intaglio prints in and around Taos, New Mexico, where she has lived and worked most of her life. A particularly telling example is her *Processional—Taos* (No. 77). John Steuart Curry's *Prize Stallions* (No. 32) and Stevan Dohanos' *State Fair* (No. 39) creatively recall the celebrations which were the annual highlight for much of rural America and which, sadly, are becoming a thing of the past. The very essence of small-town America is captured by Mabel Dwight in *Dusk* (No. 42), as citizens of a typical town gather under a streetlight at Clover and Elm to share the latest gossip and other significant news.

Howard Cook's brilliant wood engraving *Railroad Sleeping* (No. 28) summons up the whole spirit of the locomotive and its cars, though we see only the headlight, as the train has "turned in" for the night beside the station house. Mr. Cook told us, "I cut that one out of mahogany; never again!" A horse, a dog and a couple of cows are interested bystanders outside a small-town church as the bride and groom emerge after the ceremony in Doris Lee's enchanting *Country Wedding* (No. 85). We do not know of another of Thomas Nason's hundreds of wood engravings that achieves the velvety richness, subtle shadings or tones of light that place his *Factory Village* (No. 106) at the very pinnacle of the wood engraver's art. Nothing, it seems, could be more lonely than Edward Hopper's etching *The Lonely House* (No. 68), at the edge of a town, large or small, with two children playing against one of its blank walls rising in solitude even beyond the picture's border—and that loneliness in Hopper's hands is, of course, universal. Universal, too, is the human warmth radiating from George Bellows' *Sunday, Going to Church* (No. 10), even though he particularized his emotions in terms of the Bellows family in Columbus, Ohio (hardly a small town, except in the spirit conveyed here by the artist), going to church in their splendid carriage.

"THE PEOPLE, YES"

While much critical and popular attention has been paid to the portrayal of the American Scene itself in twentieth-century American printmaking, considerably less notice has been taken of the superb work done by printmakers of this period in portraying the people who inhabit these scenes, investing them with the breath of life. Reflecting the pulsating spirit that animates these works, the portraits are seldom posed likenesses; rather, they are of people working, playing, loving—always full of animation.

A book of poems, *The People, Yes*, by Carl Sandburg, comes to mind. The realism in Sandburg's poetry was one with the realism displayed by American printmakers of the time. Sandburg's book was published in 1936, at the very time American realist printmaking was at its height.

Sandburg closes his book:

> The people know the salt of the sea
> and the strength of the winds
> lashing the corners of the earth.
> The people take the earth
> as a tomb of rest and a cradle of hope . . .
> In the darkness with a great bundle of grief the people
> march.
> In the night, and overhead a shovel of stars for keeps,
> the people march:
> "Where to? What next?"[17]

One of the prints in this collection is a portrait of a woman with a puzzled face standing on a New York street. The work of Douglas Gorsline, it is titled, *Where Next?* (No. 53). In another part of his book, Sandburg wrote of "work gangs." He could have had in mind Irwin D. Hoffman's *The Stokers* (No. 65) and their intense activity in feeding the flames. Lovers are seen by the printmakers in various ways. Federico Castellón sees them sitting together, a pair almost a part of the desert landscape around them, in *Taos Tryst* (No. 21). One cannot be sure that the man and woman at dinner pictured in *Table d'Hôte* (No. 87), by Charles Locke, are lovers. His eyes and hers—even though you cannot see hers—suggest the song Josh White used to sing, which he introduced, "Now, I'm going to sing a song about two very dangerous types of people: men and women." *Vanity Fair* is near at hand in a lithograph by Ellison Hoover, *New French Hat* (No. 66).

The people come in all shapes and sizes. A small one, *The Truant* (No. 124), rendered in sparse and poignant drypoint lines by Albert Sterner, appears totally penitent as he is being given his comeuppance. People of an entirely different sort are *Hecklers* (No. 64), given lusty life by Joseph Hirsch. Though the hecklers Hirsch portrays seem to be operating in the balcony of some legislative chamber, they stand for the world's hecklers, whether at a ballgame, commencement exercise or at any of the ever-growing number of places and occasions in which this form of protest appears.

One category of portraiture by American printmakers which has received considerable attention is the self-portrait. One powerful example is Ivan Albright's *Self Portrait at 55 East Division Street* (No. 4).

Among the people who elicited the best efforts of George Bellows were family and friends, of whom he did numerous lithographs. *Elsie, Emma and Marjorie* (second stone) (No. 11), an animated, elegant piece, pictures Emma Bellows (center) with Elsie Speicher (left) and Marjorie Henri (right). Their husbands are seen, dimly, at rear left.

In a recent letter, Paul Cadmus has written,

> The etchings of my mature years, fourteen in all—that is, after student days—were all done between 1934 and 1953. With the exception of two, they were faithful reproductions of previously executed paintings. [*Two Boys on a Beach No.* 2 (No.

20) was partially based on a painting of 1936.] The reason for reproducing my paintings [in etchings] was initiated when *The Fleet's In!* [1934] was suppressed as it was about to be exhibited at the Corcoran in Washington. I was reported to have said at the time of the furor: "They may destroy the painting but they will have a sweet time eating copper." This may have been apocryphal journalese; I don't remember. I continued this method of dissemination, as did Hogarth with his *Rake's Progress* and other works, as a way of earning a living after the pictures [paintings] had left my hands. When the etchings were originally issued they were very inexpensive—nine to fifteen dollars—now they are scarce and collector's items.[18]

SATIRE AND CARICATURE

American printmakers followed and enriched a long and honored tradition in art when they used their talents as weapons in the cause of political, economic or social justice. So did Goya, Daumier, Forain, Hogarth and many others before them. As in so many other areas of printmaking, the Americans used a wide range of graphic techniques to plunge the spears of satire into the objects of their displeasure. American political satire with a sting is exemplified in lithographs by William Gropper, *A New Bill* (No. 55), and by Philip Evergood, *Still Life* (No. 46). Lucy Lippard has written that Evergood

> made the lithograph more vitriolically satirical and more topical [than his painting of the same subject]. The figures are seen from a greater distance and more detail is included—most importantly, a copy of the *New York Times* with Pearl Harbor blazoned across the headlines. The capitalist couple . . . ignore the news as they pick at their luxurious breakfast beside the enormous, ironically fertile bouquet. Their faces are openly caricatured and the title seems to apply less to the flowers than to the figures.[19]

In the same arena, the American printmakers of the first half of the twentieth century more gently satirized many of their fellow inhabitants of the American Scene, saying, in effect, "What fools these mortals be!" With these Americans, for the most part, there was an underlying current of sympathy for the objects of their satire that gave a warmth to their depictions of the human comedy. This is evident in the work of Adolf Dehn (*Jimmy Savo*, No. 36), Mabel Dwight (*Queer Fish*, No. 43), Caroline Durieux (*Bourbon Street—New Orleans*, No. 40), Peggy Bacon (*Crosspatch*, No. 6), or Clement Haupers (*Metro 1st Class*, No. 59).

ARCHITECTURAL PRINTS

Highlights of the period are the brilliant etchings and lithographs interpreting architectural wonders on both sides of the Atlantic. The indefatigable Joseph Pennell led the way, as he found the specific character, personality and spirit of each subject. That is why his prints are so much more than illustration, of which he was also a master. We have chosen one of his etchings, *St. Paul's, Fleet Street, London* (No. 111), and a lithograph from his famous *Panama Canal* series, *The End of the Day, Gatun Lock* (No. 110).

Books should be written about John Taylor Arms; his more than 400 magnificent etchings, most of architectural subjects, are only a part of his contribution to American art. More than anyone else in the period 1900–50, he was the leaven, the inspiration, the friend, the champion of American printmaking at every turn. In 30 years of leadership, he made the Society of American Etchers into a national and highly respected organization; he and Stow Wengenroth served on the first Pennell Fund Committee at the Library of Congress, overseeing the purchase of prints "for the nation" with Mr. Pennell's money; he was juror and publicist for countless print shows and exhibitions; he wrote books, still important today, on prints and printmaking. The two Arms prints pictured in this book, *Venetian Filigree* (No. 3), pure etching, and *Early Morning, North River* (No. 2), etching with aquatint, exemplify only two of the many categories of prints from his hand. Besides his European and American architectural achievements, he created many richly beautiful aquatints printed in color, some of them imaginative and romantic; he etched lovely rural scenes, mostly of Maine subjects; he made four large etchings of battleships for the U.S. Navy during World War II; he gave numerous lecture-demonstrations all around the country at which he would draw (with one hand, shading with the other), etch and print a plate before an audience—usually in a little over two hours—keeping up a nonstop lecture on the history of etching. Arms and his two friends Samuel Chamberlain (*Skyscrapers of Menton*, No. 22) and Louis Conrad Rosenberg (*Aya Sophia No. 2*, No. 114) were known as the three "M.I.T. men," all three being former students at, or otherwise affiliated with, the Massachusetts Institute of Technology. All three achieved mastery in the rich field of architectural etching.

Between 1905 and 1910 John Marin created treasures in the same field, etching European scenes and structures in a traditional manner (*L'Opéra, Paris*, No. 94). He began his stylized etchings of American subjects in 1911.

Other traditionalists in this field working in the first decades of this century included Ernest Roth, represented by his etchings *San Gregorio, Venice* (No. 116) and *Queensboro Bridge* (No. 117), and Herman Webster (*Porte de Marmousets*, No. 128).

Among the brilliant achievements in the etching of the big city during this period, in addition to Roth's *Queensboro Bridge*, are Howard Cook's *Times Square Sector* (No. 29), Armin Landeck's *Restaurant* (No. 83) and Gerald K. Geerlings' *Jewelled City* (No. 52). (Any of these could have been categorized under American Scene—Urban, but their architectural content was foremost in their composition.) Architectural lithography also reached heights in such works as Armin Landeck's *North River Vista* (No. 82), Louis Lozowick's *Brooklyn Bridge* (No. 92) and Charles Sheeler's *Industrial Series No. 1* (No. 119).

UNIVERSAL AND SYMBOLIC THEMES

The prints in all of the categories discussed previously are grounded in American realism; even the etchings of European buildings had the previously mentioned "vitality, fresh air and frankness" that stamped prints "made by an American." We conclude our account with a group in which American realism is present, but with a difference. In Milton Avery's *Riders in the Park* (No. 5) neither the riders nor the park seem specifically American, yet the spirit of the piece is. The same can be said of the mother and child in Jean Charlot's *First Steps* (No. 24), the symbolic nymphs in Arthur B. Davies' *Fountain of Youth* (No. 35), the young girl in Arthur William Heintzelman's *My Little Model* (No. 62), the woman in Allen Lewis' *Lady on the Stairs* (No. 88), the trials and tribulations of those trying to transport a load of logs in Reynold Weidenaar's *Home from the Forest* (No. 129) and the magnificent portrait, the *Abbot of Grottaferrata* (No. 135), etched by Franklin T. Wood.

Nude studies such as *Girl Dressing* (No. 79) by Yasuo Kuniyoshi, *Morning Paper* (No. 98) by Alessandro Mastro-Valerio and *Summer Morning* (No. 109) by Doel Reed seem, finally, to be universally rendered depictions of the female figure, though with thoroughly American overtones. In the Doel Reed work, for example, one glimpses a Southwest landscape through the two windows in the background.

Clare Leighton's *Ploughing* (No. 86) depicts an English farm, but it could have been done as well here in America, as the subject is, of course, universal. Troy Kinney's *Lopokova and Nijinski in "Les Sylphides"* (No. 76) depicts those great dancers, who were universal favorites, animated by an unmistakable American spirit. Last—but first in the hearts of many of his countrymen—Rockwell Kent has a very American angel bestowing *Godspeed* (No. 74) on the ship below, in a most compelling wood engraving, and those unfortunate folk present in *Solar Fade-Out* (No. 75), from Kent's *End of the World* series, look rather American.

"Wasn't that a time!," as The Weavers used to sing. Seldom, if ever, in the history of printmaking has there been the cauldron of activity and breadth of achievement seen between 1900 and 1950 in the United States. Hundreds of skilled printmakers created thousands of fine prints. From our readings of the period, and from conversations with artists who were part of it, we have learned that these men and women were friends: They were fellow members of the many print societies around the nation, they served together on juries at exhibitions, they taught side by side at art schools. For example, the catalog of the Art Students League of New York for the winter season, 1933–1934, lists Reginald Marsh as Vice-President of the League and Peggy Bacon as a Board Member. Instructors included Thomas Hart Benton, Alexander Brook, Warren Chappell (who taught the woodcut class), John Steuart Curry, Anne Goldthwaite, George Grosz, Yasuo Kuniyoshi, Charles Locke (who taught etching and lithography), William McNulty, Kenneth Hayes Miller, Raphael Soyer and William Zorach. (And you could have studied with any of them for between $11 and $18 per month!) The friendships, the teacher-and-student interactions, the cross-fertilization of ideas that ebbed and flowed among this myriad of artists, individualists all, made for an exciting era, to be sure, and resulted in what can only be called a Golden Age of American Prints.

NOTES

See the Selected Bibliography for full citations of works mentioned in abbreviated form here.

1. Among the many books and other publications on American modernist art are: John I. H. Baur, *Revolution and Tradition in Modern American Art*, Cambridge, Massachusetts: Harvard University Press, 1951; Lloyd Goodrich, *Pioneers of Modern Art in America: The Decade of the Armory Show, 1910–1920*, New York: Frederick A. Praeger for the Whitney Museum of Art, 1963; Barbara Rose, *American Art Since 1900: A Critical History*, New York: Frederick A. Praeger, 1967.
2. Karen F. Beall, *American Prints in the Library of Congress*.
3. Peter Morse, *John Sloan's Prints*, p. 134.
4. Eugene Speicher, quoted in Emma S. Bellows, *George Bellows: His Lithographs*, p. 33.
5. Jerome Myers, *Artist in Manhattan*, p. 48.
6. Elizabeth Robins Pennell, in her introduction to Louis A. Wuerth, *Catalogue of the Etchings of Joseph Pennell*, pp. xviii and xix.
7. Jerome Myers, *op. cit.*, p. 165.
8. John Sloan, quoted in Peter Morse, *op. cit.*, p. 247.
9. *Ibid.*, p. 340.
10. Reginald Marsh, quoted by Lloyd Goodrich in his introduction to Norman Sasowsky, *The Prints of Reginald Marsh*, p. 10.
11. Thomas Hart Benton, *An American in Art*, pp. 147–148.
12. Grant Wood, *Revolt Against the City*, Number One in the "Whirling World Series." Iowa City, Iowa: Clio Press, 1935, pp. 38 and 26.
13. John Steuart Curry, "What Should the American Artist Paint?," *Art Digest*, September 1935, p. 29.
14. Benton, *op. cit.*, pp. 148 and 155.
15. *Ibid.*, p. 150.
16. Susan A. Hutchinson, in *Fine Prints of the Year, 1933*, p. 14.
17. Carl Sandburg, *The People, Yes*, New York: Harcourt, Brace and Company, 1936, pp. 285–286.
18. From a letter written by Mr. Paul Cadmus to Mr. John Axelrod in 1982, quoted here with the permission of Mr. Cadmus and Mr. Axelrod.
19. Lucy R. Lippard, *The Graphic Work of Philip Evergood*, pp. 29–30.

NOTE ON THE PRINTS

The captions give the following information: artist's name, title of print, date, medium, edition size, dimensions and reference to a standard catalog of the artist's prints. Additional facts, when warranted, are also included.

Since the title of No. 54 could not be ascertained, a descriptive title is given in brackets. Dimensions, taken from platemark to platemark for etchings and other intaglio prints and from the extremities of the image for lithographs and woodblock prints, are given in inches, height before width. The edition size listed is the number of impressions in the published state; we do not include trial proofs or states earlier than the published state. The catalog references are detailed in the section of the Selected Bibliography titled "Catalogs of the Artists' Prints," which is arranged alphabetically by artist.

Most of the prints pictured in this book were made between 1900 and 1950. Two were created before 1900: Nos. 102 and 103, by Charles Mielatz, were made in 1891 and 1892, respectively. They are included because in them Mielatz pioneered the realism in prints of New York that became such a vital factor in American printmaking following the turn of the century. At the other end of the time frame, because they are totally in the spirit of American realist prints of the period 1900–1950, we have included four prints that were done after 1950—in 1951, 1952 or 1953: by Charles Burchfield (No. 17), John Rogers Cox (No. 34), Armin Landeck (No. 83) and Lynd Ward (No. 127).

GREAT AMERICAN PRINTS
1900-1950

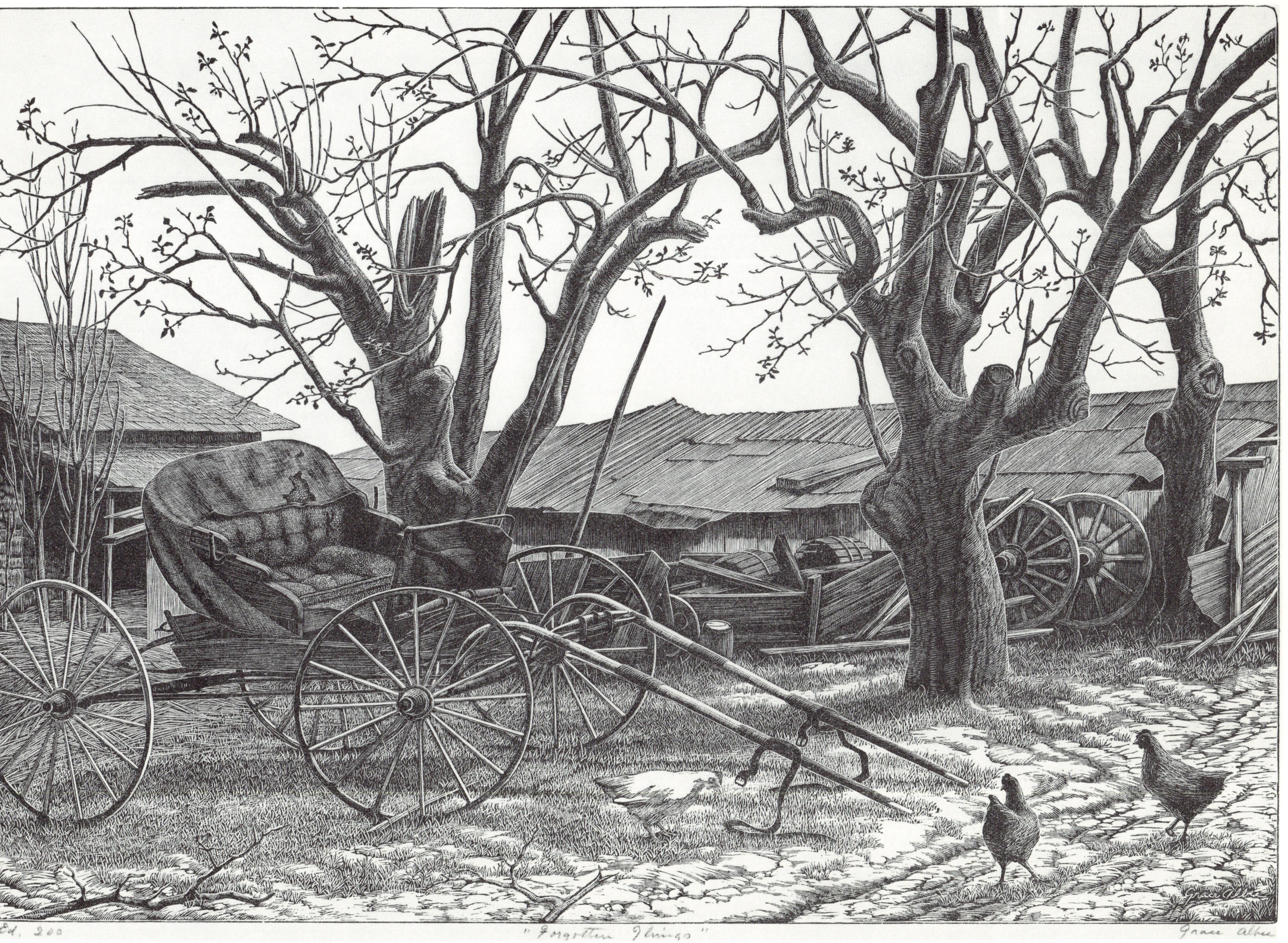

1. Grace Thurston Arnold Albee. *Forgotten Things*, 1942. Wood engraving. Edition 210. 8 × 11¼.

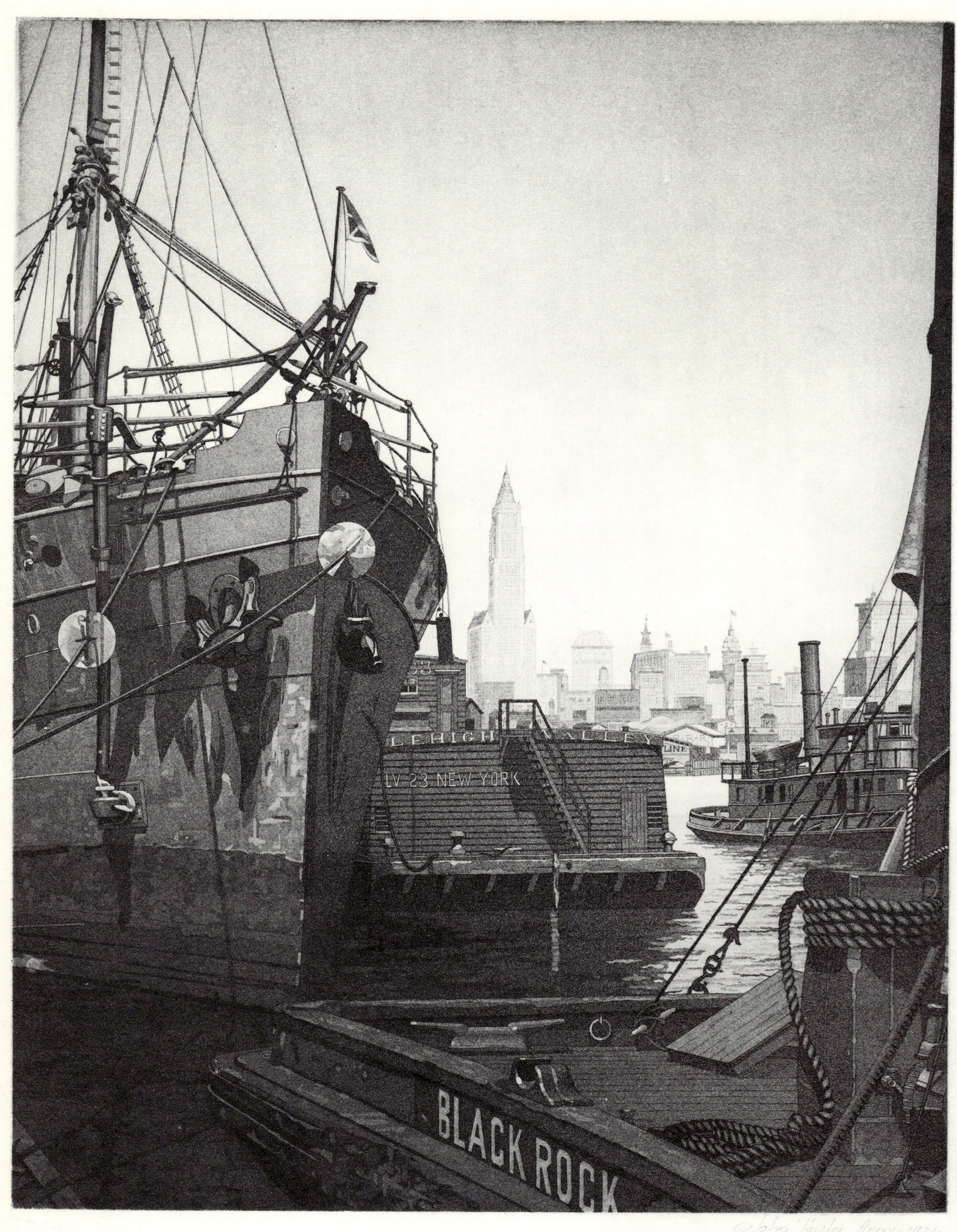

2. JOHN TAYLOR ARMS. *Early Morning, North River* (New York City), 1921. Etching. Edition 48 in black and white, 27 in color. 9½ × 7½. Arms 102, Fletcher 100.

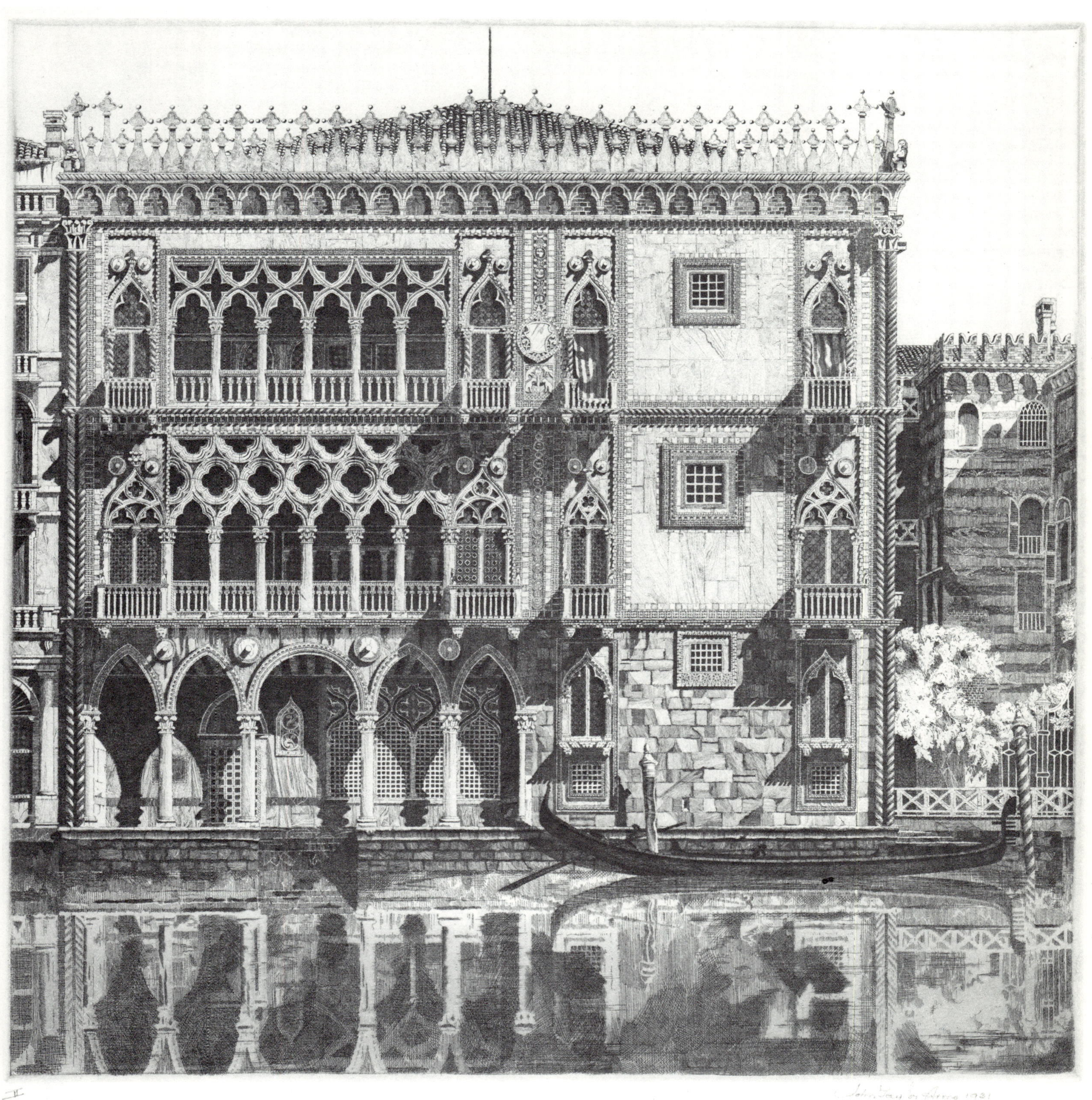

3. JOHN TAYLOR ARMS. *Venetian Filigree*, 1931. Etching. Edition 152. 10¾ × 11. Arms 237, Fletcher 235.

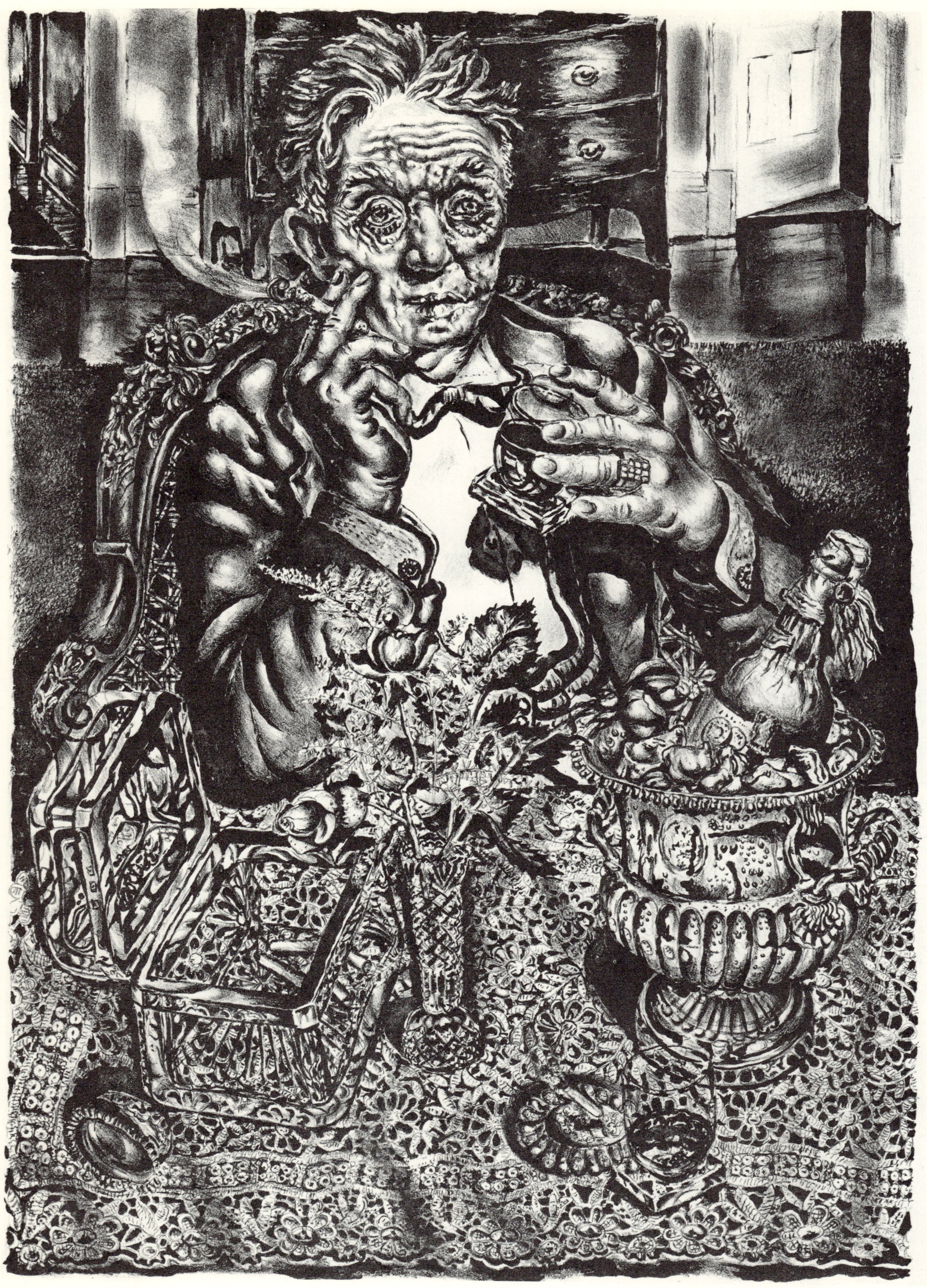

4. Ivan Le Lorraine Albright. *Self Portrait at 55 East Division Street* (Chicago), 1947. Lithograph. Edition 250. 14⅛ × 10⅛. Grayson 13.

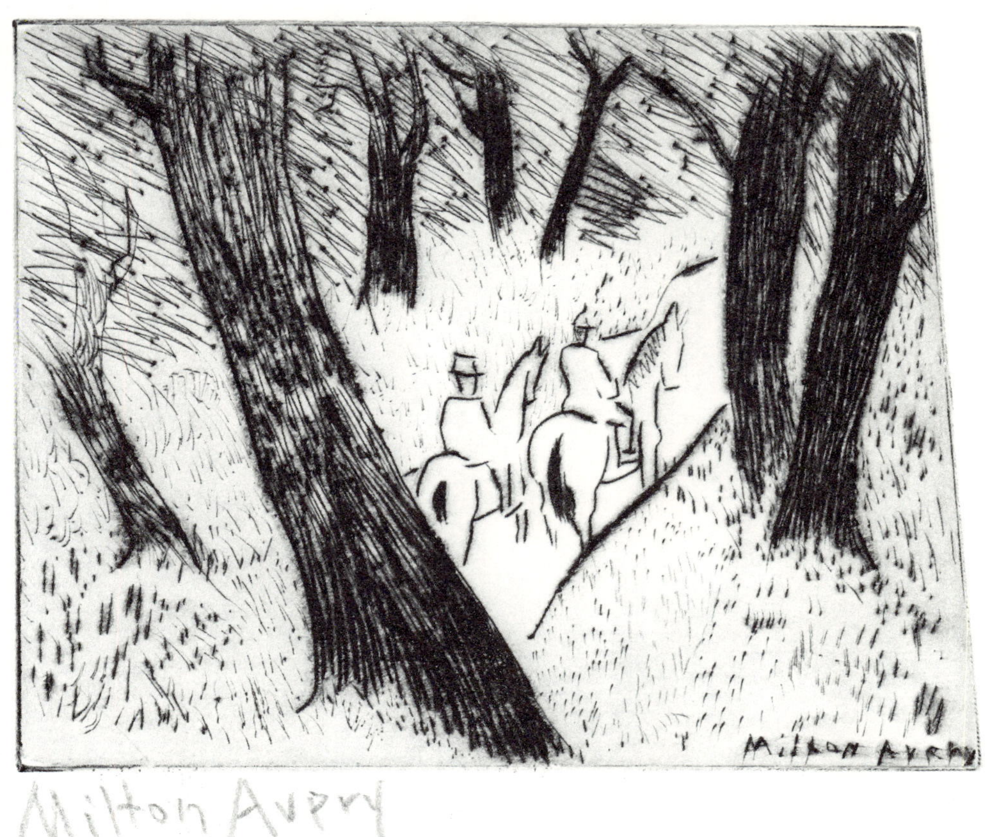

5. MILTON AVERY. *Riders in the Park,* 1934. Drypoint. Edition of 100 published in *Laurels Portfolio No. 4,* 1948. $3\frac{15}{16} \times 5$. Lunn 6.

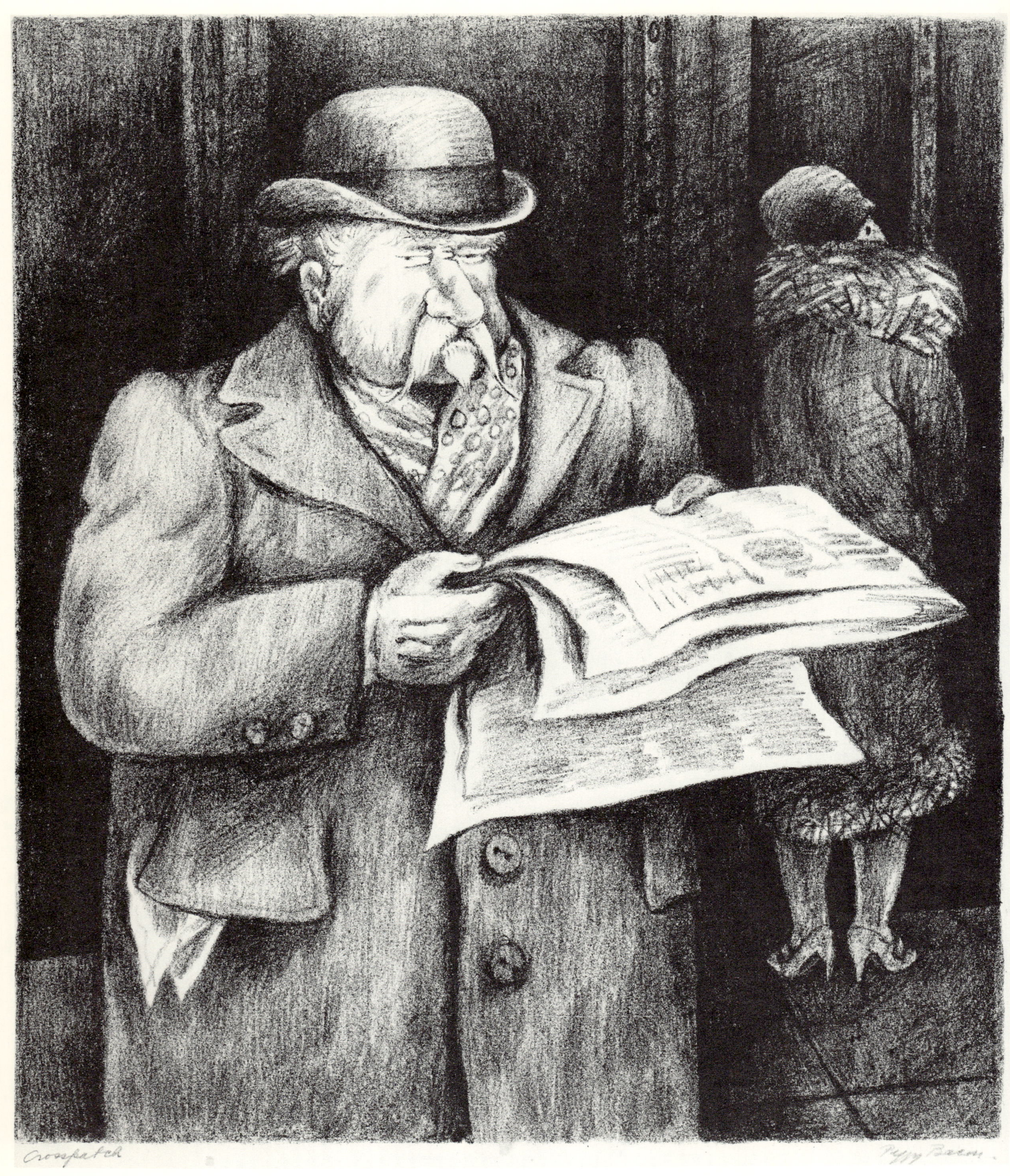

6. PEGGY BACON. *Crosspatch* (or *The Titan*), 1929. Lithograph. 14¾ × 13. Flint 87.

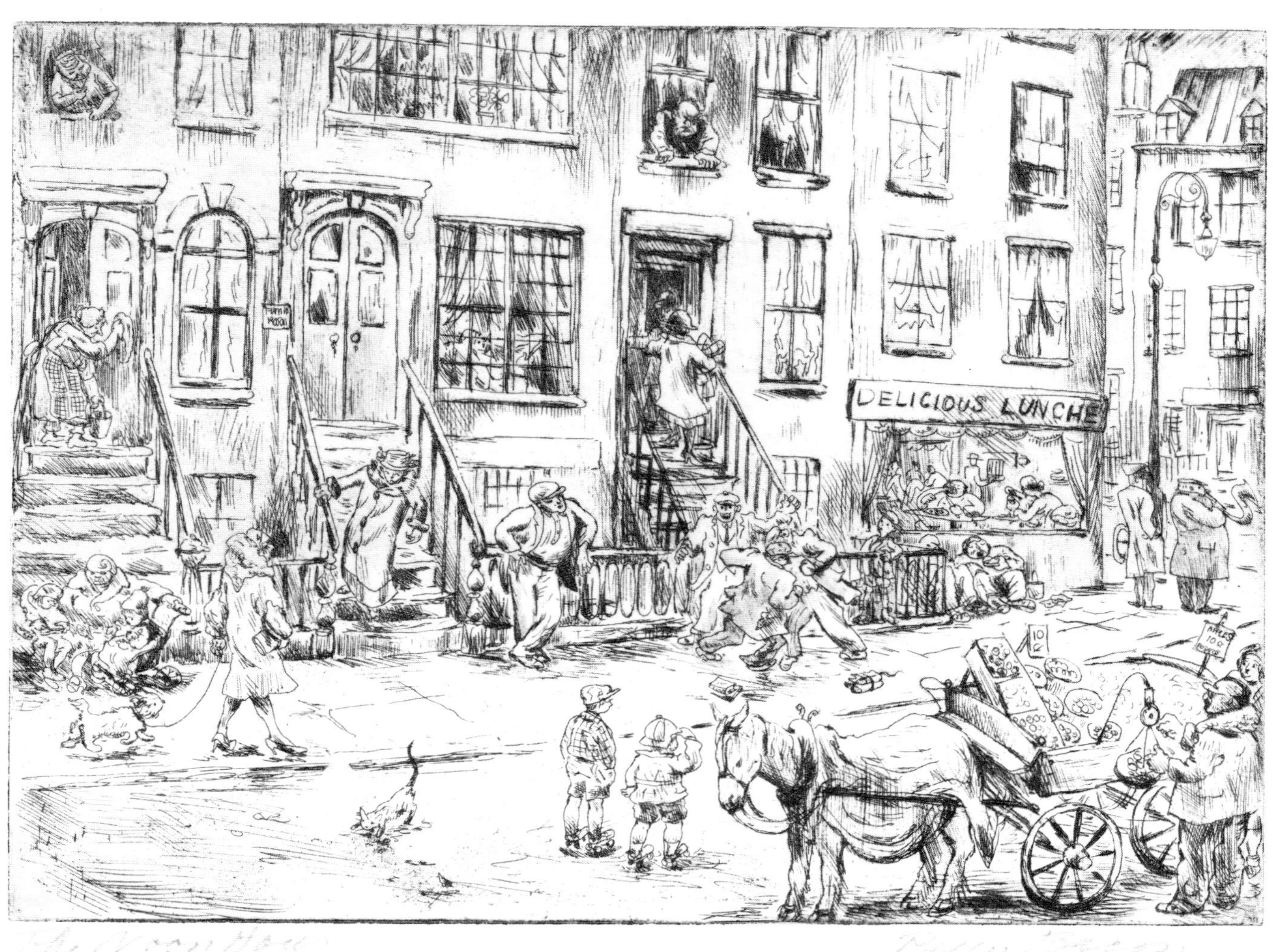

7. PEGGY BACON. *The Noon Hour* (New York City), 1931. Etching. 5 × 7. Flint 101.

8. Albert Winslow Barker. *The Fertile Earth*, 1938. Lithograph. Edition 50. $14\frac{5}{8} \times 10\frac{3}{4}$. Barker 196.

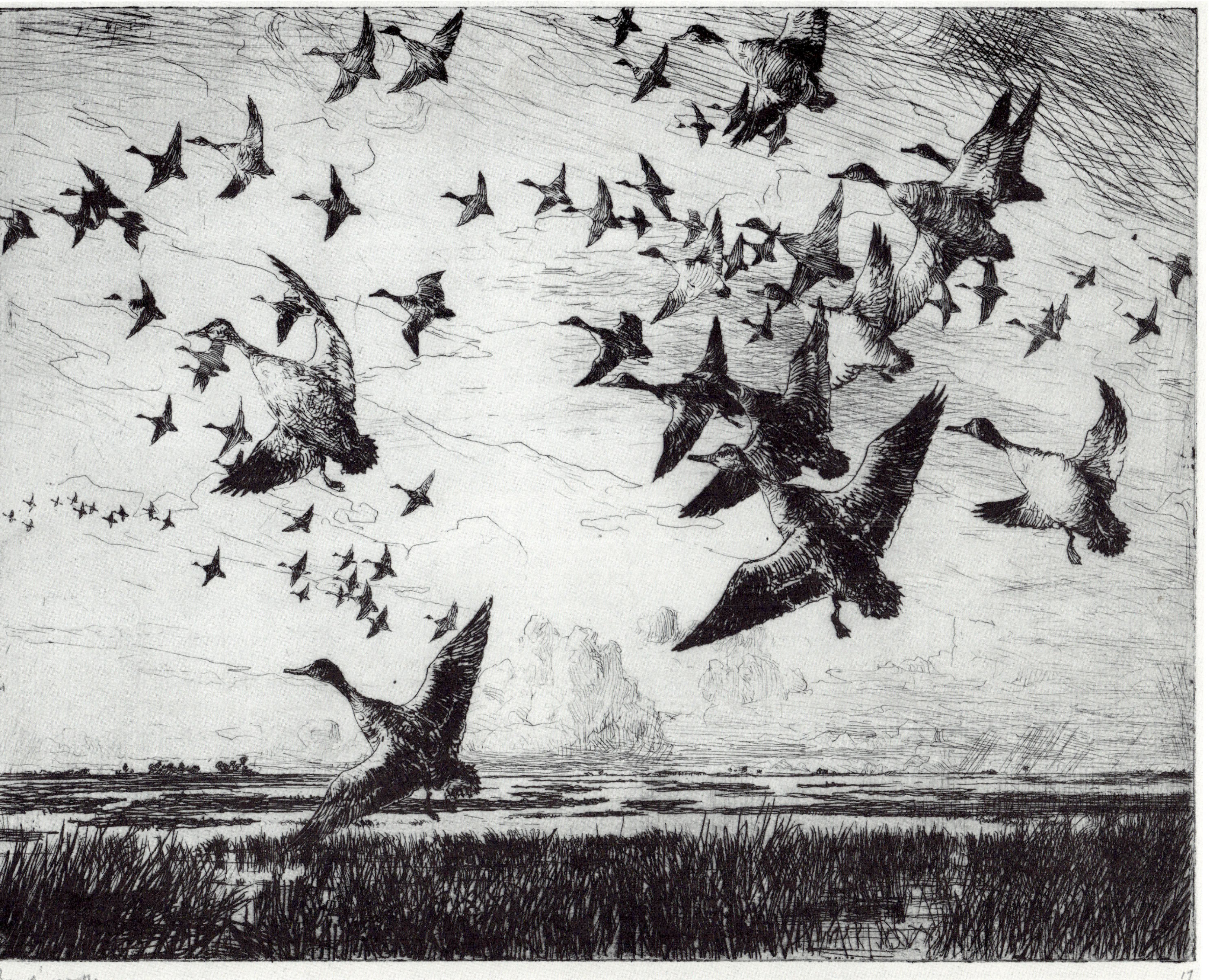

9. Frank Weston Benson. *Morning Flight,* 1919. Etching. Edition 150. 7⅞ × 9⅞. Paff 152.

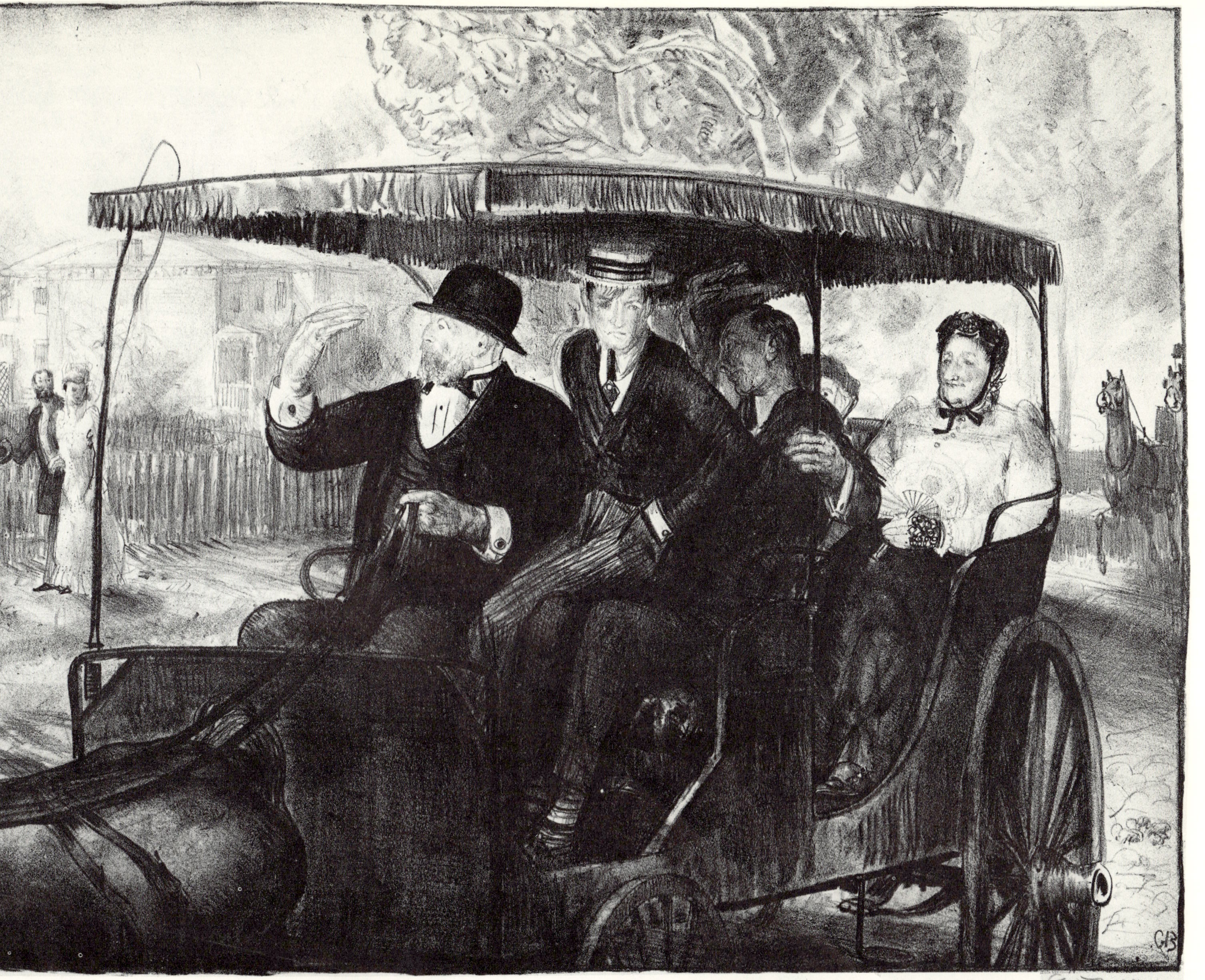

10. GEORGE WESLEY BELLOWS. *Sunday, Going to Church* (Columbus, O.), 1921. Lithograph. Edition 54. 12⅛ × 14⅞. Bellows 154, Mason 73.

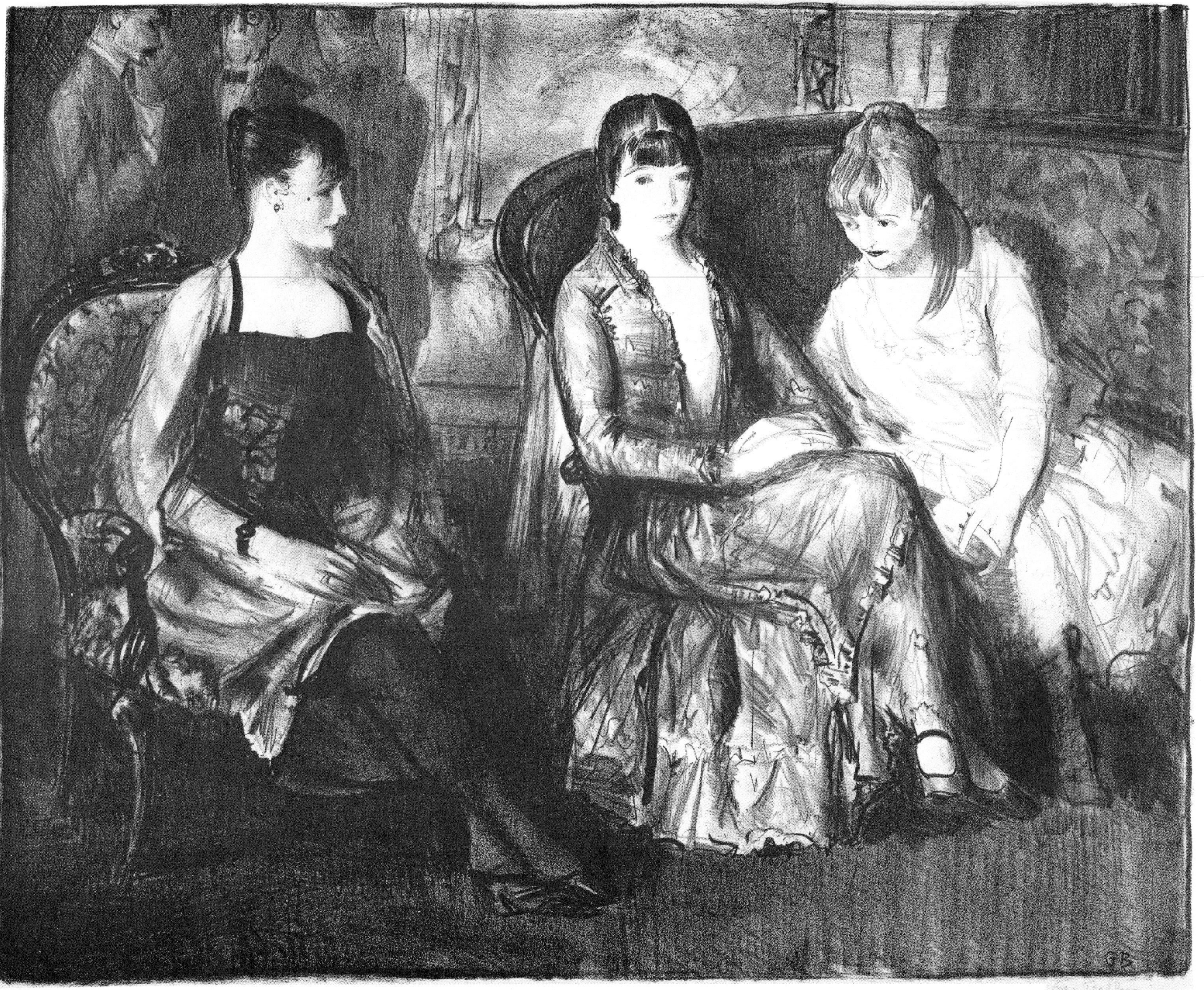

11. George Wesley Bellows. *Elsie, Emma and Marjorie* (second stone), 1921. Lithograph. Edition 64. 11⅜ × 13⅞. Bellows 4, Mason 104.

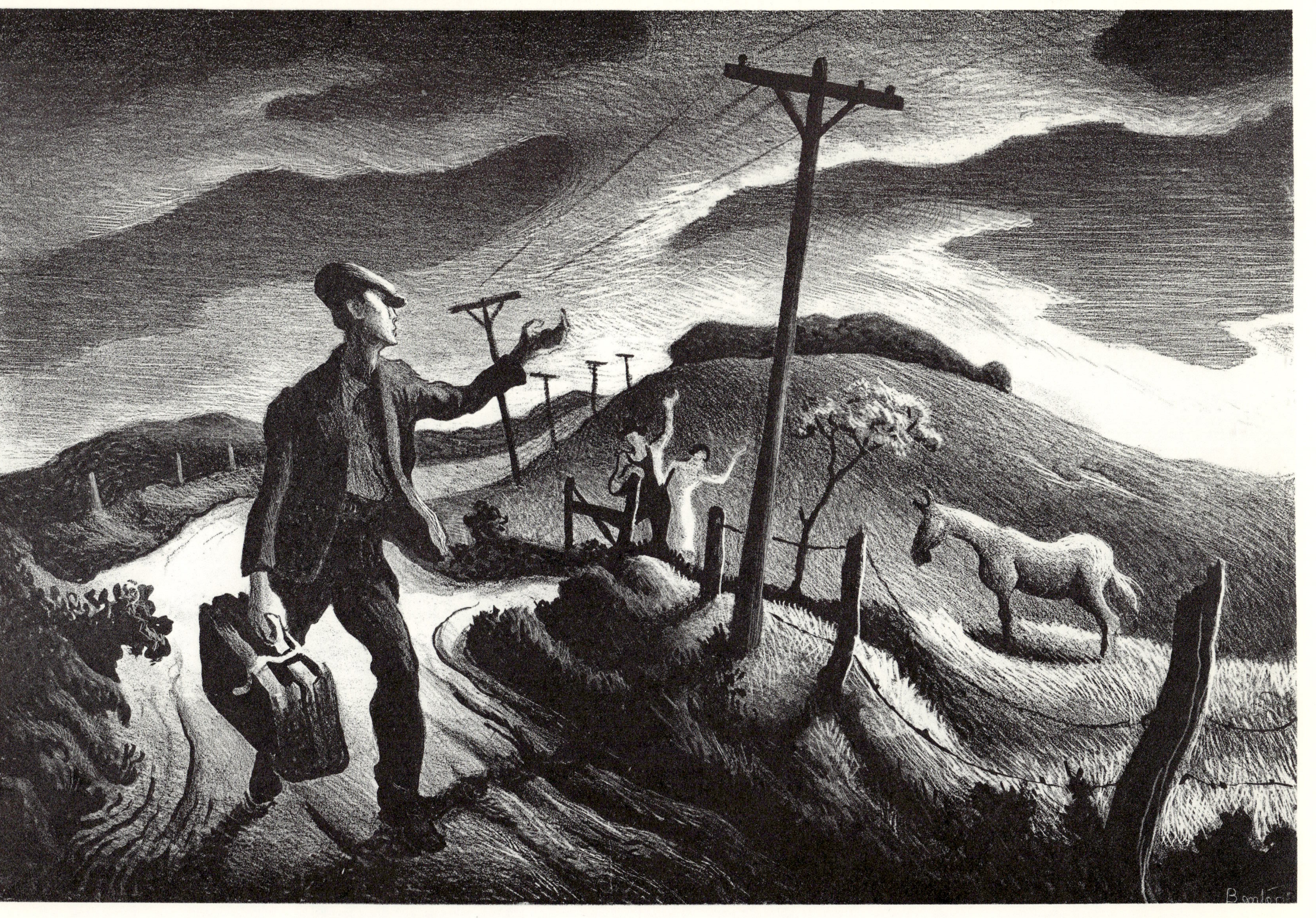

12. Thomas Hart Benton. *The Boy*, 1948. Lithograph. Edition 250. 9½ × 13¾. Fath 72.

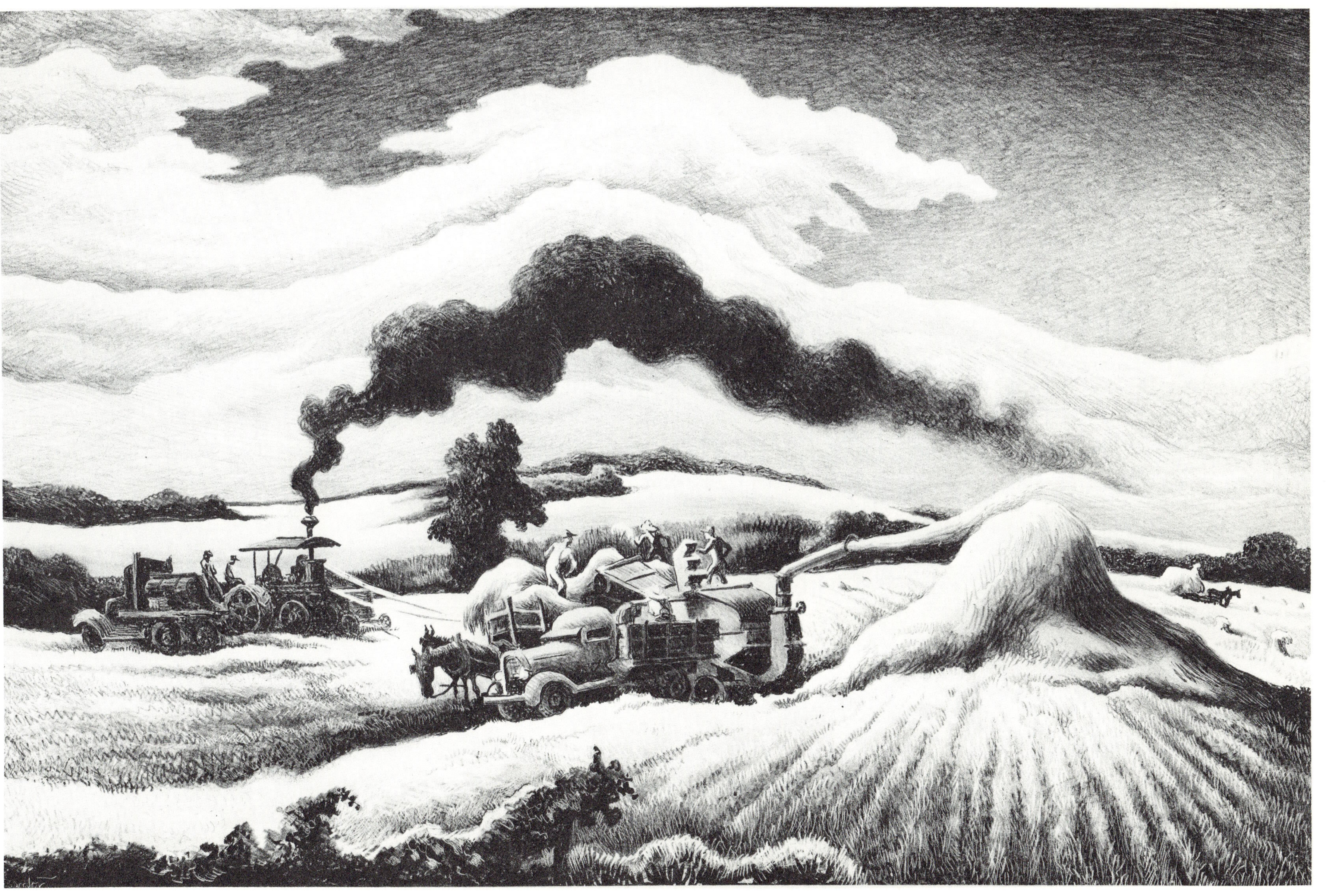

13. Thomas Hart Benton. *Threshing*, 1941. Lithograph. Edition 250. 9¼ × 14. Fath 48.

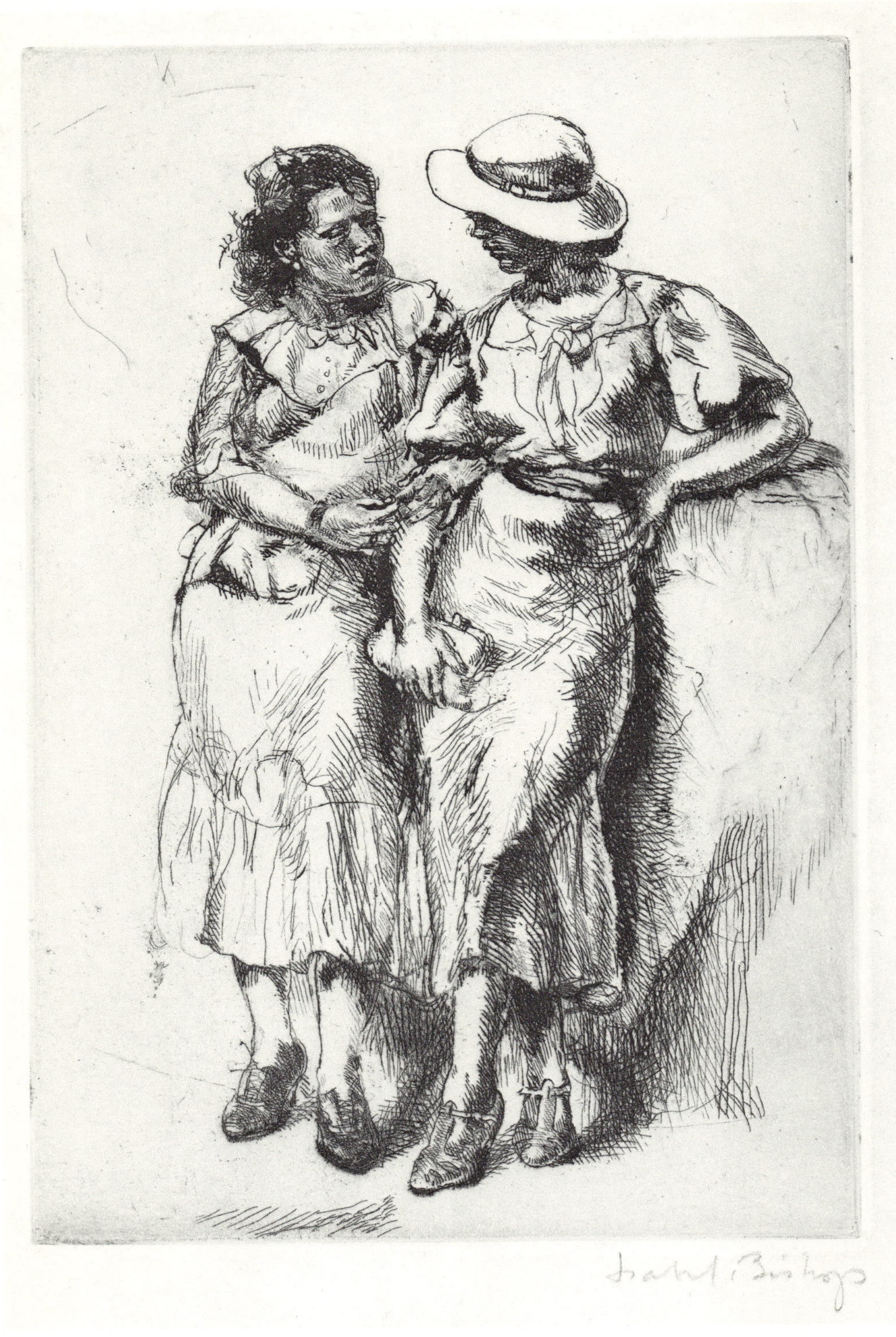

14. ISABEL BISHOP. *The Noon Hour*, 1935. Etching. Original edition 40. 6⅞ × 4⅞. Arizona 103.

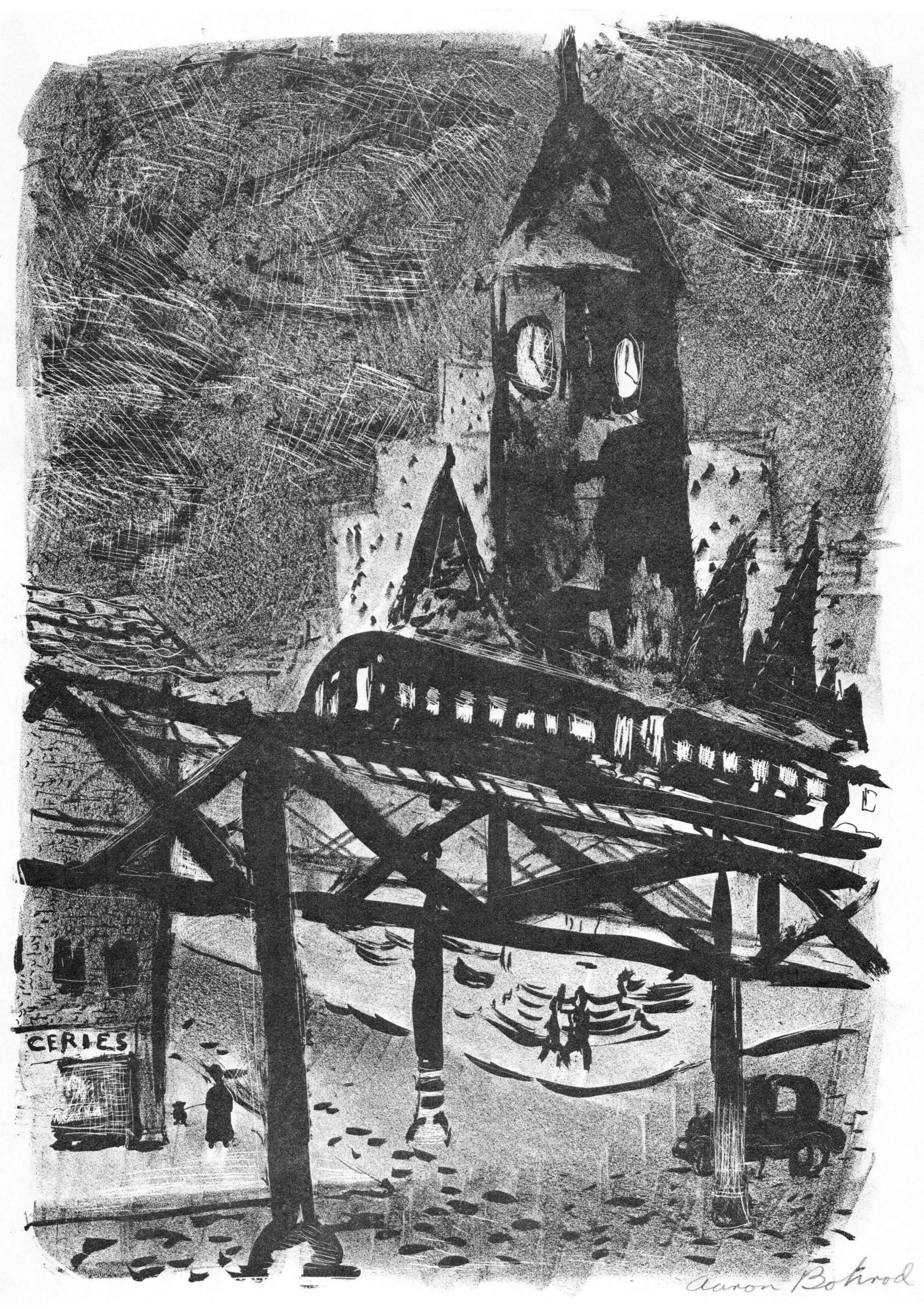

15. Aaron Bohrod. *Jefferson Market* (New York City), 1931. Lithograph. Edition "less than 10." 13½ × 9½.

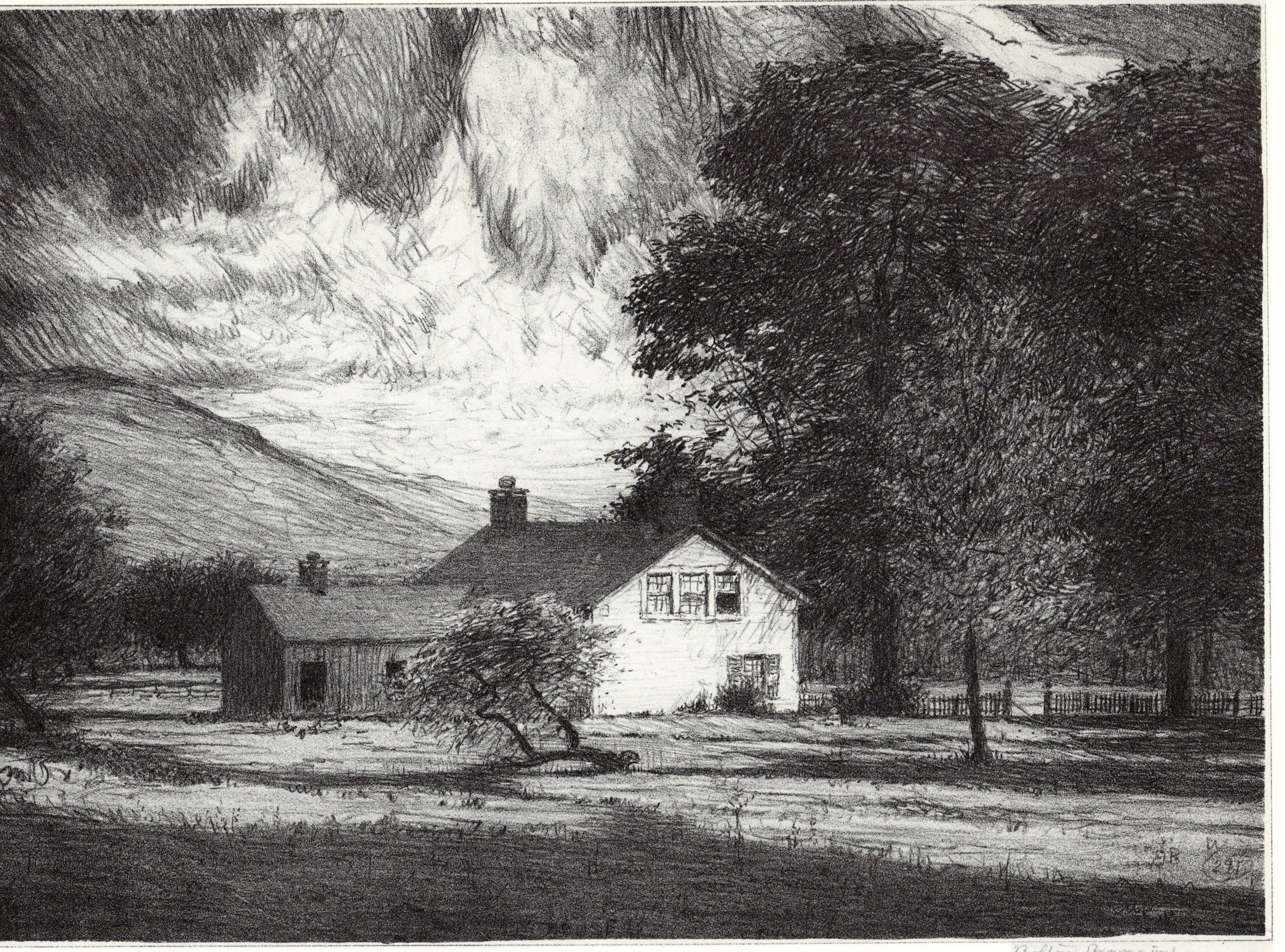

16. Bolton Coit Brown. *My House* (Woodstock, N.Y.), 1921. Lithograph. Edition ca. 29. 10 × 13½.

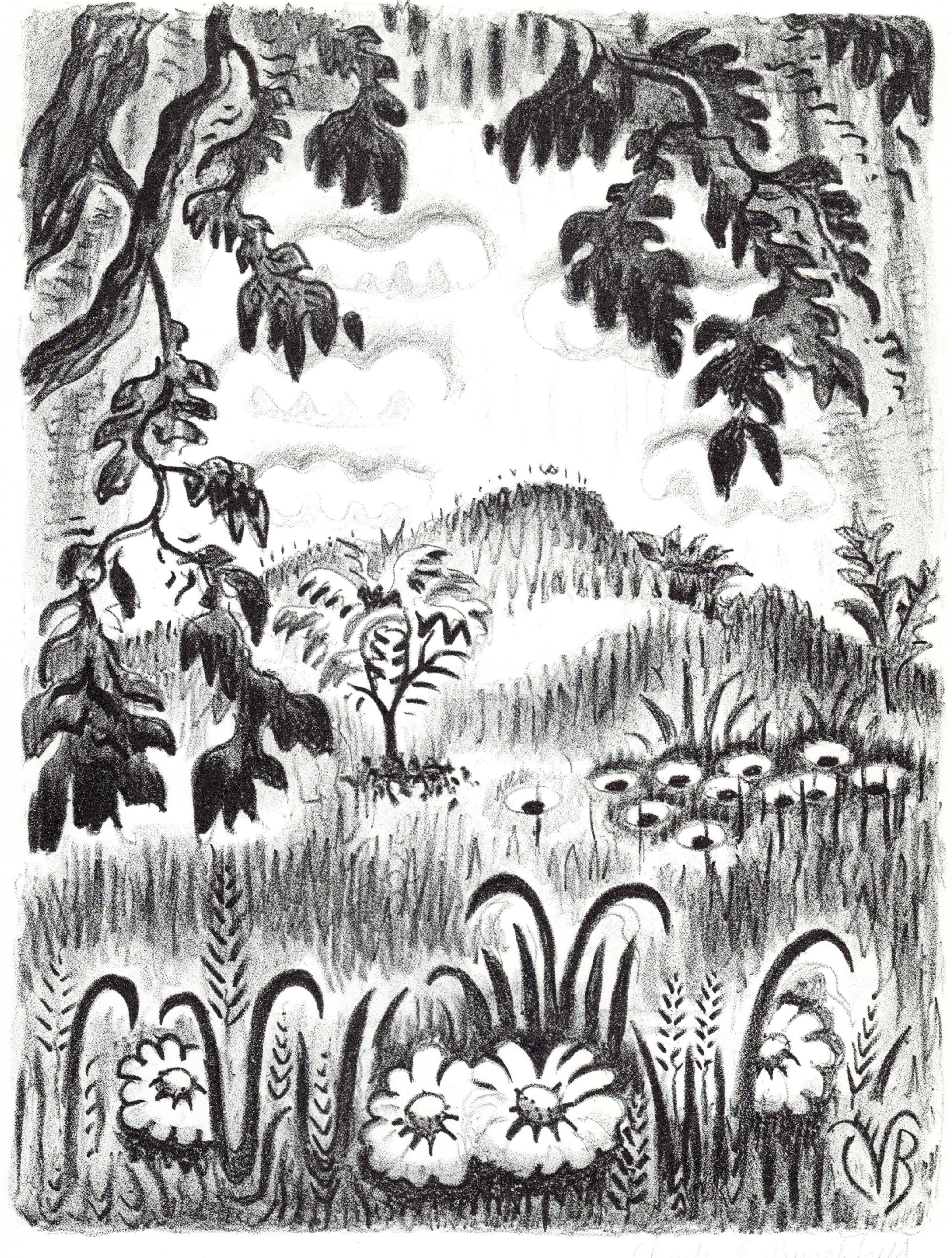

17. Charles Ephraim Burchfield. *Summer Benediction*, 1951–52. Lithograph. Edition 260, publication of the Print Club of Cleveland for 1953. $12 \times 9\frac{1}{16}$.

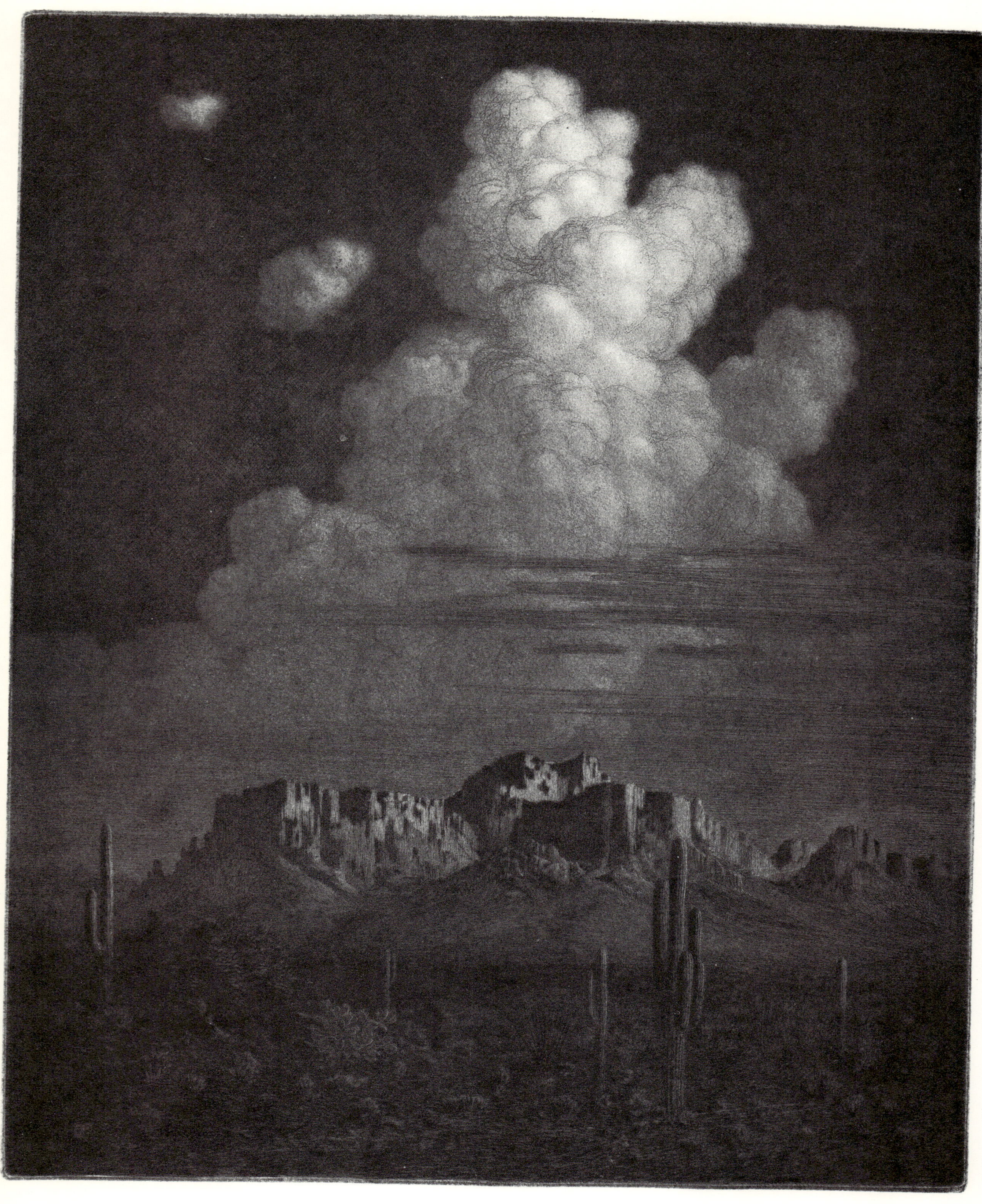

18. George Elbert Burr. *Superstition Mountain, Apache Trail, Arizona, Night (No. 2)*, 1931. Drypoint and aquatint. 11¾ × 9¾. Seeber 325.

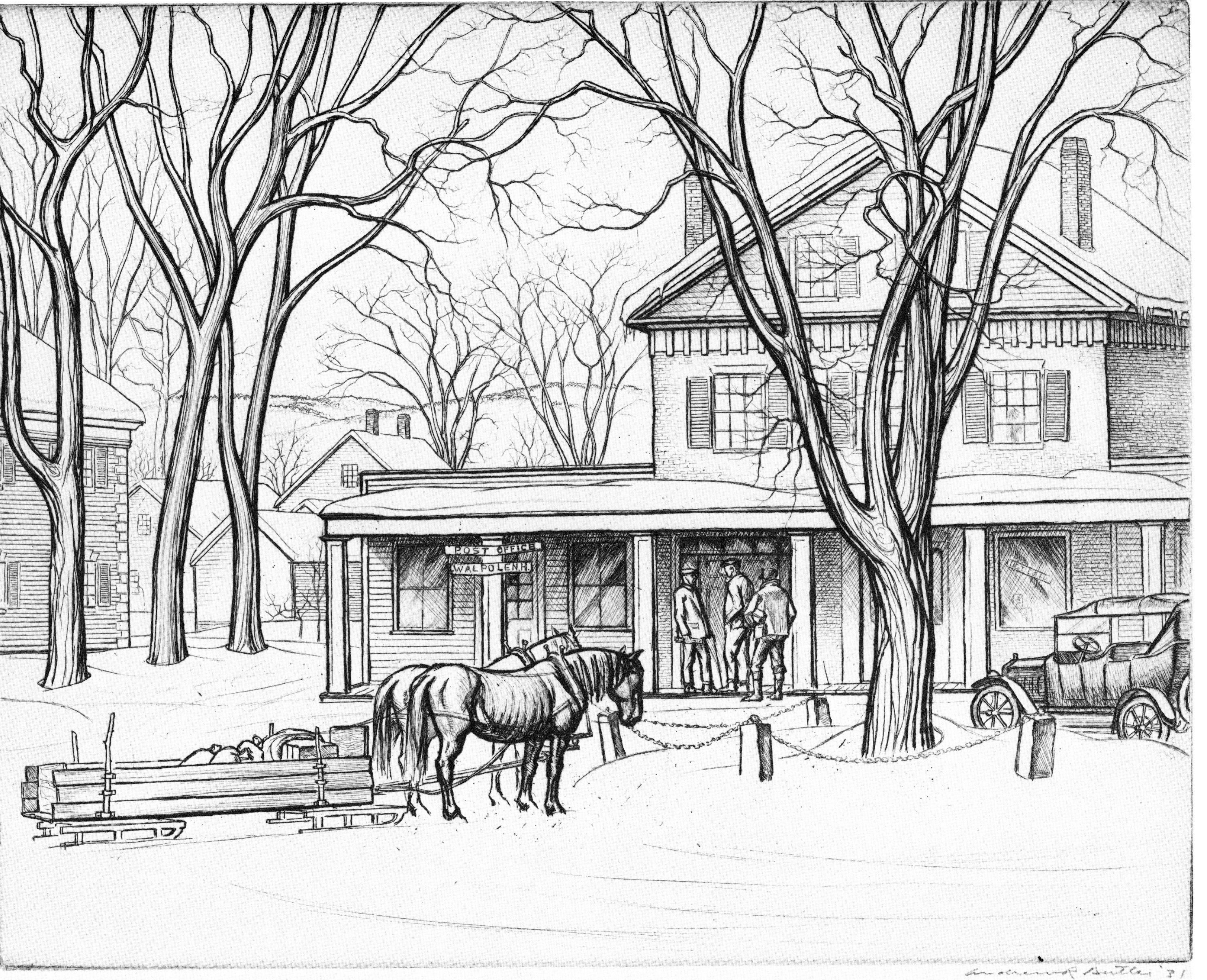

19. ANDREW R. BUTLER. *Winter at Walpole* (or *The Country Store*), 1931. Etching. 8½ × 10½.

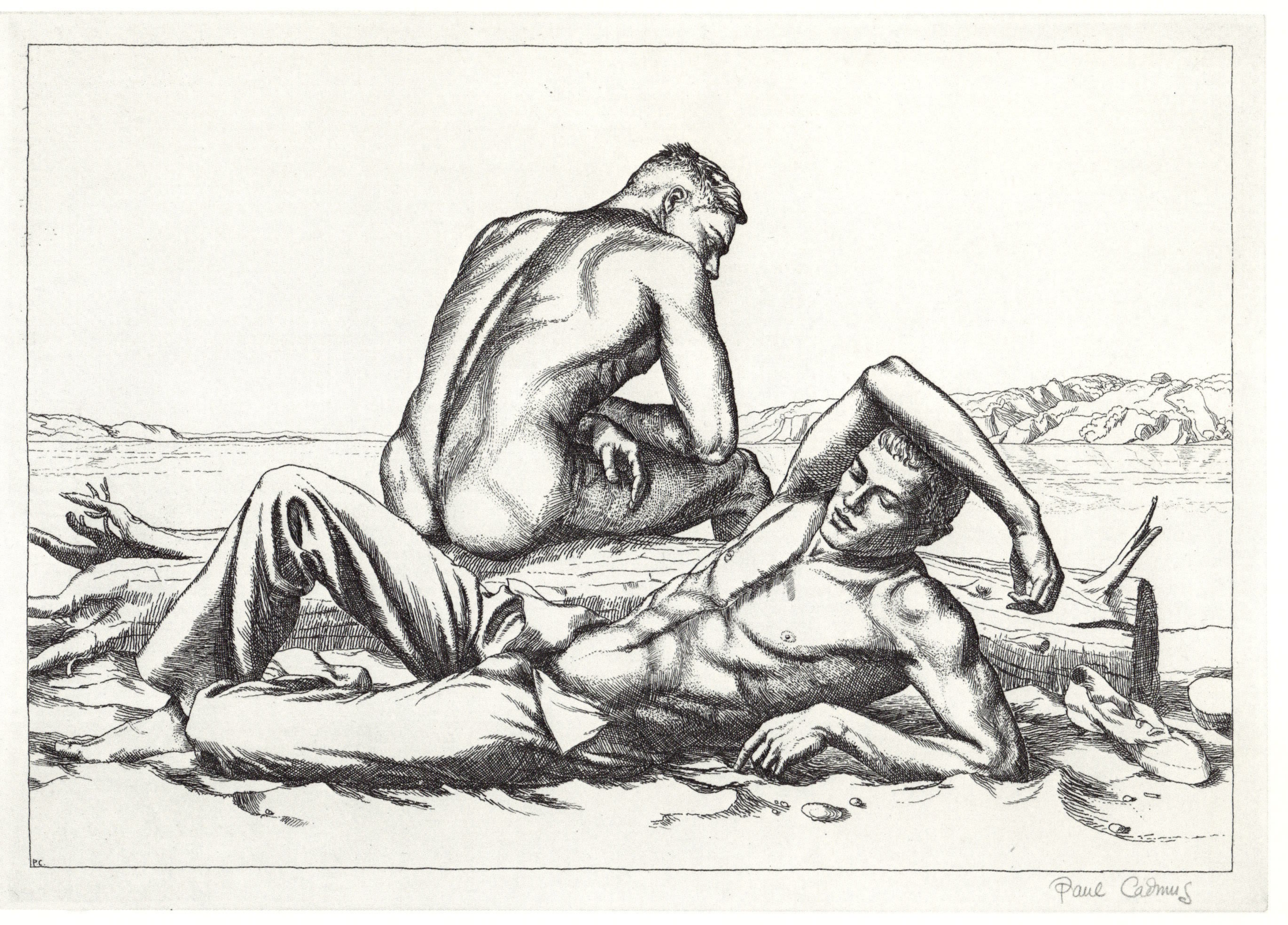

20. Paul Cadmus. *Two Boys on a Beach No. 2*, 1939. Etching. Edition 151, for Print Club of Albany, 1939. 6⅜ × 9. Brooklyn 86.

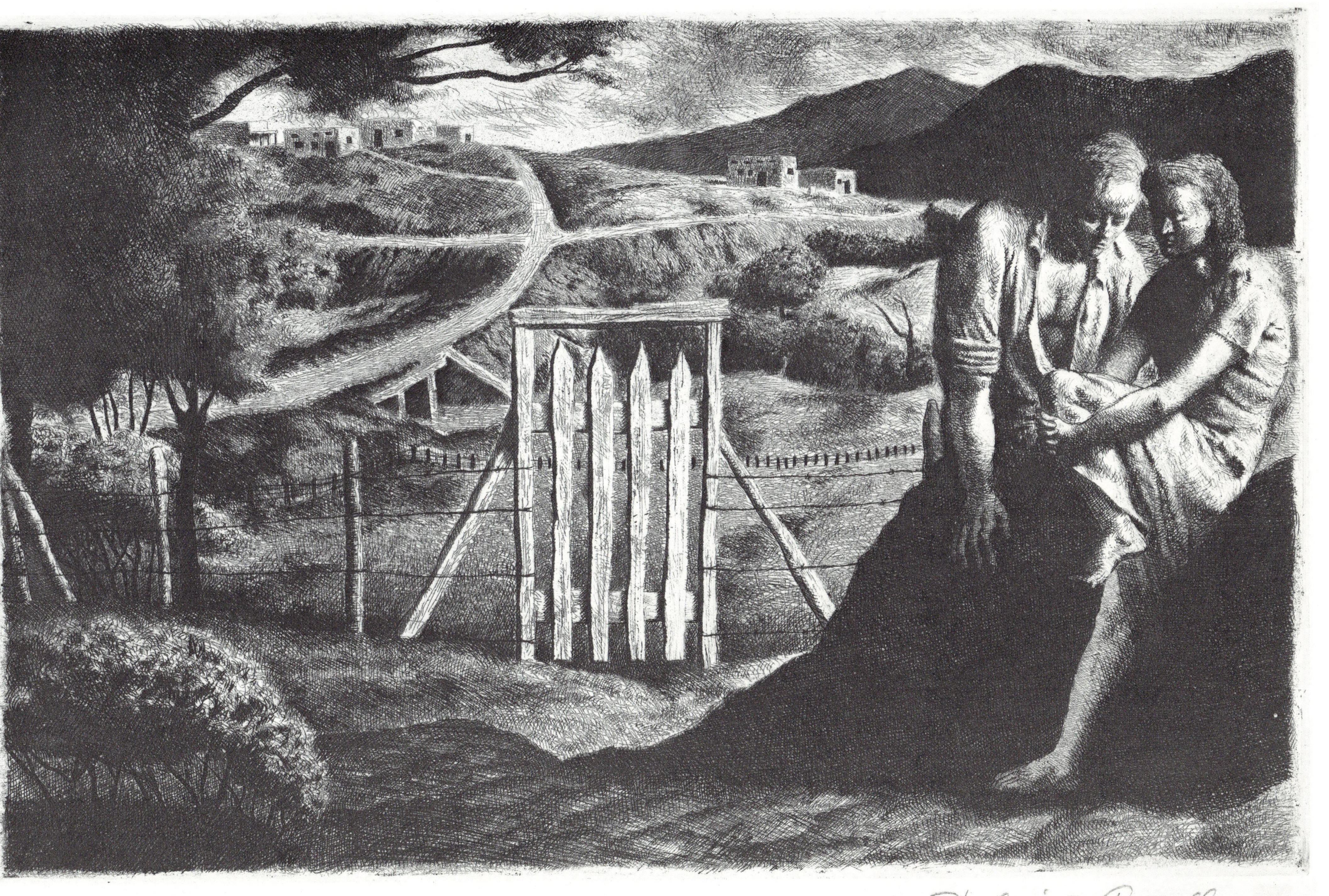

21. Federico Castellón. *Taos Tryst*, ca. 1942. Etching. Edition 50. 7¾ × 11¾. Freundlich 28.

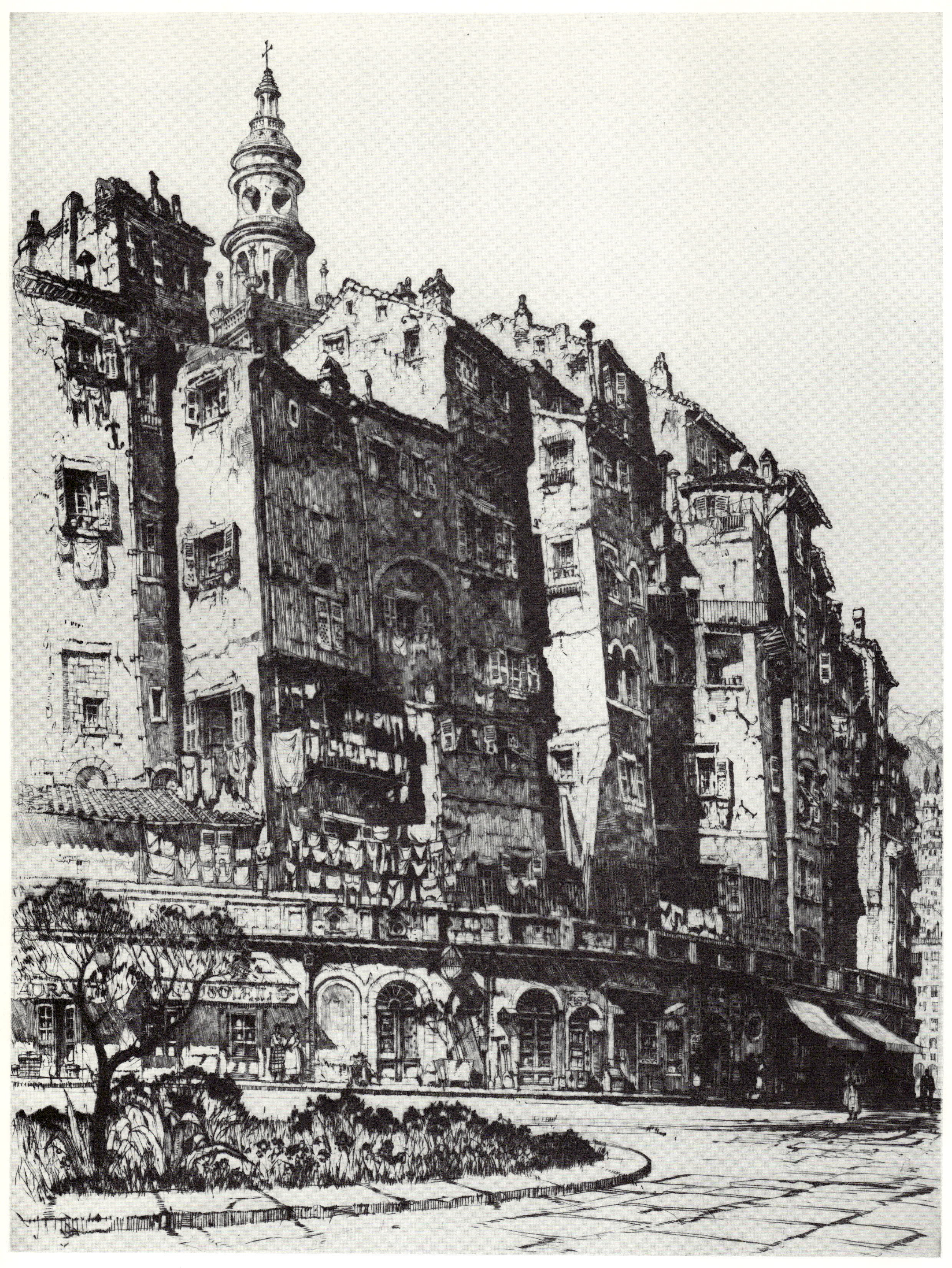

22. SAMUEL CHAMBERLAIN. *Skyscrapers of Menton*, 1930. Drypoint. Edition 100. $12\frac{5}{8} \times 9\frac{1}{2}$. Chamberlain & Kingsland 94.

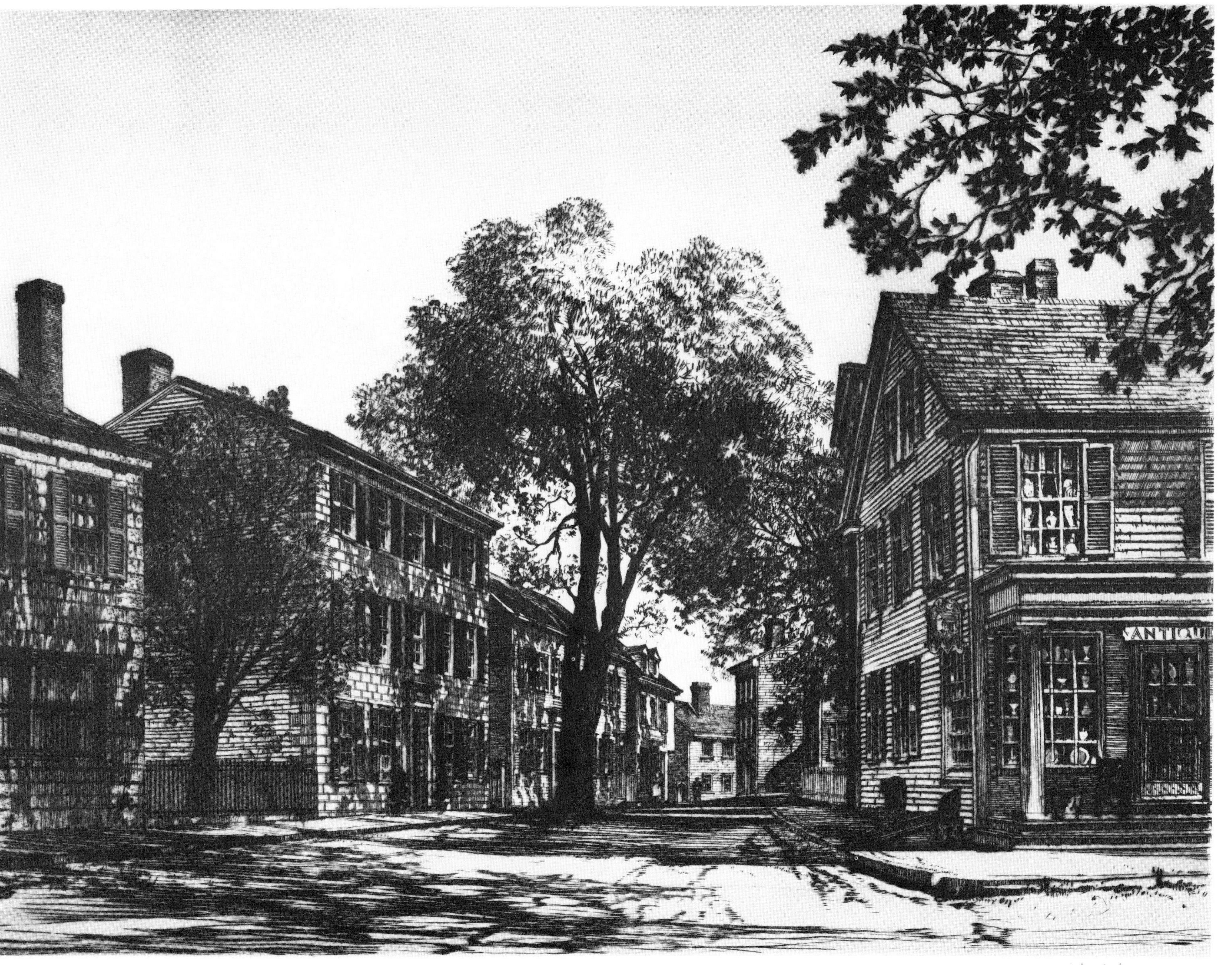

23. Samuel Chamberlain. *Summer Shadows* (Marblehead, Mass.), 1940. Drypoint. Edition 300. 8¾ × 11¼. Chamberlain & Kingsland 275.

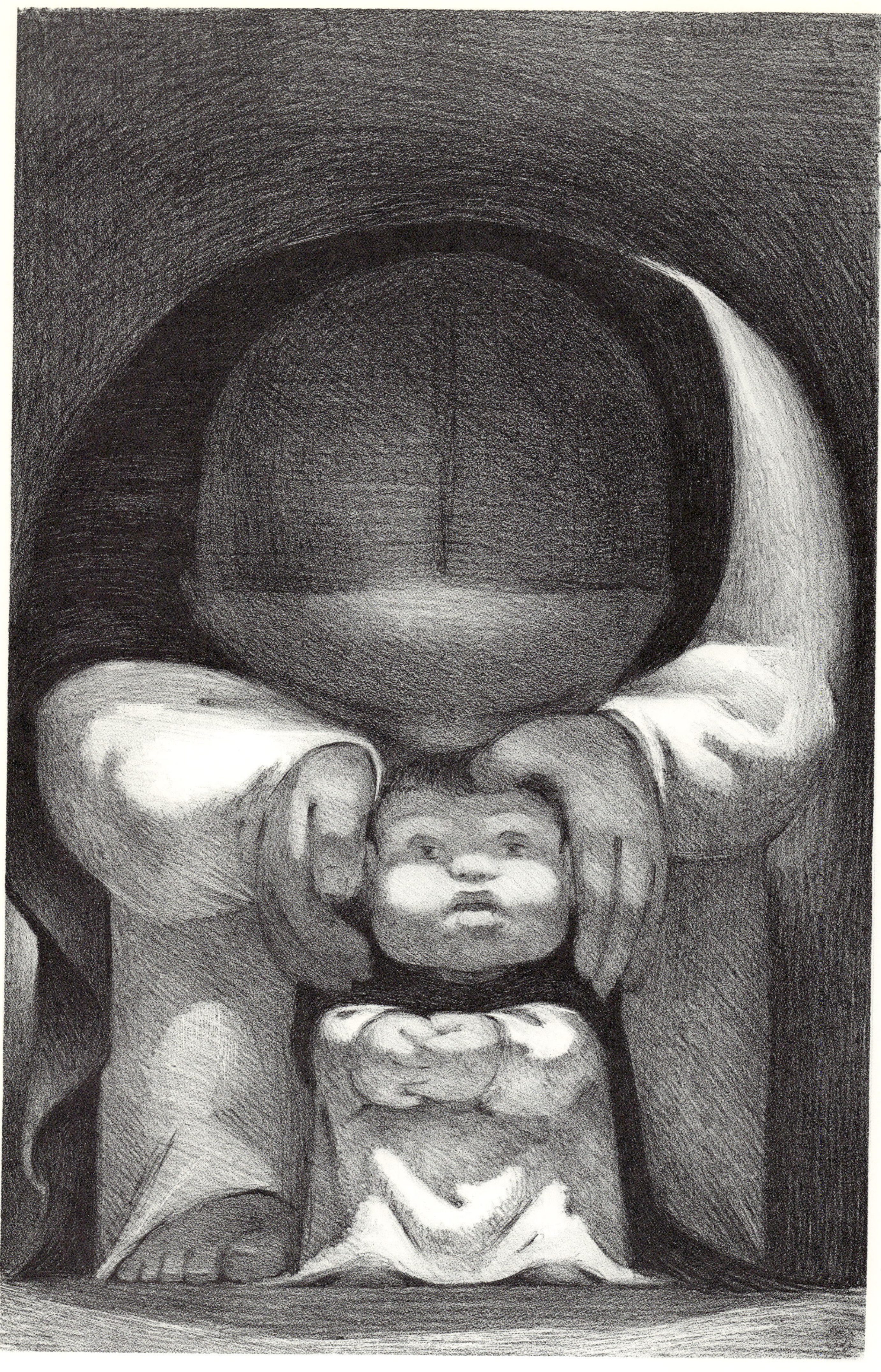

24. Jean Charlot. *First Steps*, 1936. Lithograph. Published by the American Artists Group, 1936. 14 × 9. Morse 317.

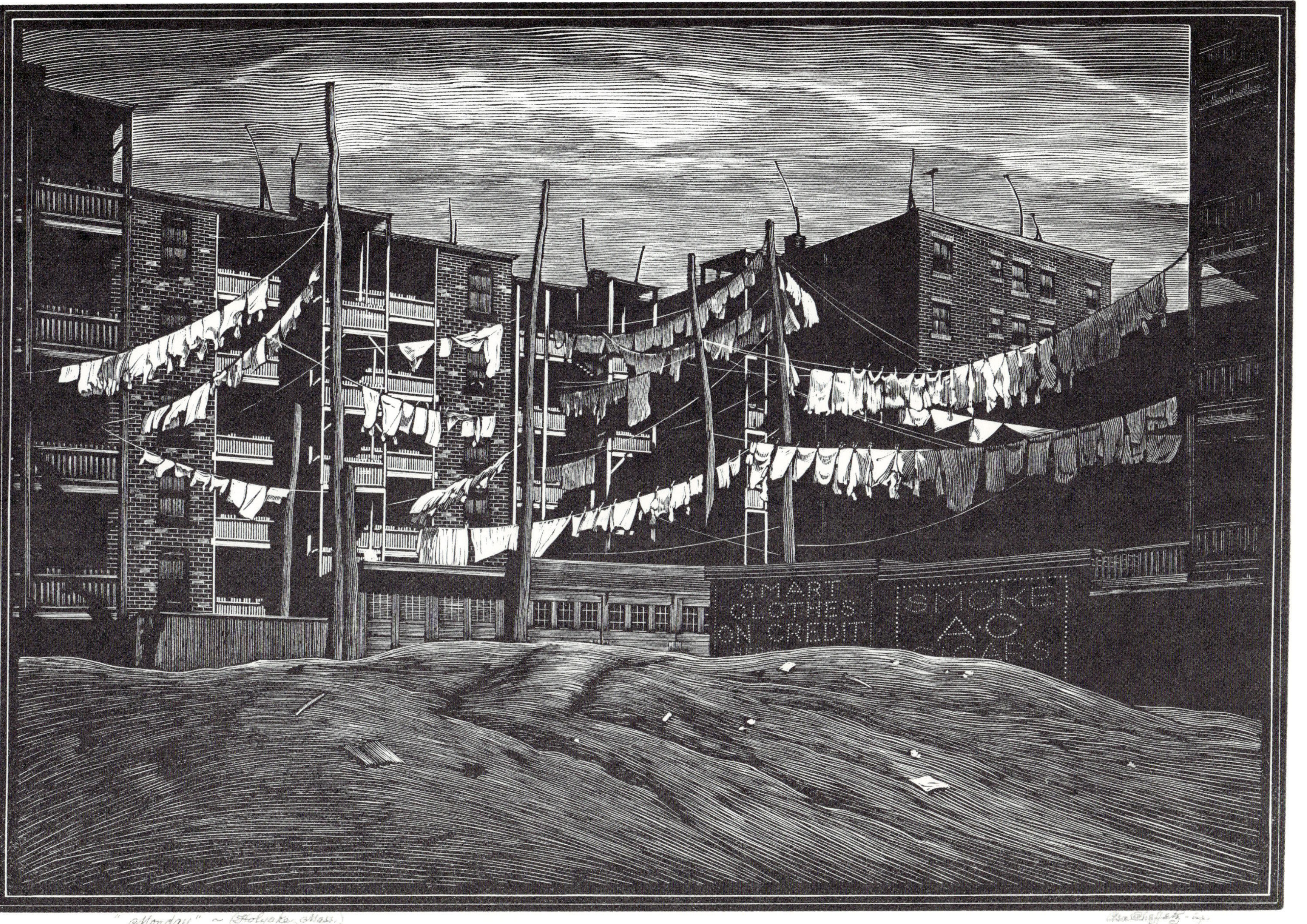

25. Asa Cheffetz. *Monday*, 1932. Wood engraving. Edition ca. 40. 7 × 10.

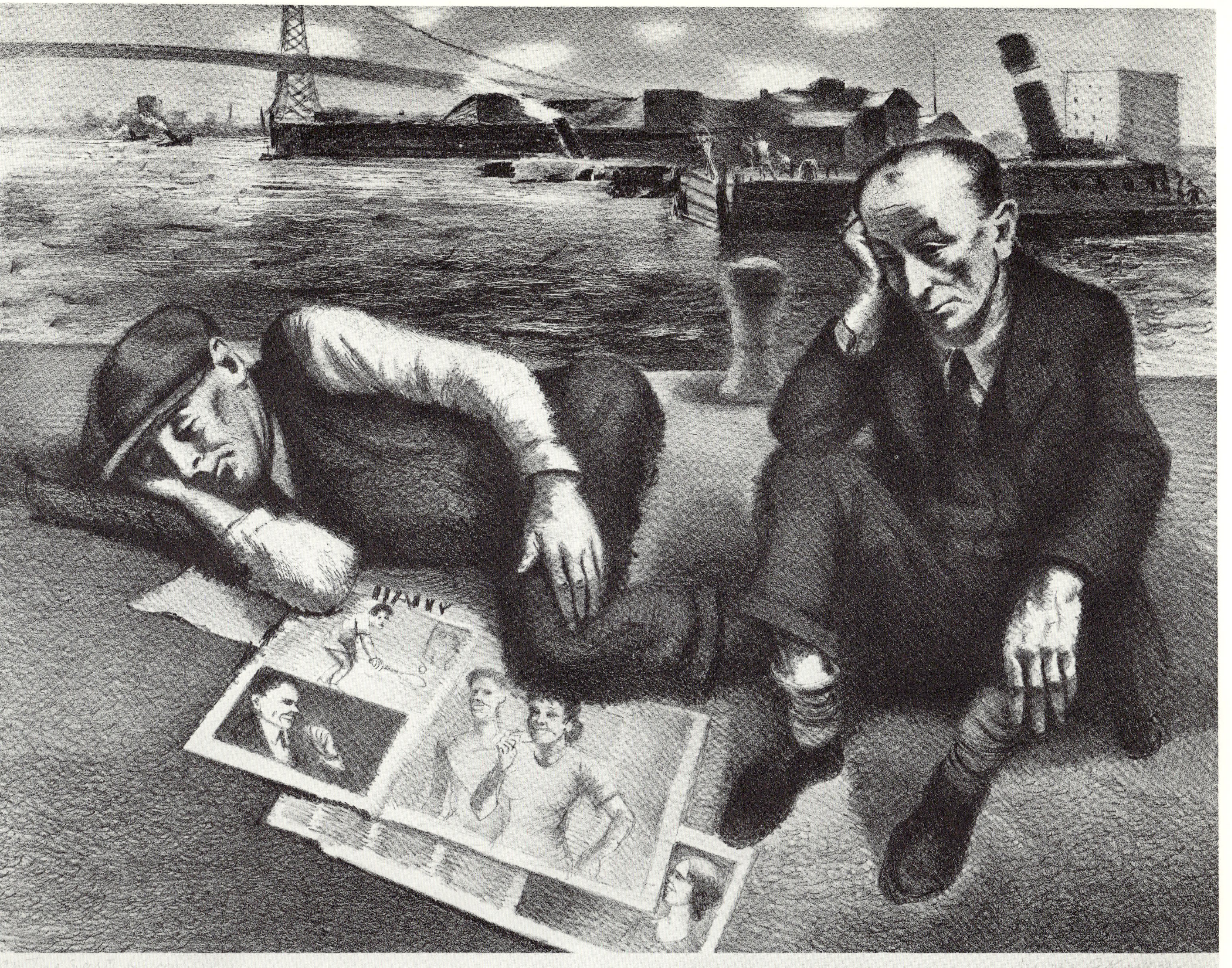

26. NICOLAI CIKOVSKY. *On the East River* (New York City), mid-1930s. Lithograph. 11⅞ × 15¼.

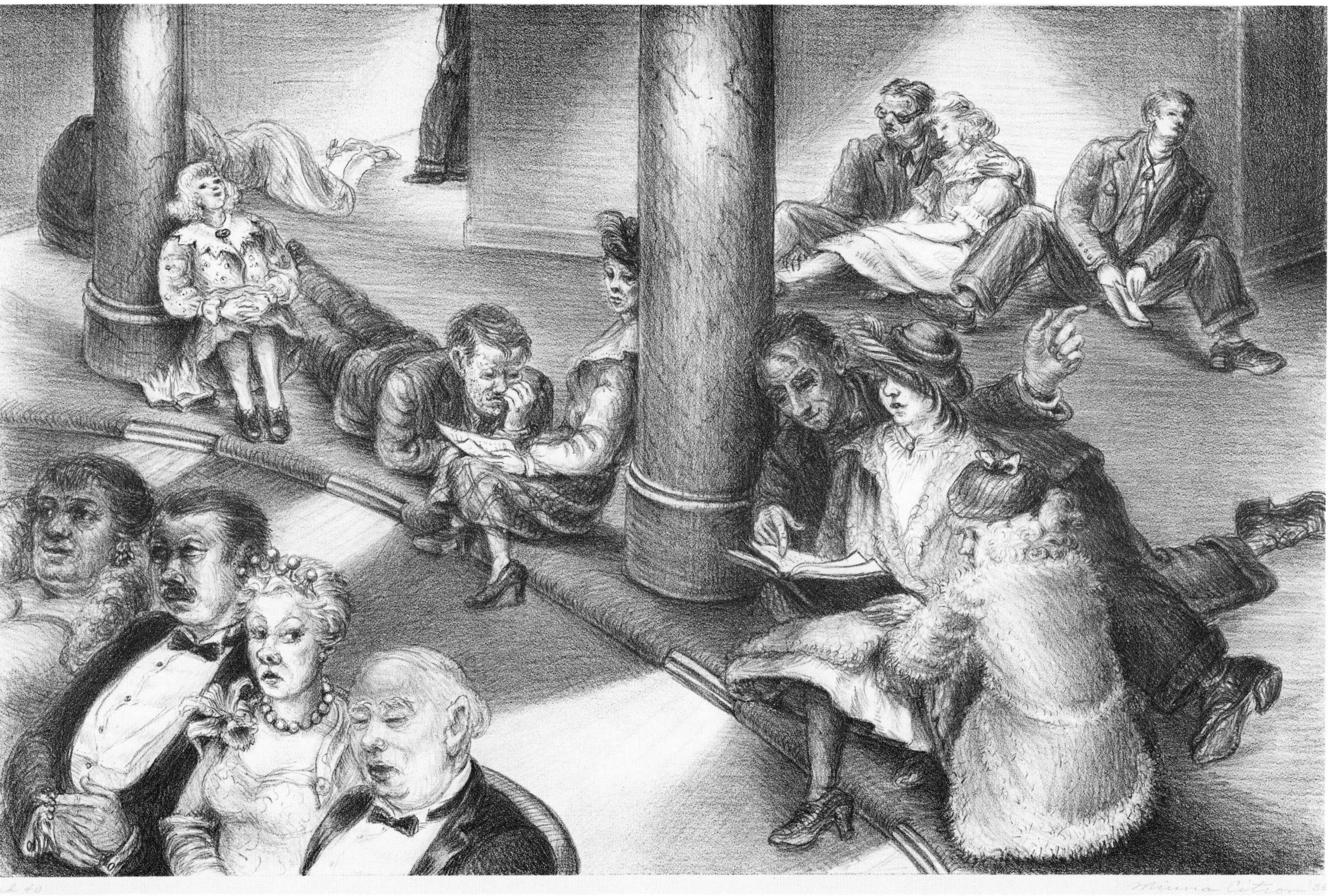

27. Minna Wright Citron. *Dress Circle—Carnegie Hall* (New York City), 1936. Lithograph. Edition 40. 8¾ × 13⅜.

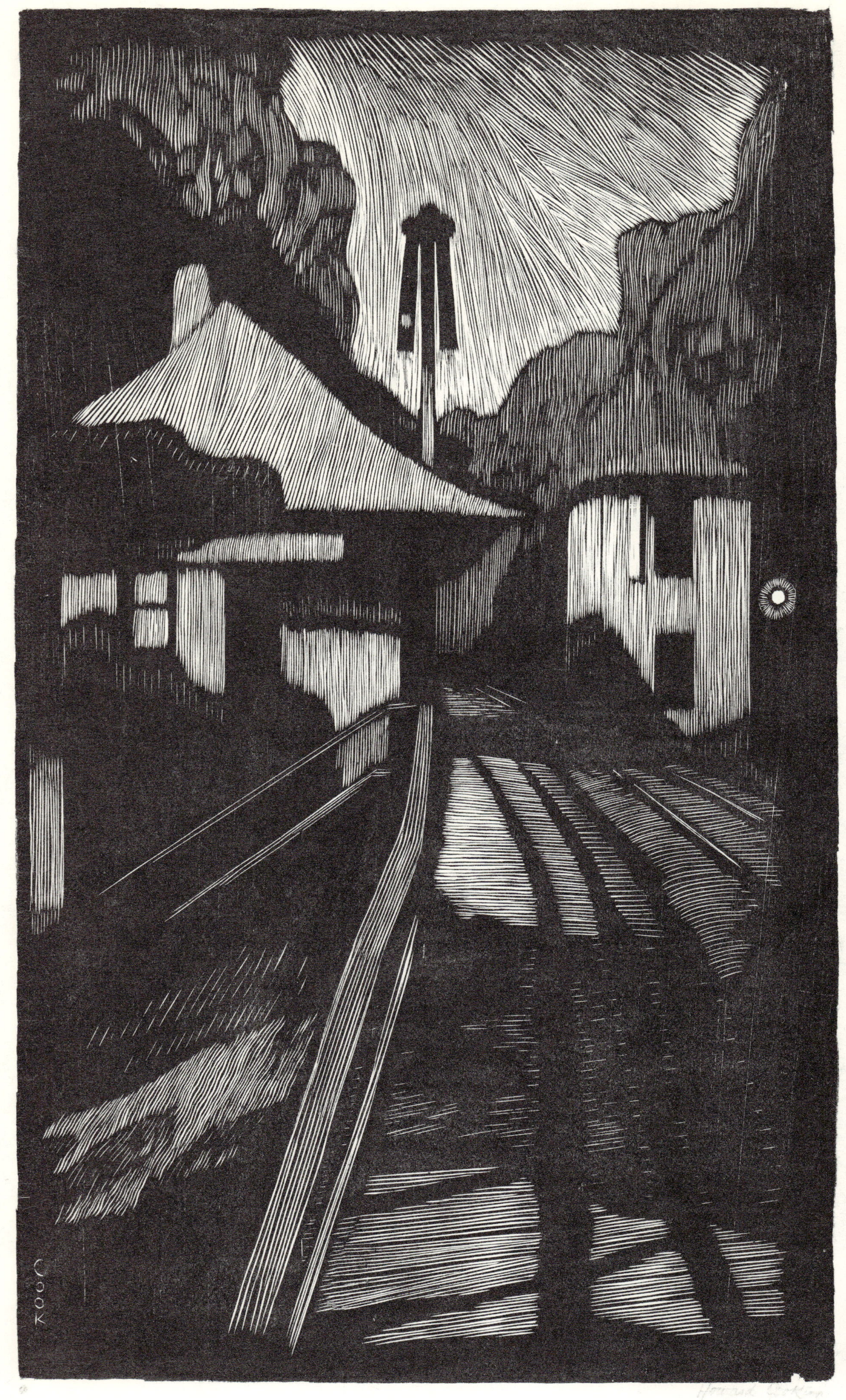

28. Howard Norton Cook. *Railroad Sleeping*, 1926. Woodcut. Edition 50. 15¼ × 9. Checkerboard 14, Duffy 29.

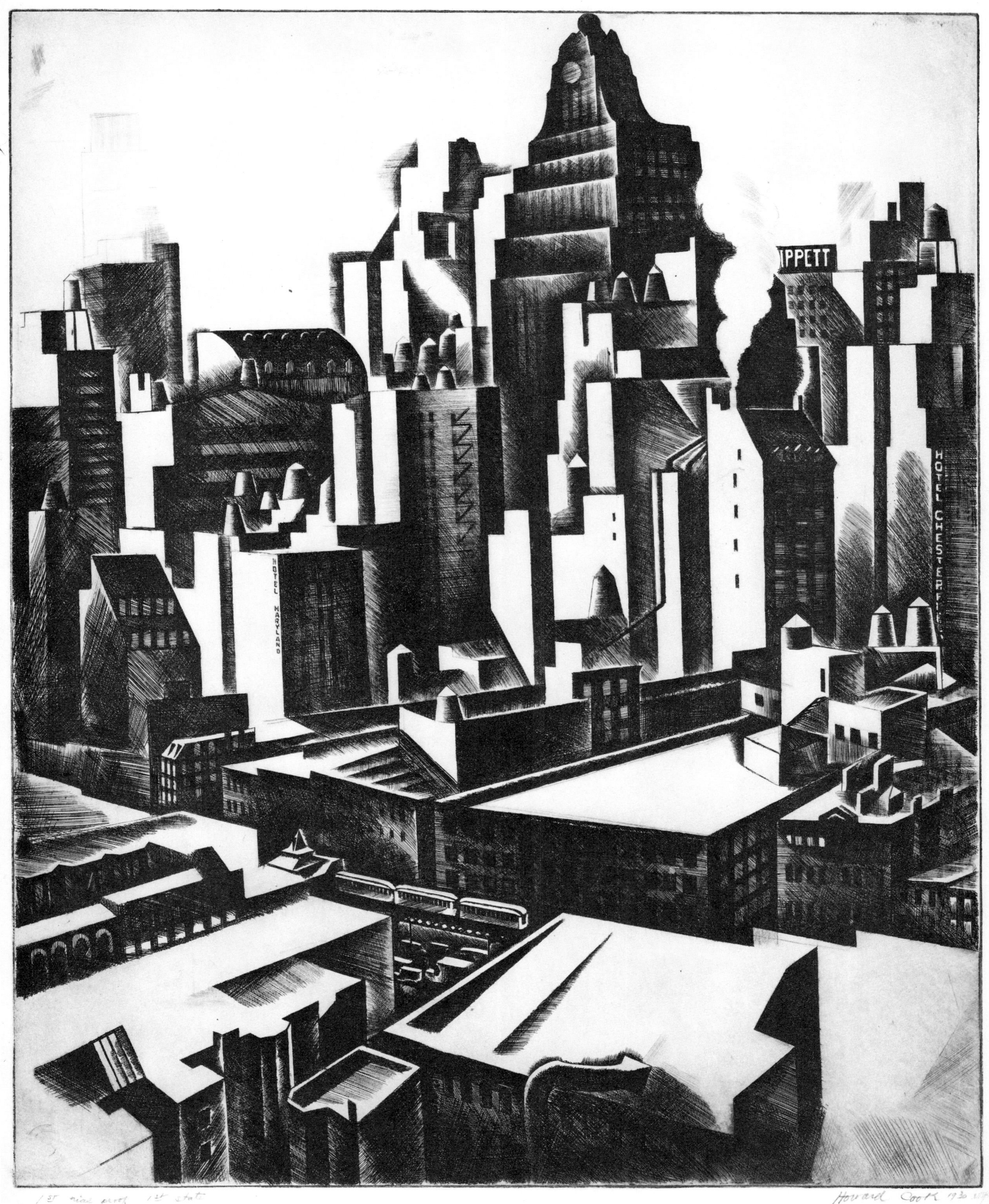

29. Howard Norton Cook. *Times Square Sector* (New York City), 1930. Etching. Edition 75; this is the first trial proof of the first state. $11\frac{7}{8} \times 9\frac{7}{8}$. Checkerboard 104, Duffy 146.

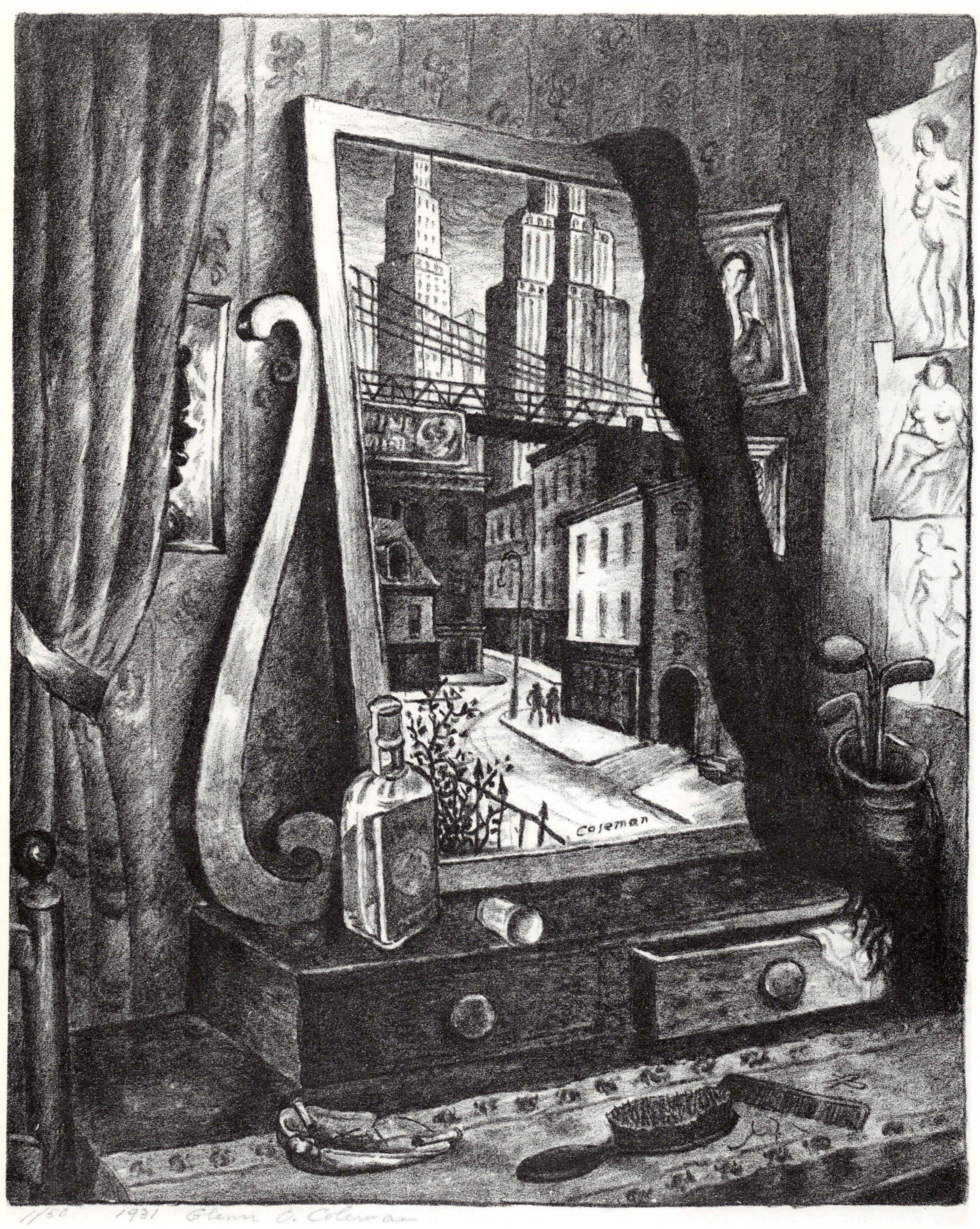

30. Glenn O. Coleman. *Still Life* (New York City), 1931. Lithograph. Edition 50. $15 \times 12\frac{1}{8}$.

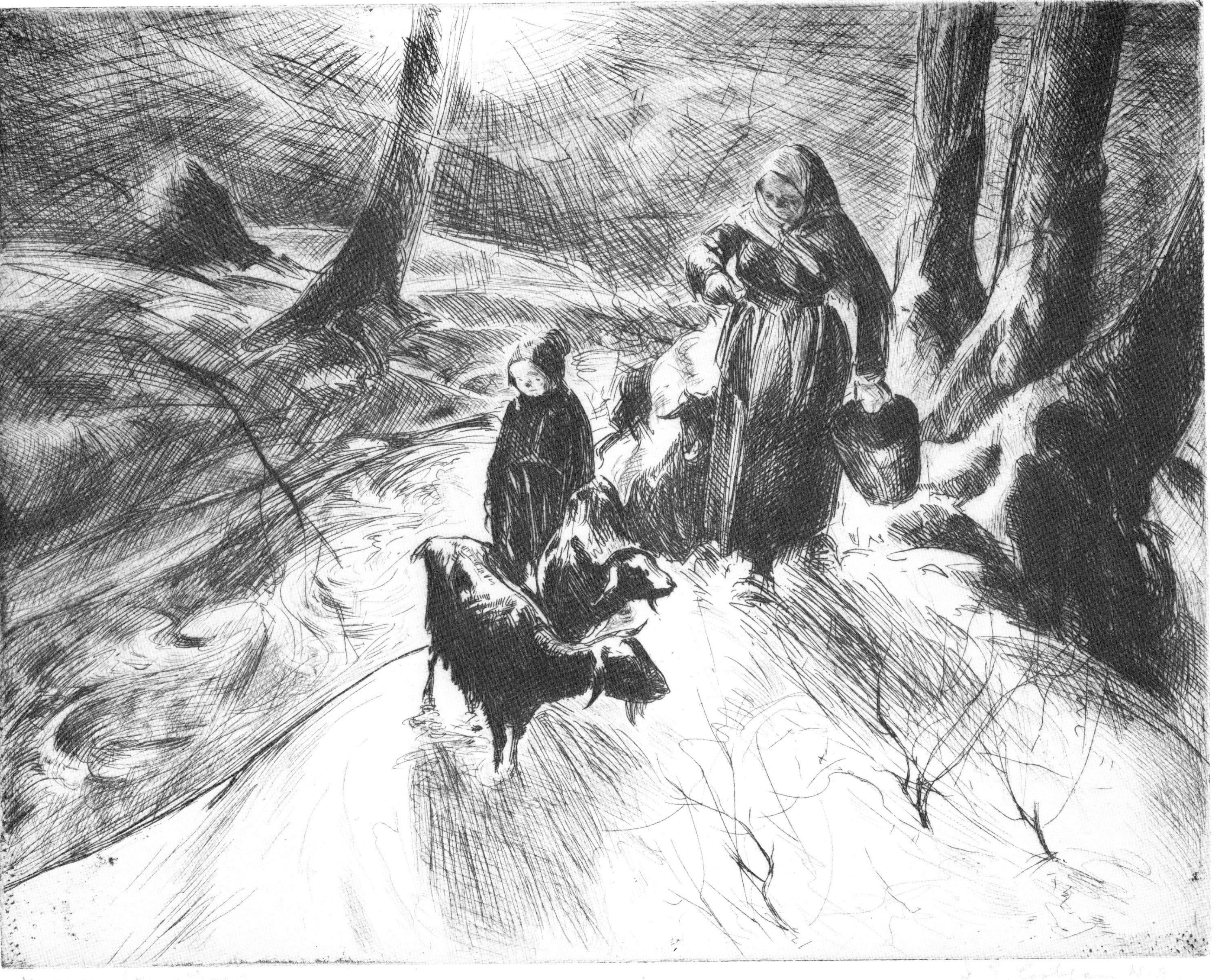

31. John Edward Costigan. *Woman, Boy, Goats*. Etching. 7⅞ × 9⅞.

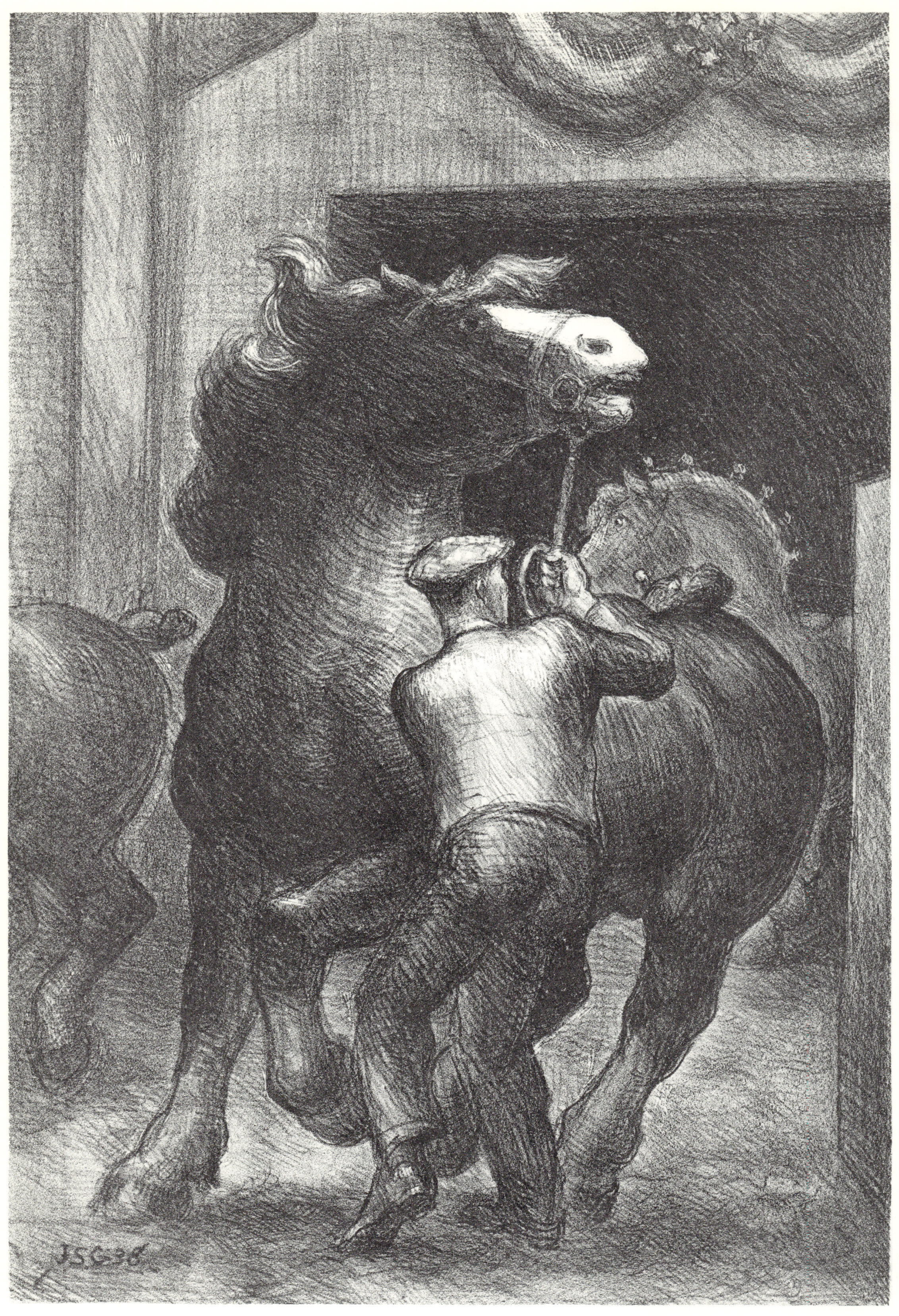

32. JOHN STEUART CURRY. *Prize Stallions*, 1938. Lithograph. Edition 250. 12¾ × 8¾. Cole 31.

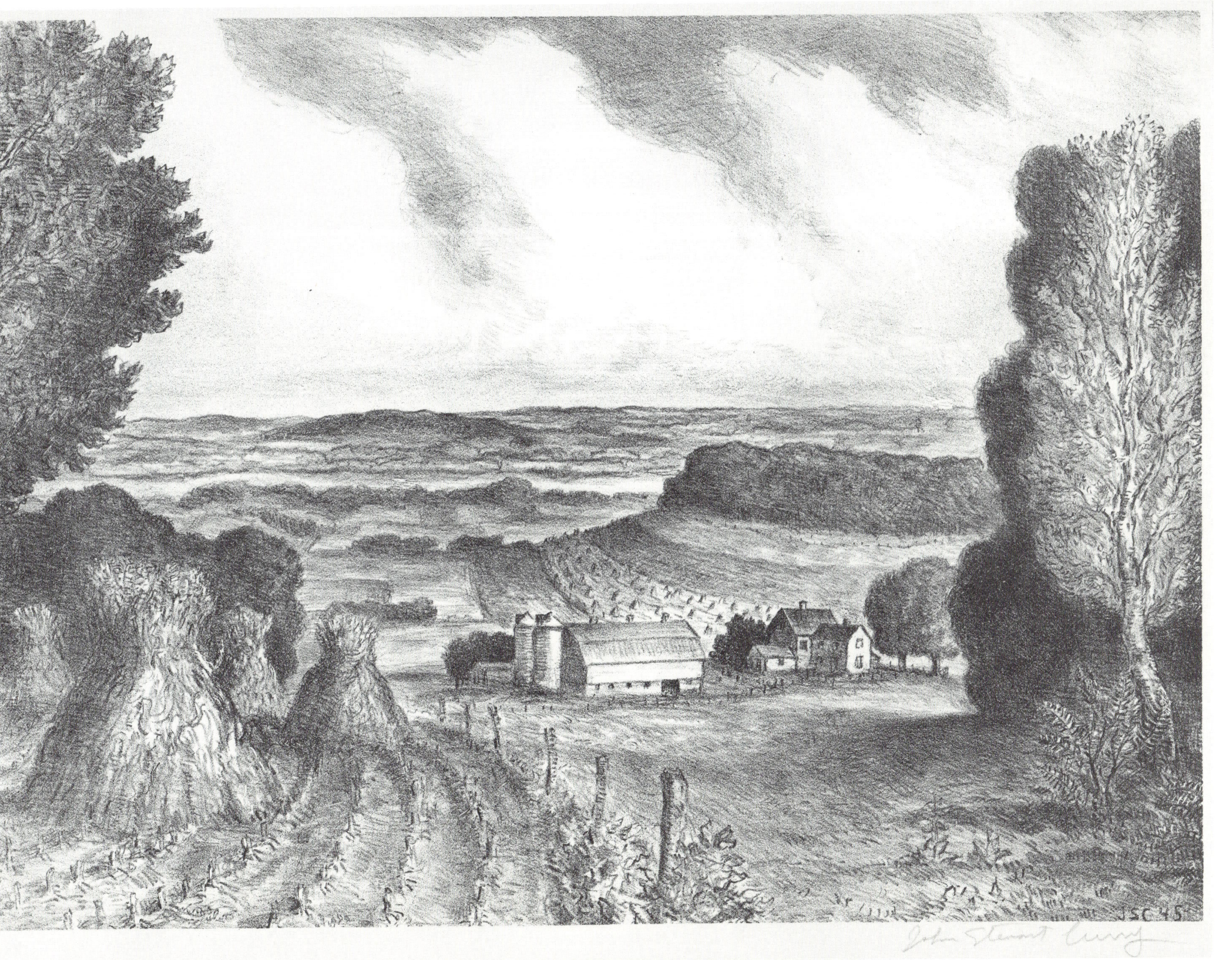

33. John Steuart Curry. *Valley of the Wisconsin*, 1945. Lithograph. Edition 250. 11⅝ × 15⅜. Cole 41.

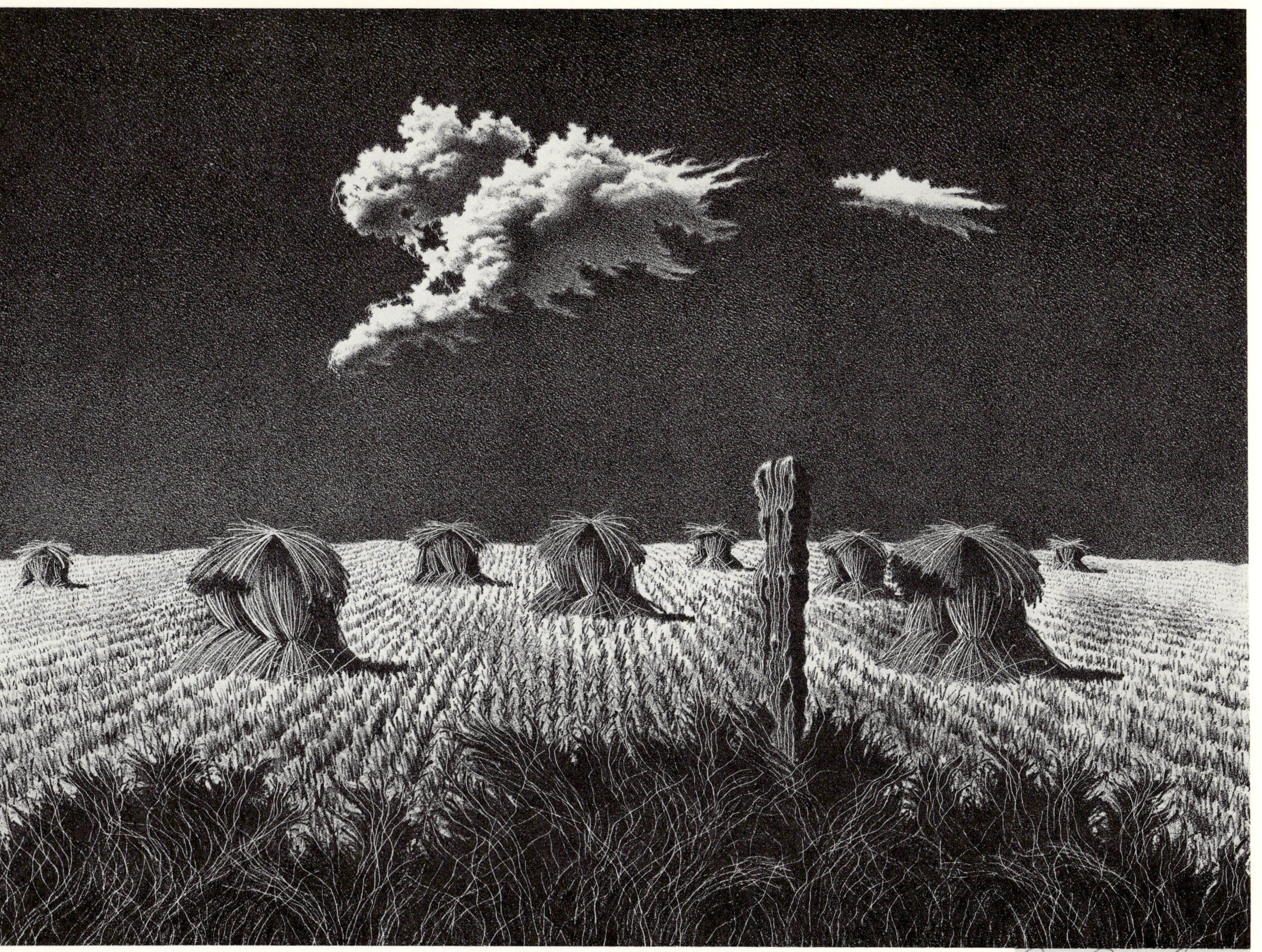

34. John Rogers Cox. *Wheat Shocks,* 1951. Lithograph. Edition 250. $8\frac{3}{4} \times 11\frac{3}{4}$.

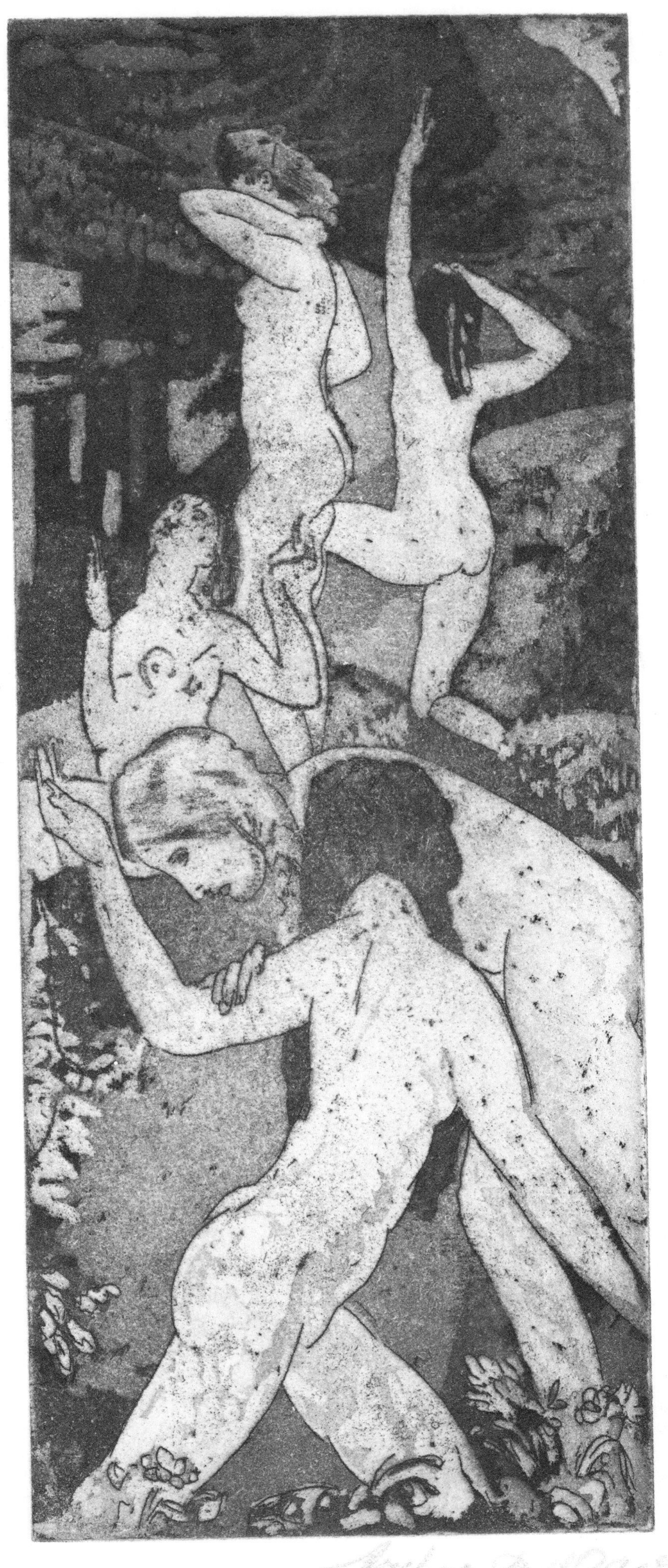

35. ARTHUR BOWEN DAVIES. *Fountain of Youth,* 1919. Soft ground, etching and aquatint. Edition 35. 10¼ × 4¼. Price 18.

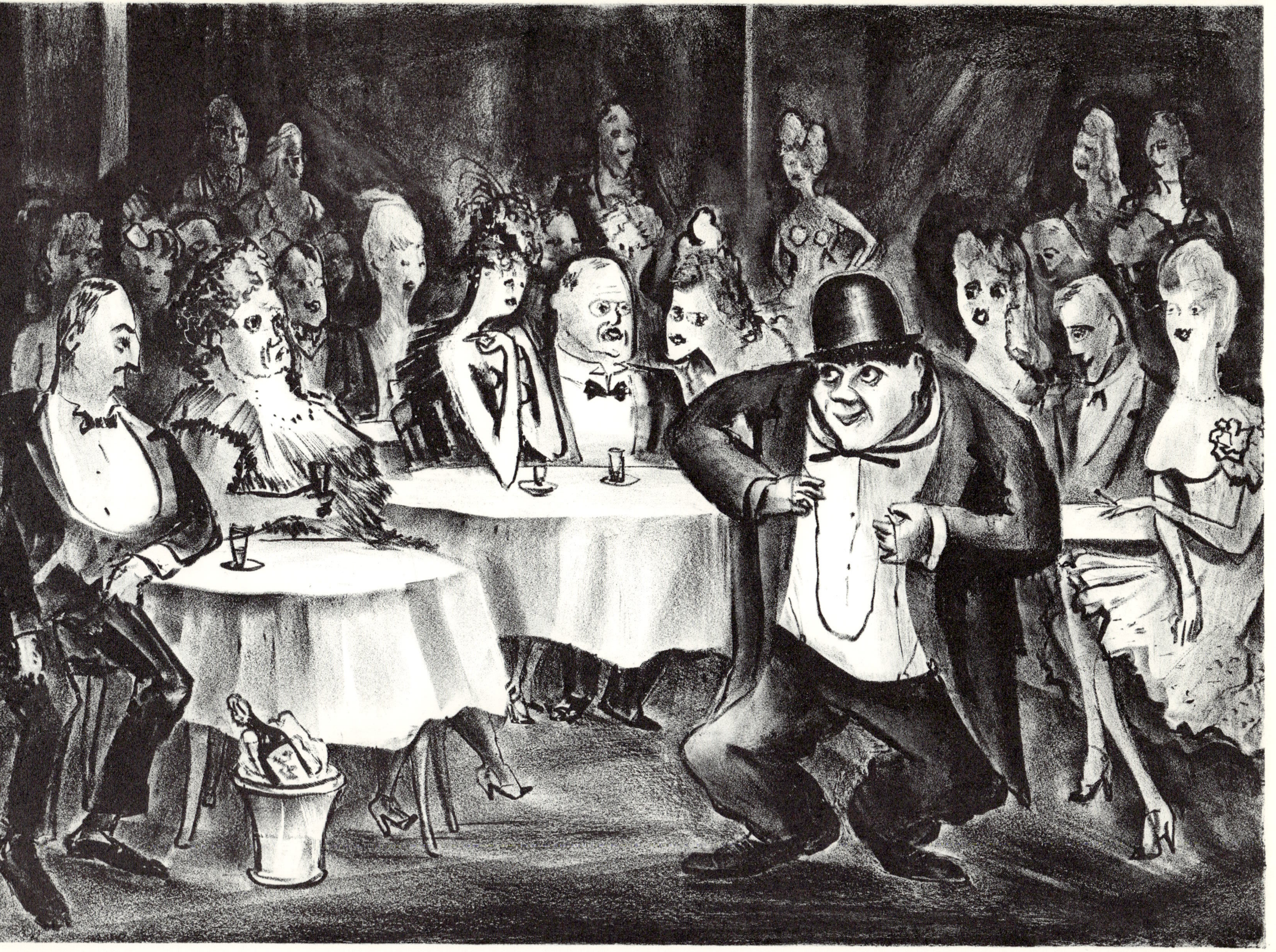

36. Adolf Dehn. *Jimmy Savo*, 1945. Lithograph. Edition 30. $12\frac{1}{2} \times 16\frac{3}{4}$.

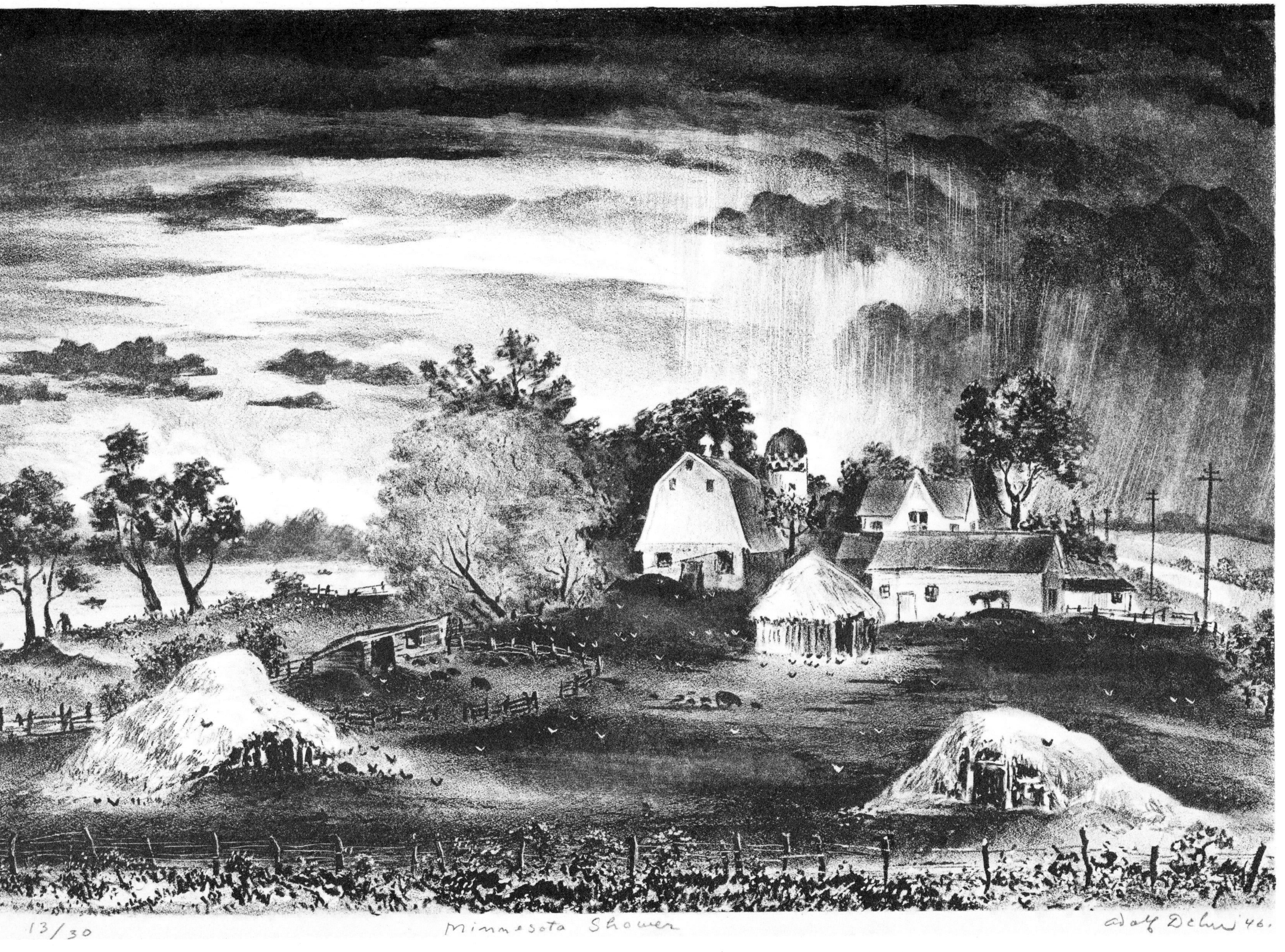

37. ADOLF DEHN. *Minnesota Shower* (or *Minnesota Farm*), 1946. Lithograph. Edition 30. 12⅜ × 17½.

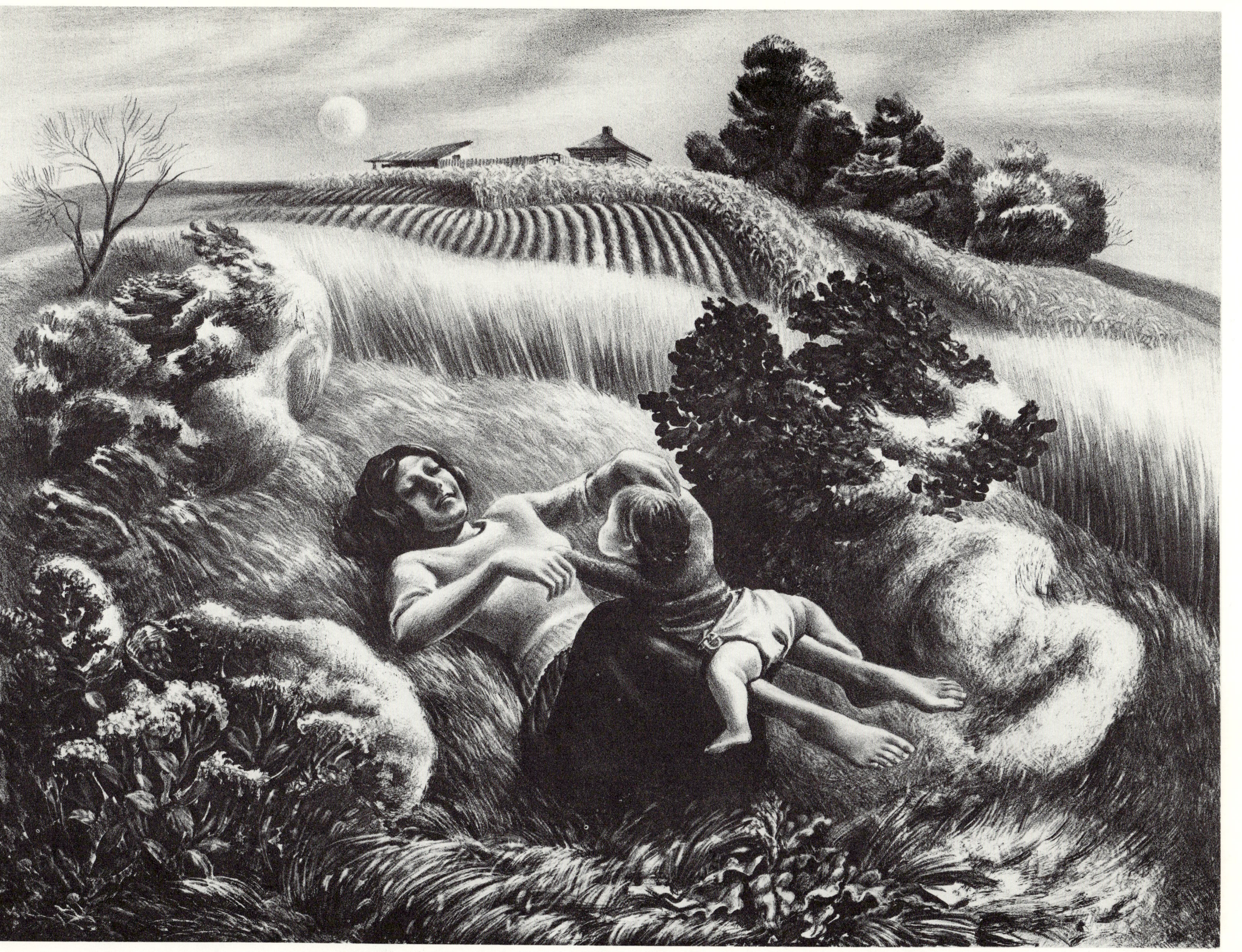

38. John Stockton DeMartelly. *Ride a Cock Horse,* Lithograph. 9¼ × 12⅛.

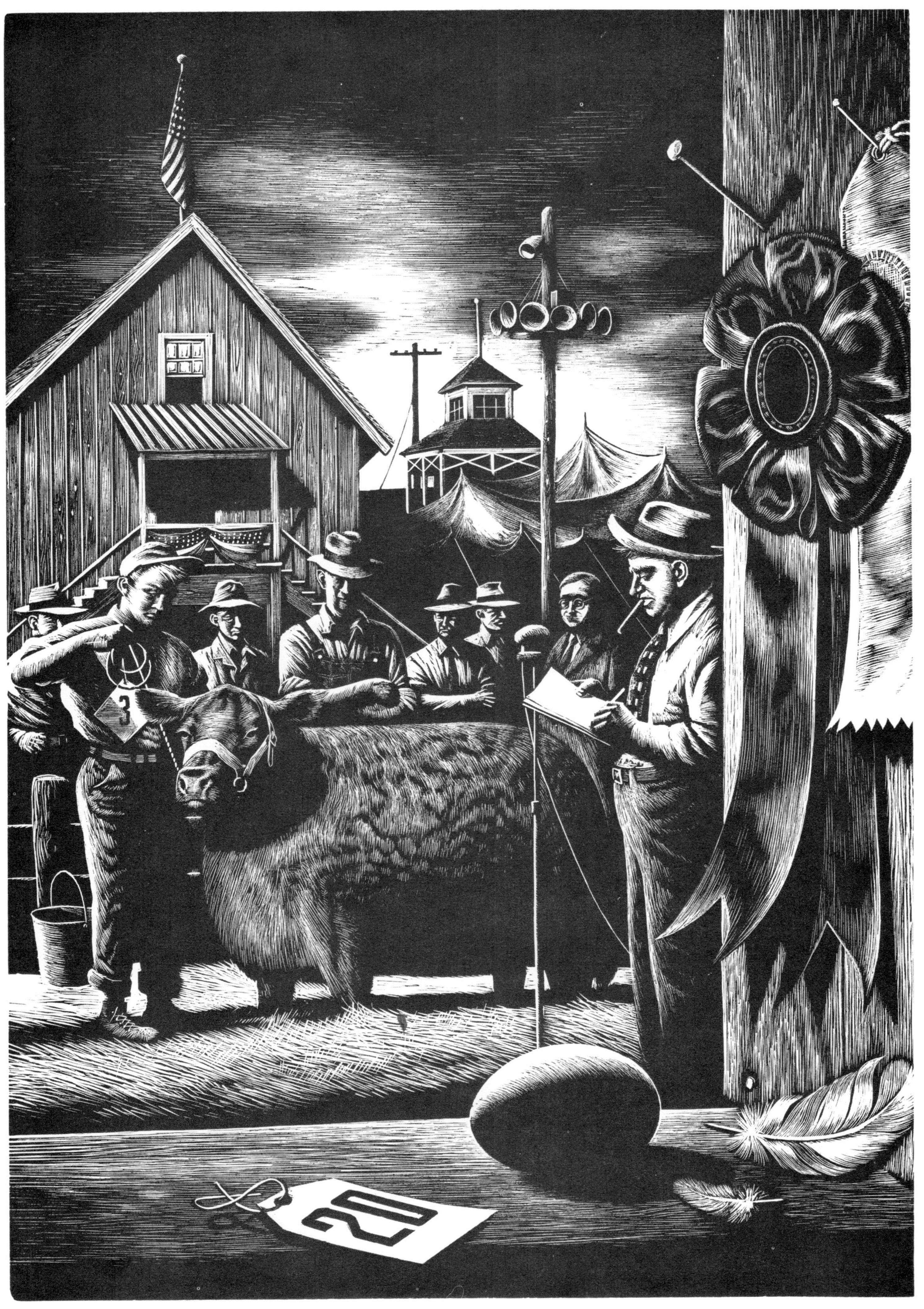

39. Stevan Dohanos. *State Fair,* 1948. Wood engraving. Edition 265, publication of the Print Club of Cleveland, 1948. $12\frac{5}{8} \times 8\frac{7}{8}$.

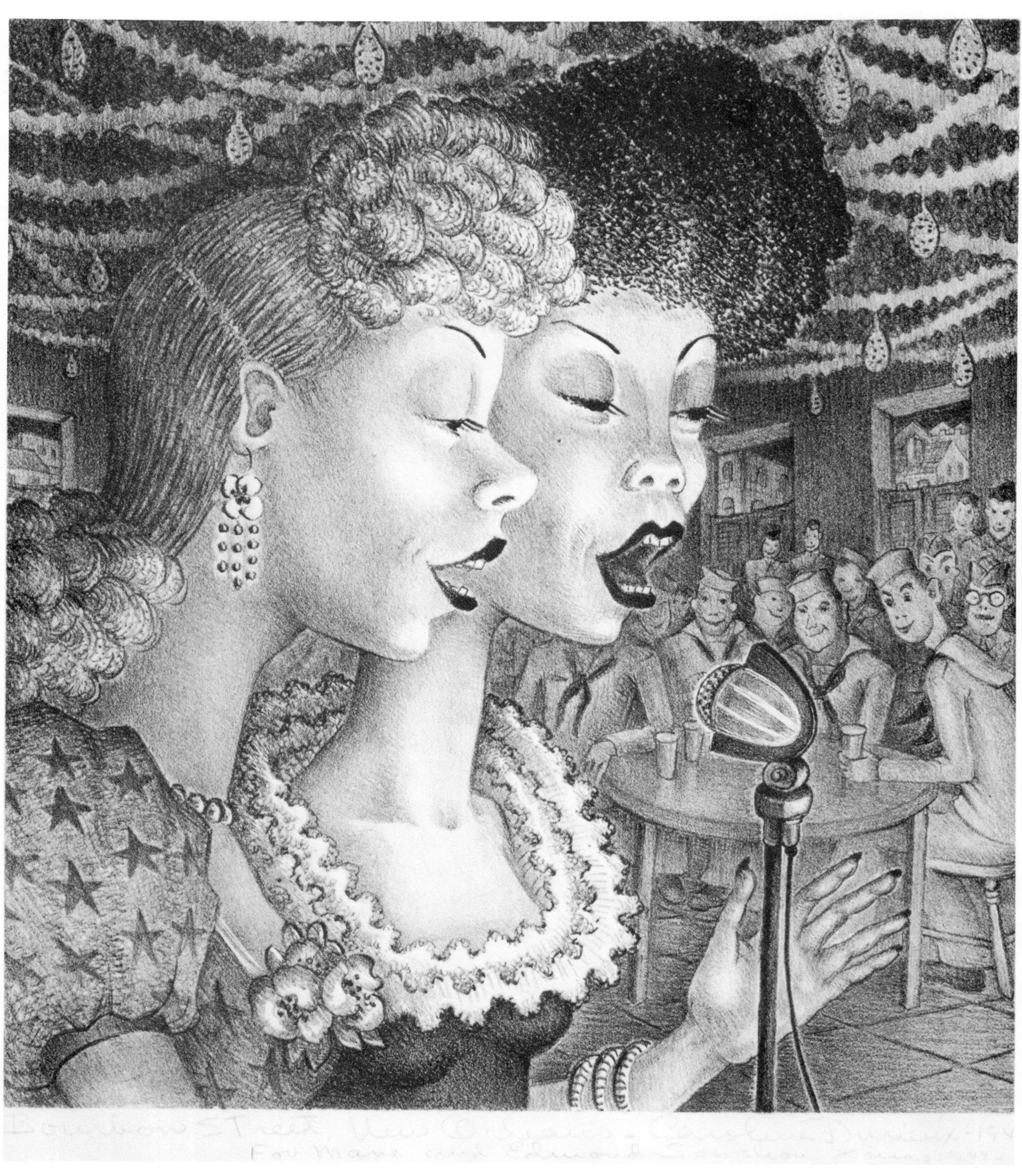

40. Caroline Wogan Durieux. *Bourbon Street—New Orleans,* 1942. Lithograph. Edition 10. 10⅝ × 10. Cox 29.

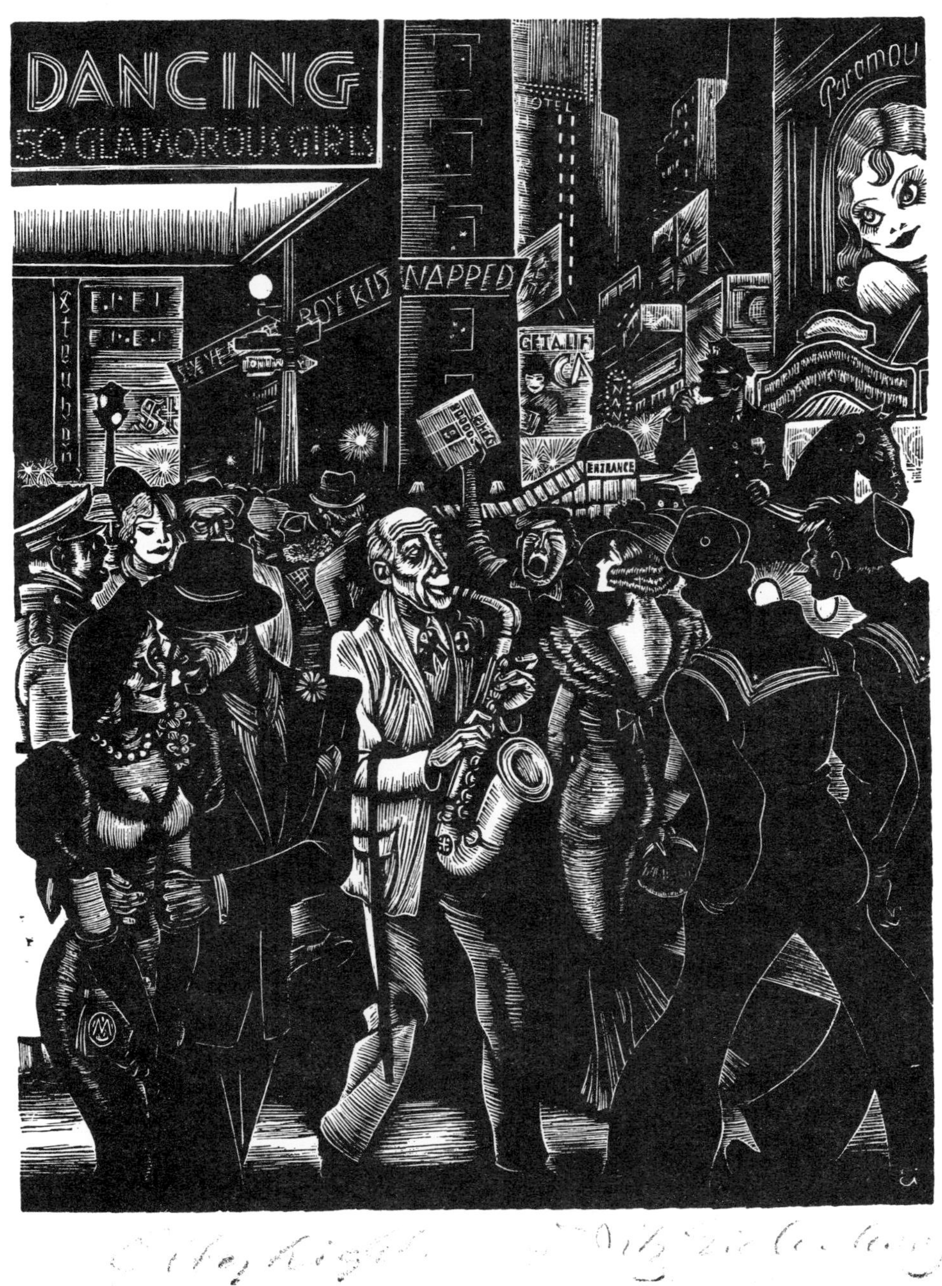

41. FRITZ EICHENBERG. *City Lights* (New York City), 1934. Wood engraving. Edition 200. $6\frac{1}{4} \times 4\frac{3}{4}$.

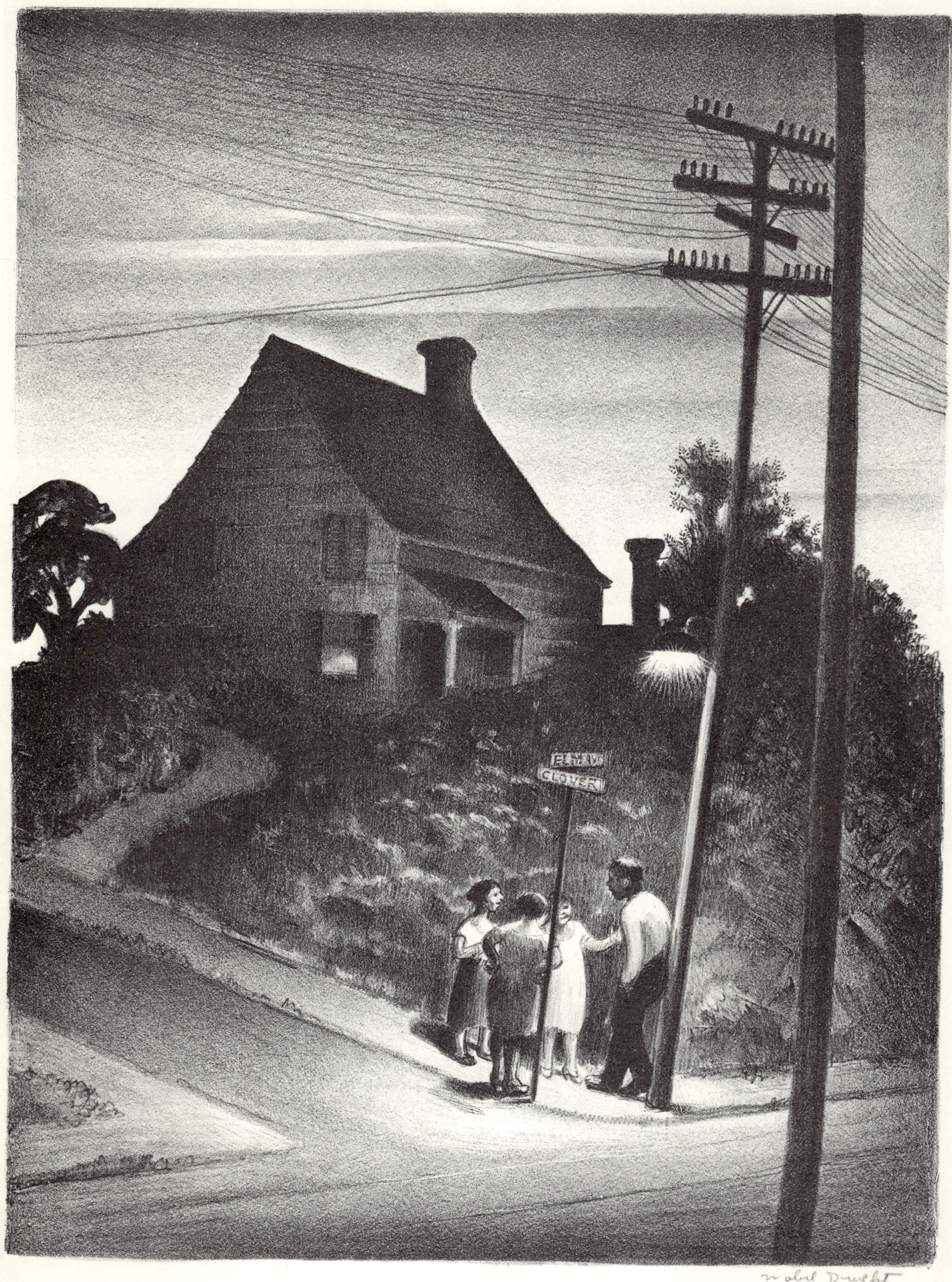

42. Mabel Dwight. *Dusk*, 1929. Lithograph. Edition 100. 13 × 9¾. Zigrosser 39.

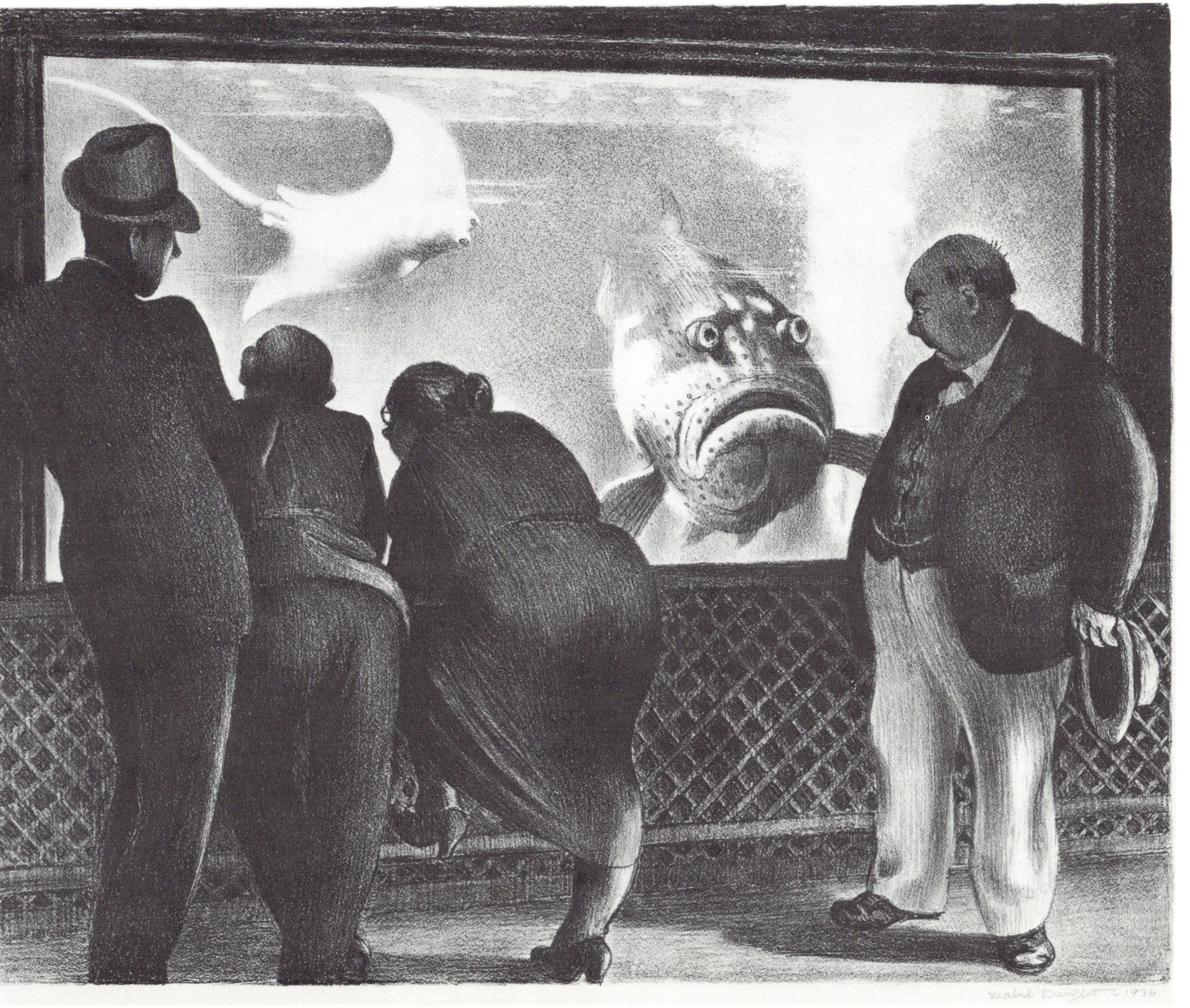

43. MABEL DWIGHT. *Queer Fish*, 1936. Lithograph. Published by the American Artists Group. 10⅝ × 13. Zigrosser 80.

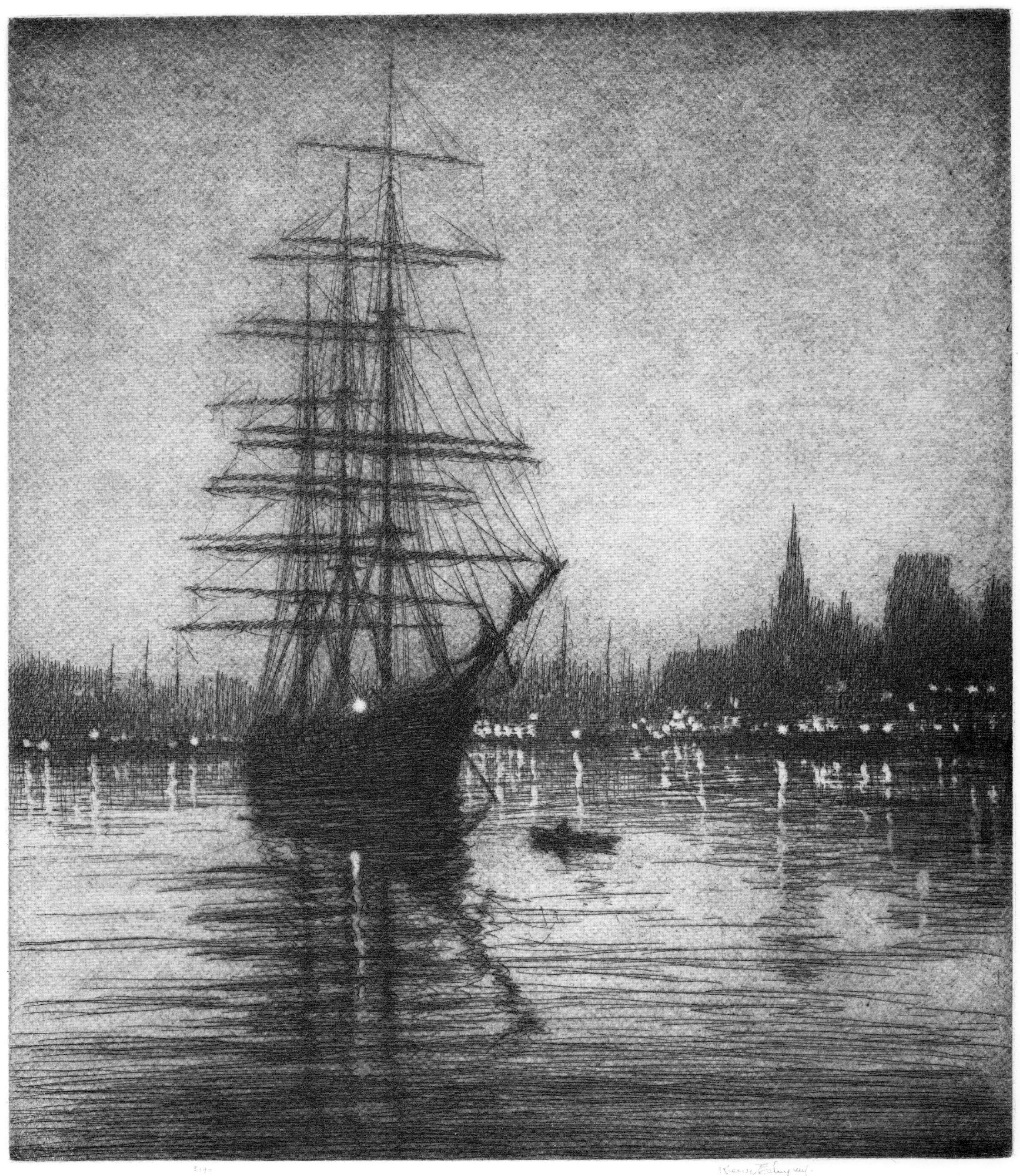

44. Kerr Eby. *Harbor Lights,* 1930. Etching and aquatint. Edition 90. 12 × 10½.

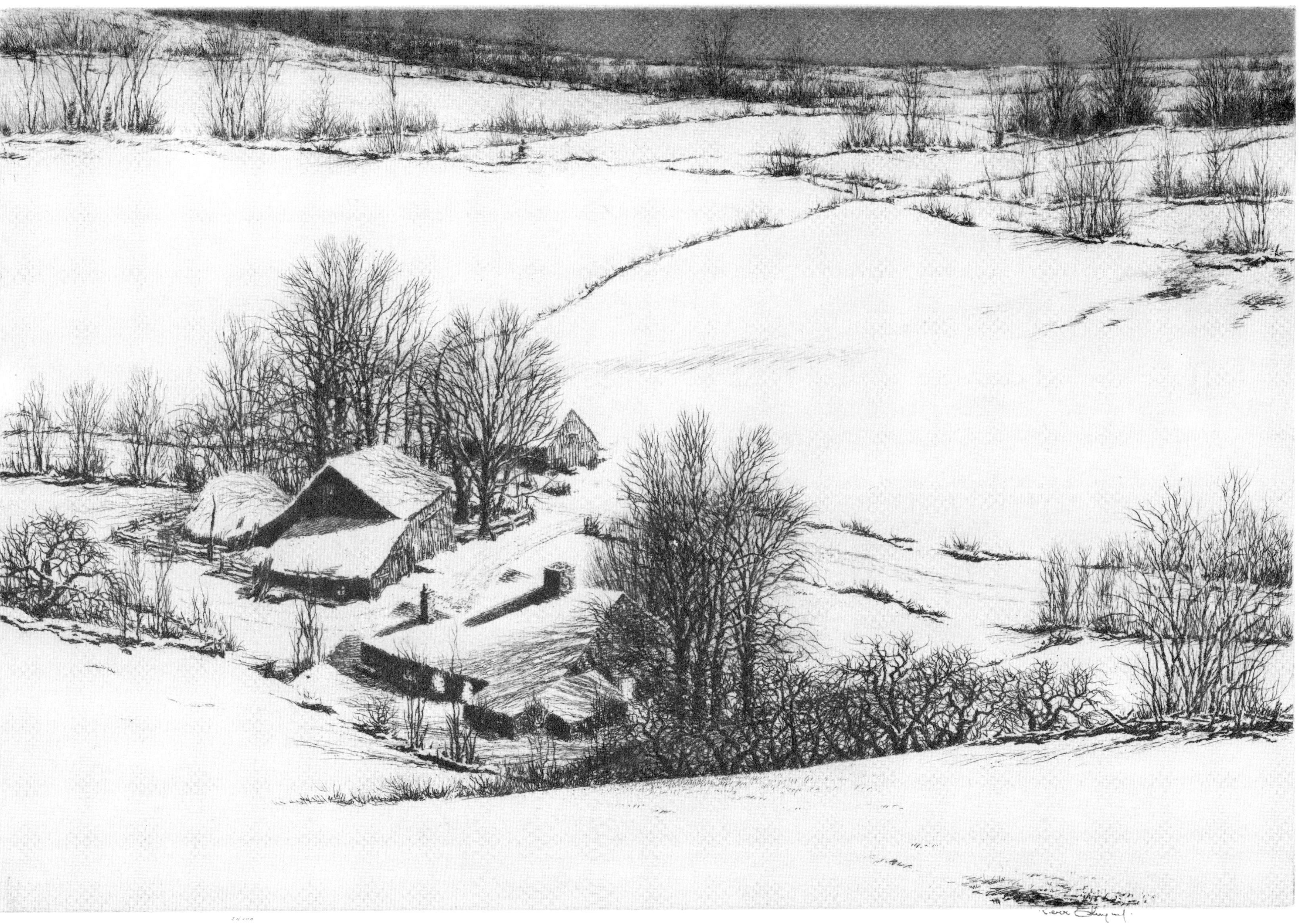

45. KERR EBY. *Still Hollow*, 1936. Etching. Edition 100. $10\frac{1}{4} \times 14\frac{11}{16}$.

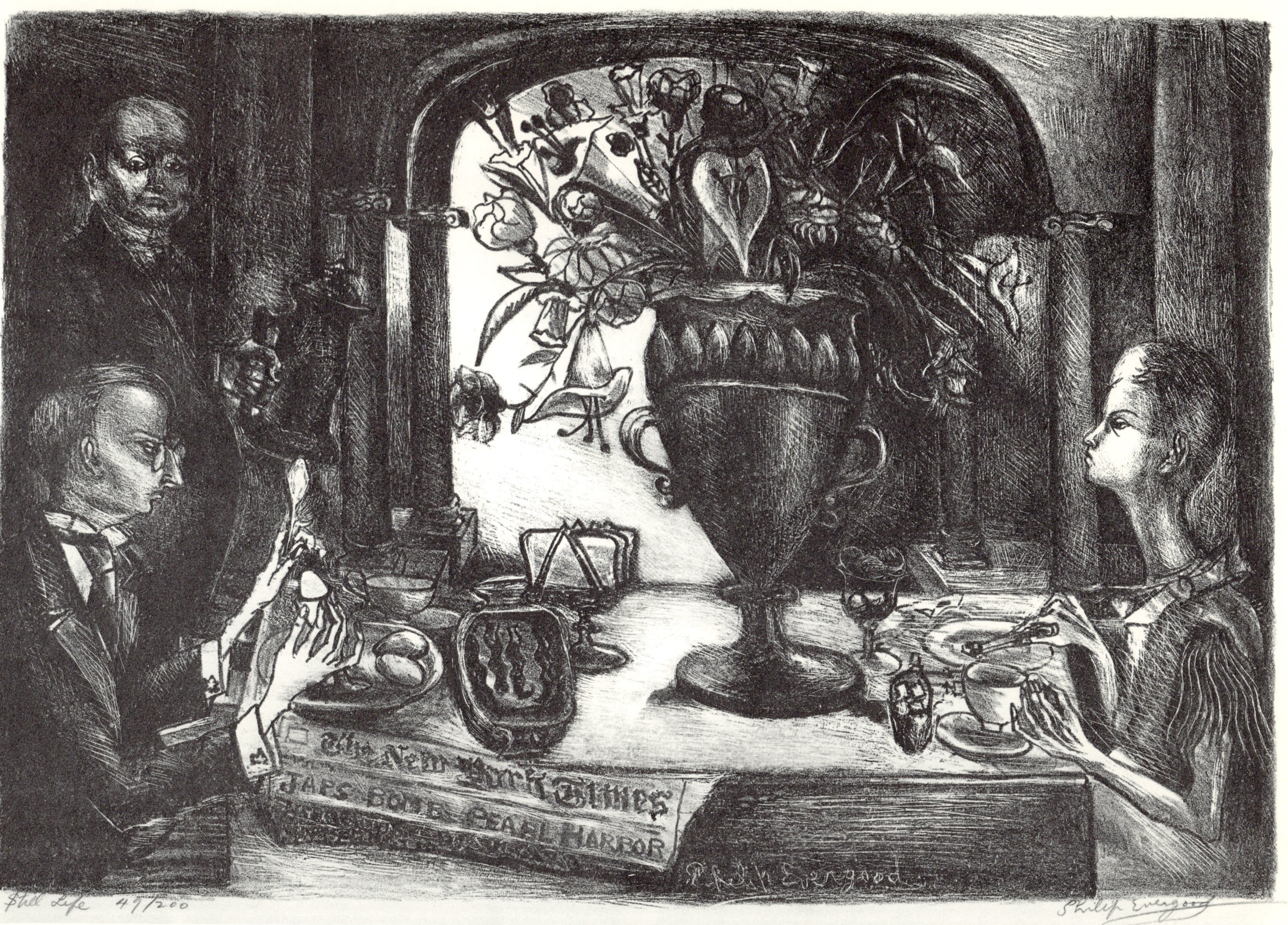

46. Philip Howard Francis Evergood. *Still Life*, 1944. Lithograph. Edition 200. $11\frac{1}{2} \times 16\frac{1}{4}$. Lippard 156.

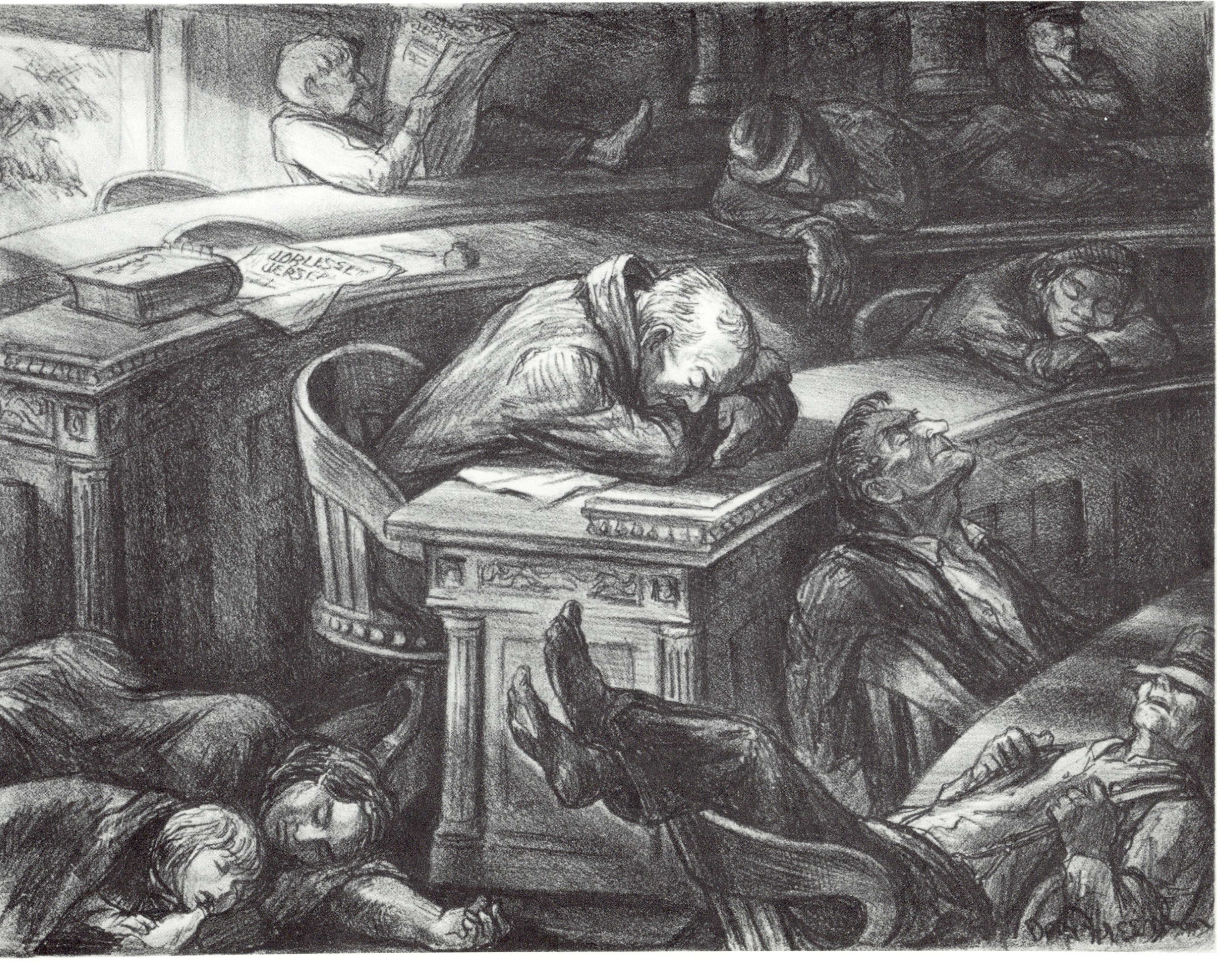

47. Don Freeman. *Dawn in the Assembly,* 1935. Lithograph. Edition 33. $8\frac{3}{4} \times 11\frac{1}{8}$.

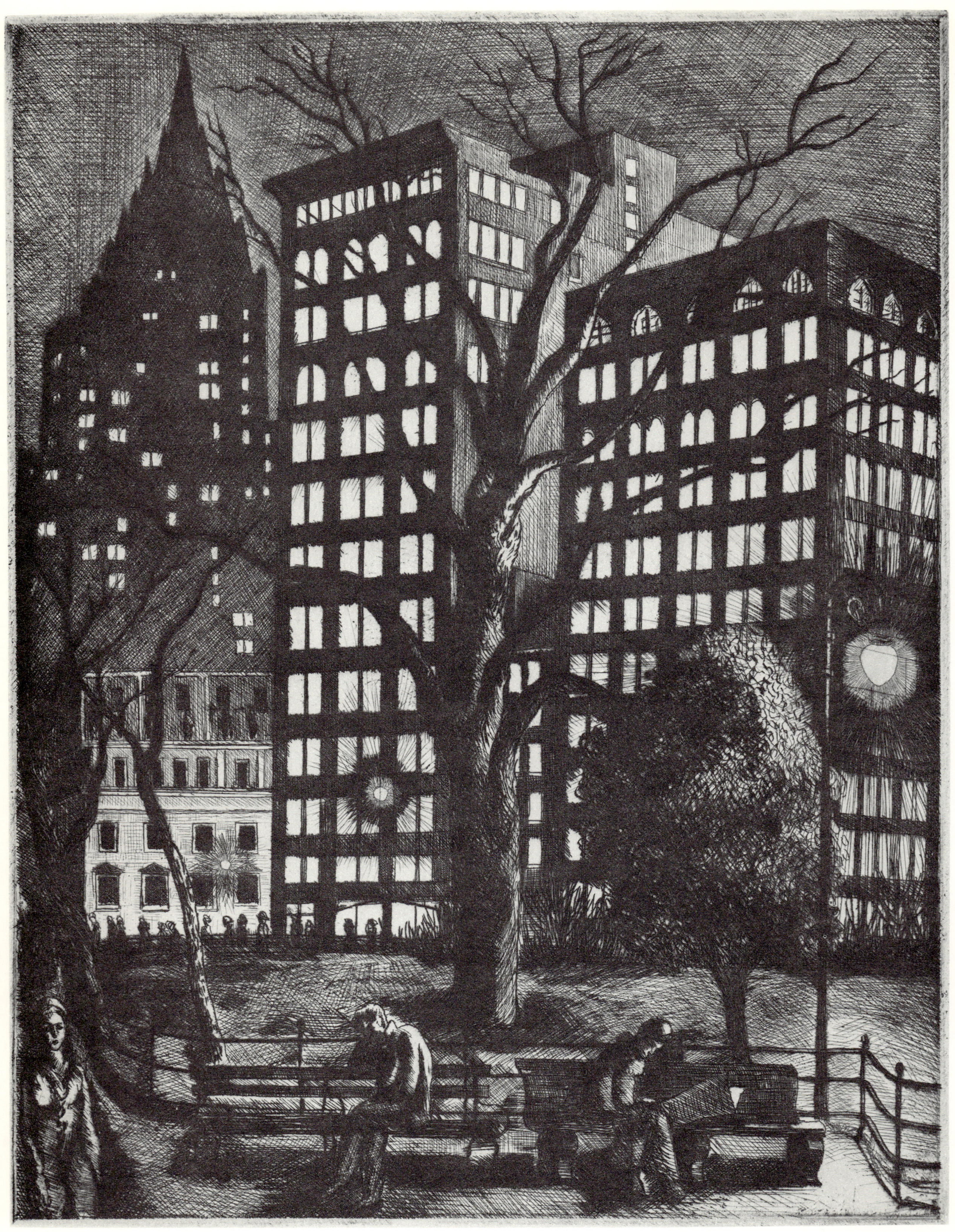

48. Ernest Fiene. *City Lights* (or *Madison Square Park*; New York City), 1932. Etching. Edition ca. 250. 11¾ × 9⅛.

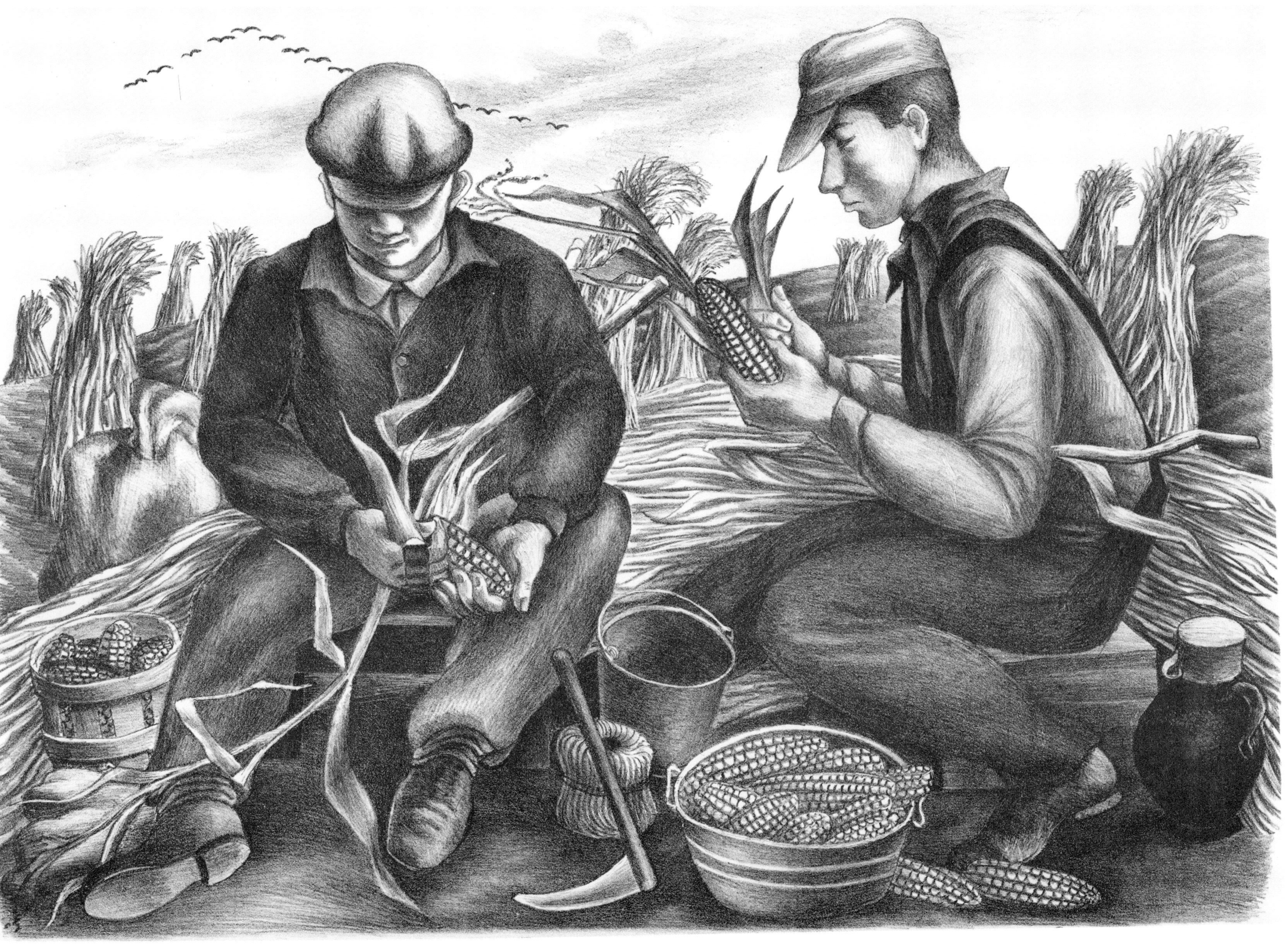

49. Ernest Fiene. *Corn Shuckers*, 1934. Lithograph. 11 × 15⅛.

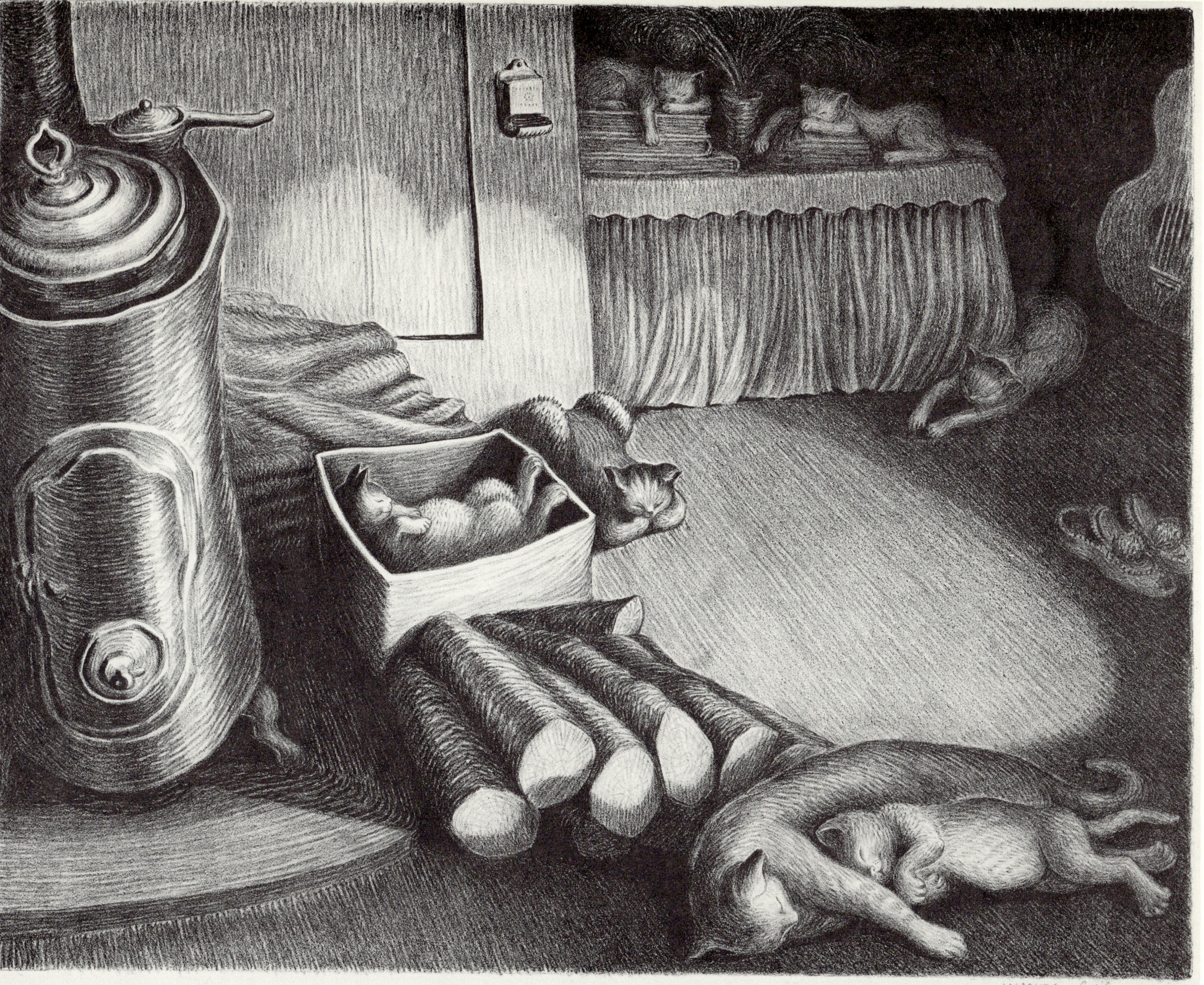

50. WANDA GÁG. *Siesta*, 1938. Lithograph. 9⅞ × 12⅛.

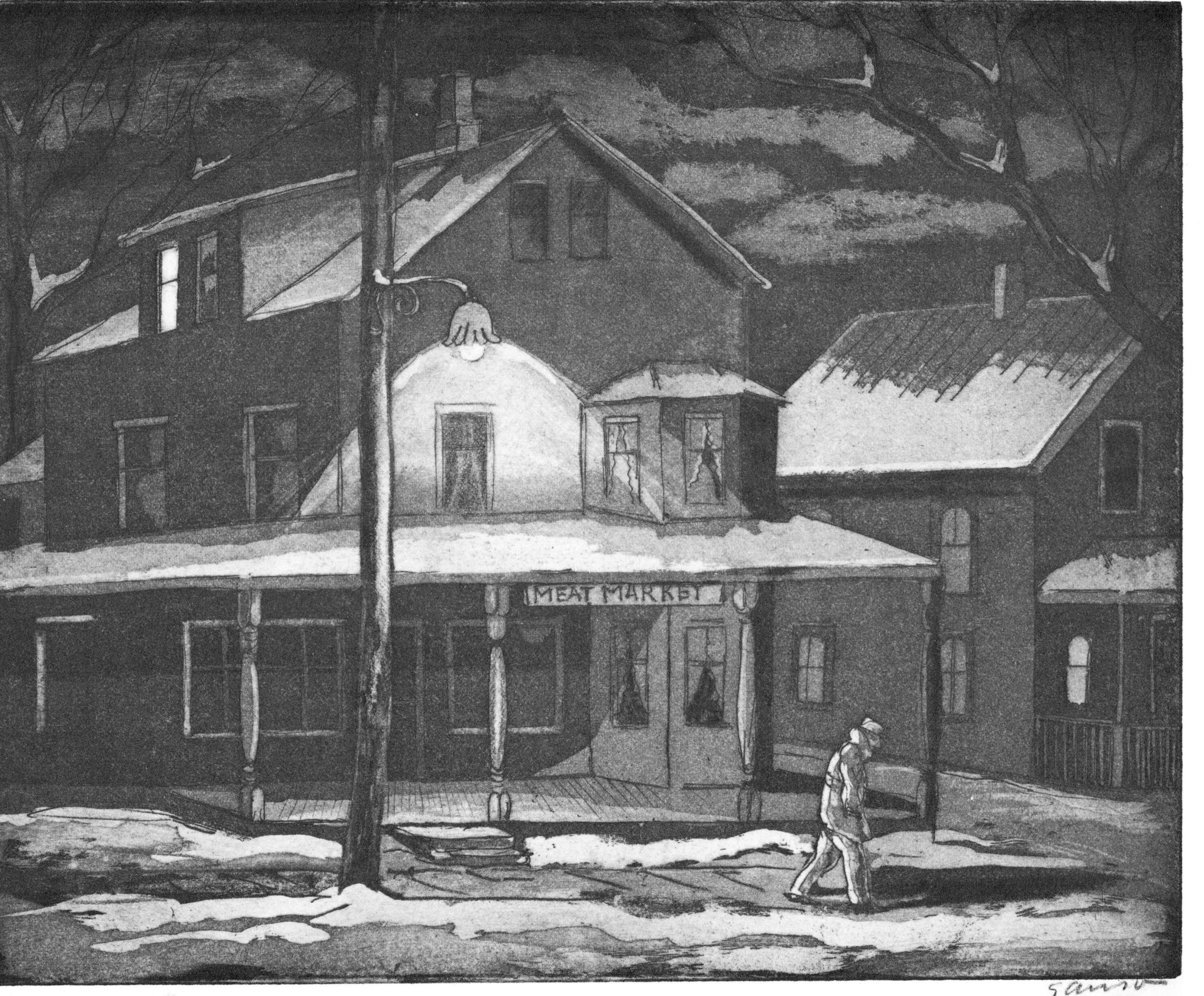

51. EMIL GANSO. *Meat Market—Woodstock* (N.Y.), 1934. Aquatint. Edition 35. 9 × 11.

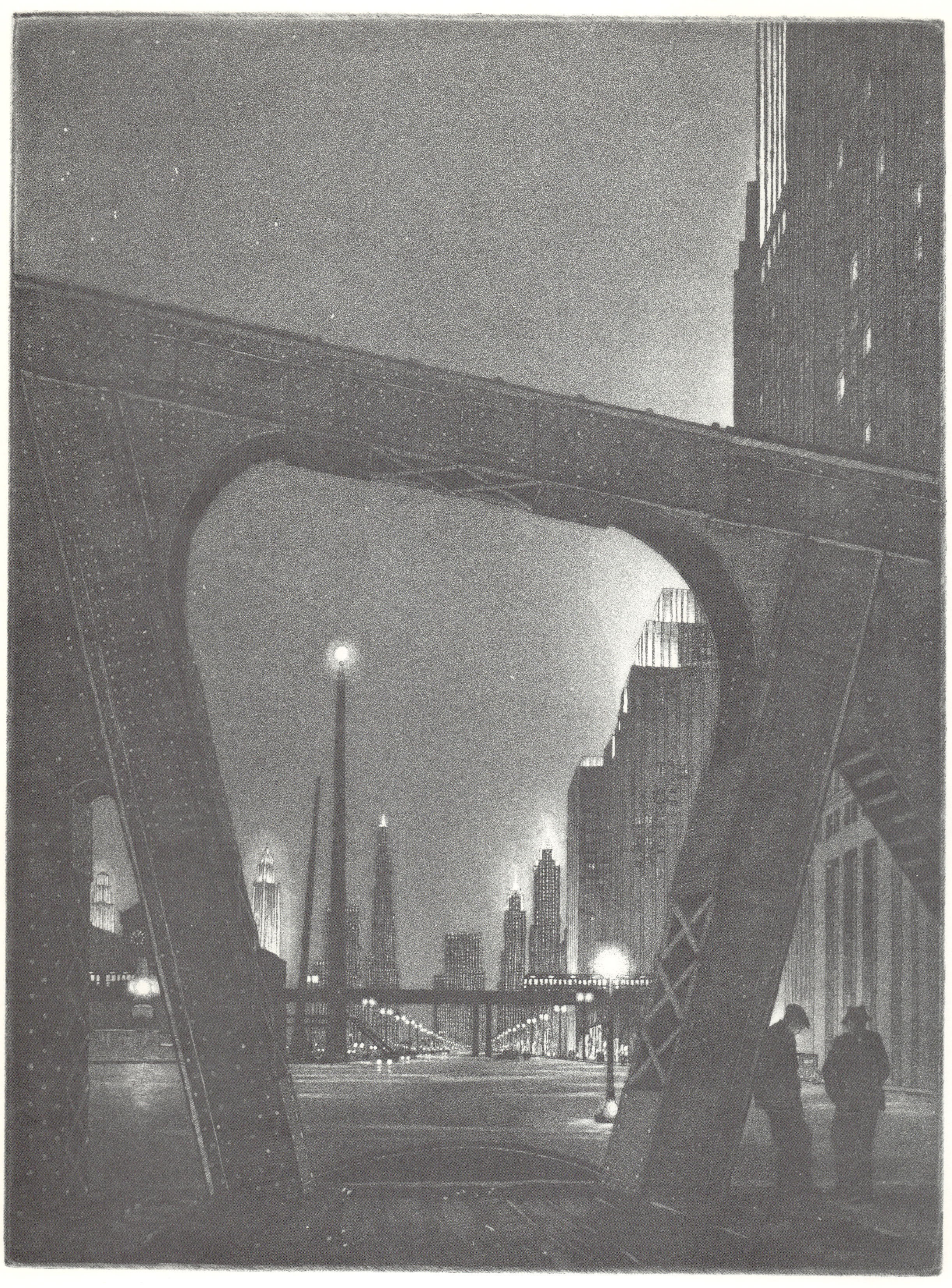

52. GERALD KENNETH GEERLINGS. *Jewelled City* (Chicago), 1931. Etching and aquatint. Edition 32. 15⅝ × 11⅝.

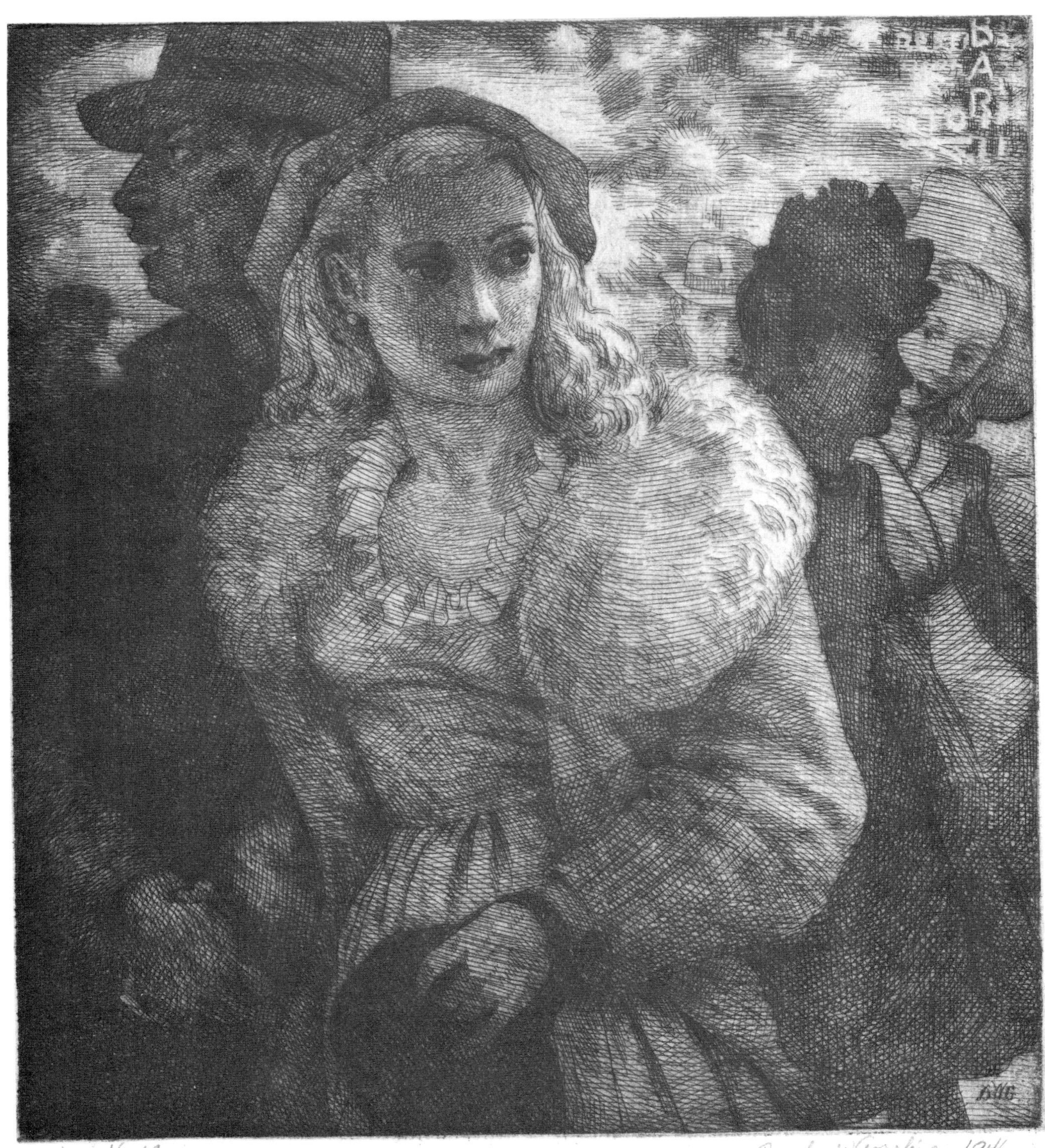

53. Douglas Warner Gorsline. *Where Next?*, 1946. Etching. $7\frac{1}{2} \times 6\frac{7}{8}$.

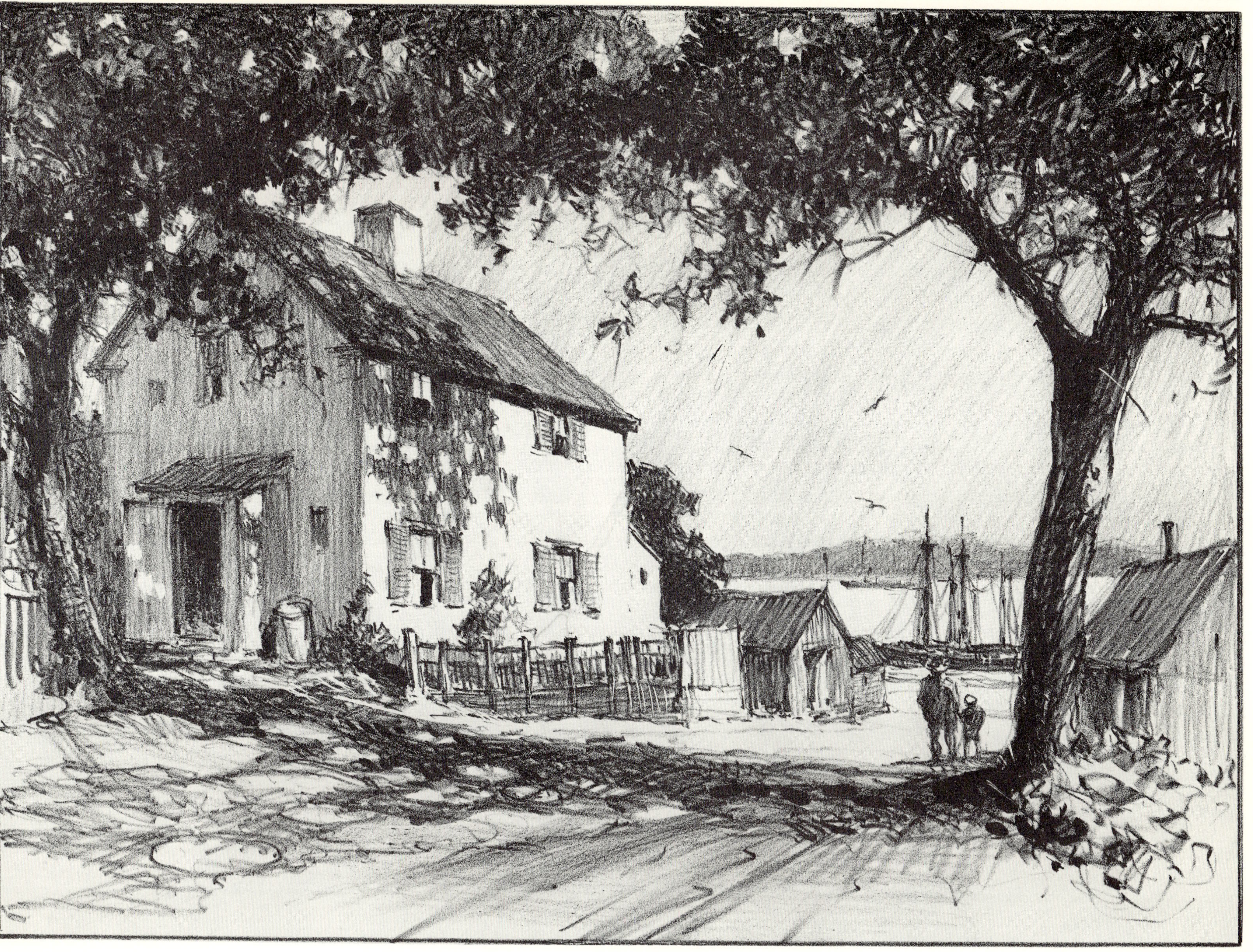

54. Gordon Hope Grant. [House by the sea]. Lithograph. 9 × 12.

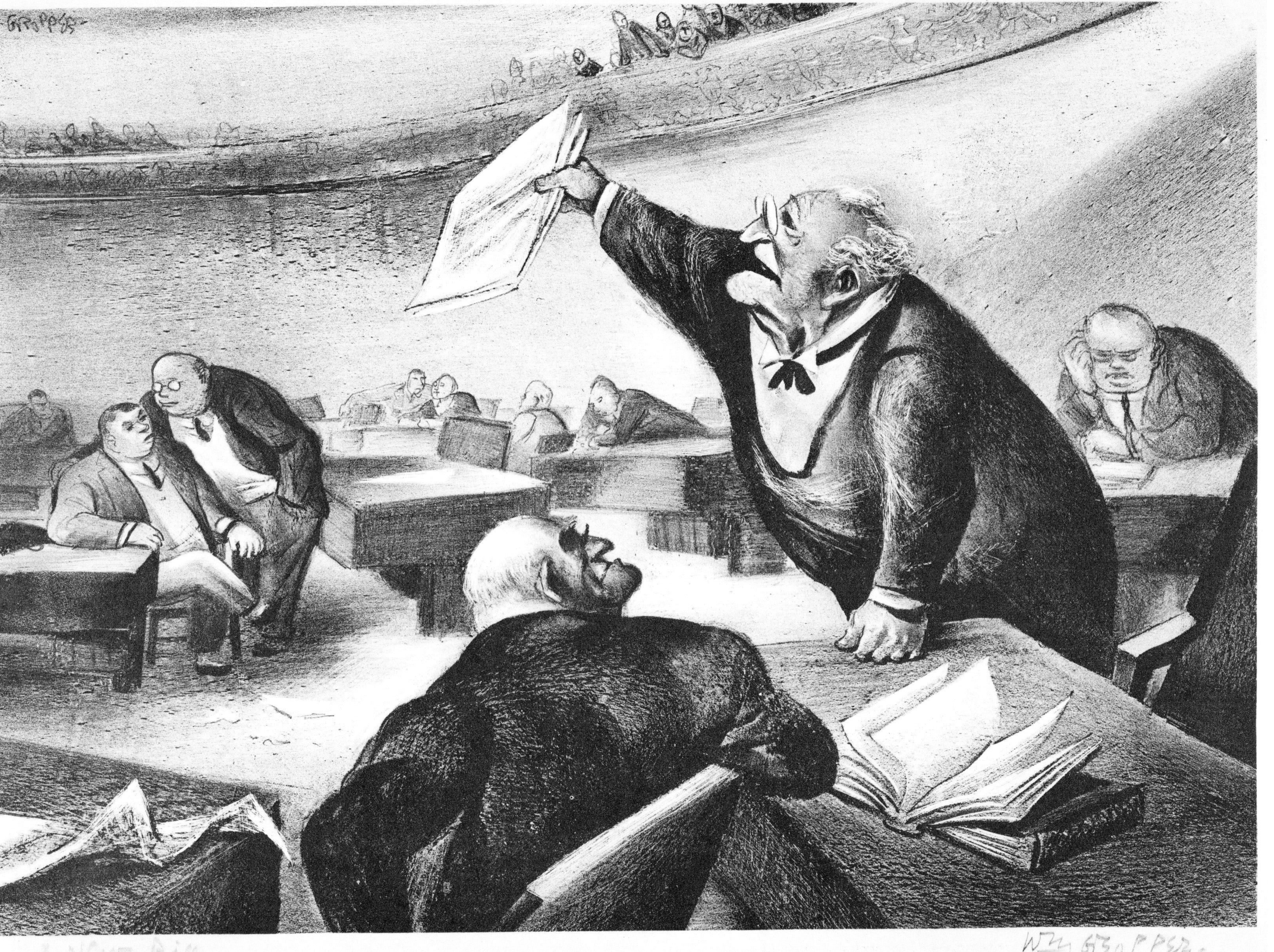

55. William Gropper. *A New Bill*, 1940–41. Lithograph. 11¾ × 15⅞.

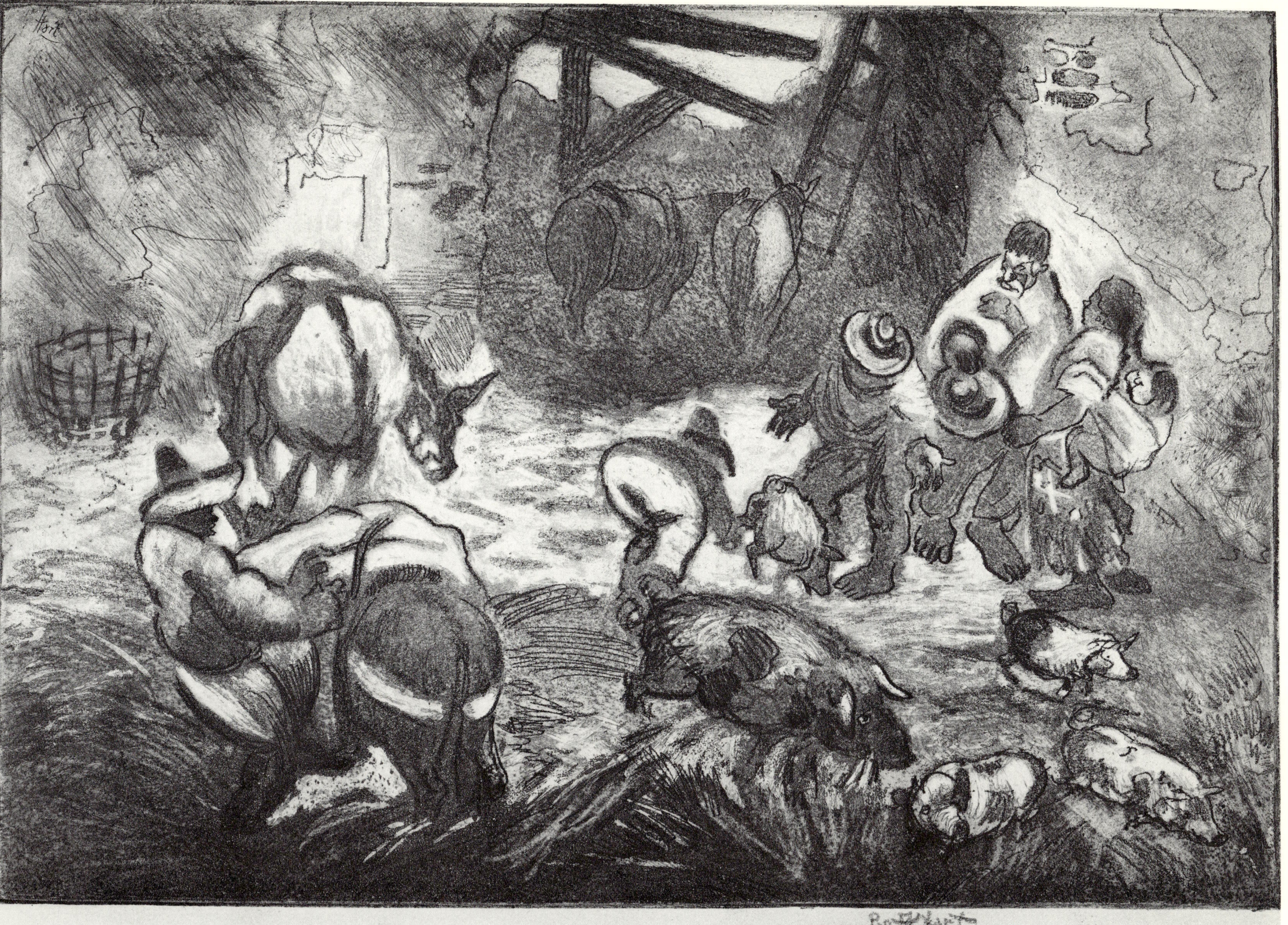

56. GEORGE OVERBURY ("POP") HART. *Pig Market, Mexico*, 1926. Aquatint and soft-ground etching. 8⅞ × 12½. Newark 200.

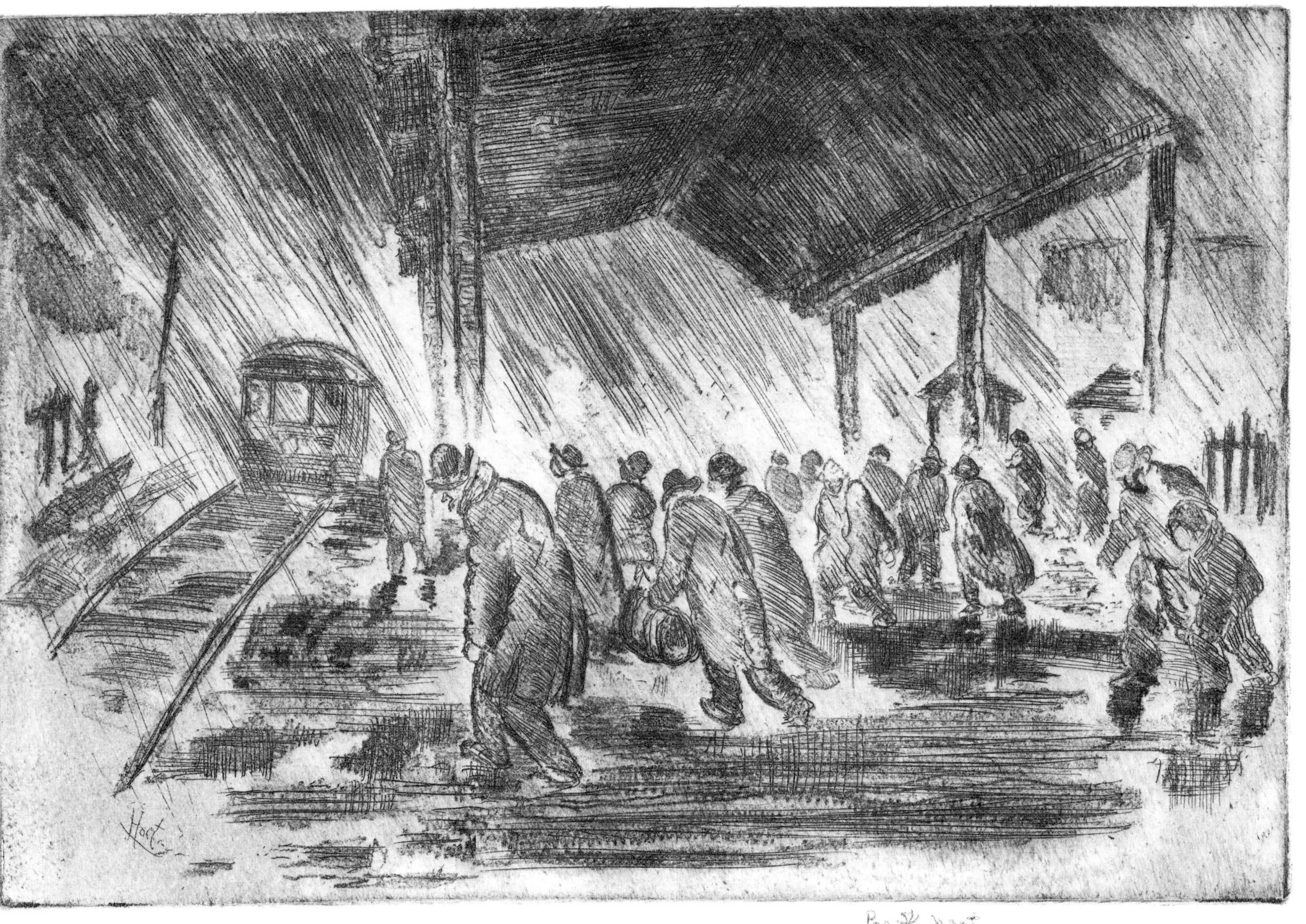

57. George Overbury ("Pop") Hart. *Working People,* 1925. Etching. 6½ × 9½. Newark 212.

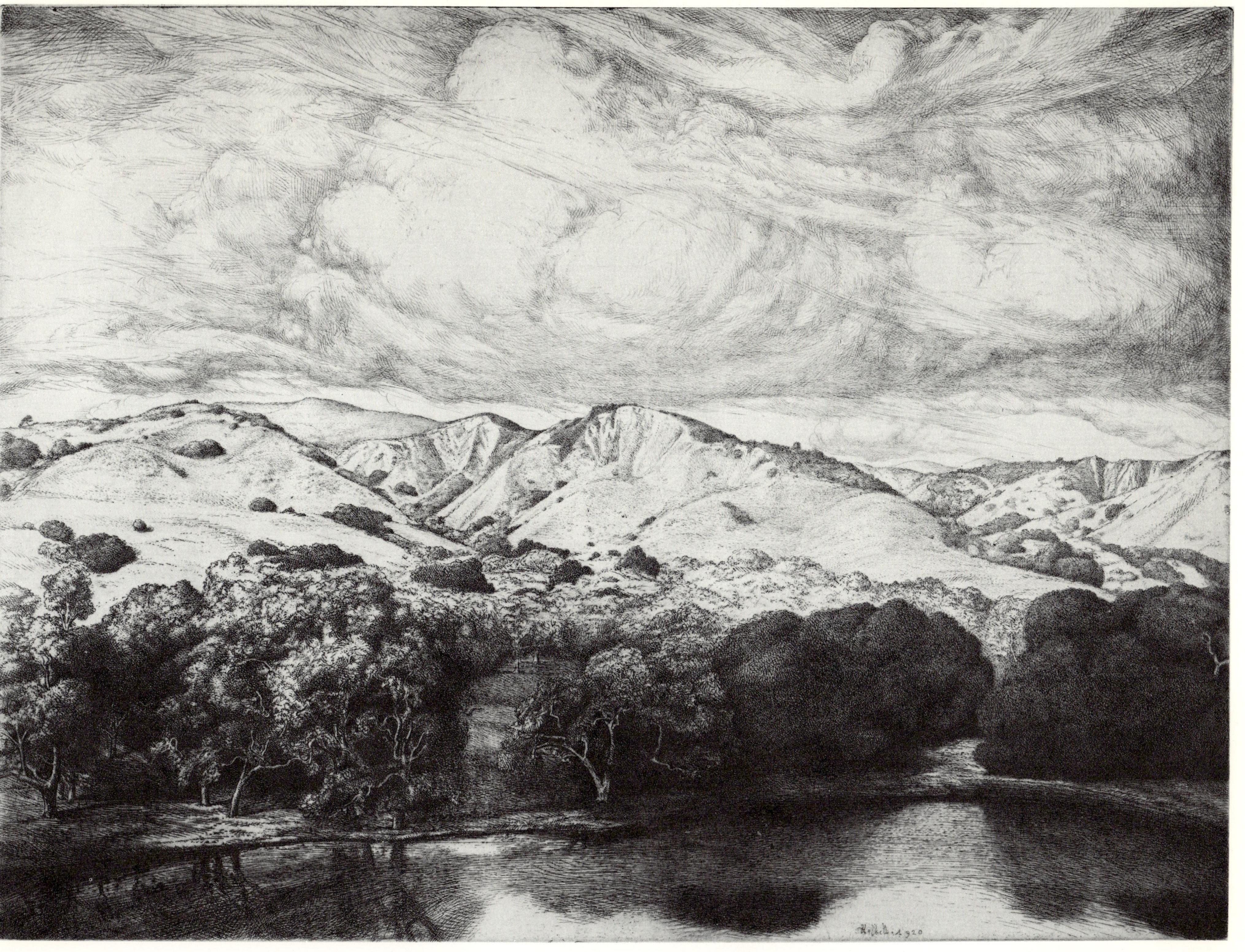

58. ERNEST HASKELL. *Mirror of the Goddess*, 1920. Etching with engraving. Edition 100. 8⅞ × 11⅝.

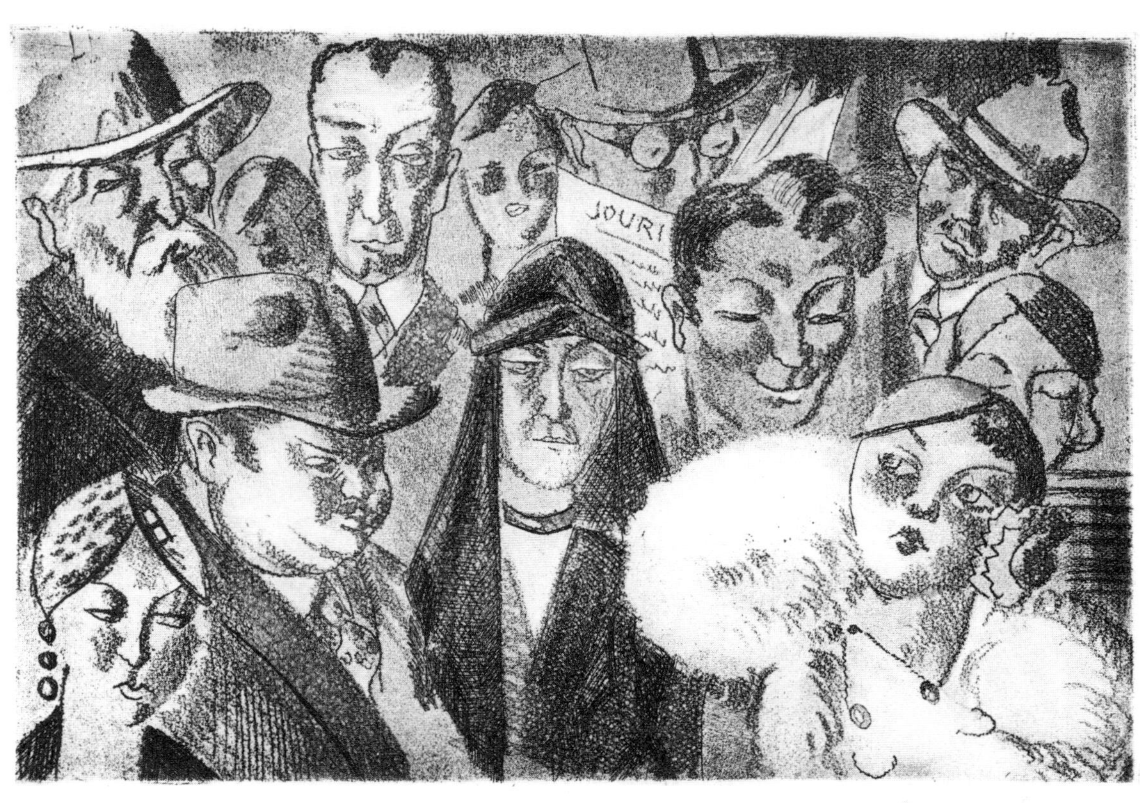

59. CLEMENT HAUPERS. *Metro 1st Class,* 1928. Soft-ground etching. Edition 20. $3\frac{7}{8} \times 5\frac{7}{8}$.

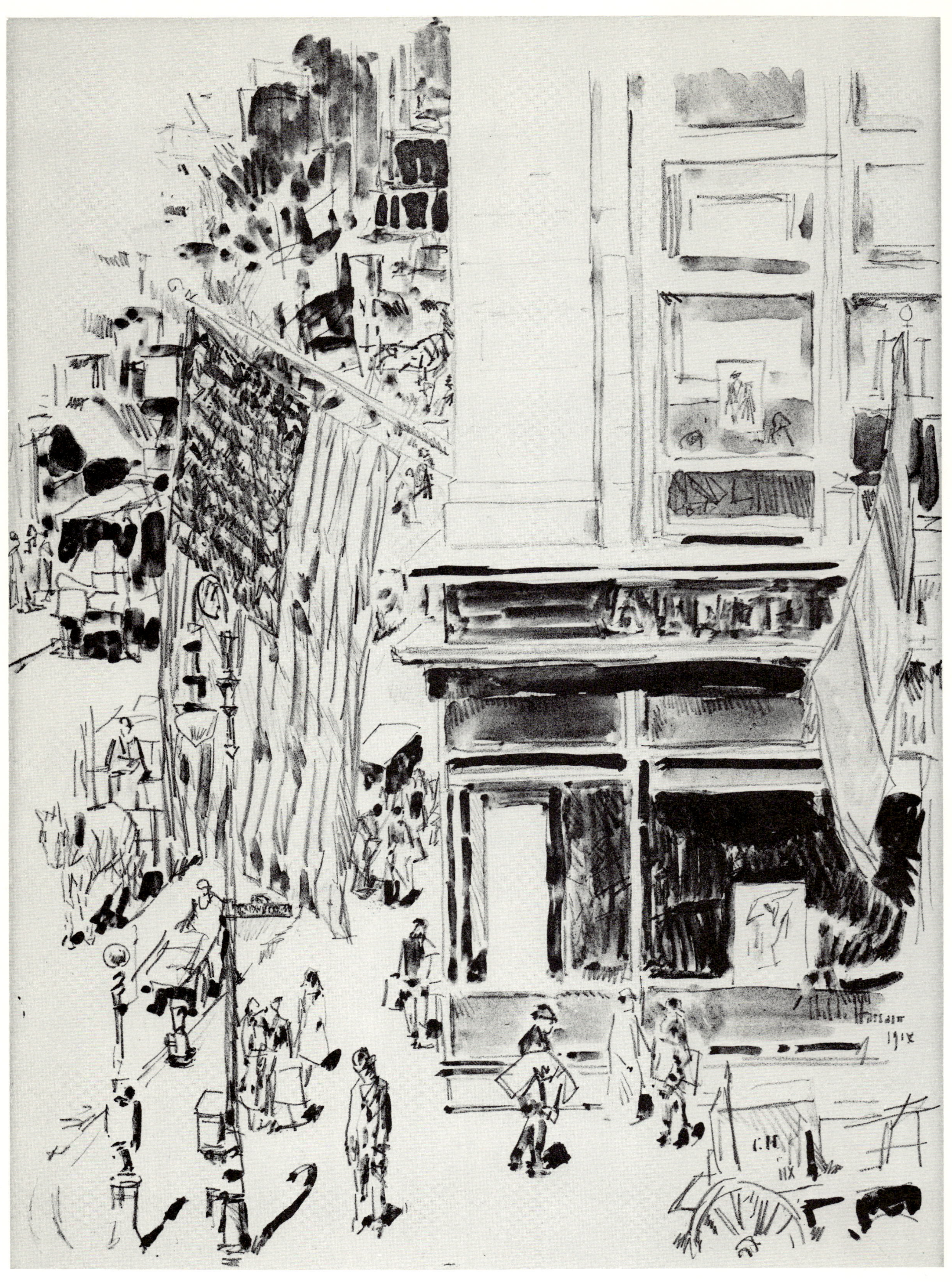

60. FREDERICK CHILDE HASSAM. *Lafayette Street* (New York City), 1918. Crayon and lithotint. Edition 59. 14½ × 11. Griffith 5.

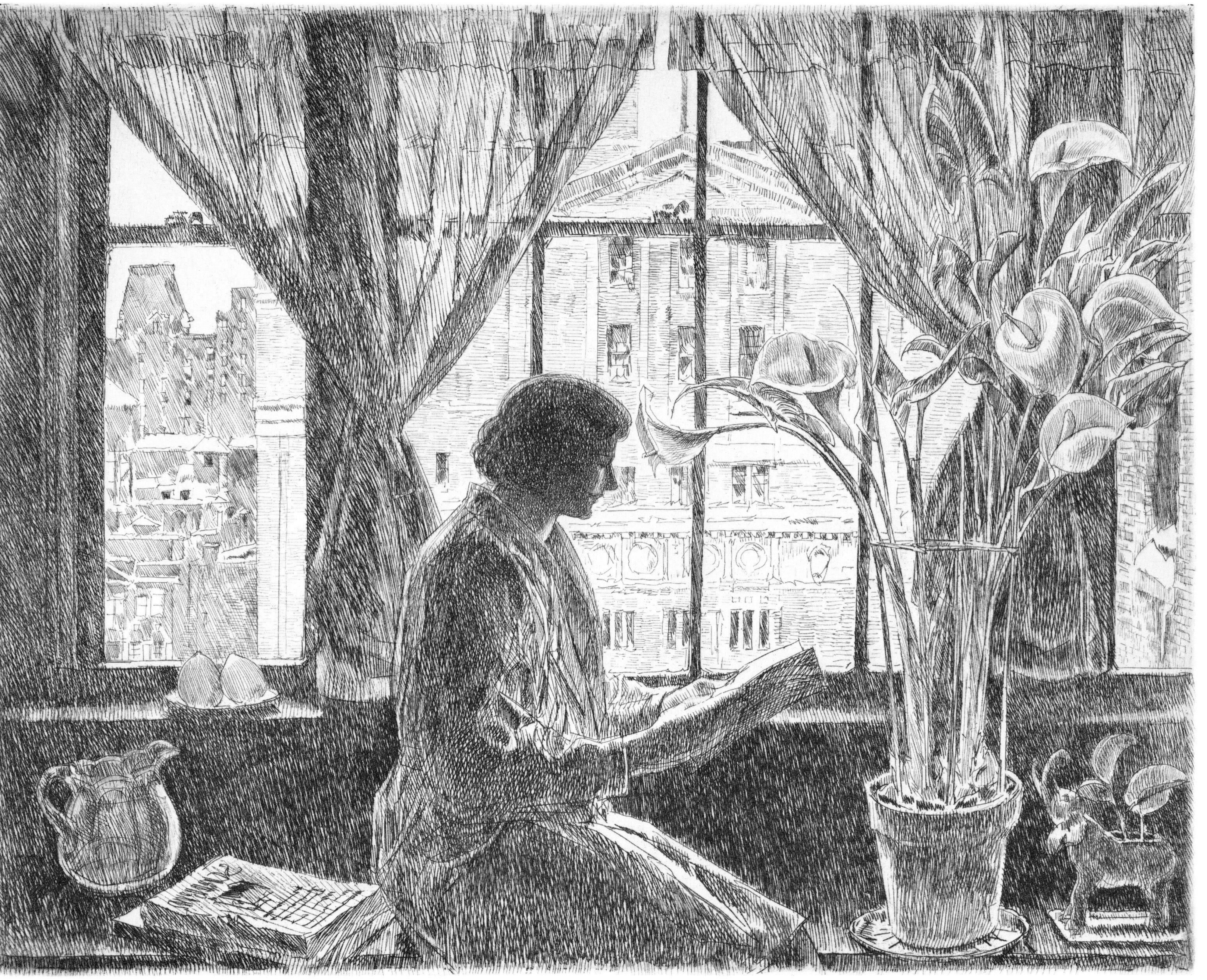

61. Frederick Childe Hassam. *Virginia and a New York Winter Window*, 1934. Etching. Edition 100. 10⅜ × 12⅞. Not in Cortissoz or Clayton.

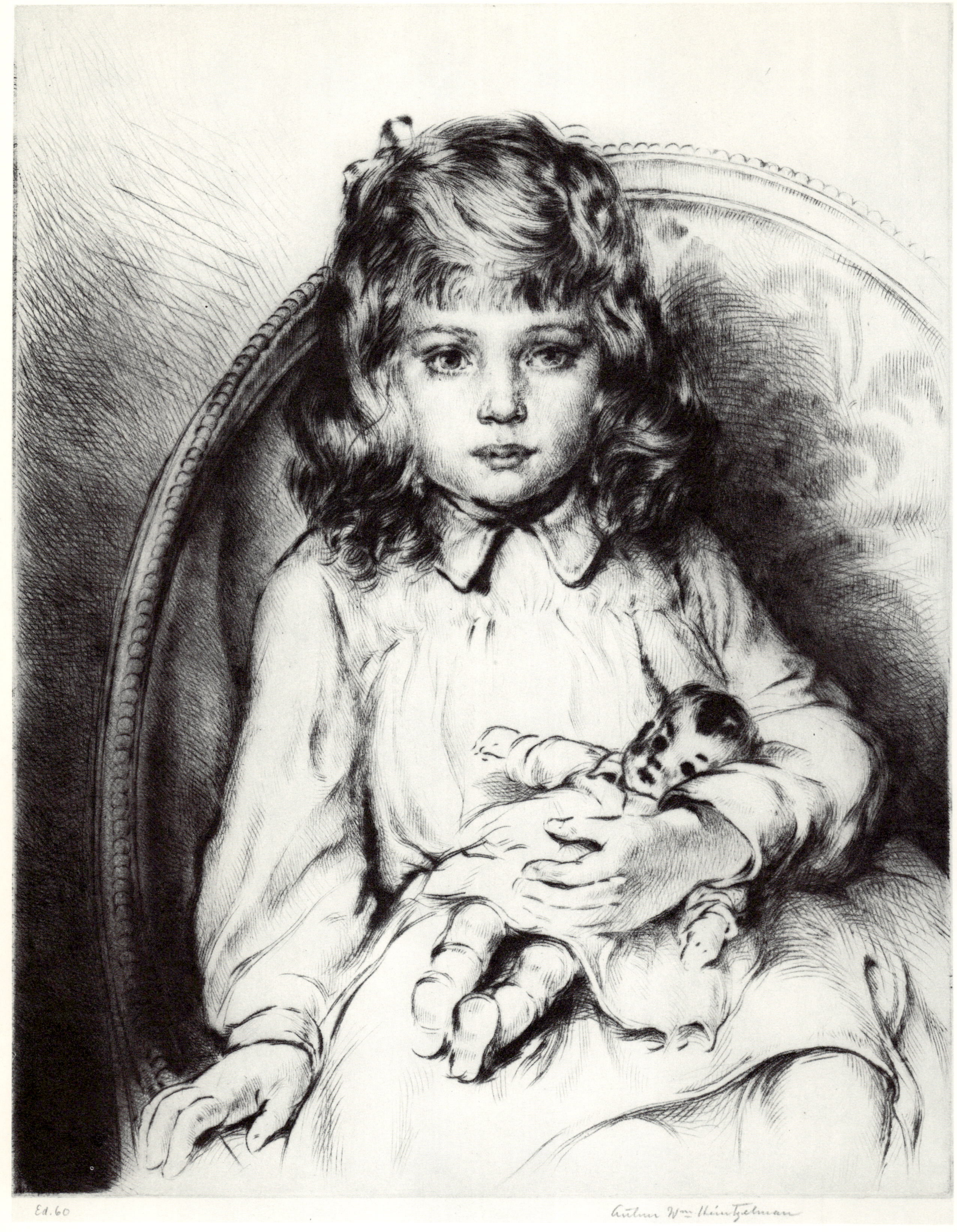

62. Arthur William Heintzelman. *My Little Model*, 1941. Drypoint. Edition 60. $11\frac{1}{2} \times 9$.

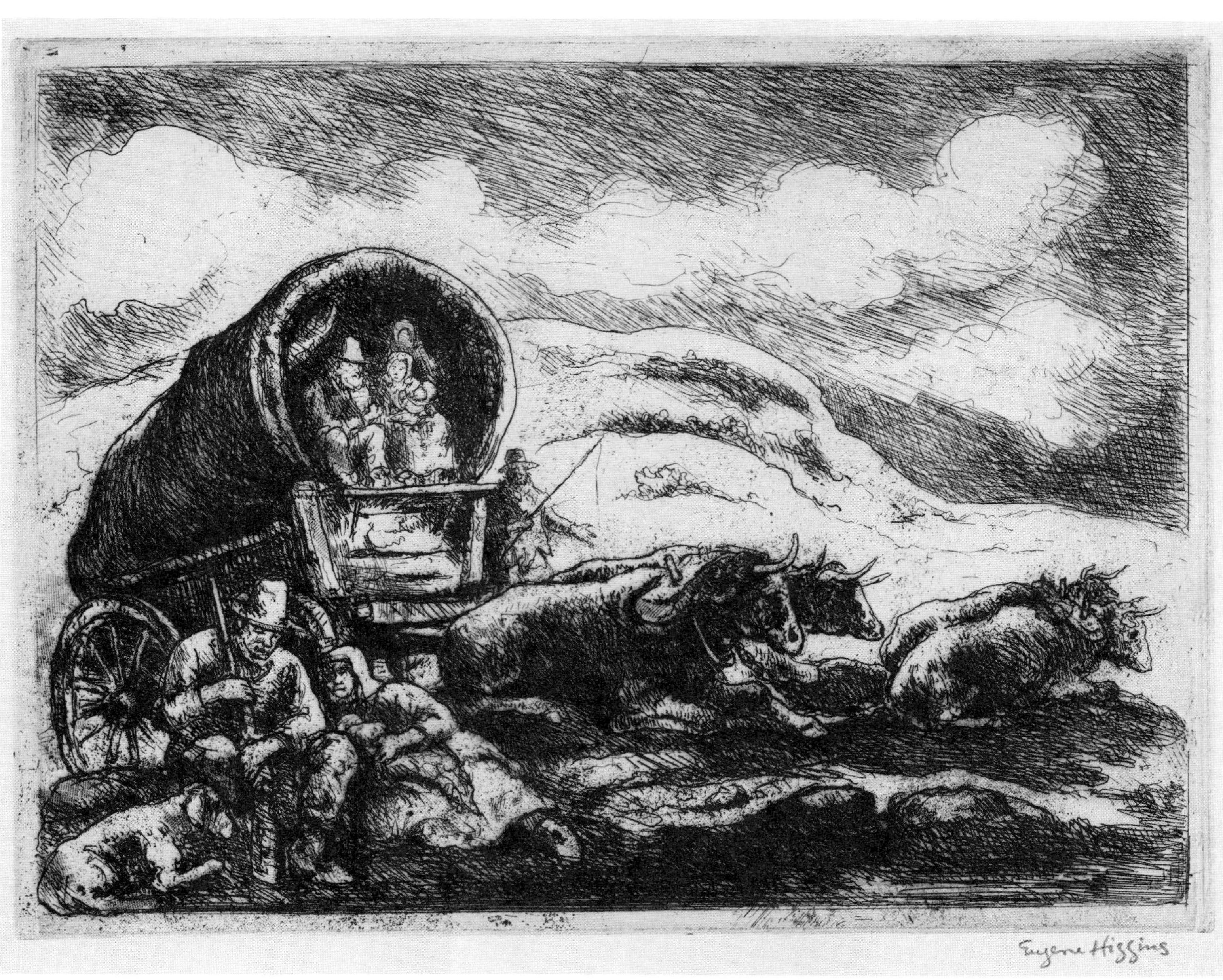

63. EUGENE HIGGINS. *Pioneers Resting*, 1937. Etching. Edition 149. 5⅞ × 7⅞.

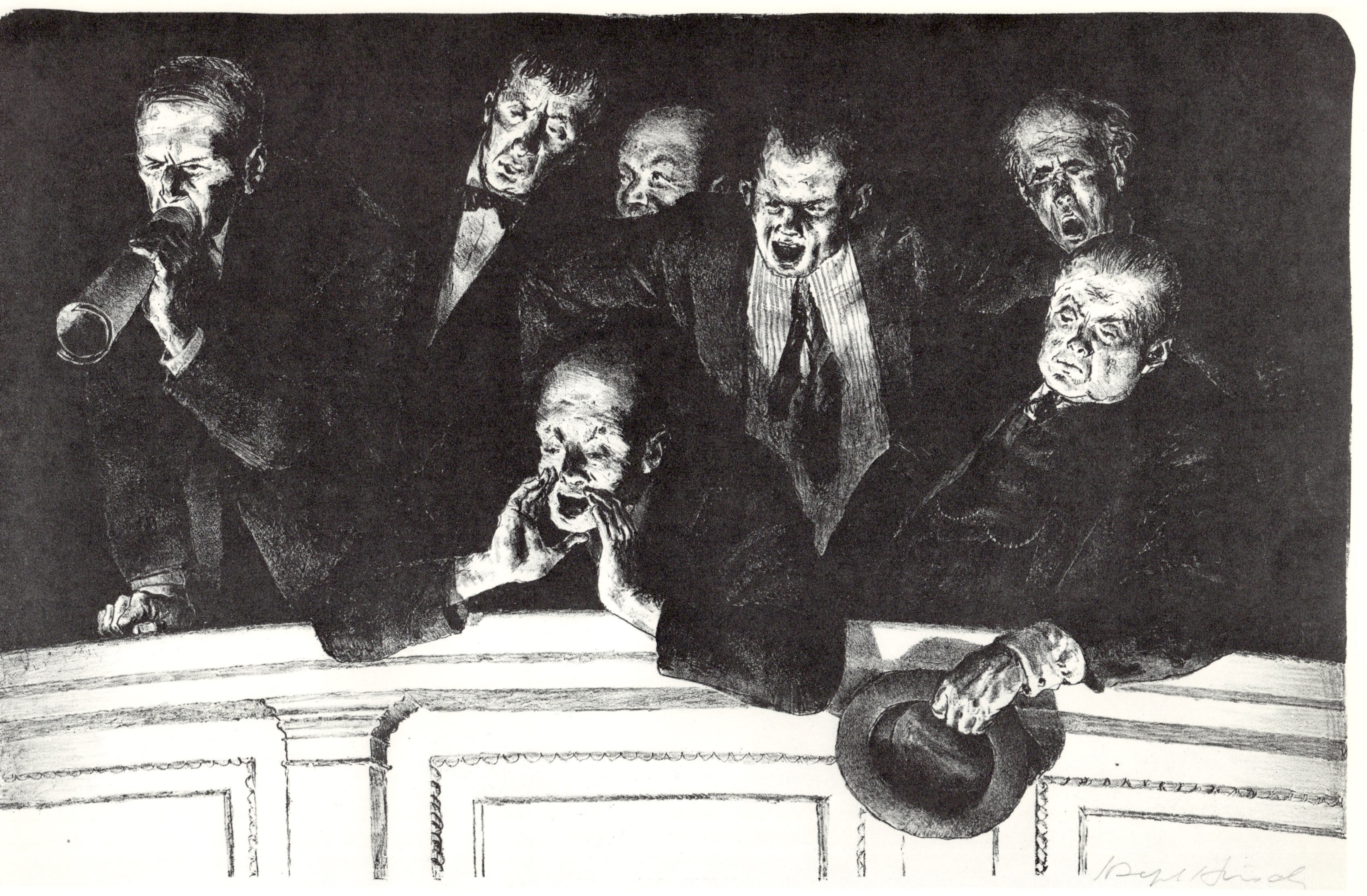

64. Joseph Hirsch. *Hecklers*, 1943–44. Lithograph. Edition 250. 10 × 15¼. Cole 7.

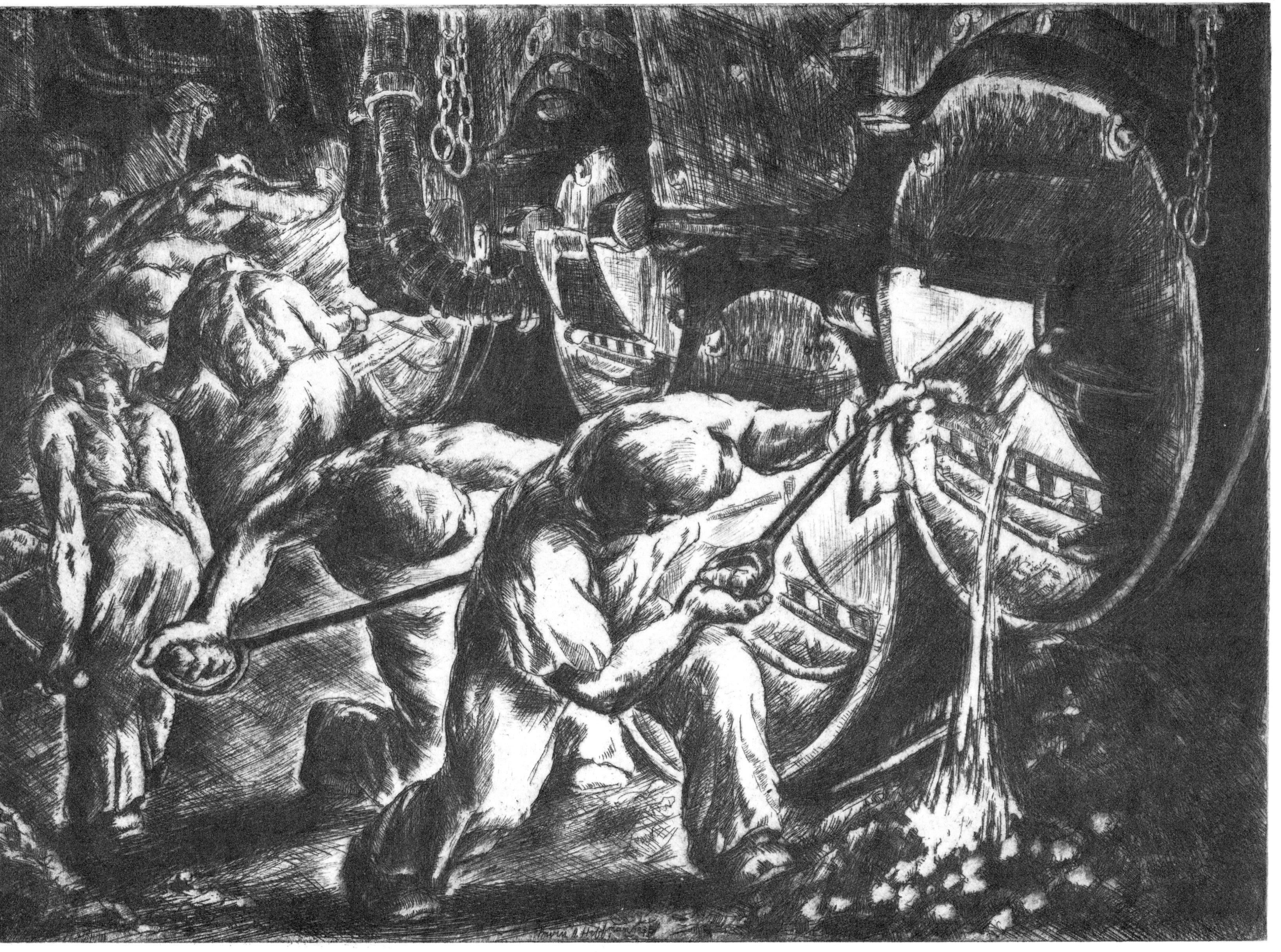

65. IRWIN DAVID HOFFMAN. *The Stokers*, 1935. Etching. Edition 100. 8 × 10⅞.

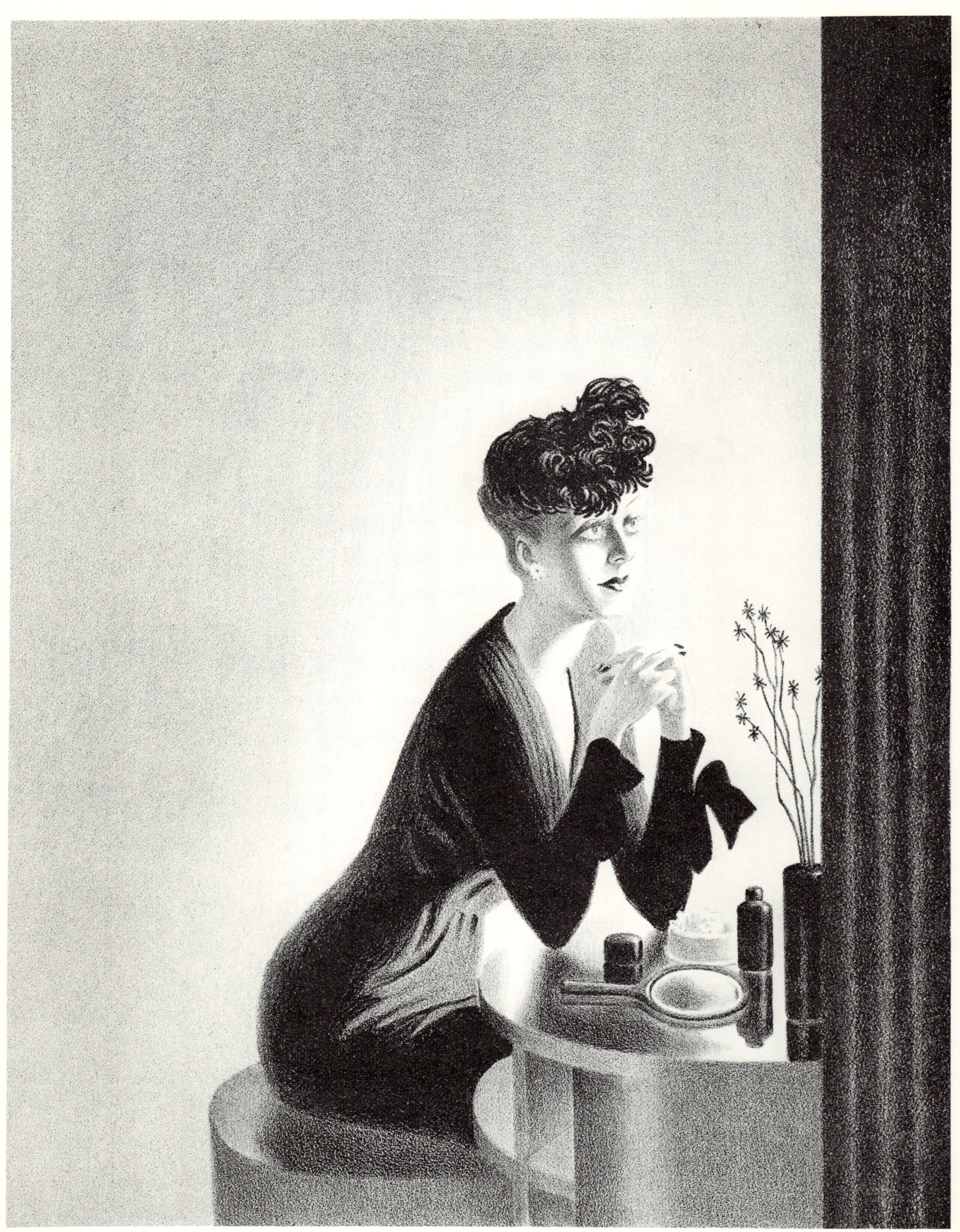

66. Ellison Hoover. *New French Hat,* late 1930s. Lithograph. 11¼ × 8$^{13}/_{16}$.

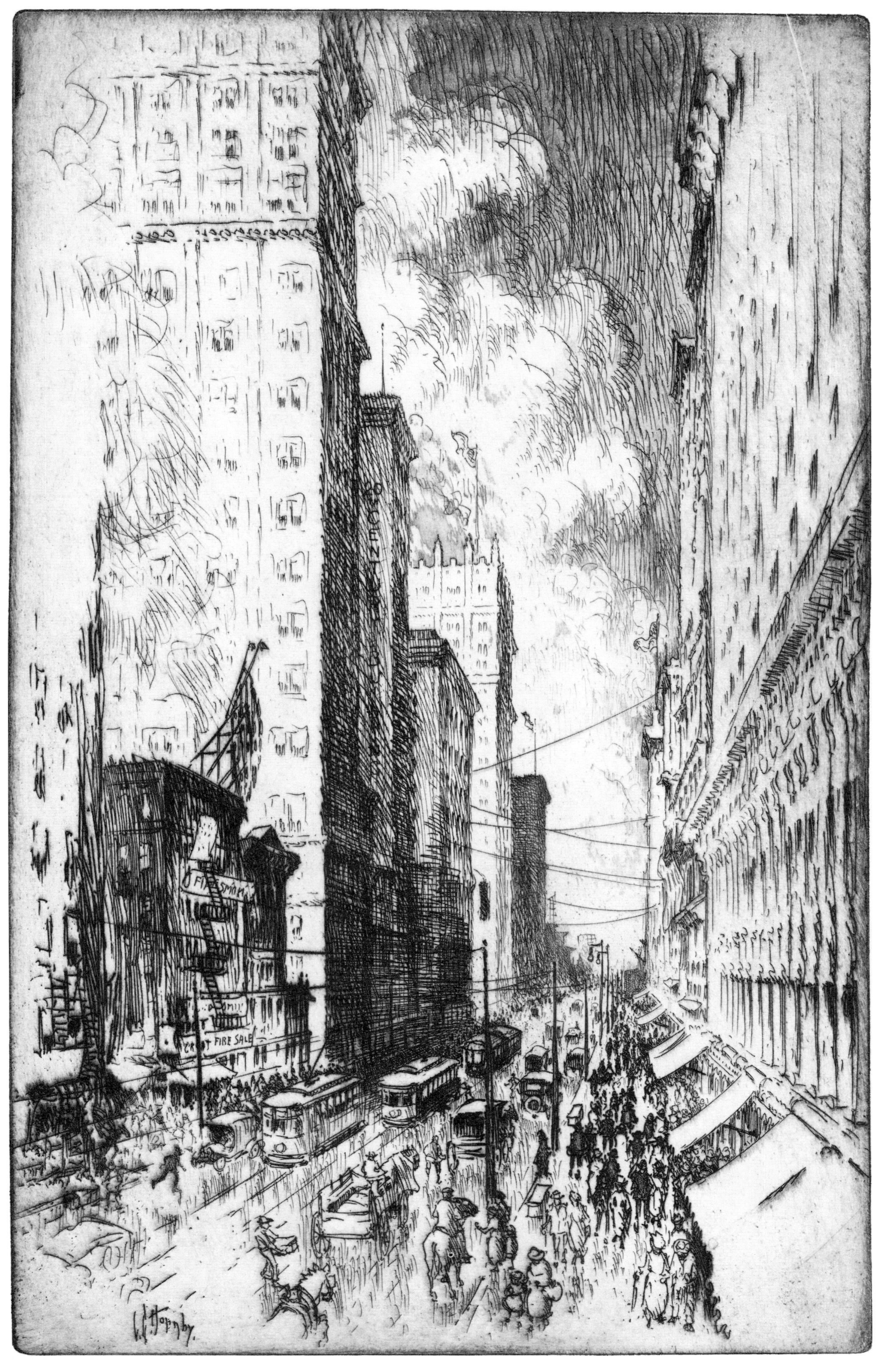

67. LESTER GEORGE HORNBY. *State Street from Van Buren Street* (Chicago), 1916. Etching. $11\frac{7}{8} \times 7\frac{5}{8}$.

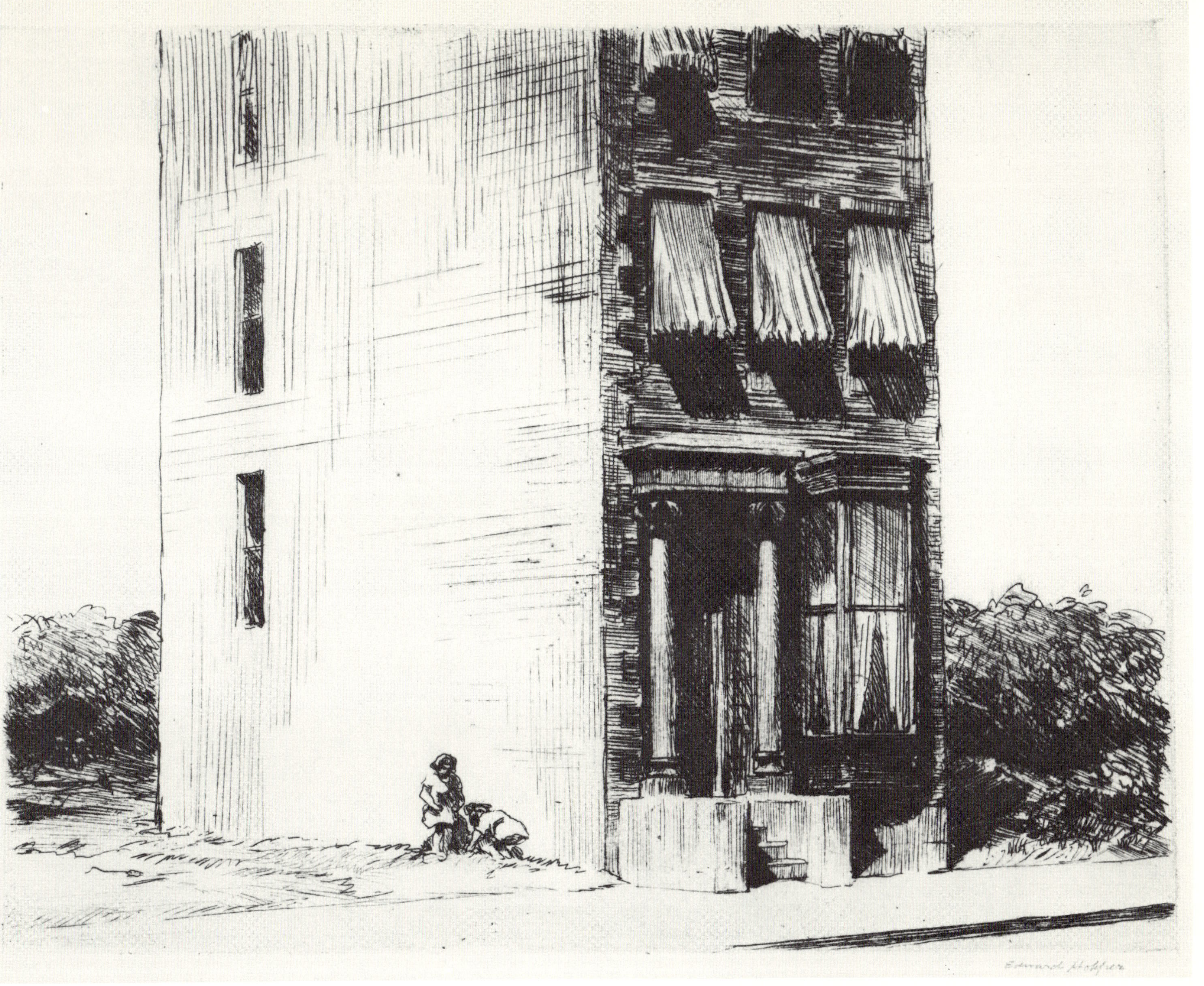

68. EDWARD HOPPER. *The Lonely House,* 1923. Etching. 8 × 10. Zigrosser 18, Levin 102.

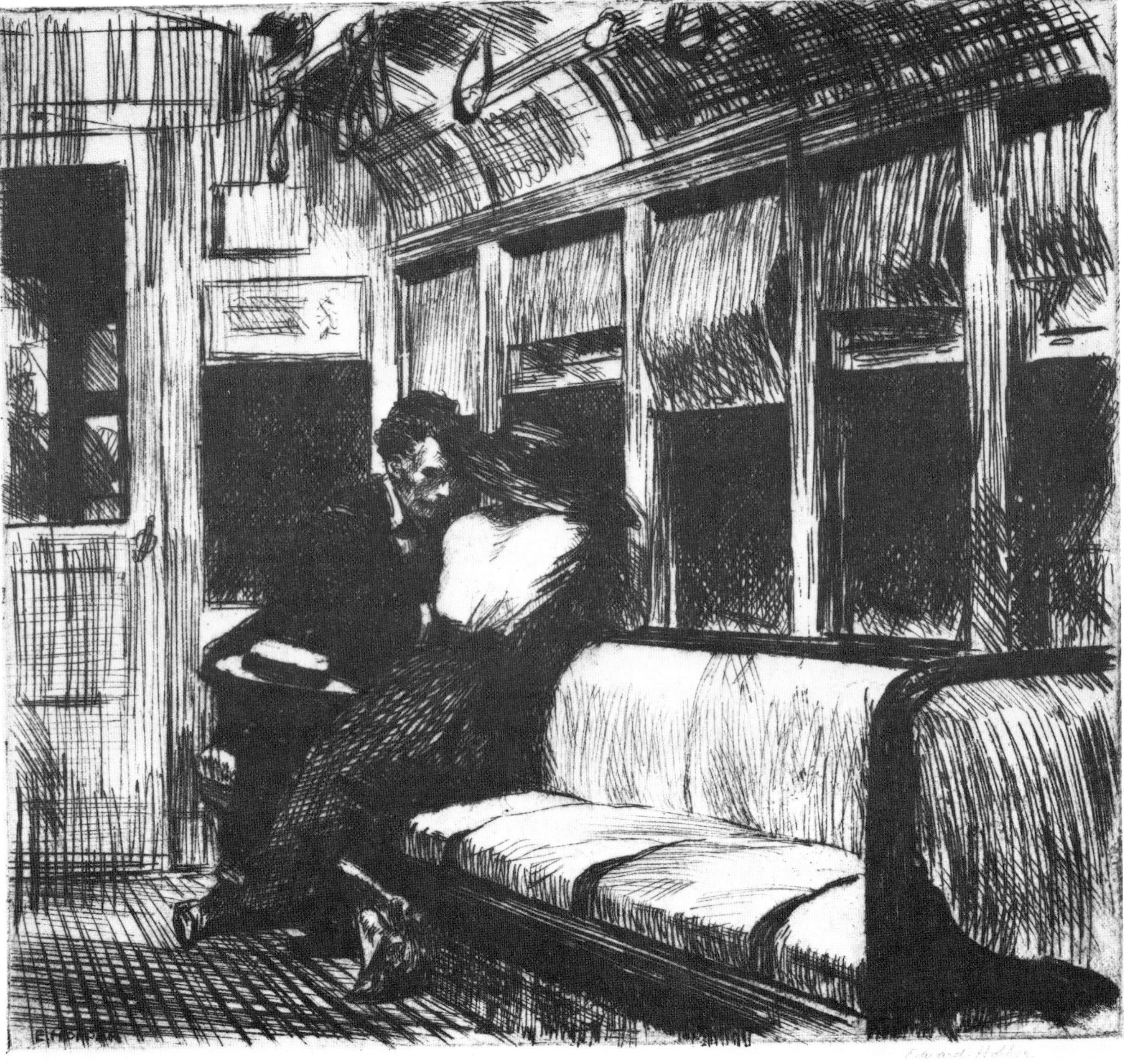

69. Edward Hopper. *Night on the El Train* (New York City). Etching. 7½ × 8. Zigrosser 21, dated 1920; Levin 56, dated 1918.

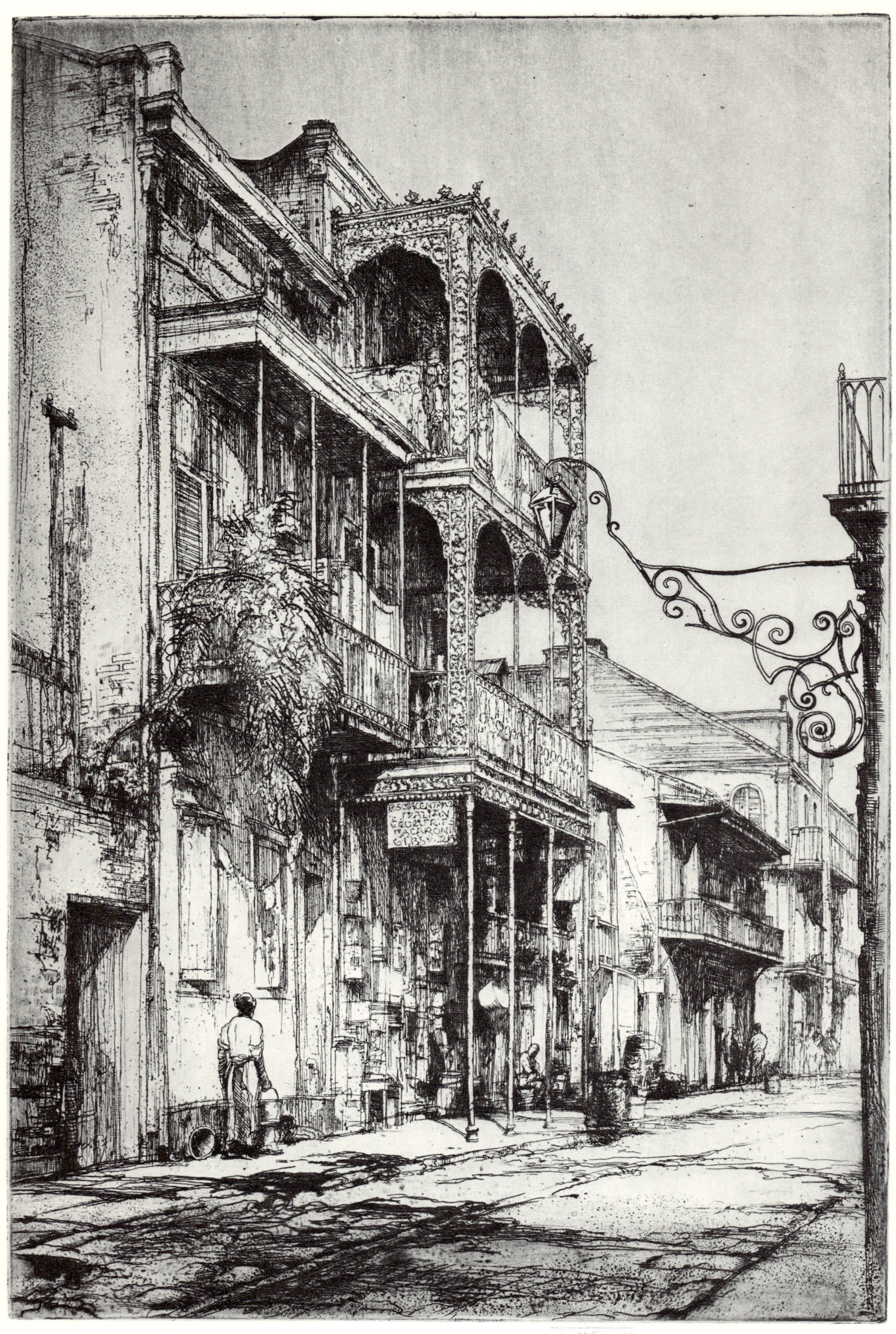

70. Earl Horter. *Creole Quarter—New Orleans*, ca. 1914. Etching. 11¼ × 7⅝.

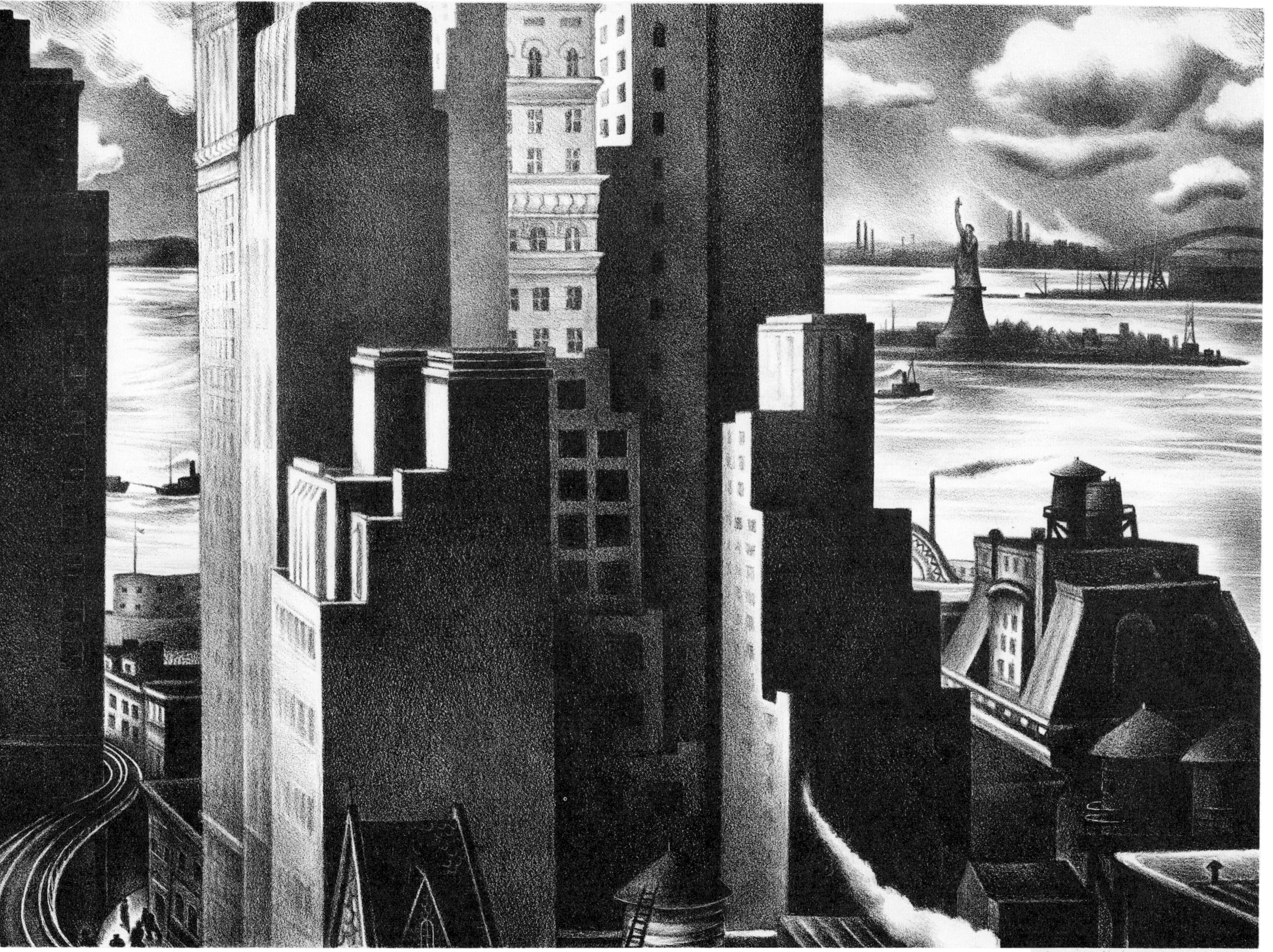

71. Victoria Ebbels Hutson Huntley. *Lower New York,* 1934. Lithograph. Edition 50. 10⅛ × 13$^{11}/_{16}$.

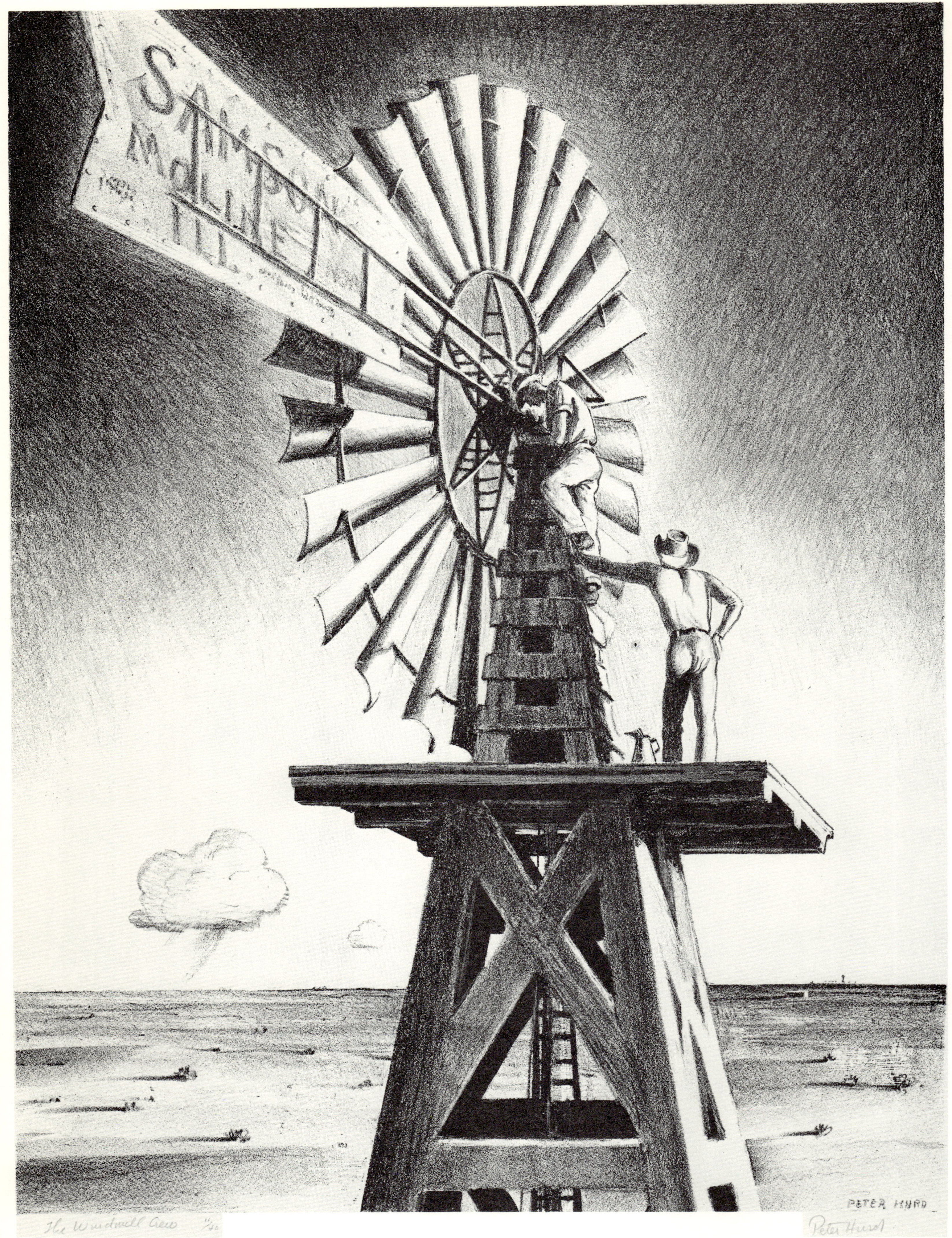

72. PETER HURD. *The Windmill Crew*, 1936. Lithograph. Edition 40. 15⅝ × 12¼. Meigs 36.

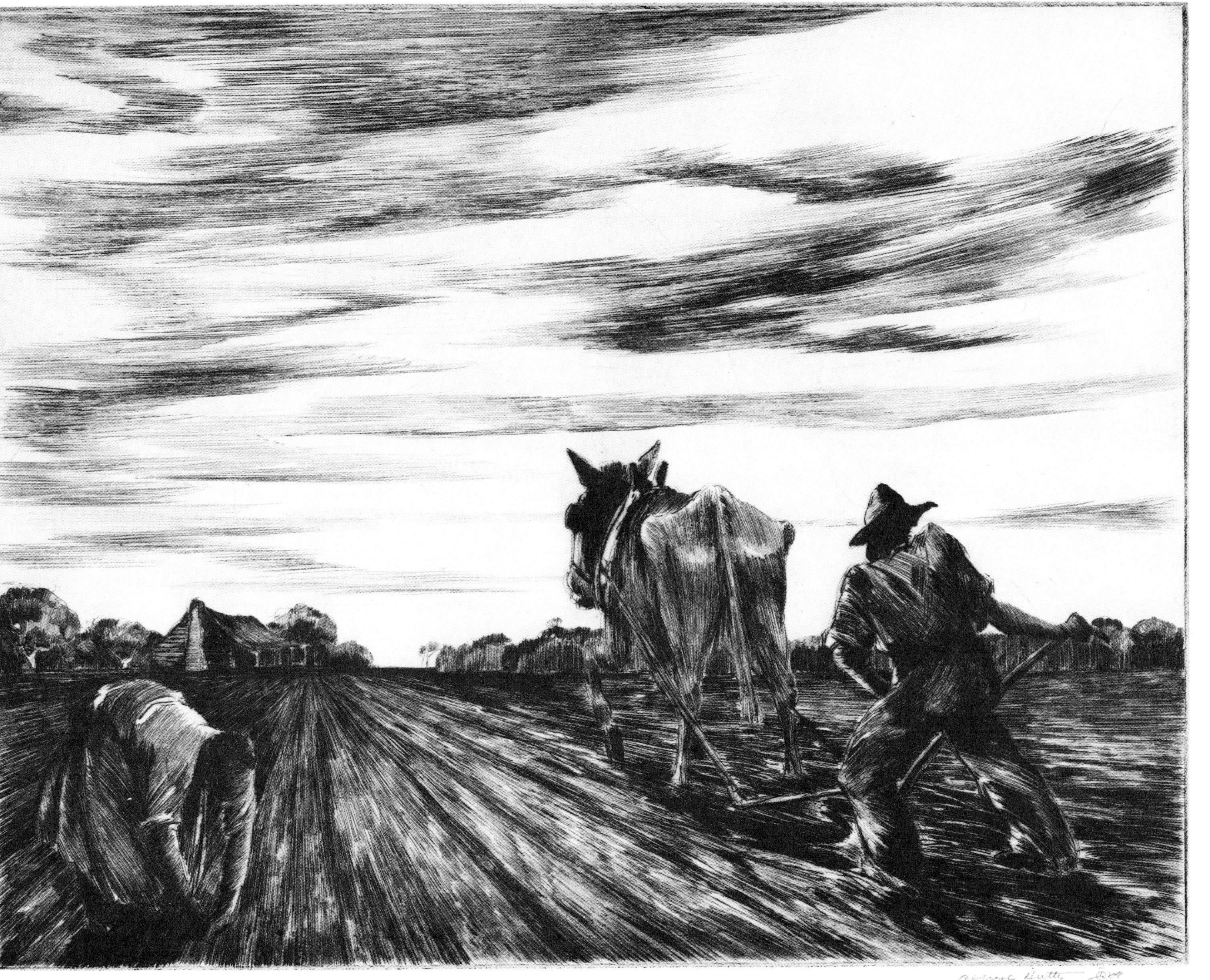

73. ALFRED HEBER HUTTY. *Rural South*, 1939. Drypoint. Edition 75. 8⅜ × 10⅜.

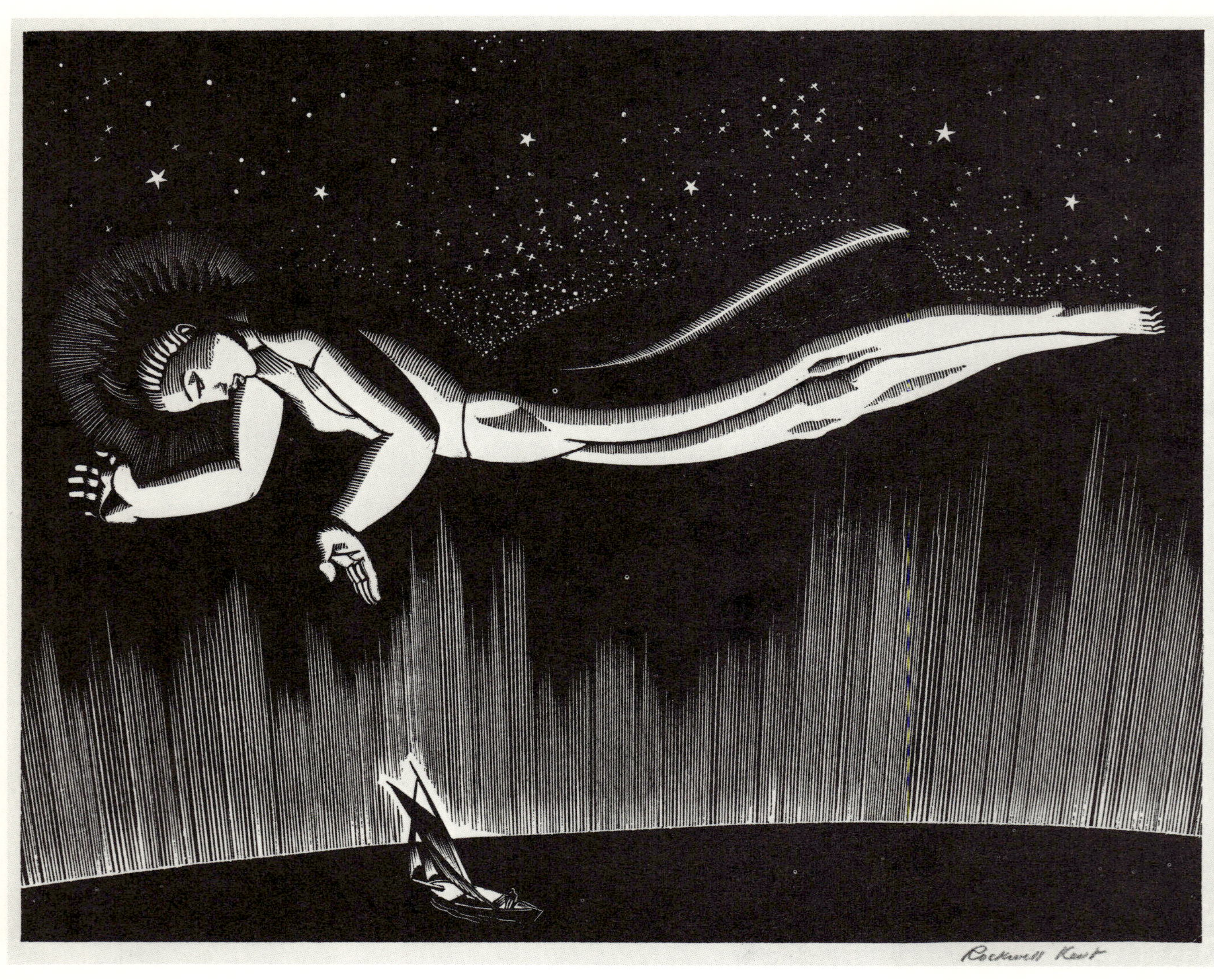

74. Rockwell Kent. *Godspeed,* 1931. Wood engraving. Edition 150, published 1932. $5\frac{5}{16} \times 6\frac{7}{8}$. Burne Jones 84.

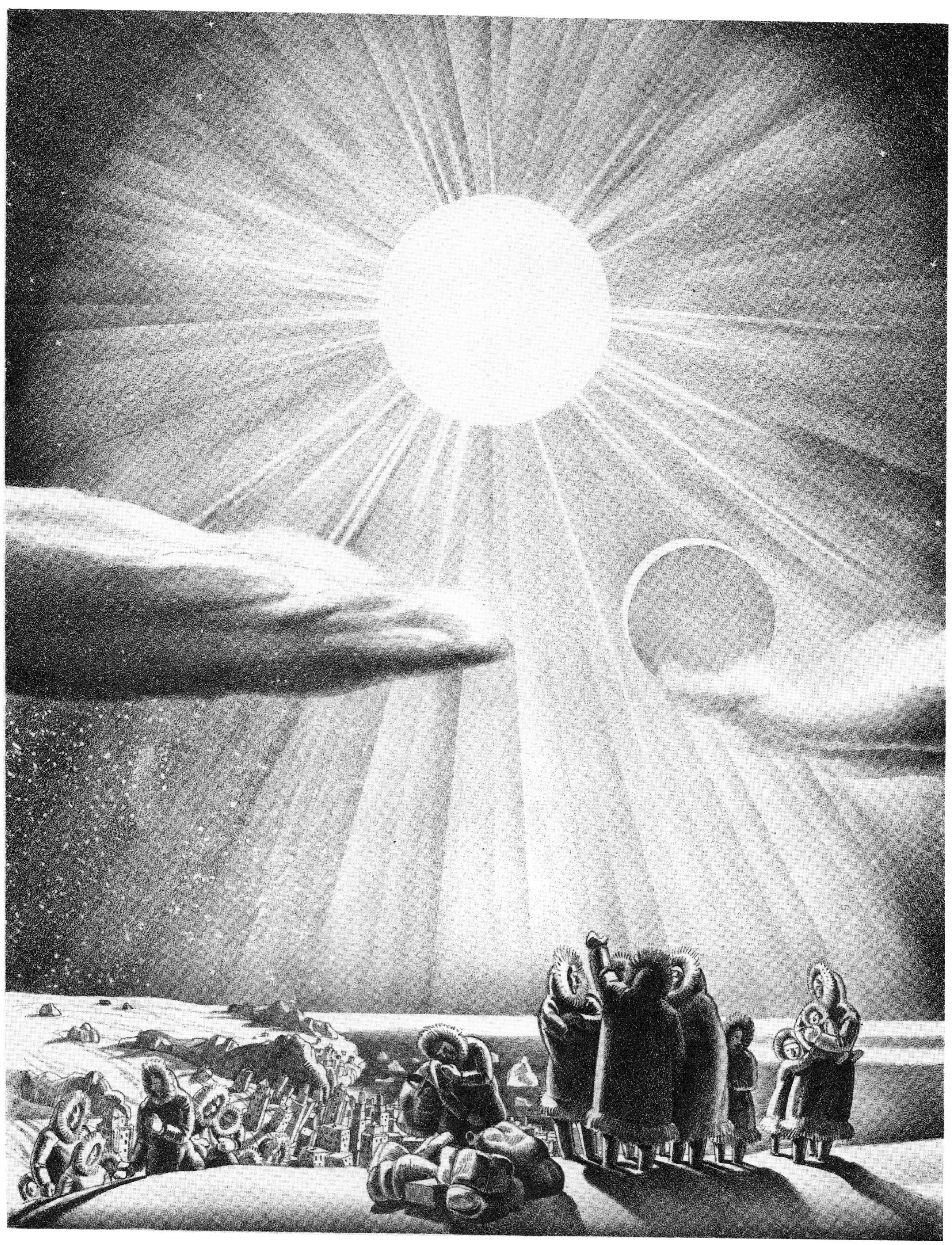

75. Rockwell Kent. *Solar Fade-Out,* 1937. Lithograph (from the *End of the World* series). 13 1/16 × 10 1/8. Burne Jones 116.

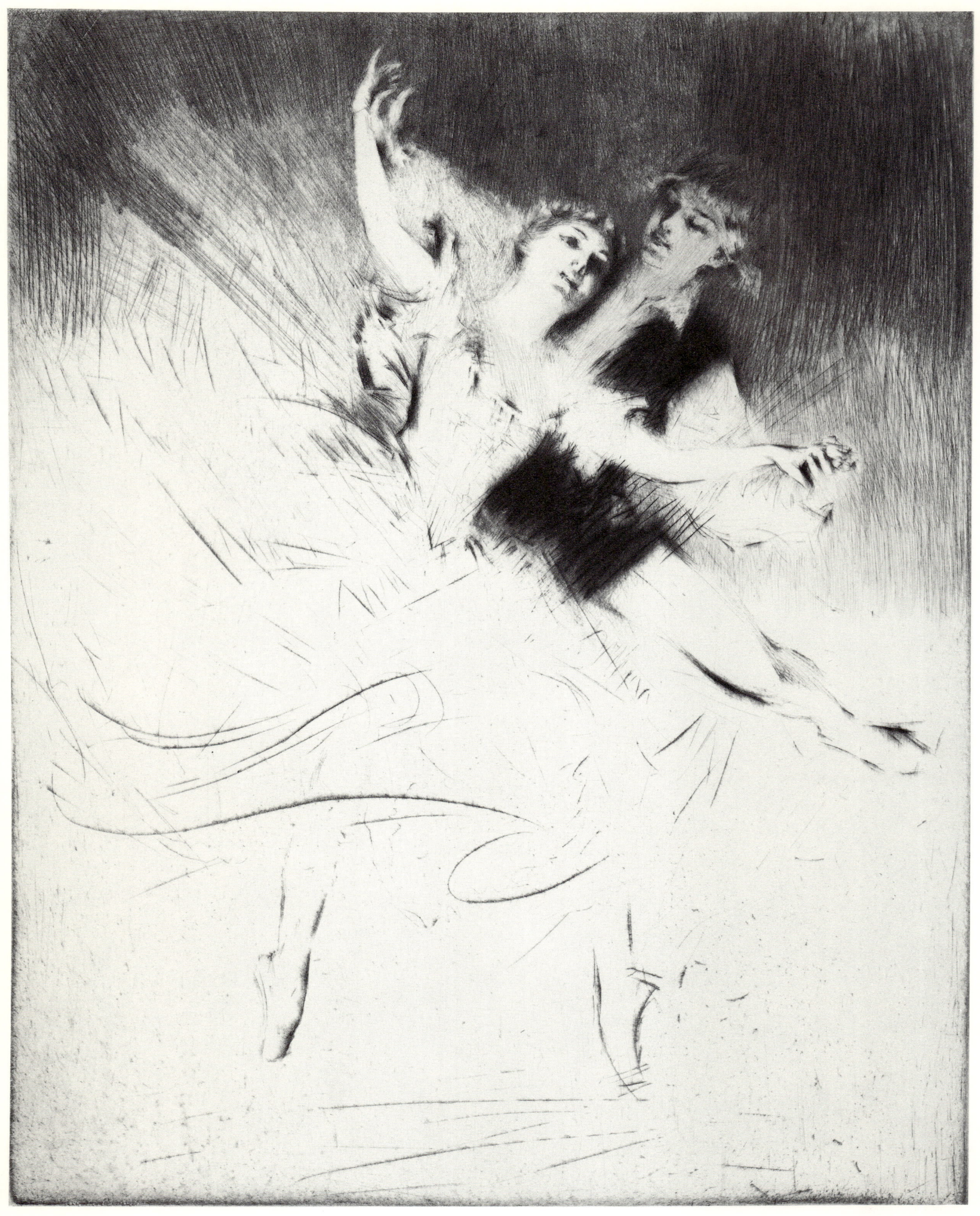

76. Troy Kinney. *Lopokova and Nijinski in "Les Sylphides,"* 1916. Drypoint. Edition 138. 11¾ × 9½. Kinney 11.

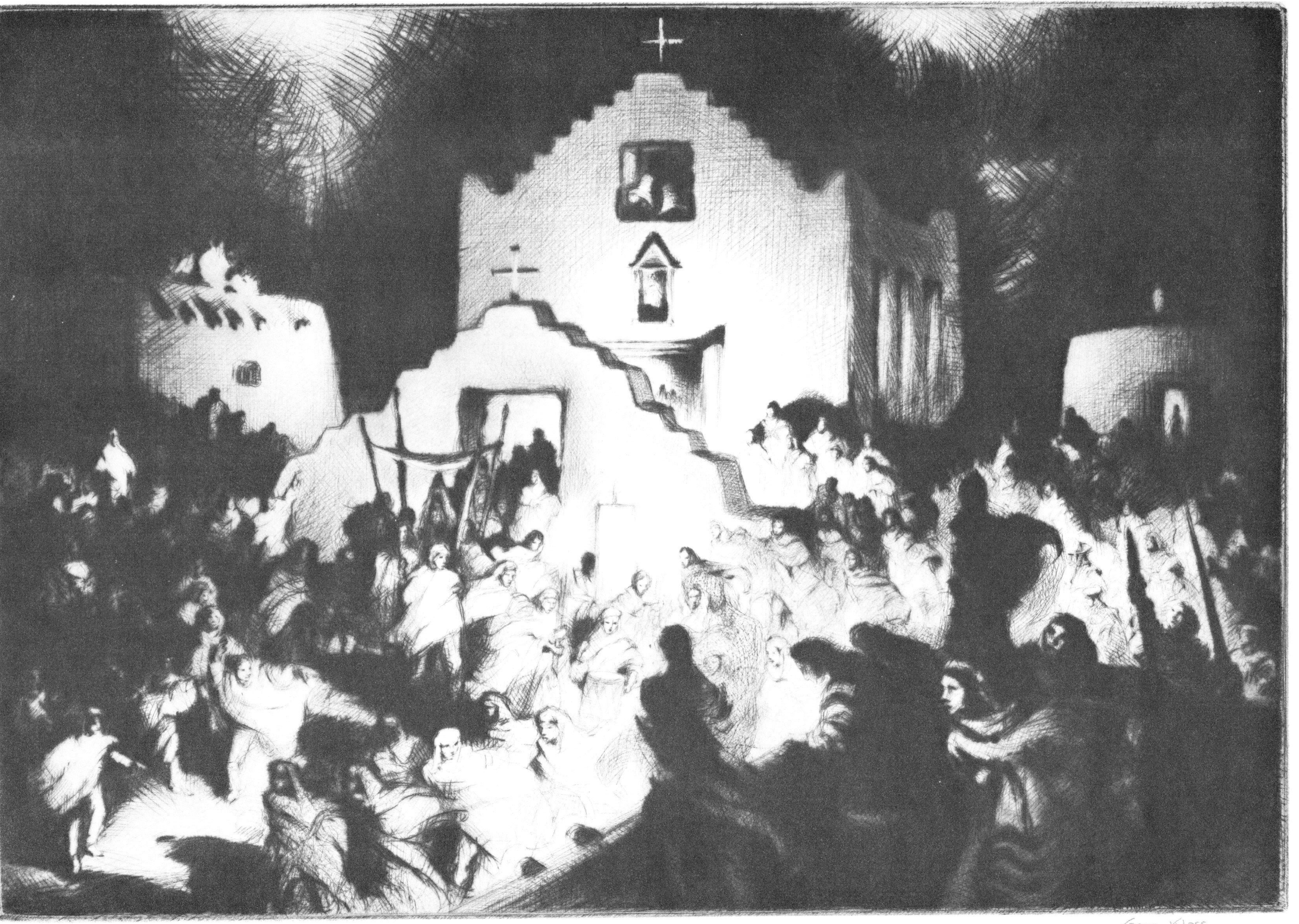

77. Gene Kloss. *Processional—Taos*, 1948. Drypoint. Edition 250. 10 × 14. Kloss 431.

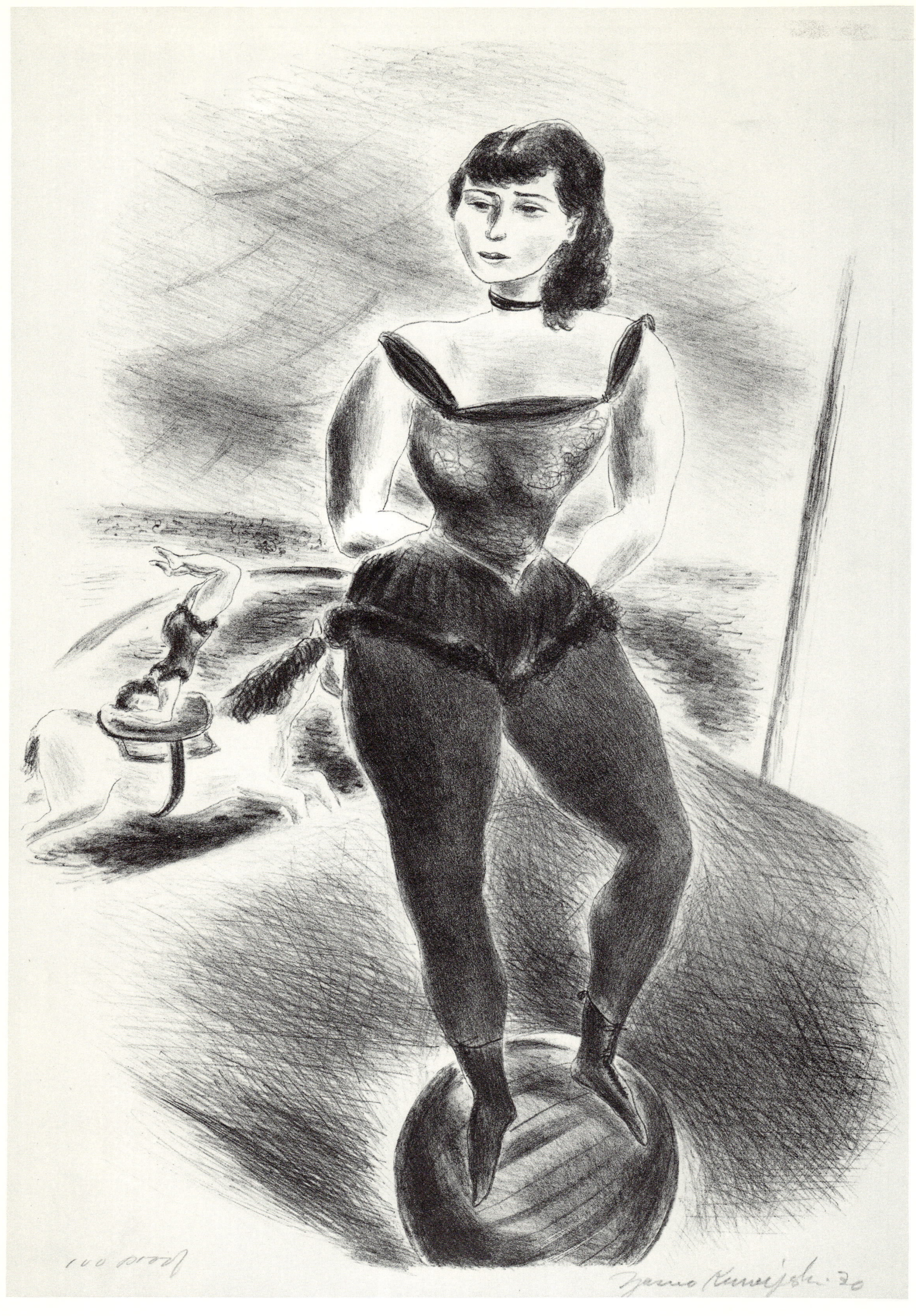

78. Yasuo Kuniyoshi. *Circus Performer Balanced on a Ball*, 1930. Lithograph. Edition ca. 110. 14⅛ × 10¼. Archives of American Art 49.

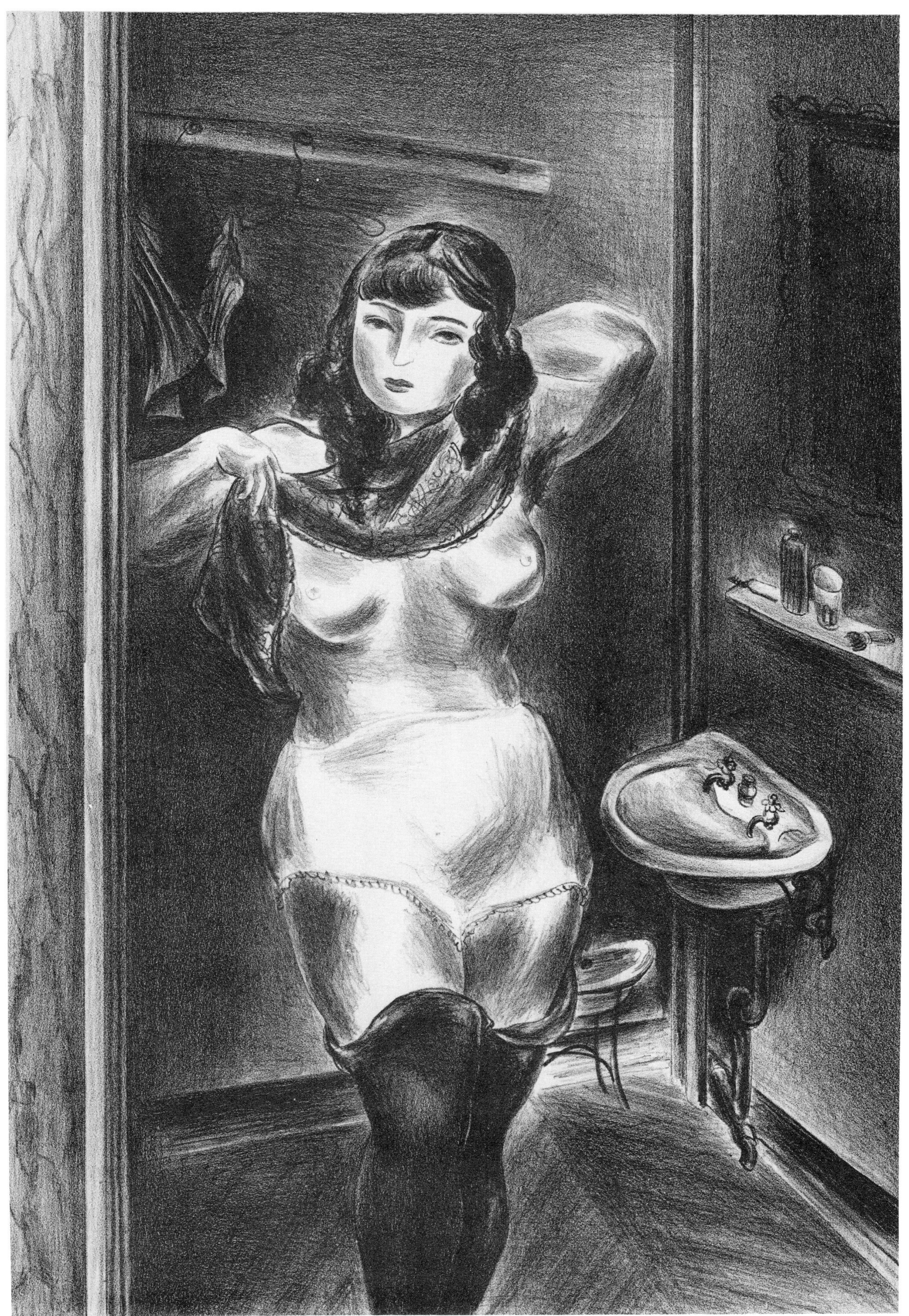

79. Yasuo Kuniyoshi. *Girl Dressing,* 1928. Lithograph. Edition 30. 12¾ × 8⅝. Archives of American Art 26.

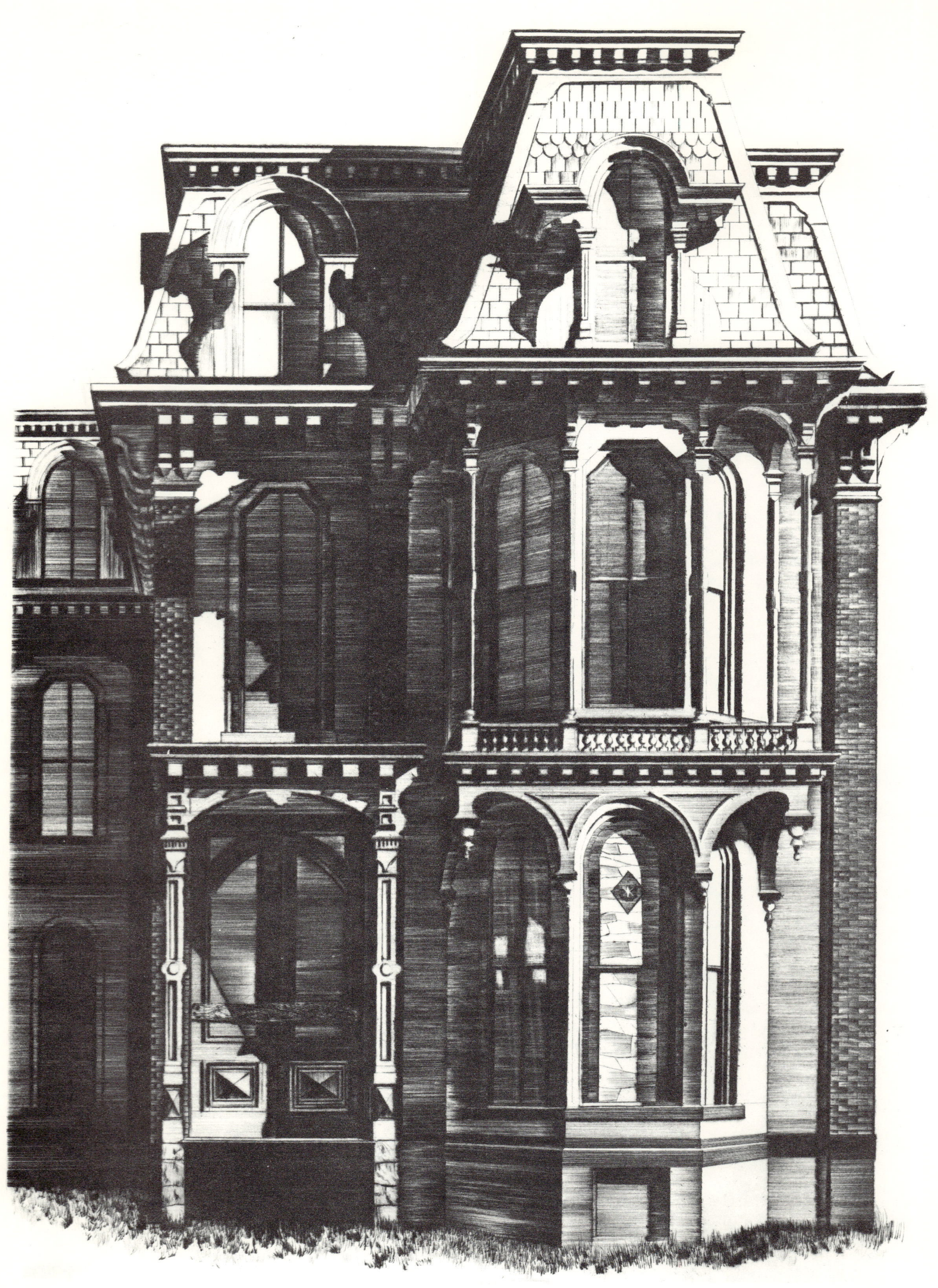

80. Lawrence Edward Kupferman. *Saratoga Springs Victorian,* ca. 1938–39. Drypoint. 13⅞ × 9¾.

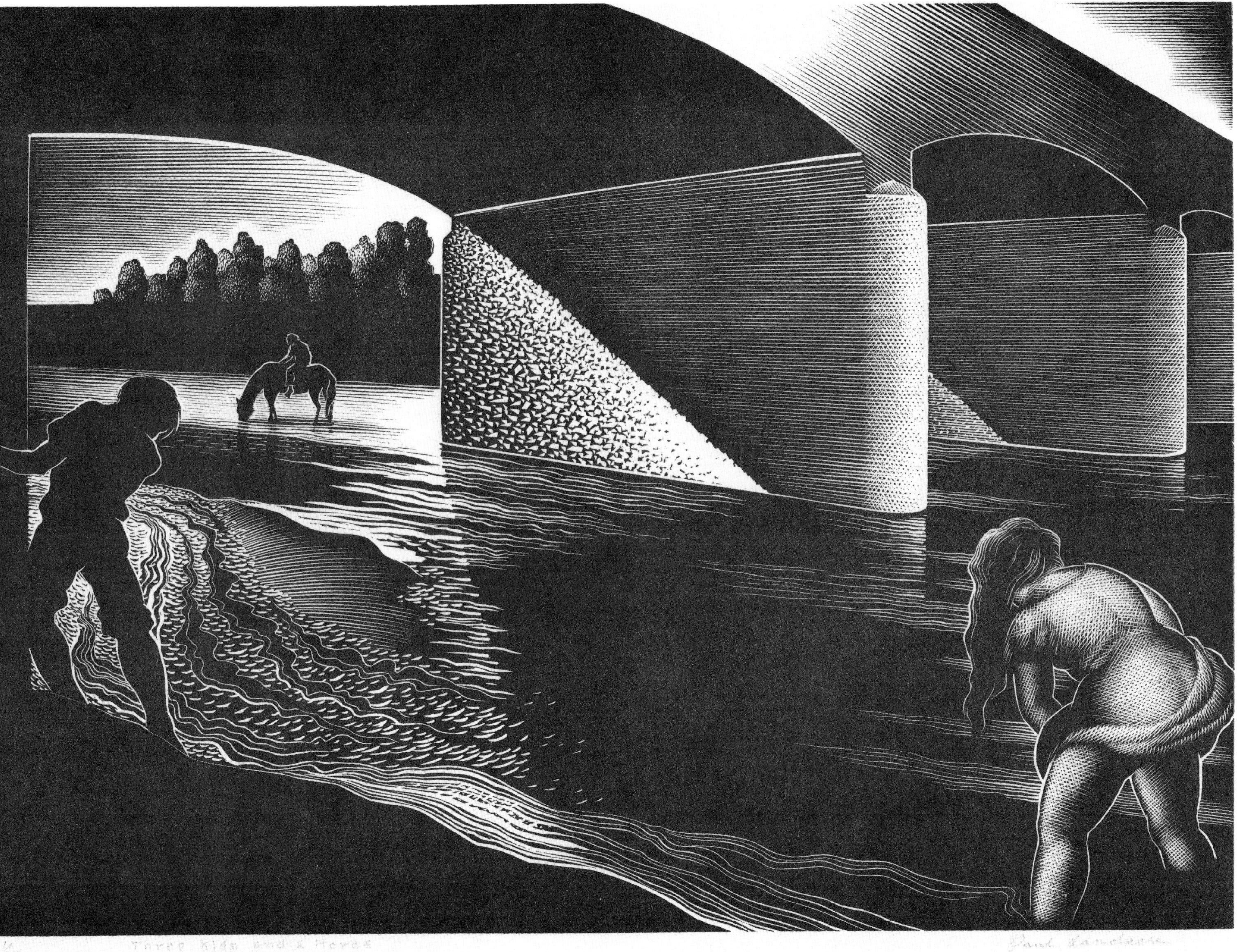

81. PAUL HAMBLETON LANDACRE. *Three Kids and a Horse*, 1943. Wood engraving. Edition 100. 7½ × 10¼.

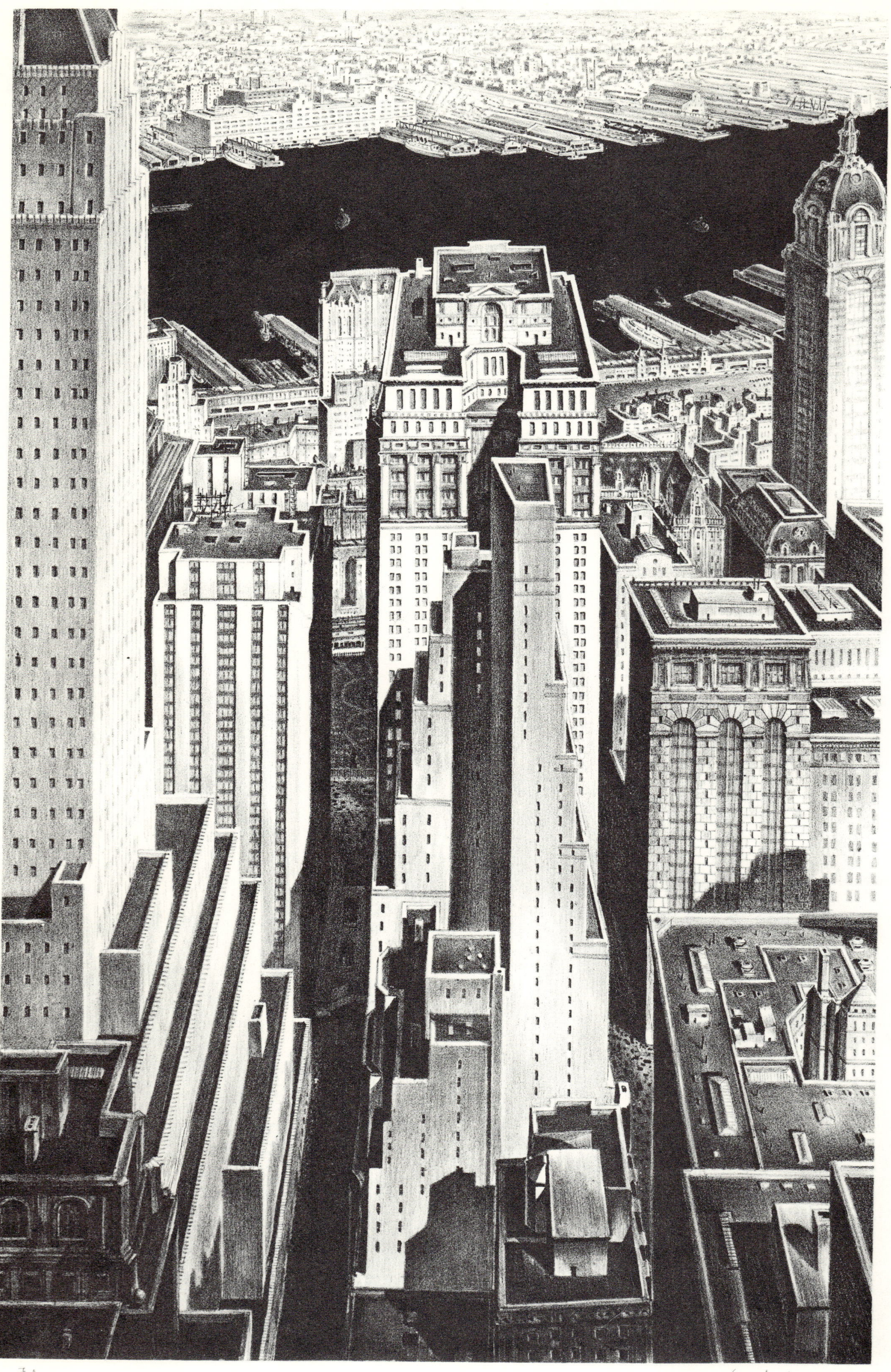

82. ARMIN LANDECK. *North River Vista* (New York City), 1932. Lithograph. Edition 10. 16 × 11¼. Kraeft 40.

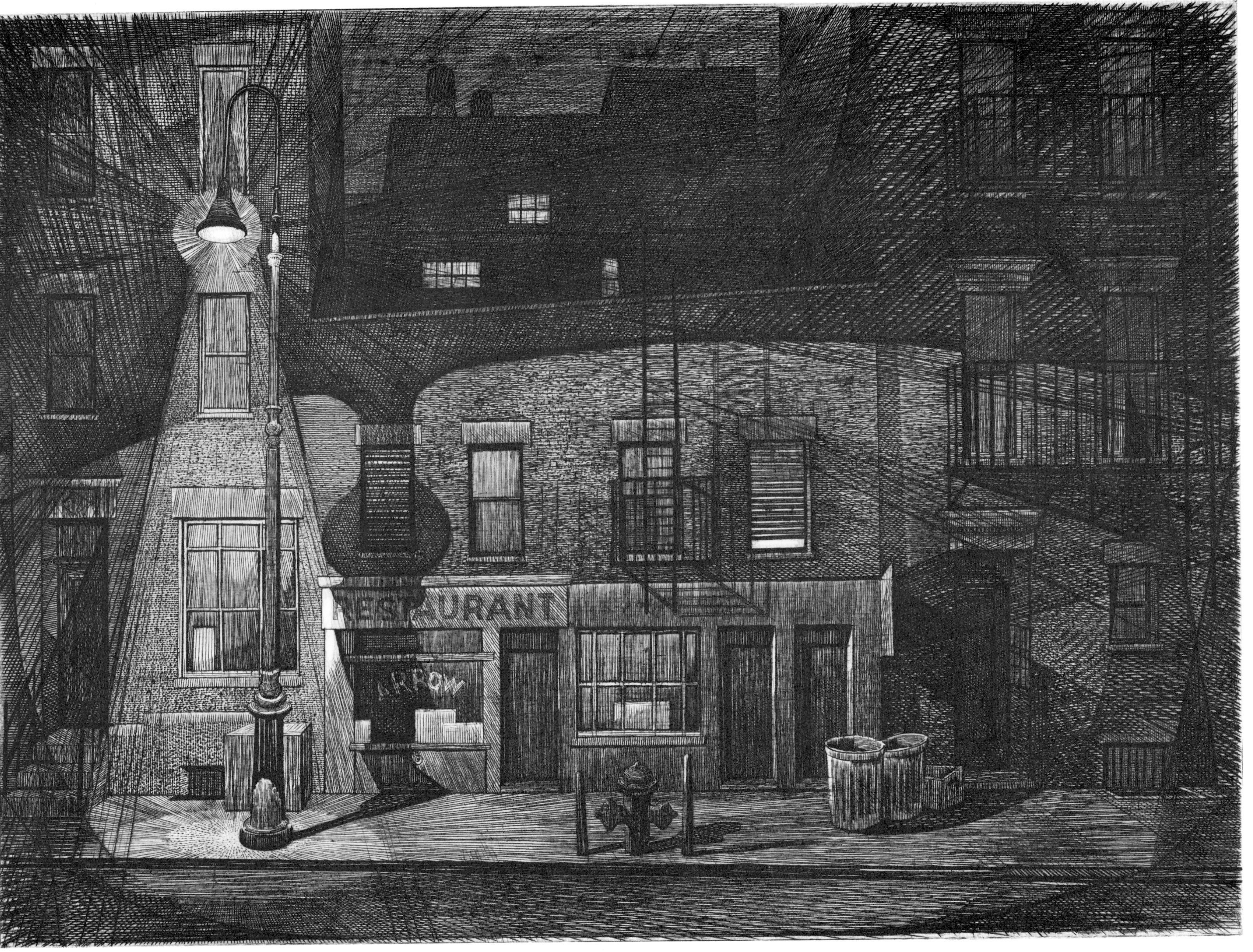

83. ARMIN LANDECK. *Restaurant* (New York City), 1951. Copper engraving. Edition 100. $11\frac{15}{16} \times 15\frac{15}{16}$. Kraeft 109.

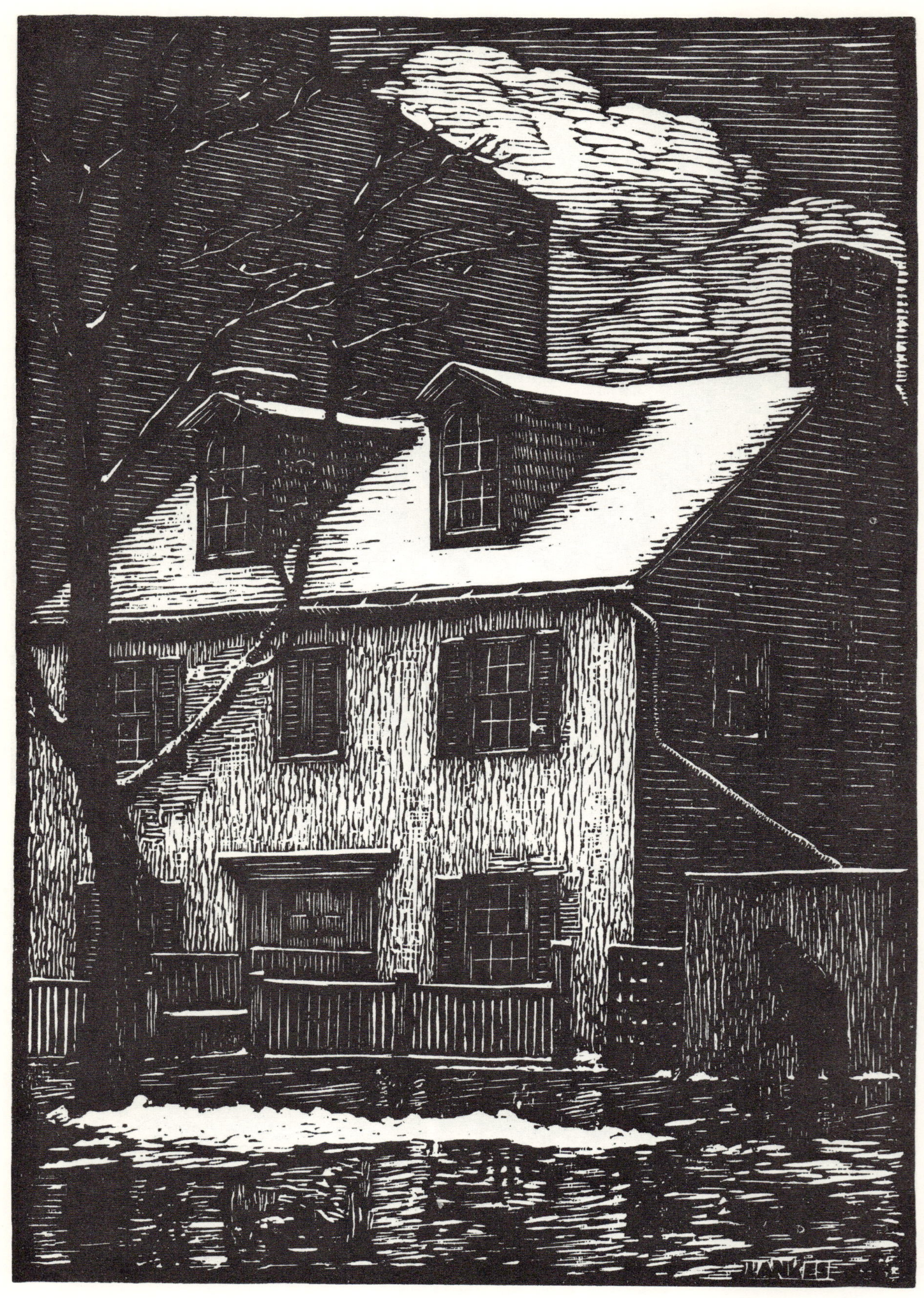

84. Julius J. Lankes. *"N" Street House, Georgetown* (Washington, D.C.), 1927. Wood engraving. $8\frac{5}{8} \times 6\frac{1}{8}$.

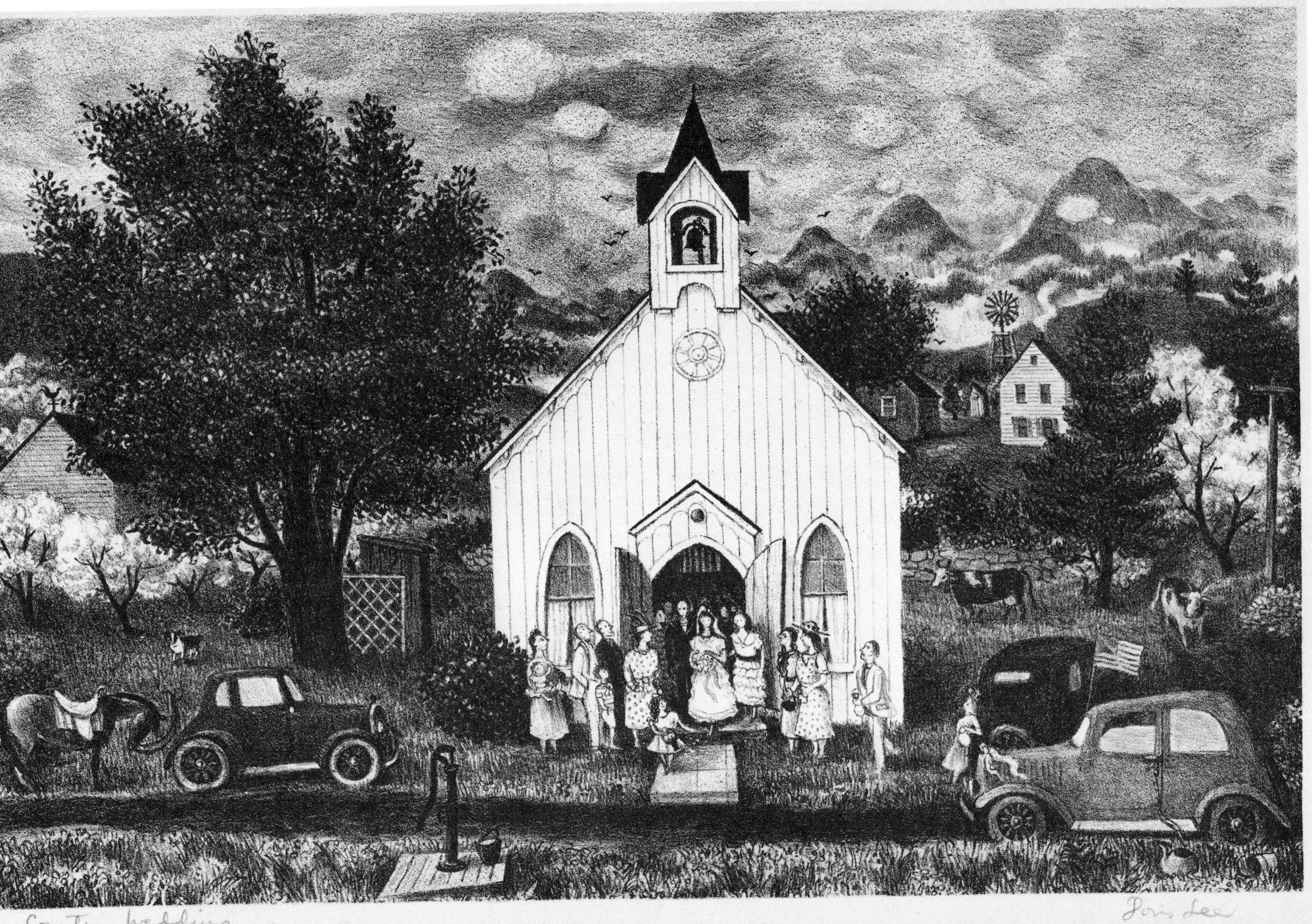

85. Doris Emrick Lee. *Country Wedding*, 1944. Lithograph. 8 × 11⅞.

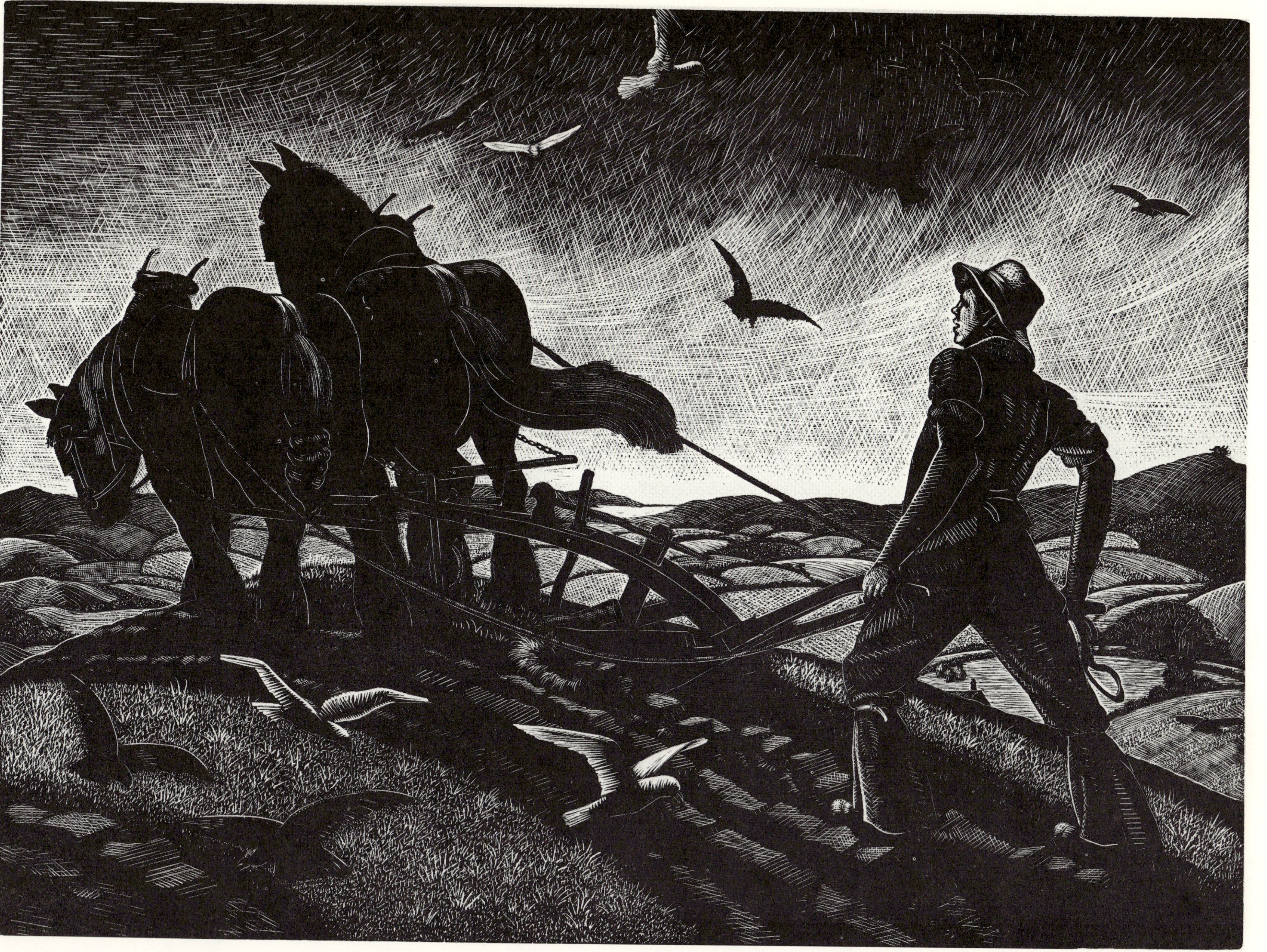

86. Clare Veronica Hope Leighton. *Ploughing*, 1933. Wood engraving. Edition 60. 7½ × 10. Boston Public Library 220.

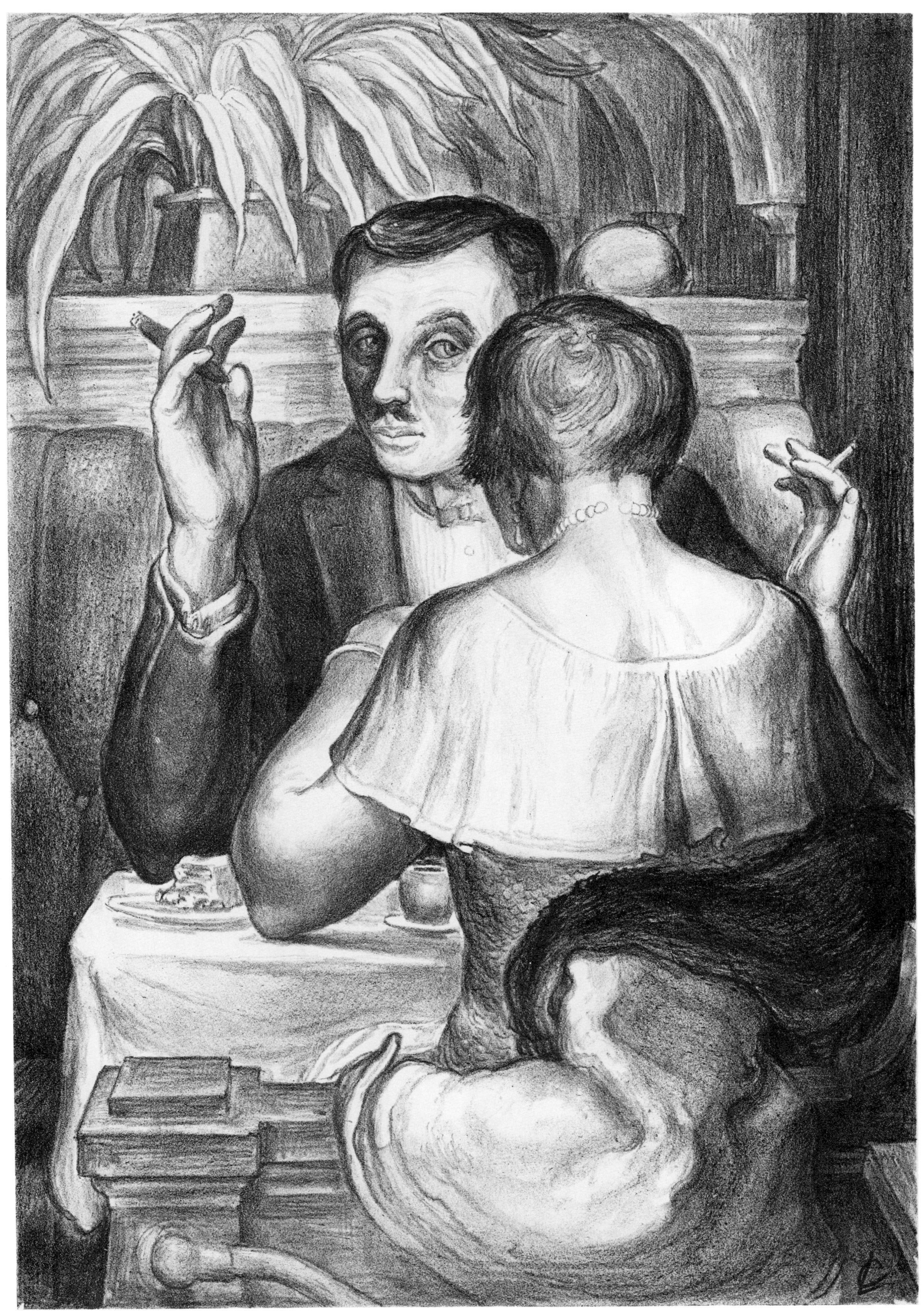

87. Charles Wheeler Locke. *Table d'Hôte.* Lithograph. Edition 40. 11⅝ × 8⅛.

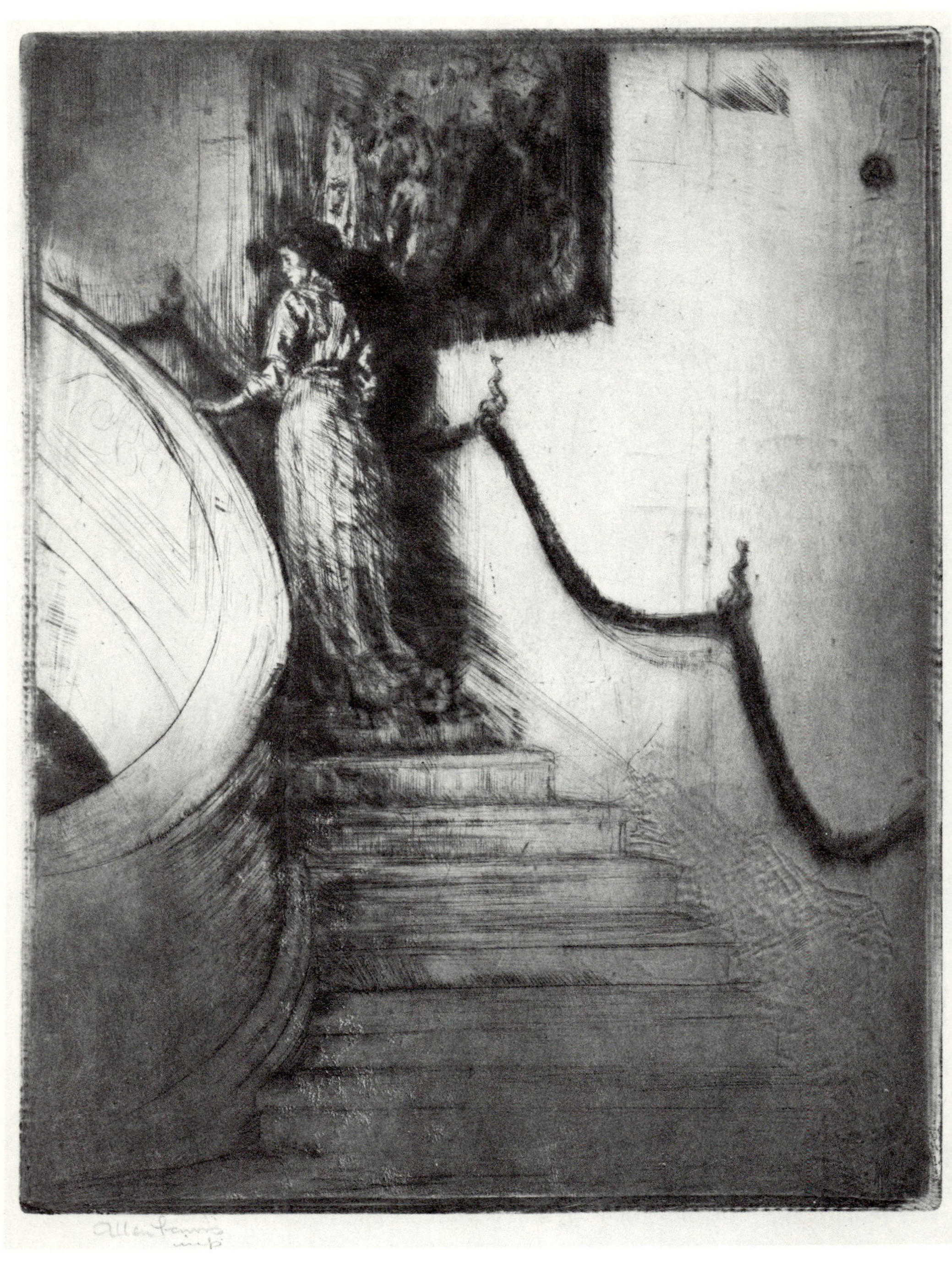

88. Arthur Allen Lewis. *Lady on the Stairs* (the artist's wife, Bessie), ca. 1912. Drypoint. $6\frac{3}{4} \times 5\frac{1}{4}$.

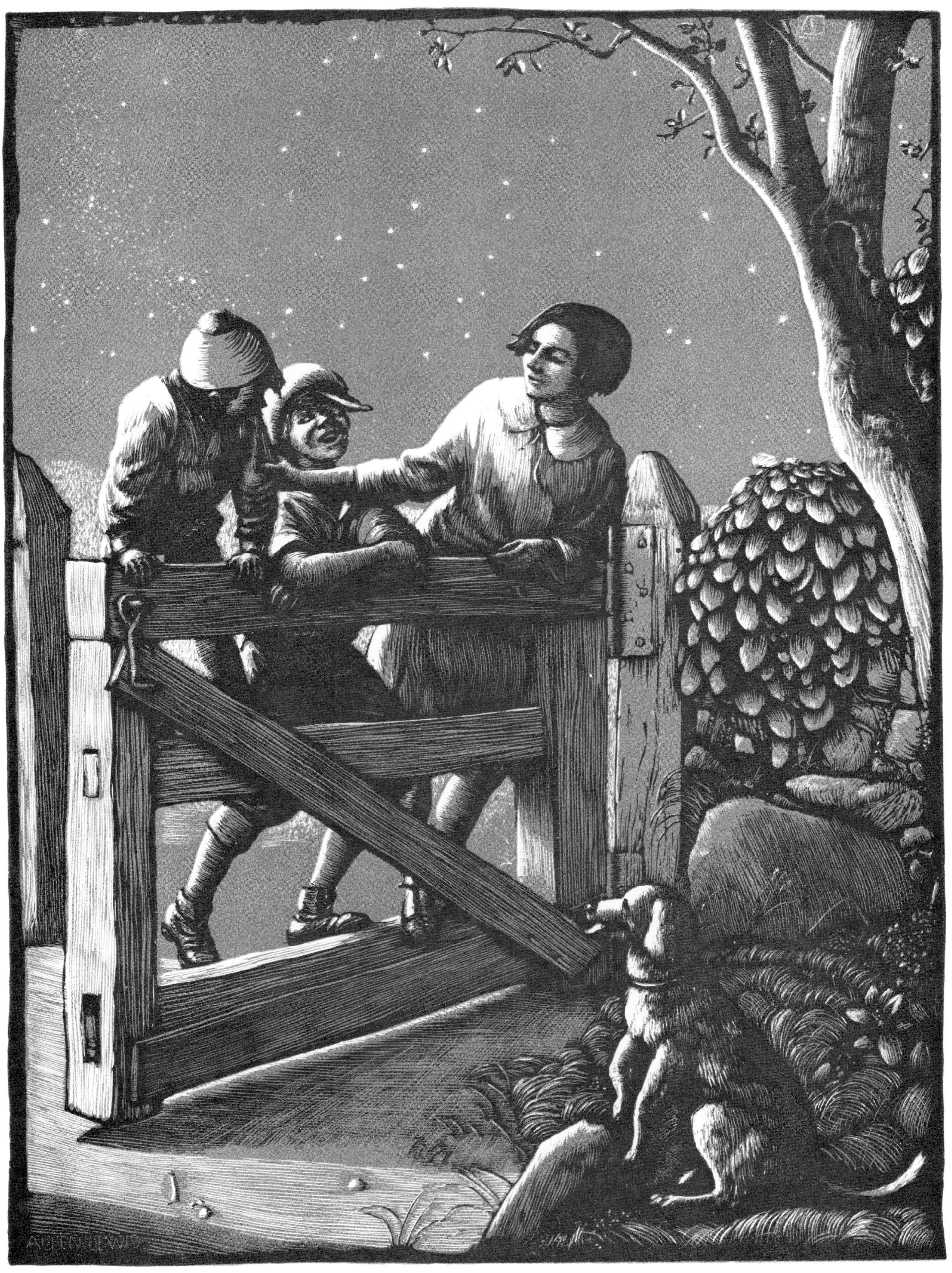

89. Arthur Allen Lewis. *Swinging the Gate,* 1936. Woodcut printed in colors. Published by the American Artists Group. 10 × 7½.

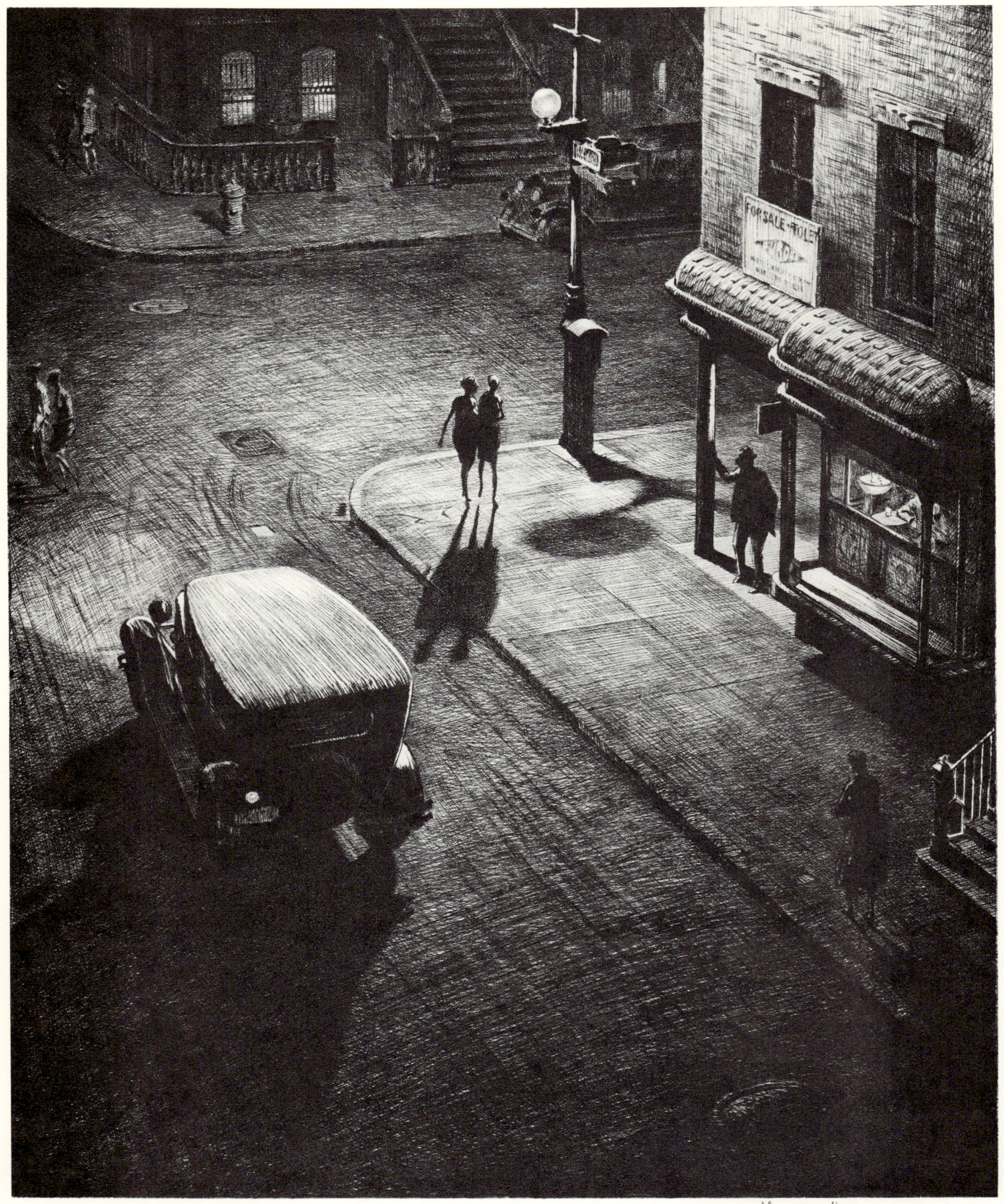

90. MARTIN LEWIS. *Relics* (New York City), 1928. Drypoint. Edition 100. $11\frac{7}{8} \times 9\frac{7}{8}$. McCarron 65.

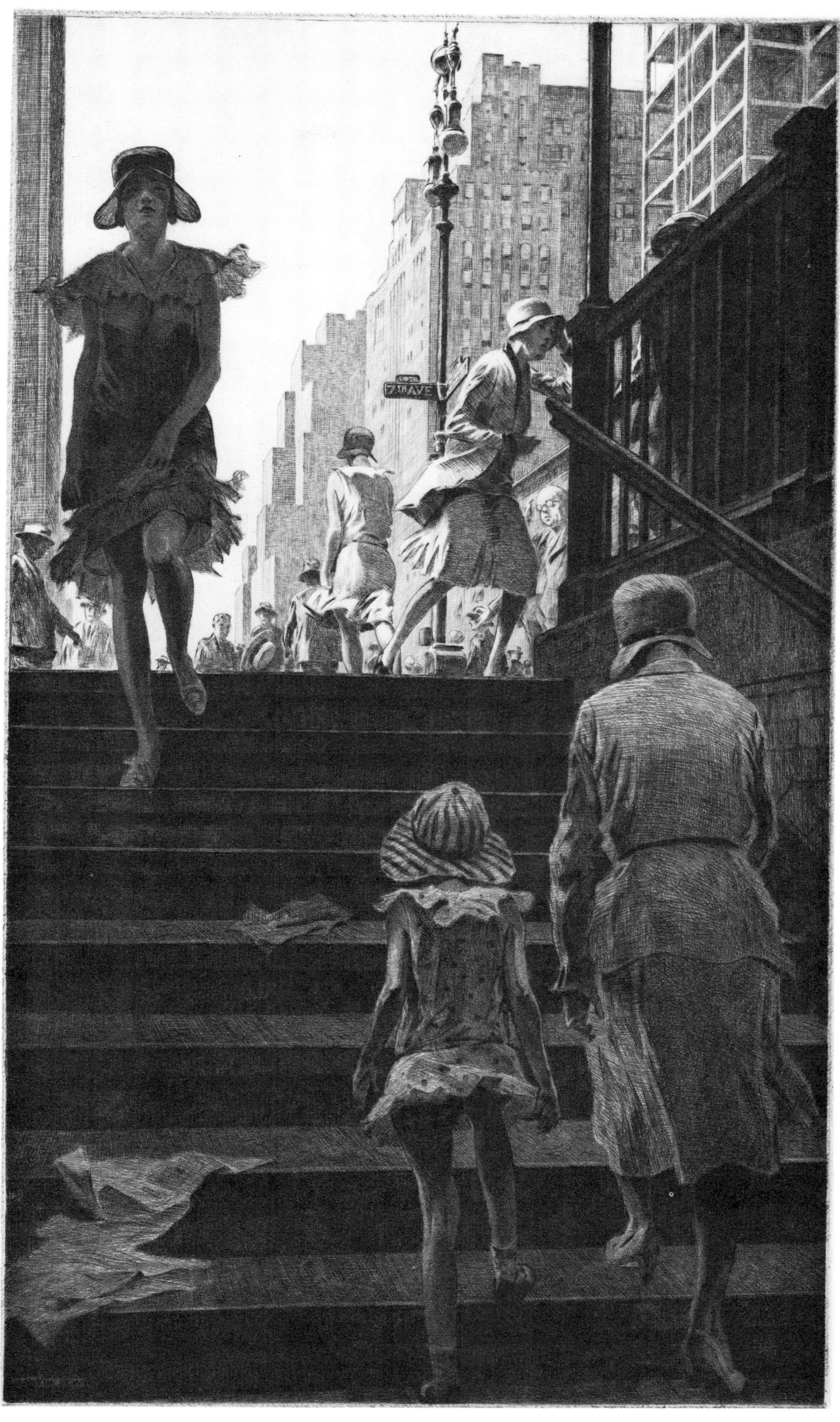

91. Martin Lewis. *Subway Steps* (New York City), 1930. Drypoint. Edition 100. 13½ × 8⅛. McCarron 96.

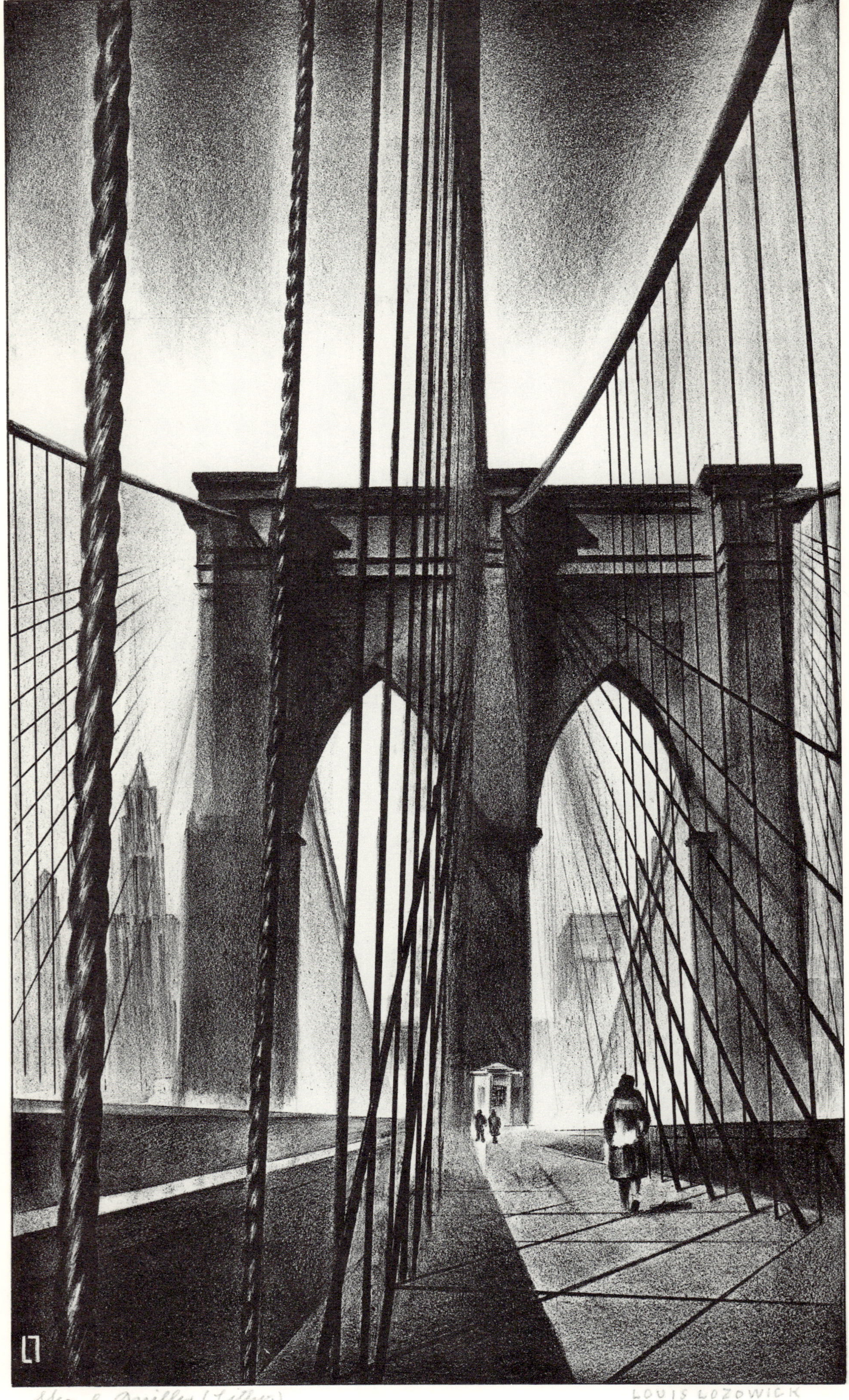

92. LOUIS LOZOWICK. *Brooklyn Bridge* (New York City), ca. 1930. Lithograph. Edition 100. $13 \times 7\frac{7}{8}$. Flint 48.

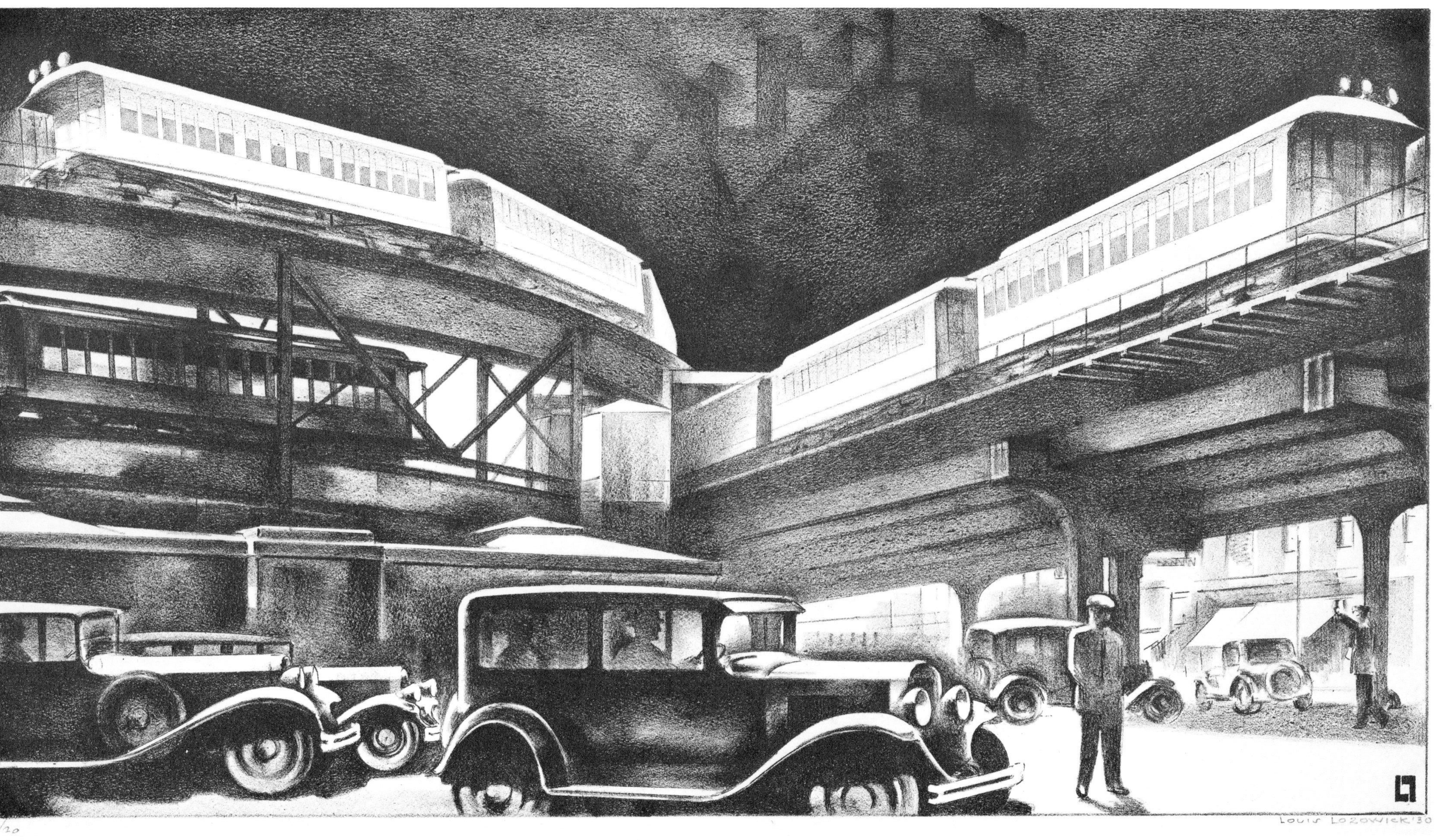

93. Louis Lozowick. *Traffic* (New York City), 1930. Lithograph. Edition 20. 9⅛ × 16⅛. Flint 72.

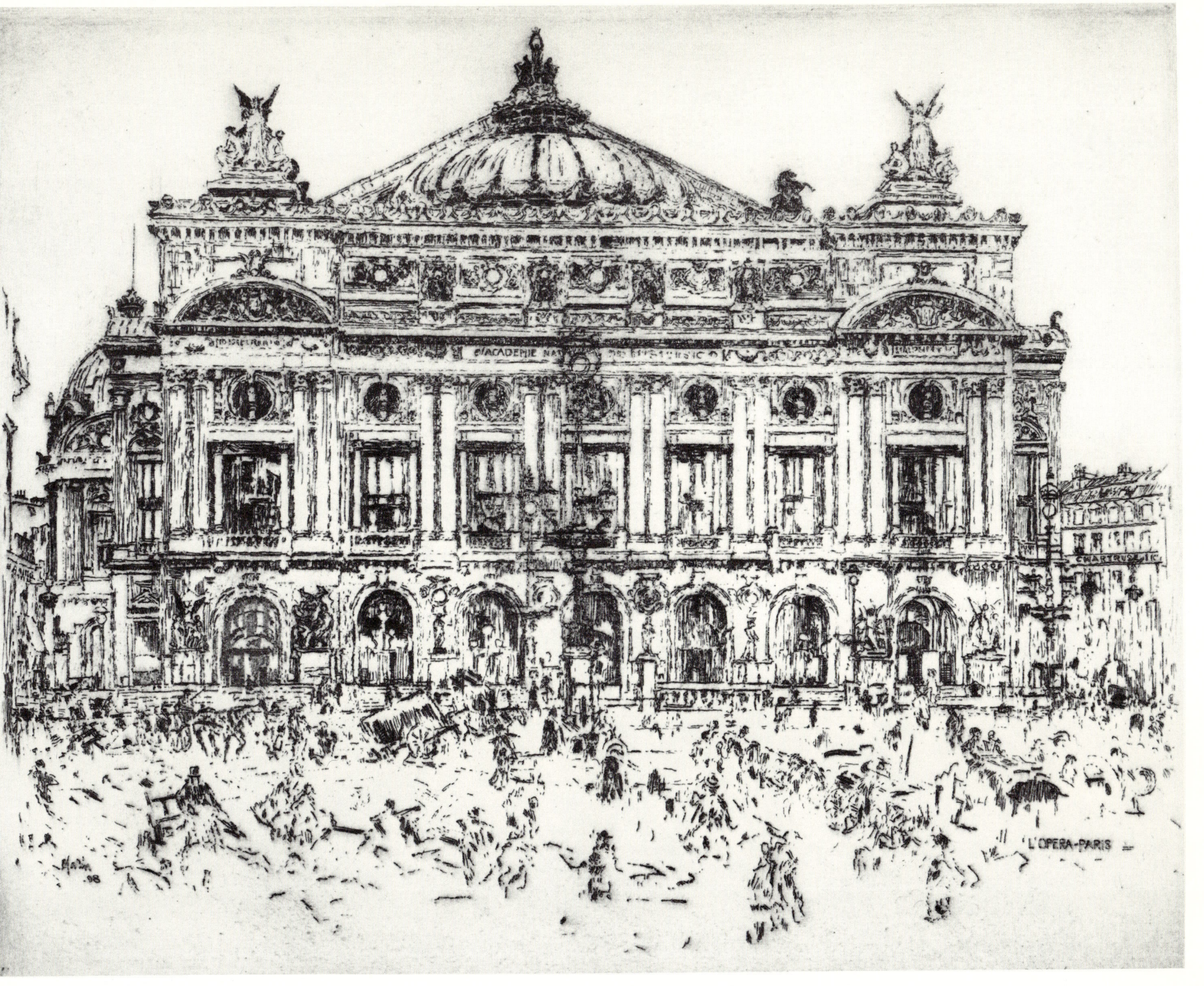

94. JOHN MARIN. *L'Opéra, Paris,* 1908. Etching. Edition ca. 30. $10\frac{13}{16} \times 13$. Zigrosser 80.

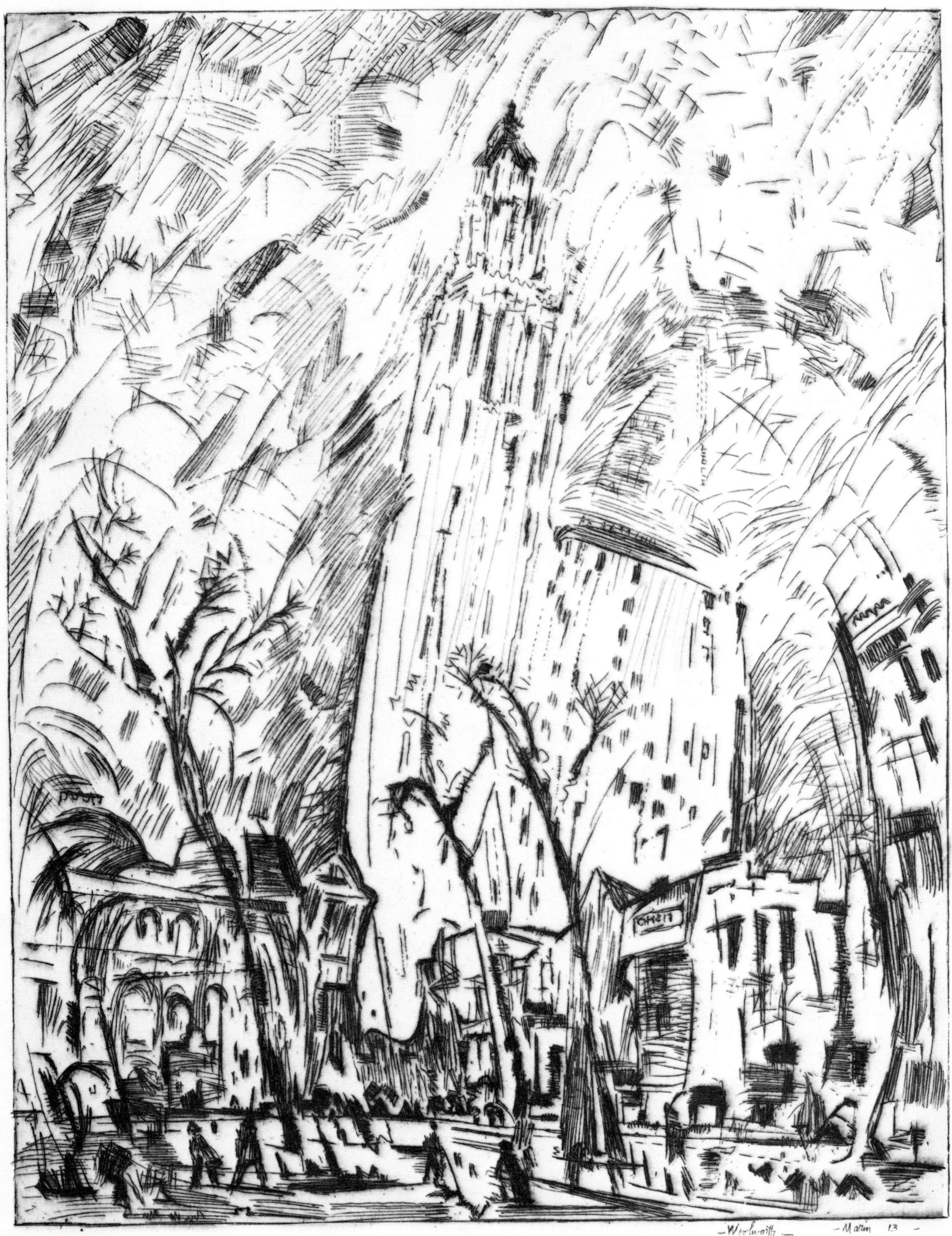

95. JOHN MARIN. *Woolworth Building (The Dance)* (New York City), 1913. Etching. Edition ca. 30. 13 × 10½. Zigrosser 116.

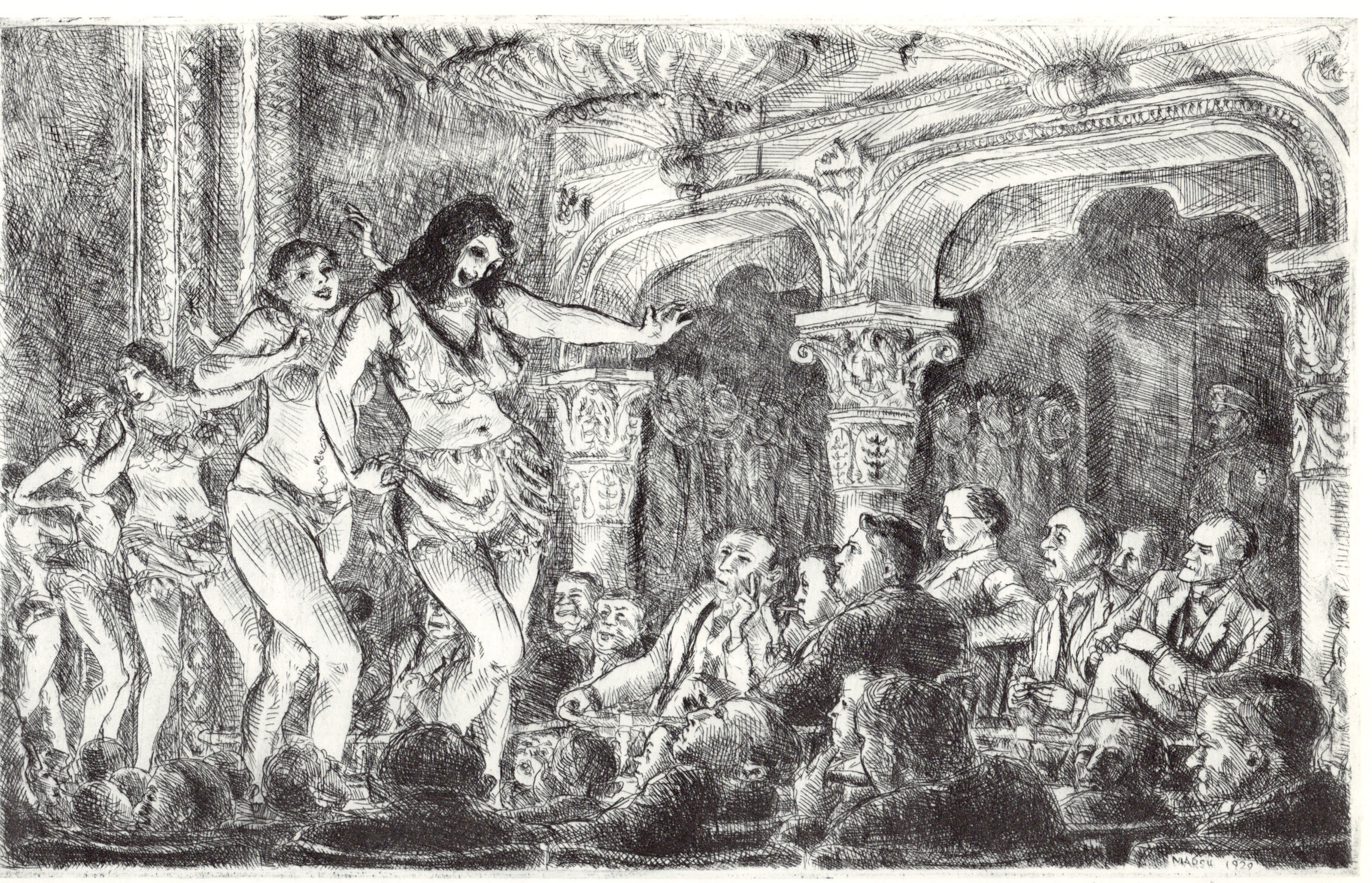

96. Reginald Marsh. *Gaiety Burlesk* (New York City), 1929. Etching. Edition ca. 13. 7 × 10¾. Sasowsky 74.

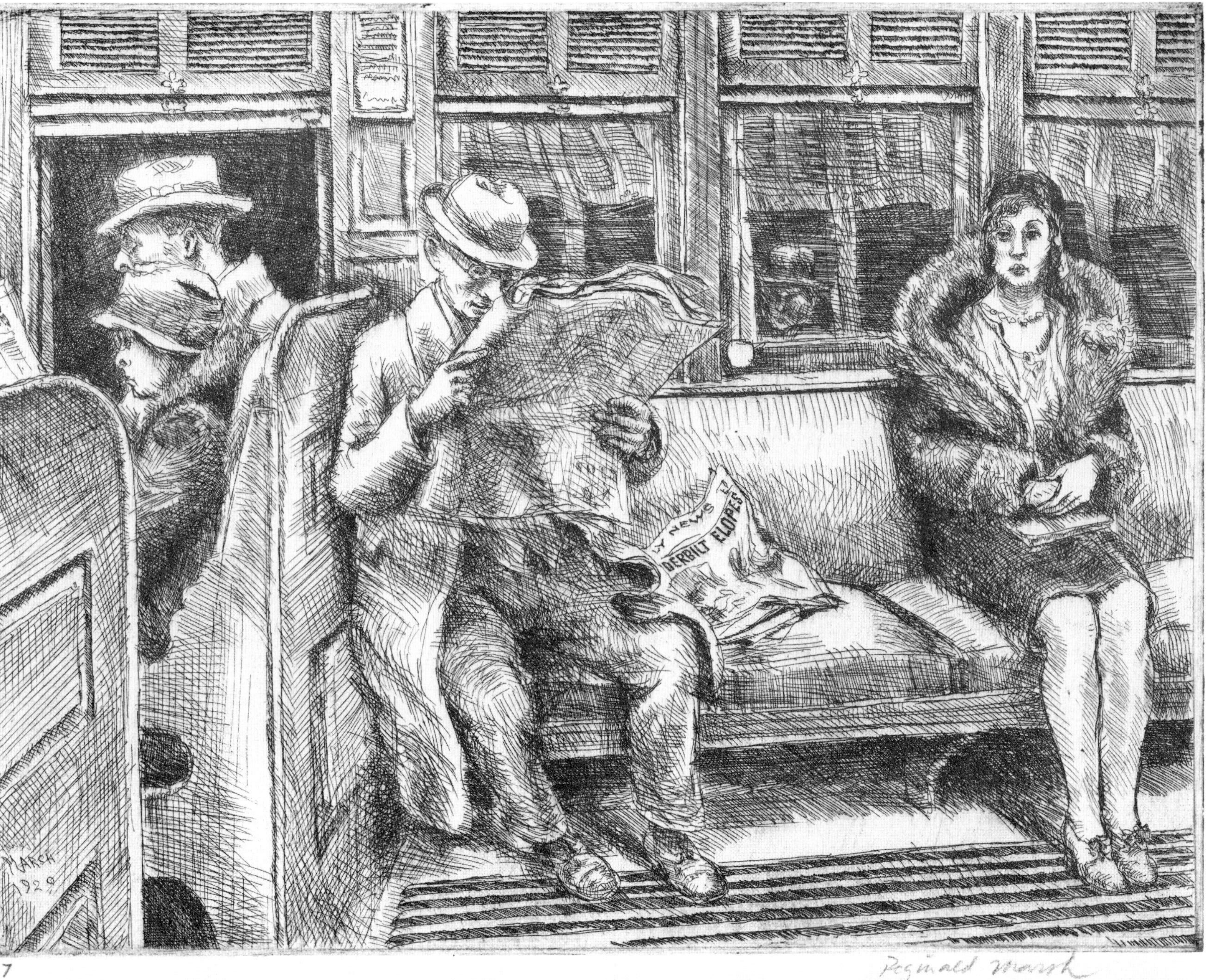

97. REGINALD MARSH. *2nd Avenue El* (New York City), 1929. Etching. Edition ca. 25. 7 × 9. Sasowsky 59.

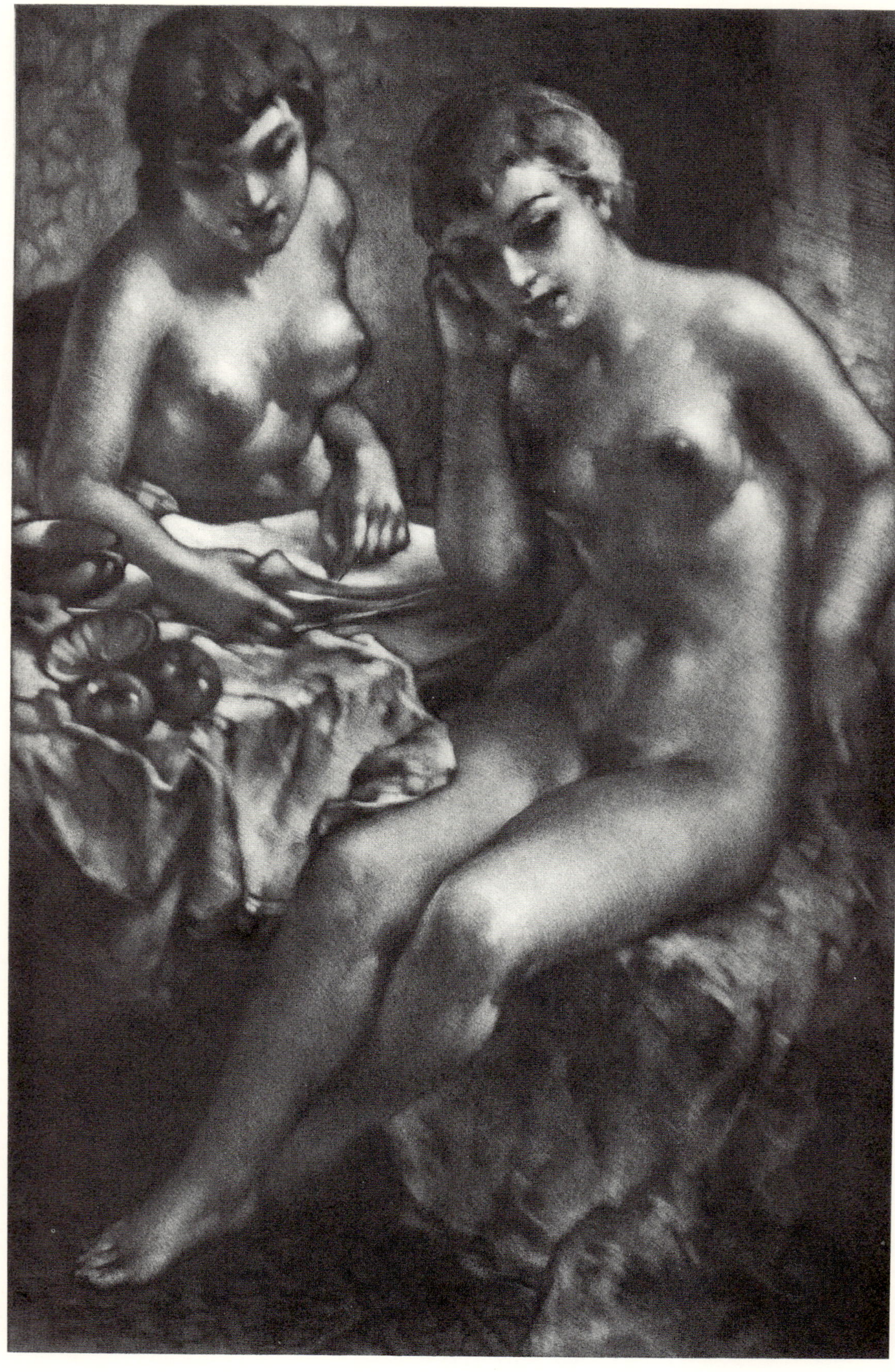

98. ALESSANDRO MASTRO-VALERIO. *Morning Paper*, 1941. Mezzotint. Presentation print of the Chicago Society of Etchers, 1941. 8⅞ × 5⅞.

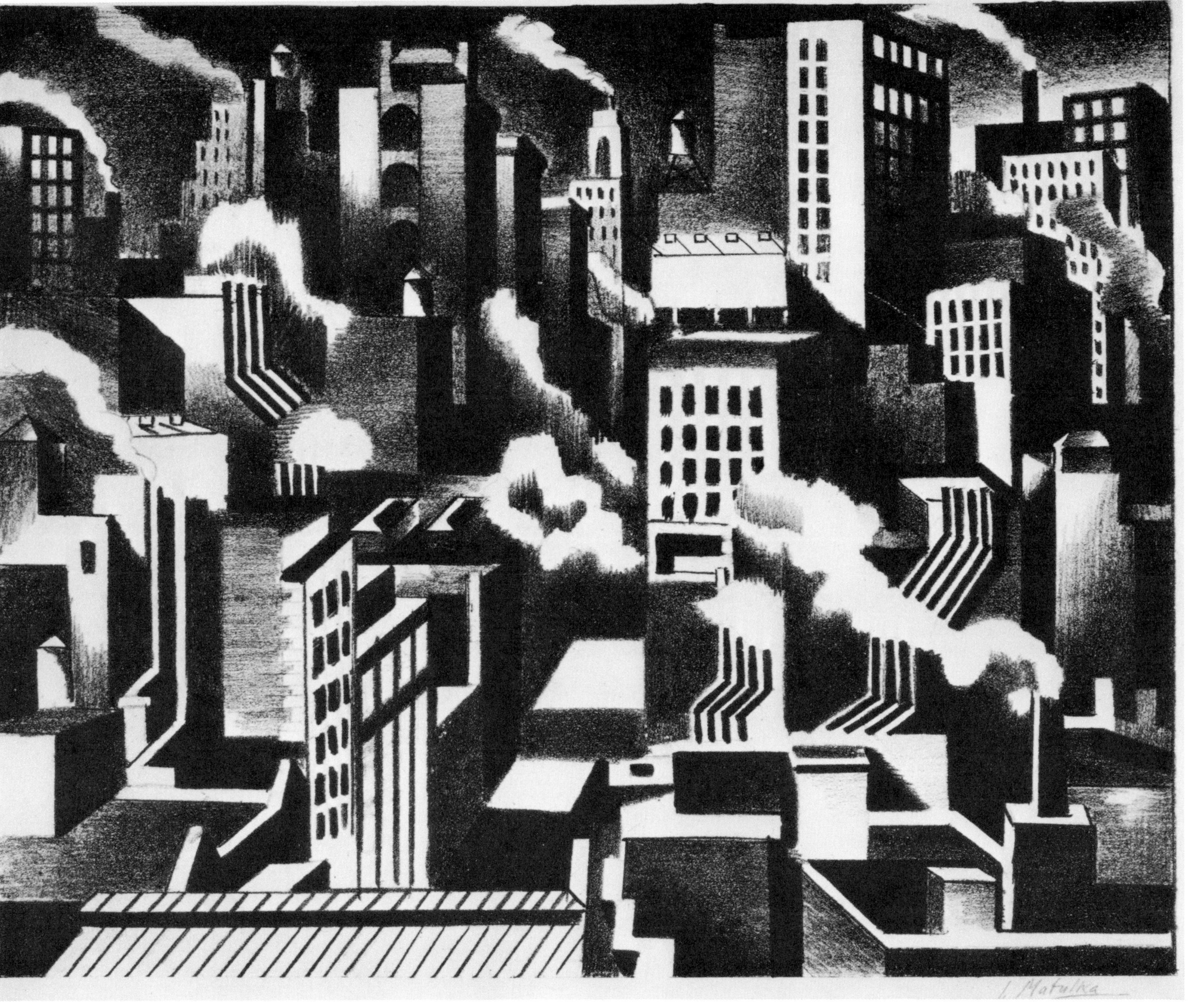

99. JAN MATULKA. *Arrangement—New York* (or *Architecture of New York; Evening*), ca. 1925. Lithograph. $13\frac{3}{16} \times 15$. Flint 32.

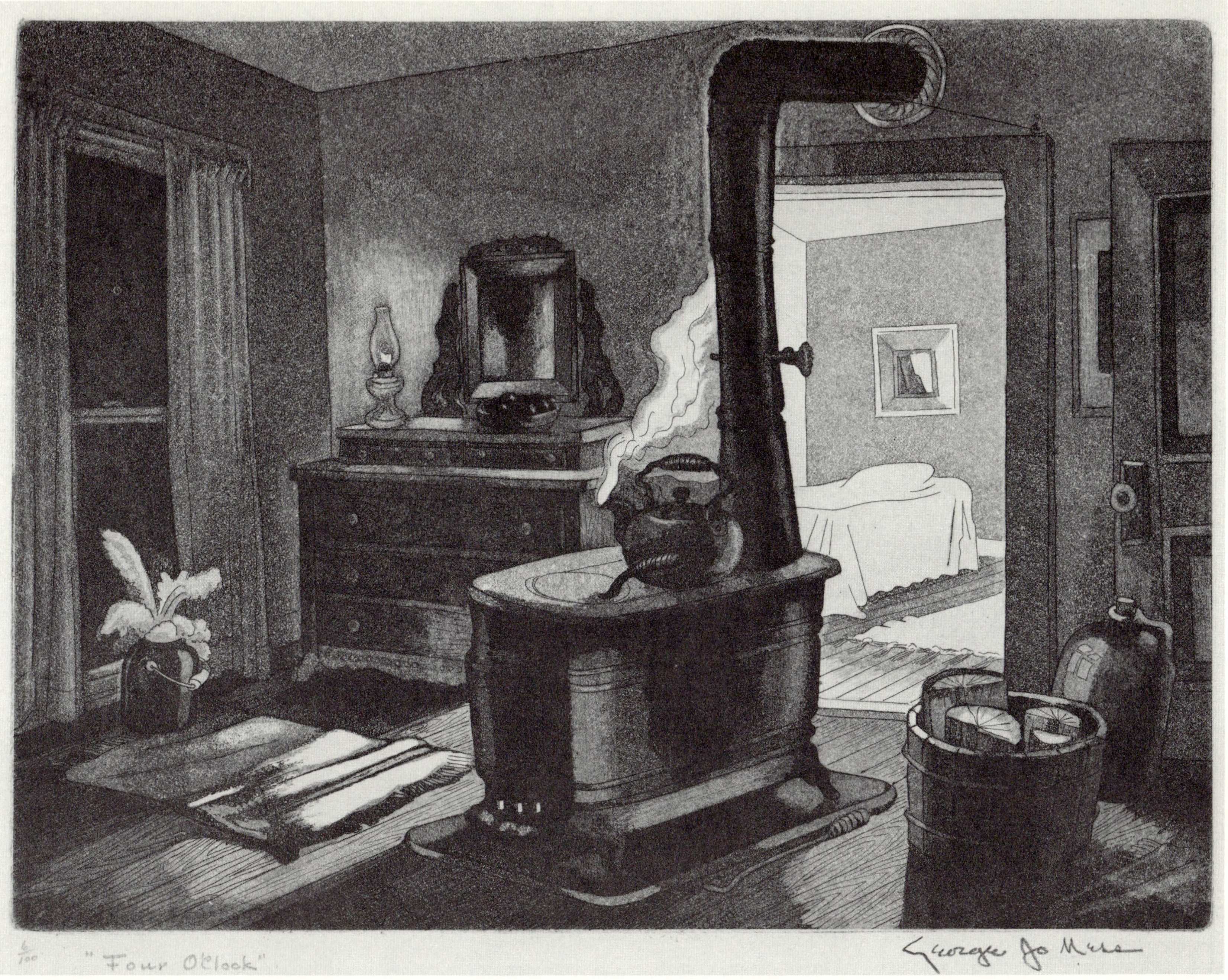

100. George Jo Mess. *Four O'Clock*, 1943. Aquatint. Edition 100. 6⅜ × 8⅜.

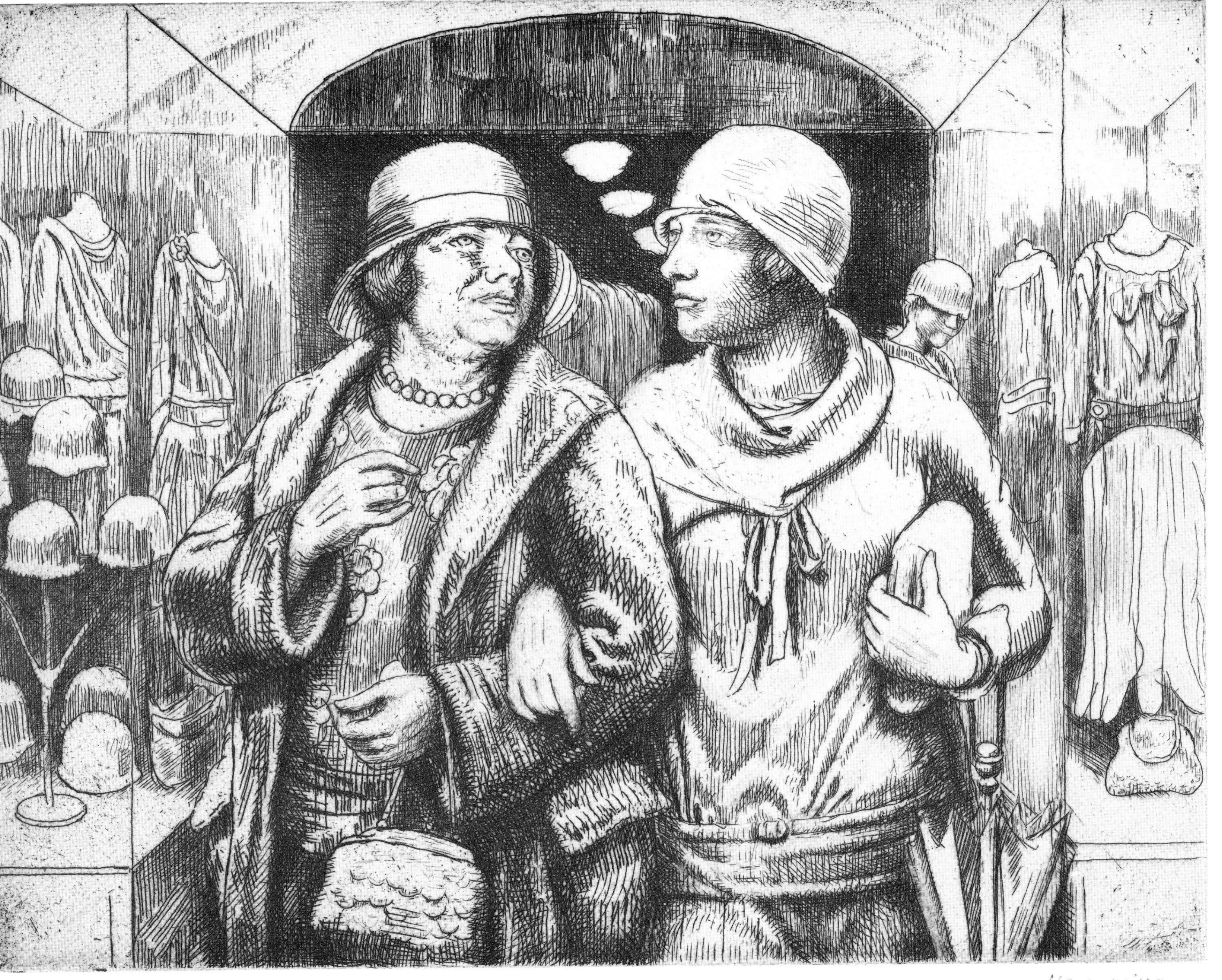

101. Kenneth Hayes Miller. *Leaving the Shop*, early 1930s. Etching. 7⅞ × 9¹³⁄₁₆.

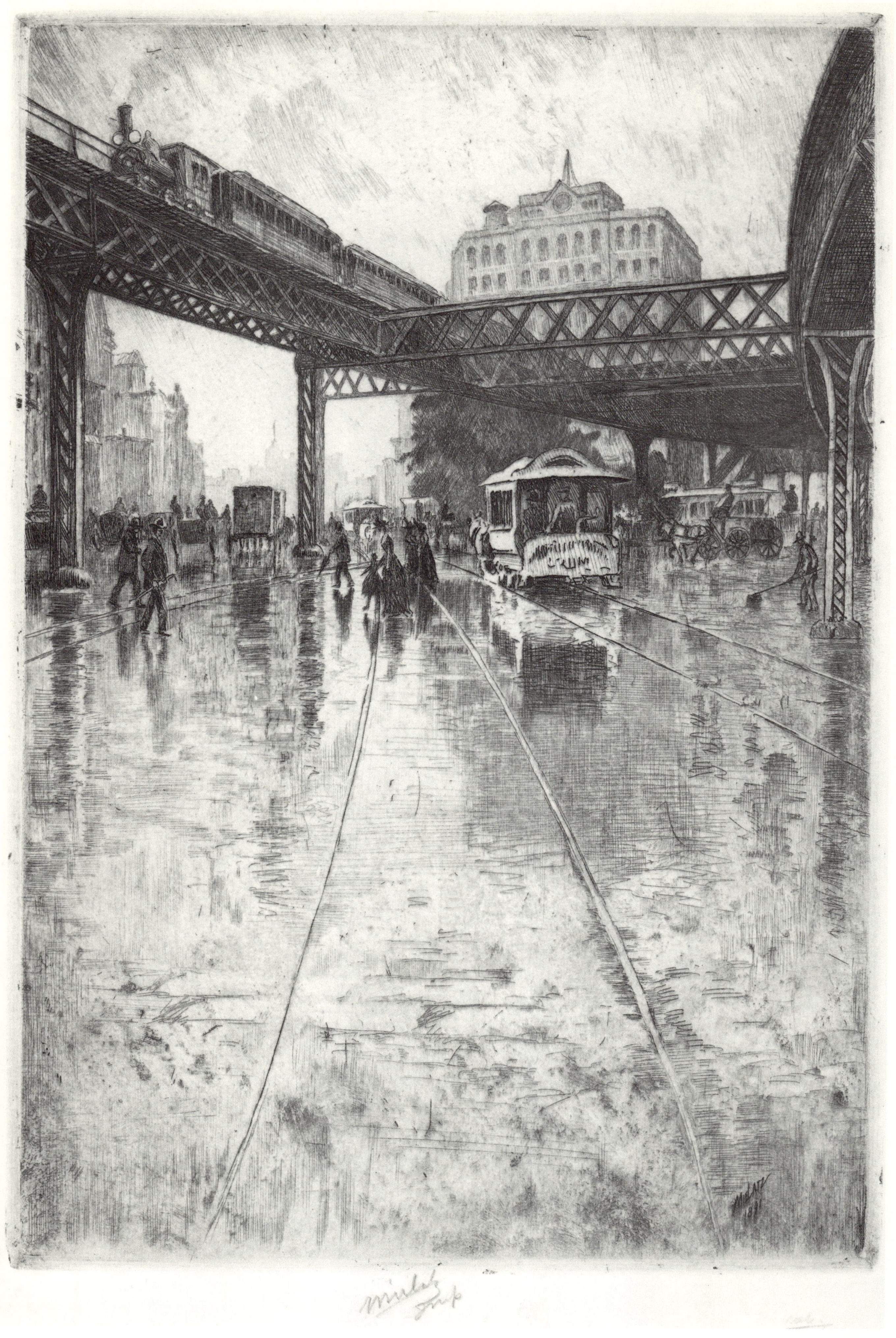

102. CHARLES FREDERICK WILLIAM MIELATZ. *In the Bowery* (New York City), 1891. Etching. 9⅞ × 6⅞.

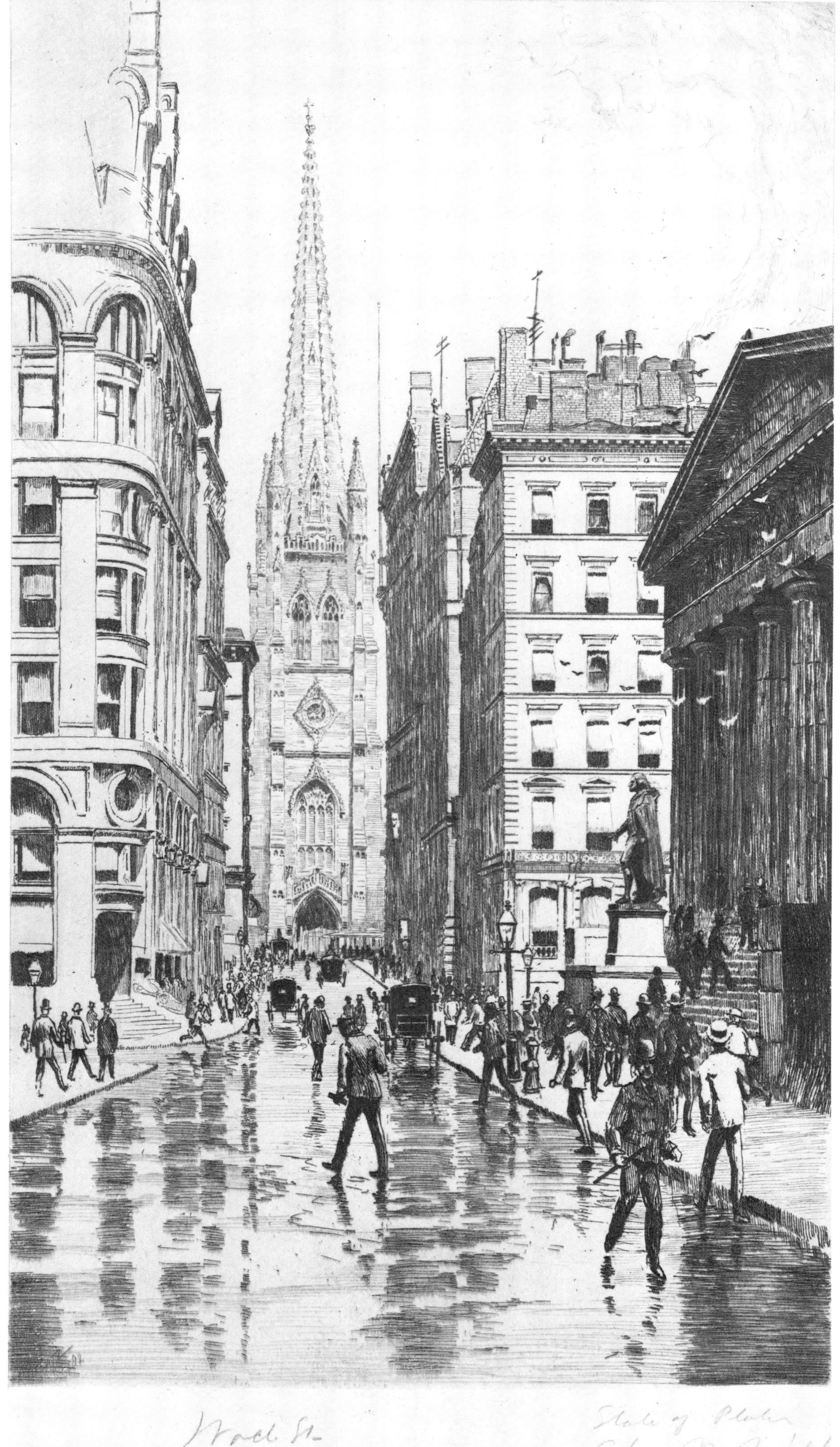

103. Charles Frederick William Mielatz. *Wall Street* (New York City), 1892. Etching. $12\frac{3}{8} \times 7\frac{3}{8}$.

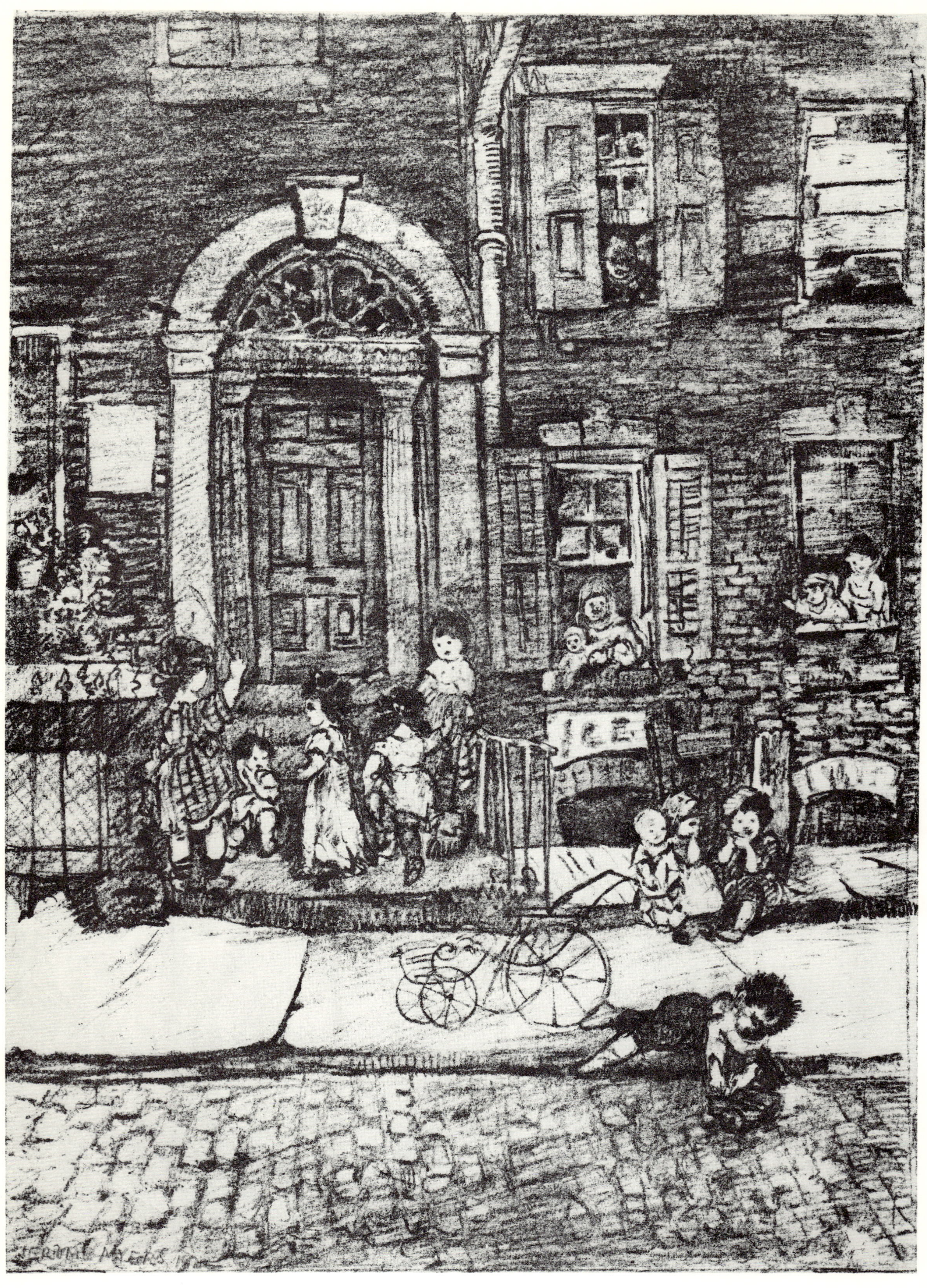

104. Jerome Myers. *An Old Doorway* (or *Old House*) (New York City). Lithograph. $15\frac{1}{2} \times 11\frac{3}{8}$.

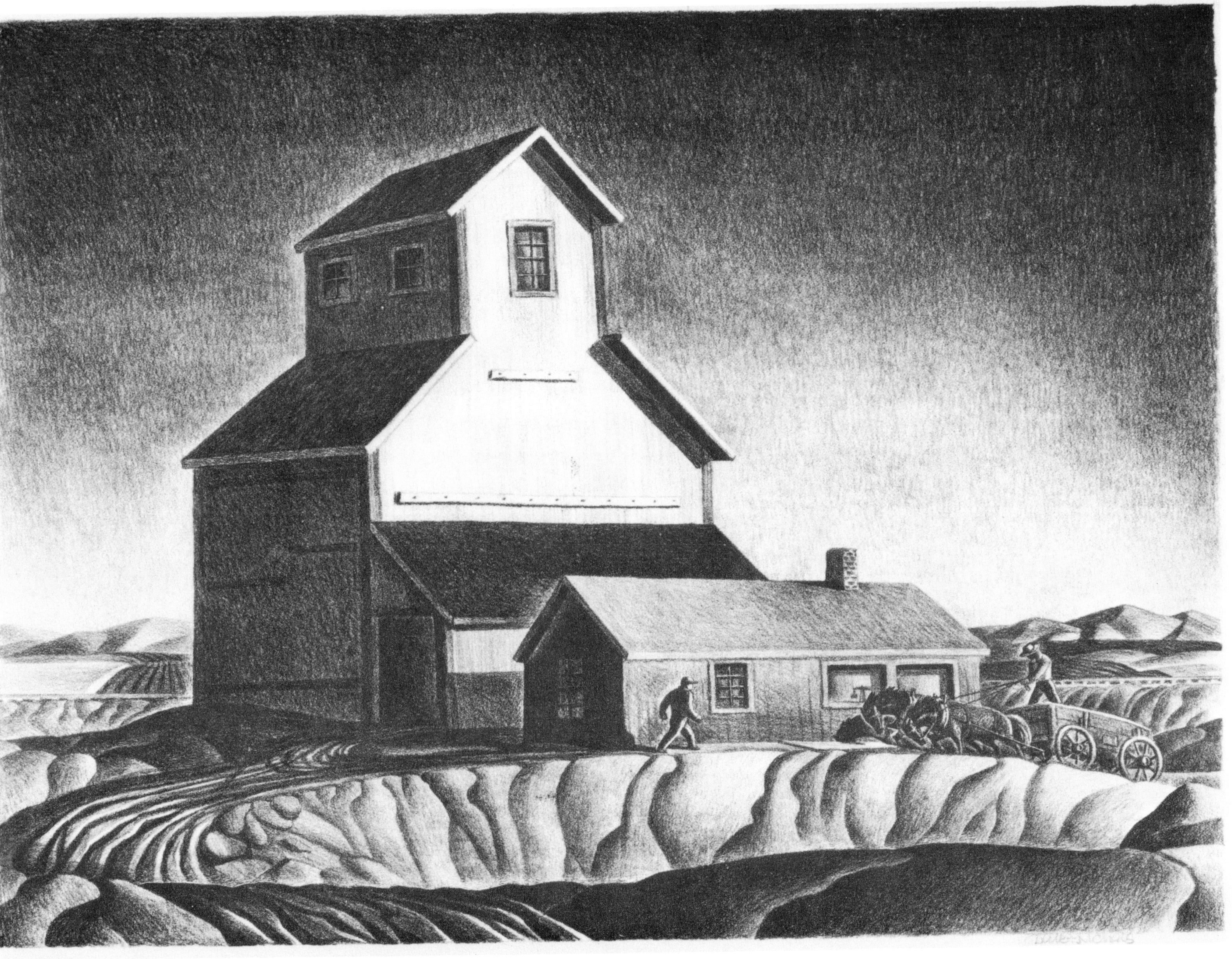

105. DALE WILLIAM NICHOLS. *Grain Elevator*, mid-1930s. Lithograph. 9½ × 12½.

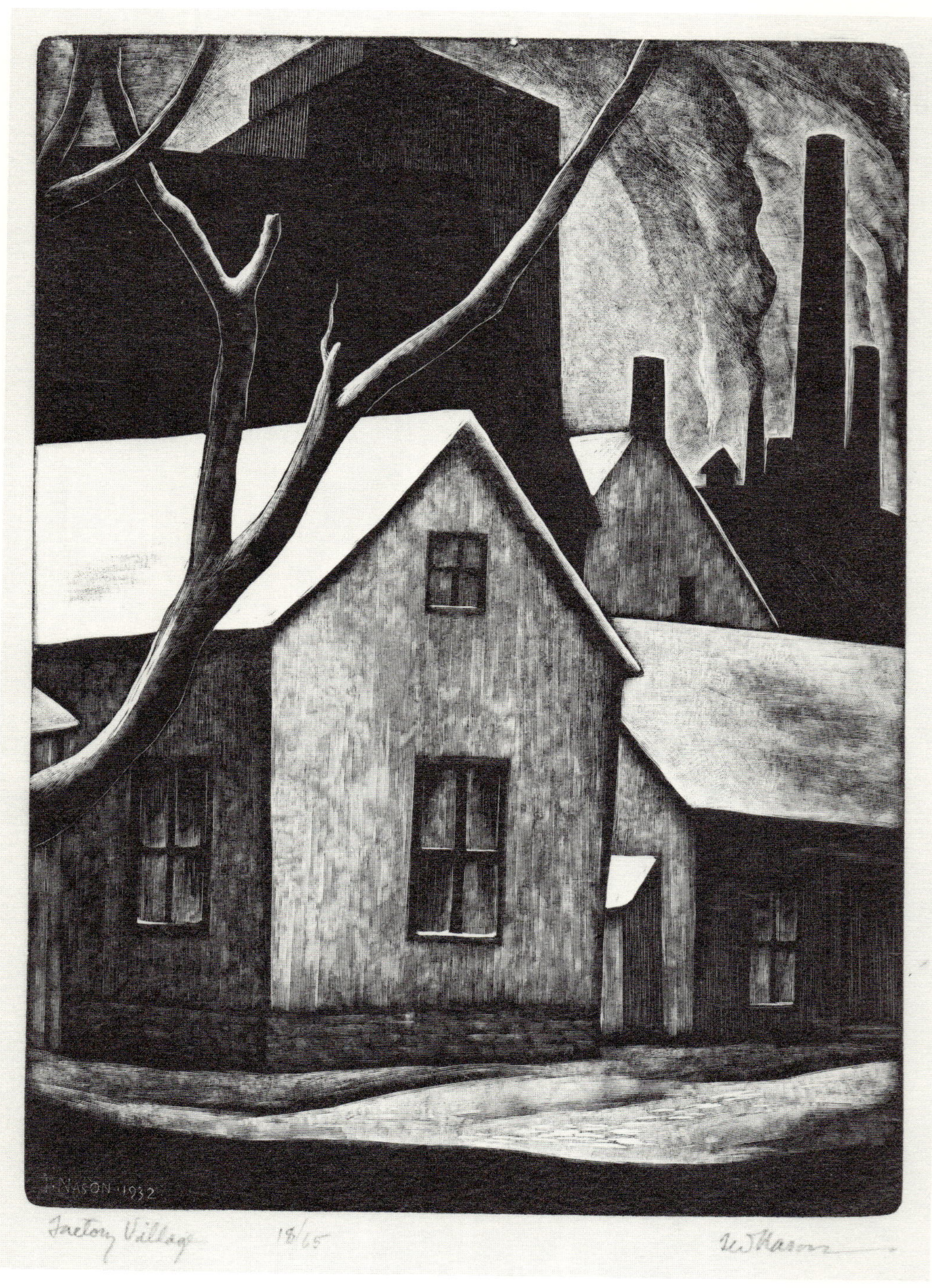

106. Thomas Willoughby Nason. *Factory Village,* 1932. Wood engraving. Edition 65. $6\frac{5}{8} \times 5$. Nason 138.

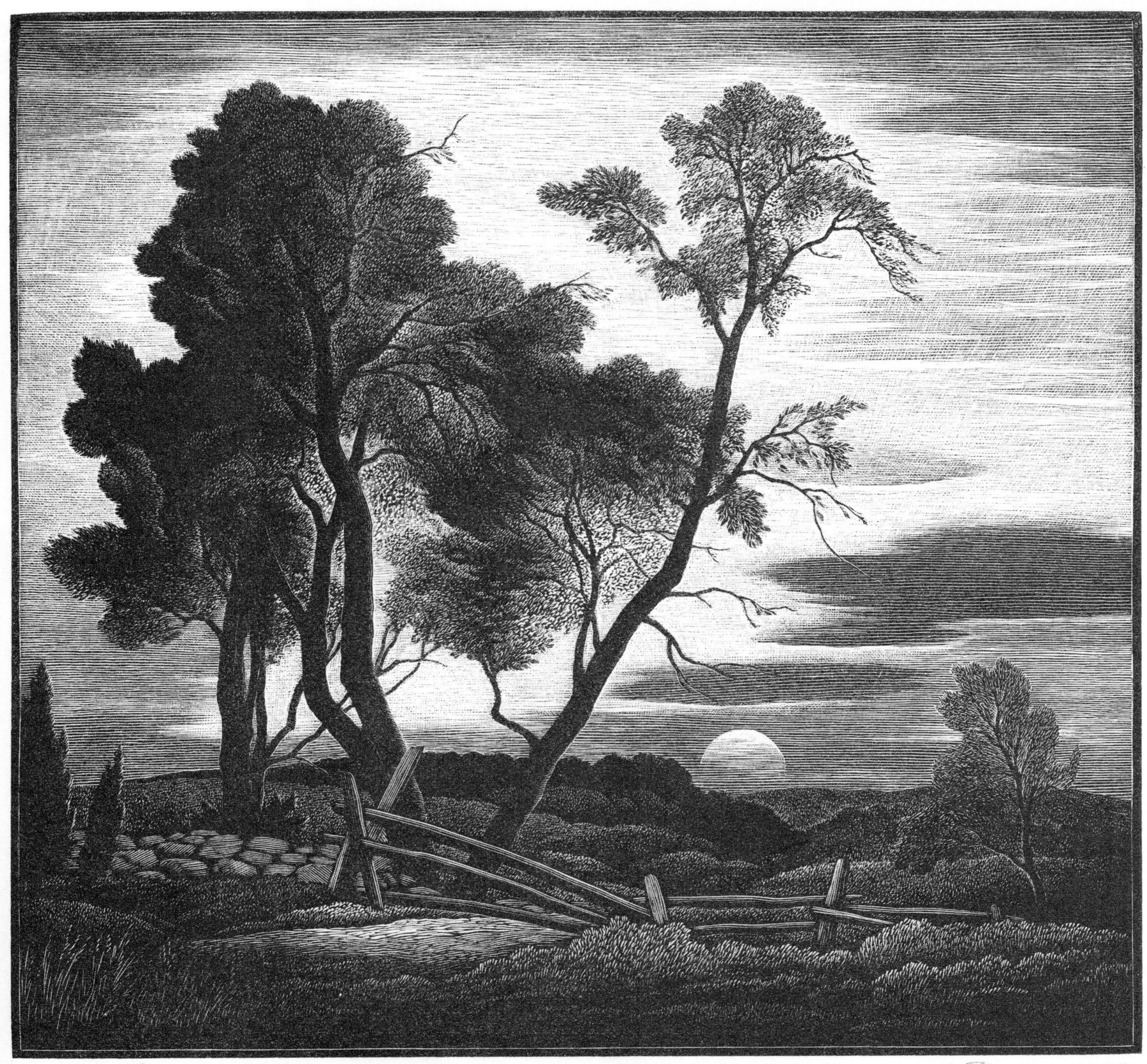

107. THOMAS WILLOUGHBY NASON. *Near Lyme, Sunset,* 1944. Wood engraving. Edition 209, presentation print of The Woodcut Society, 1945. $7 \times 7\frac{5}{8}$. Nason 336.

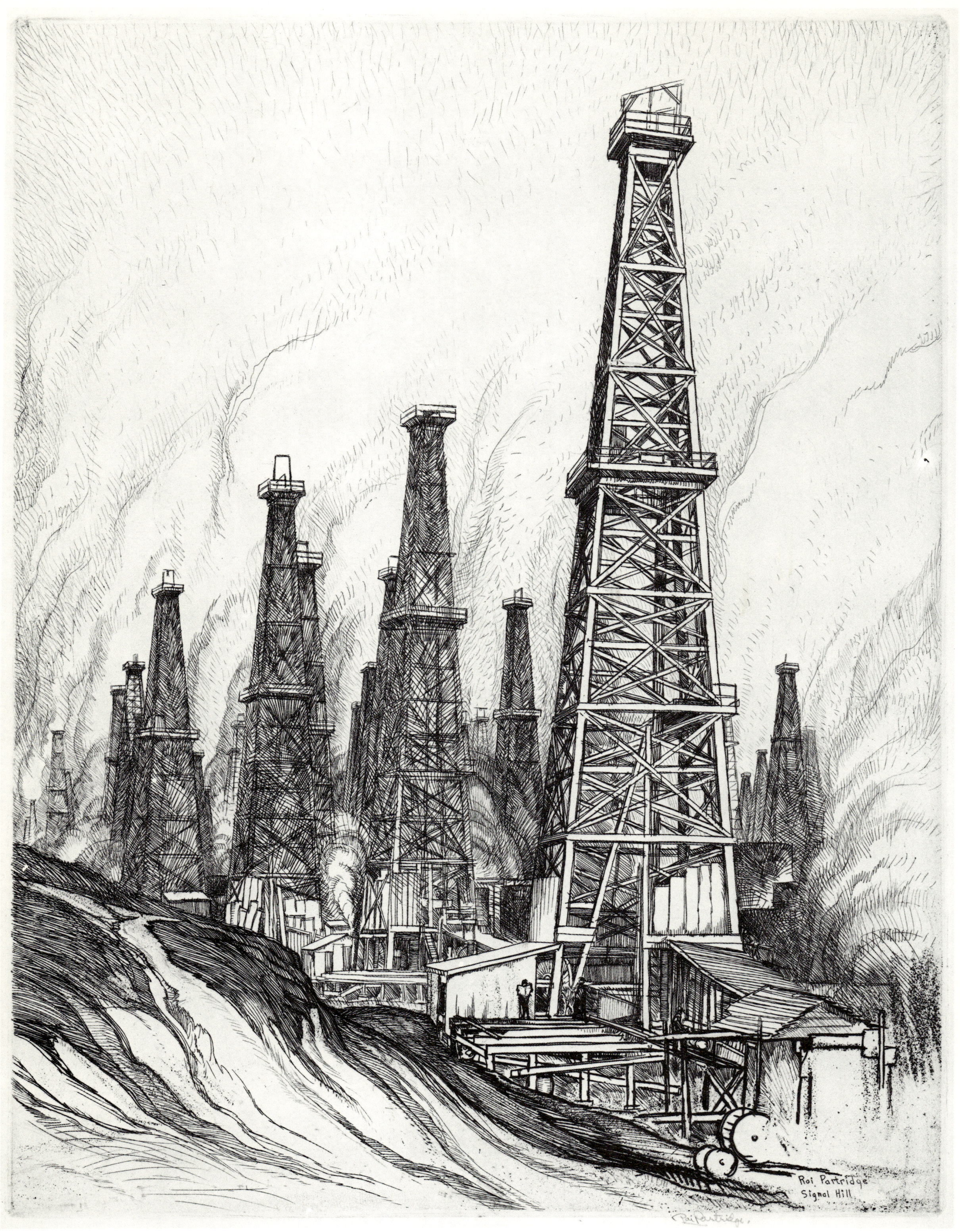

108. Roi Partridge. *Signal Hill*, 1928. Etching. Edition 16. 13¾ × 10¾.

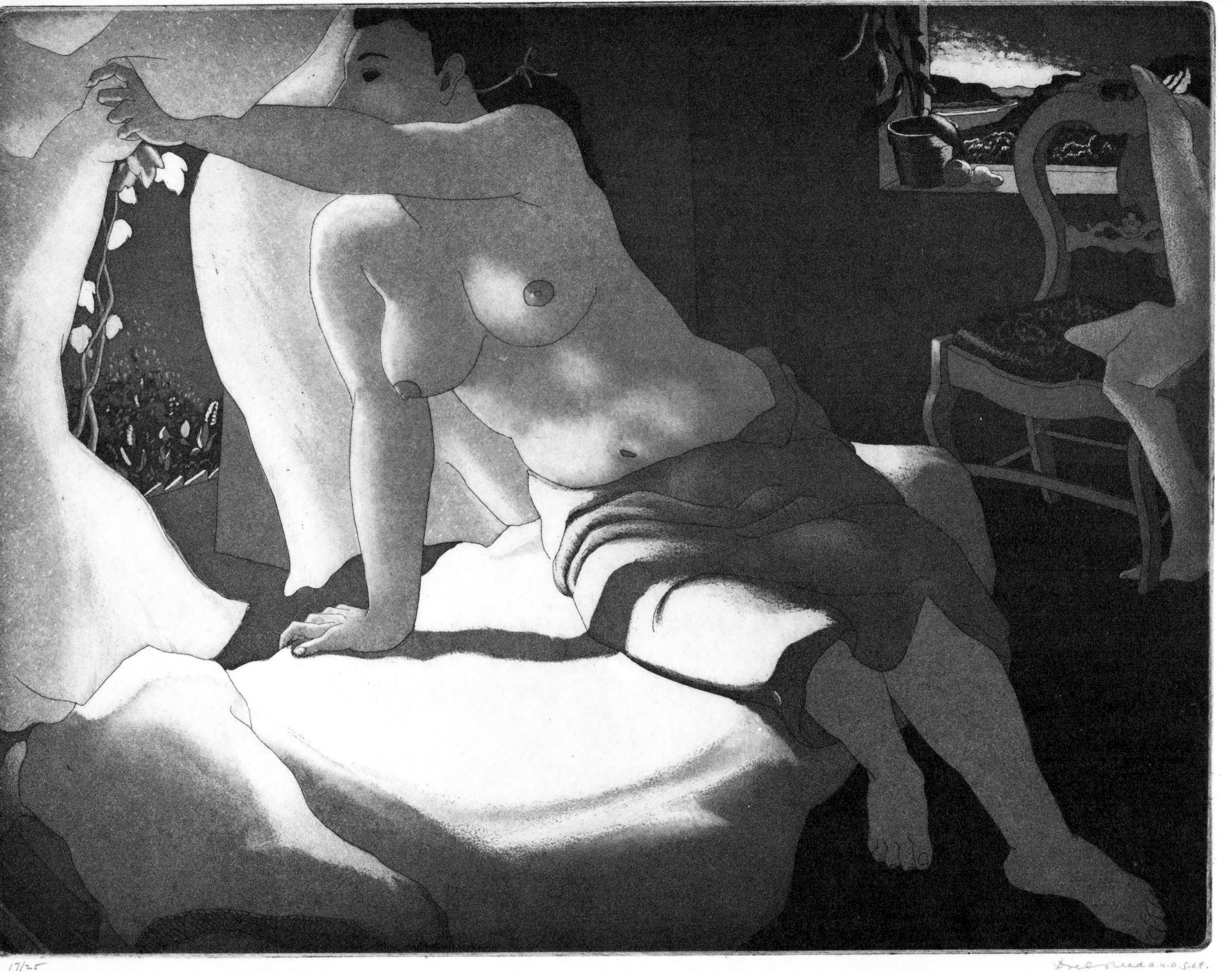

109. Doel Reed. *Summer Morning*, 1945. Aquatint. Edition 25. 13 × 16¾.

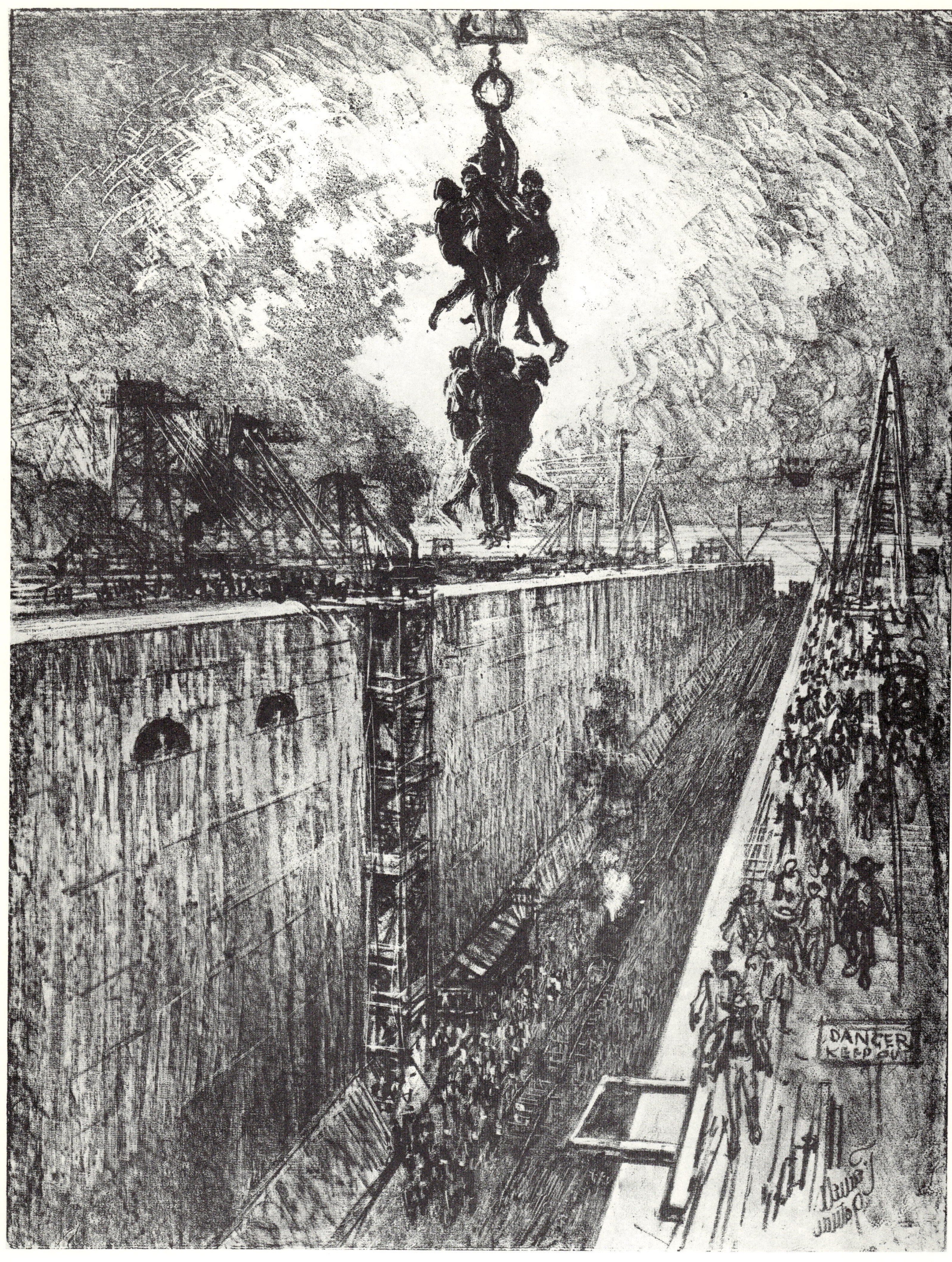

110. JOSEPH PENNELL. *The End of the Day, Gatun Lock* (from his *Panama Canal* series), 1912. Lithograph. Edition 50. 22 × 16¾. Wuerth 226.

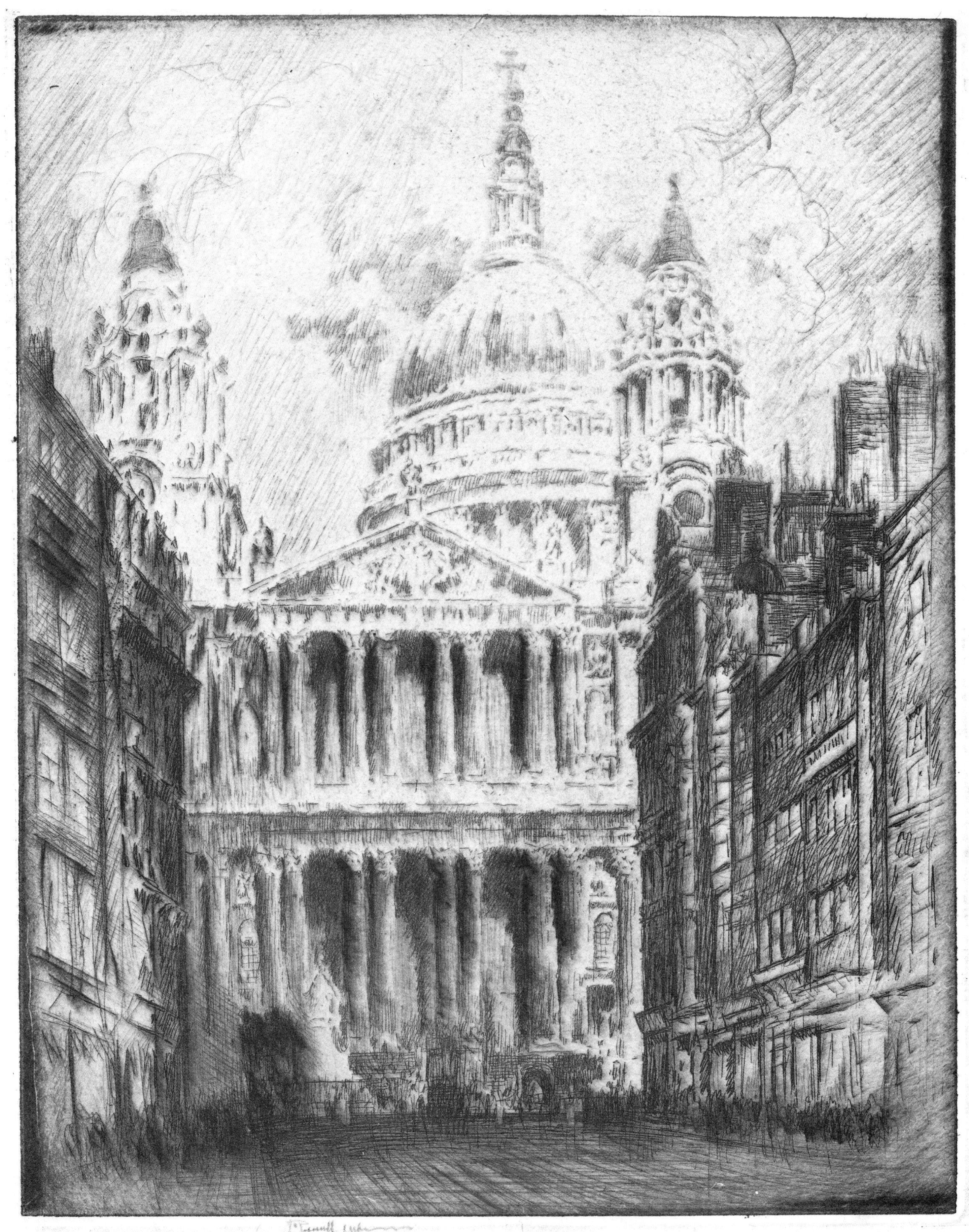

111. Joseph Pennell. *St. Paul's, Fleet Street, London*, 1905. Etching. Edition ca. 75. 11 × 8. Wuerth 353.

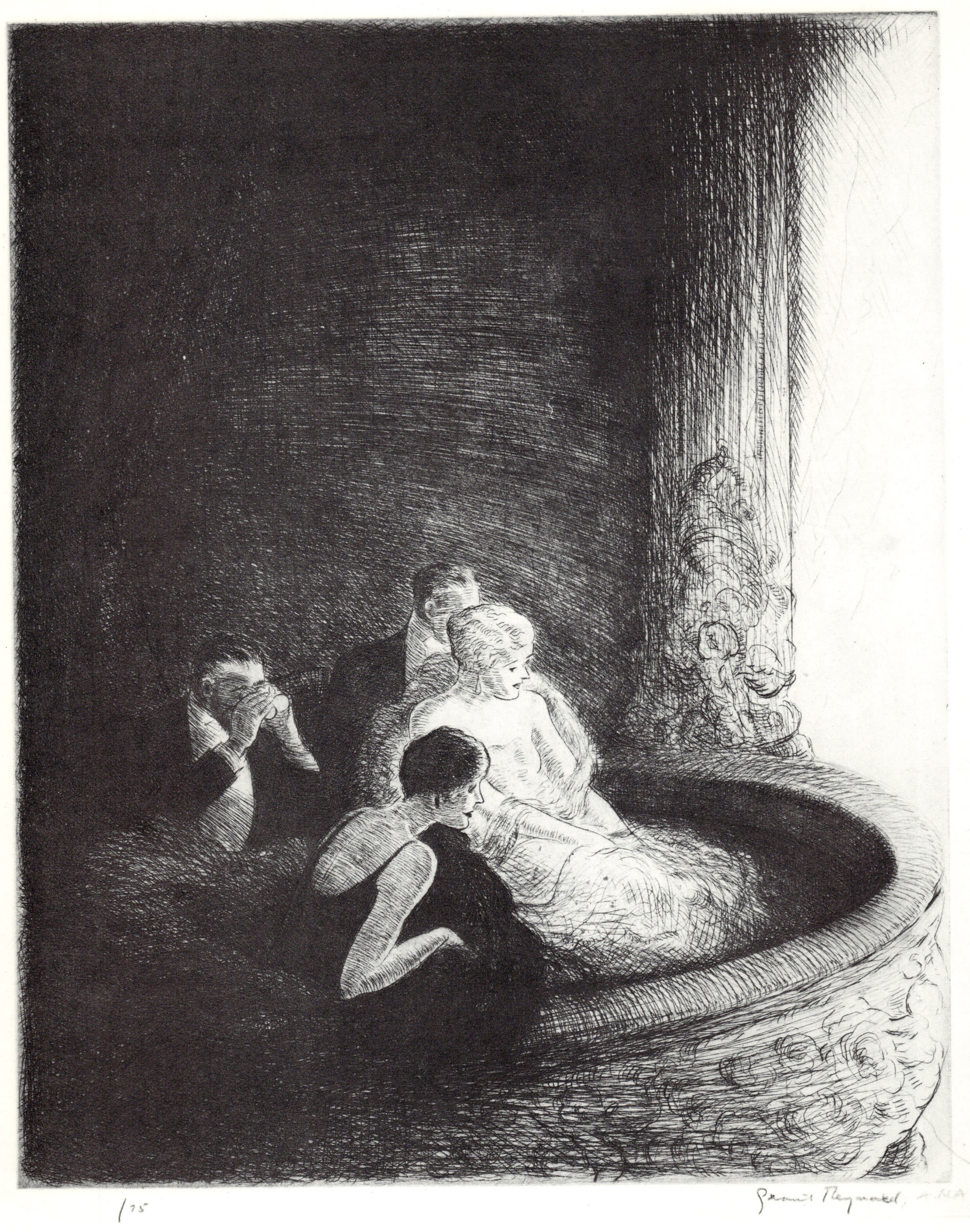

112. Grant Tyson Reynard. *The Loge*, ca. 1930. Drypoint. Edition 75. $9\frac{7}{8} \times 8$.

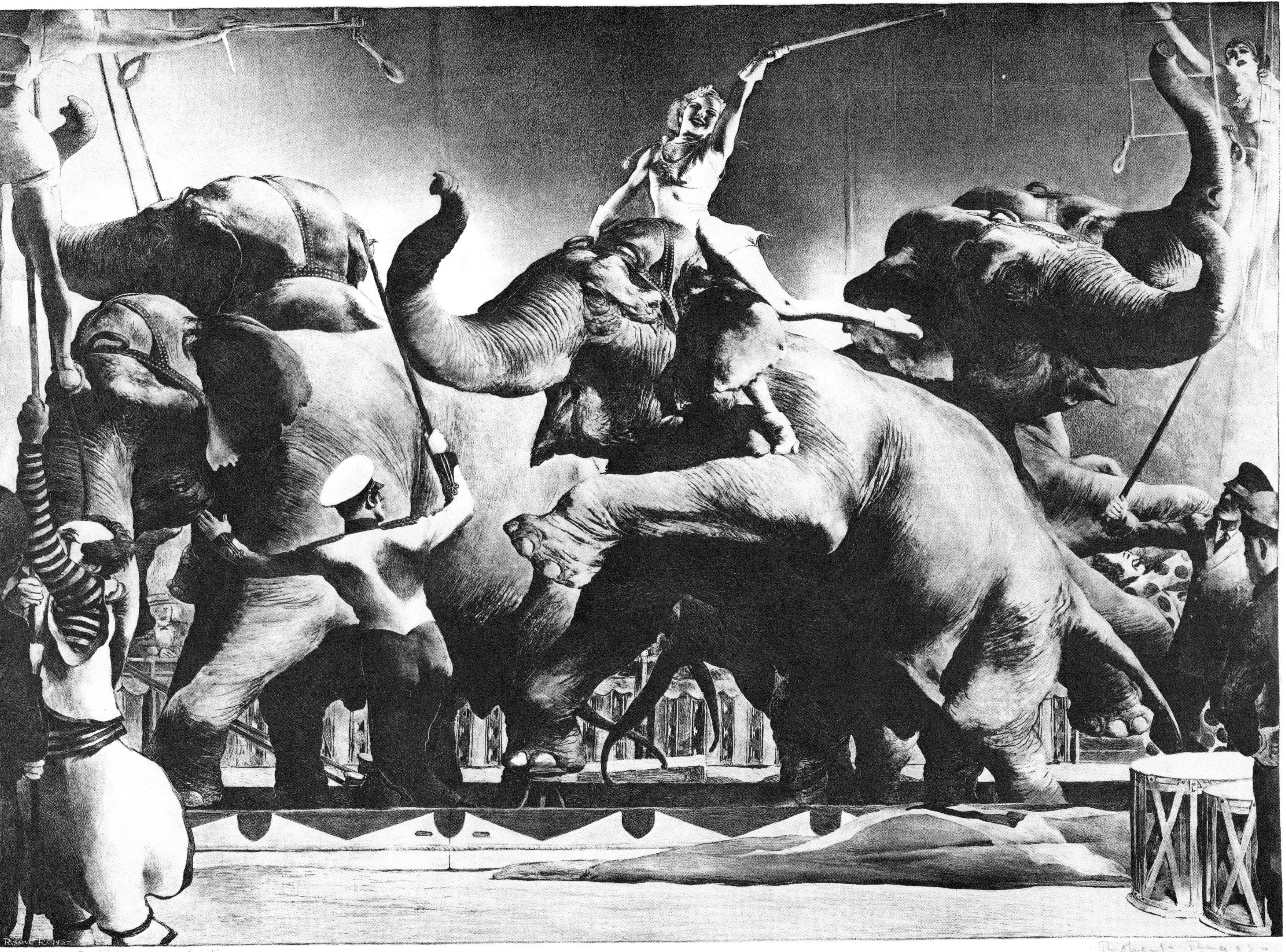

113. Robert Riggs. *Elephant Act*, 1937. Lithograph. 14¼ × 19½.

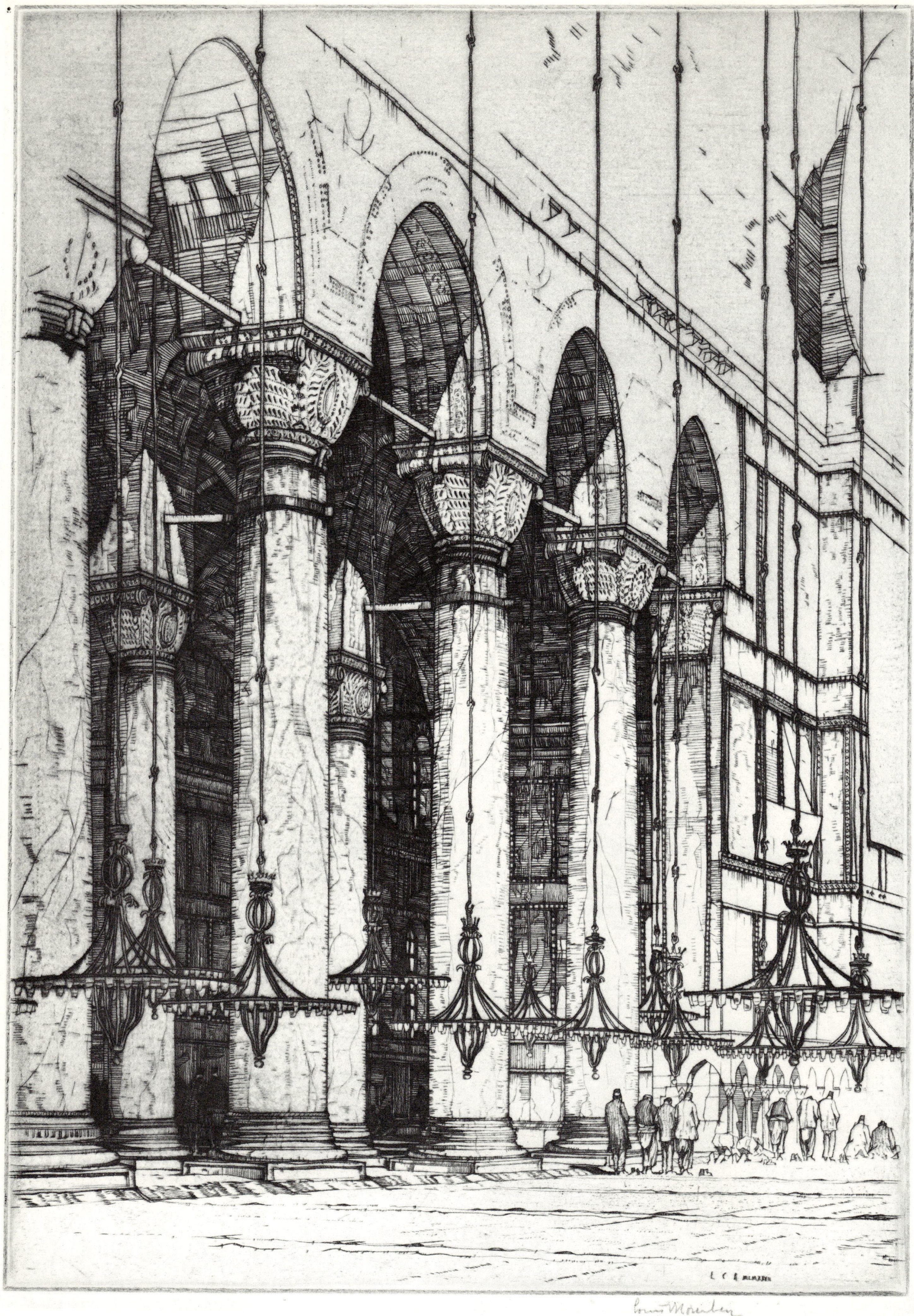

114. Louis Conrad Rosenberg. *Aya Sophia No. 2* (Istanbul), 1927. Drypoint. Edition 150. 11⅜ × 8¼. McMillan 58.

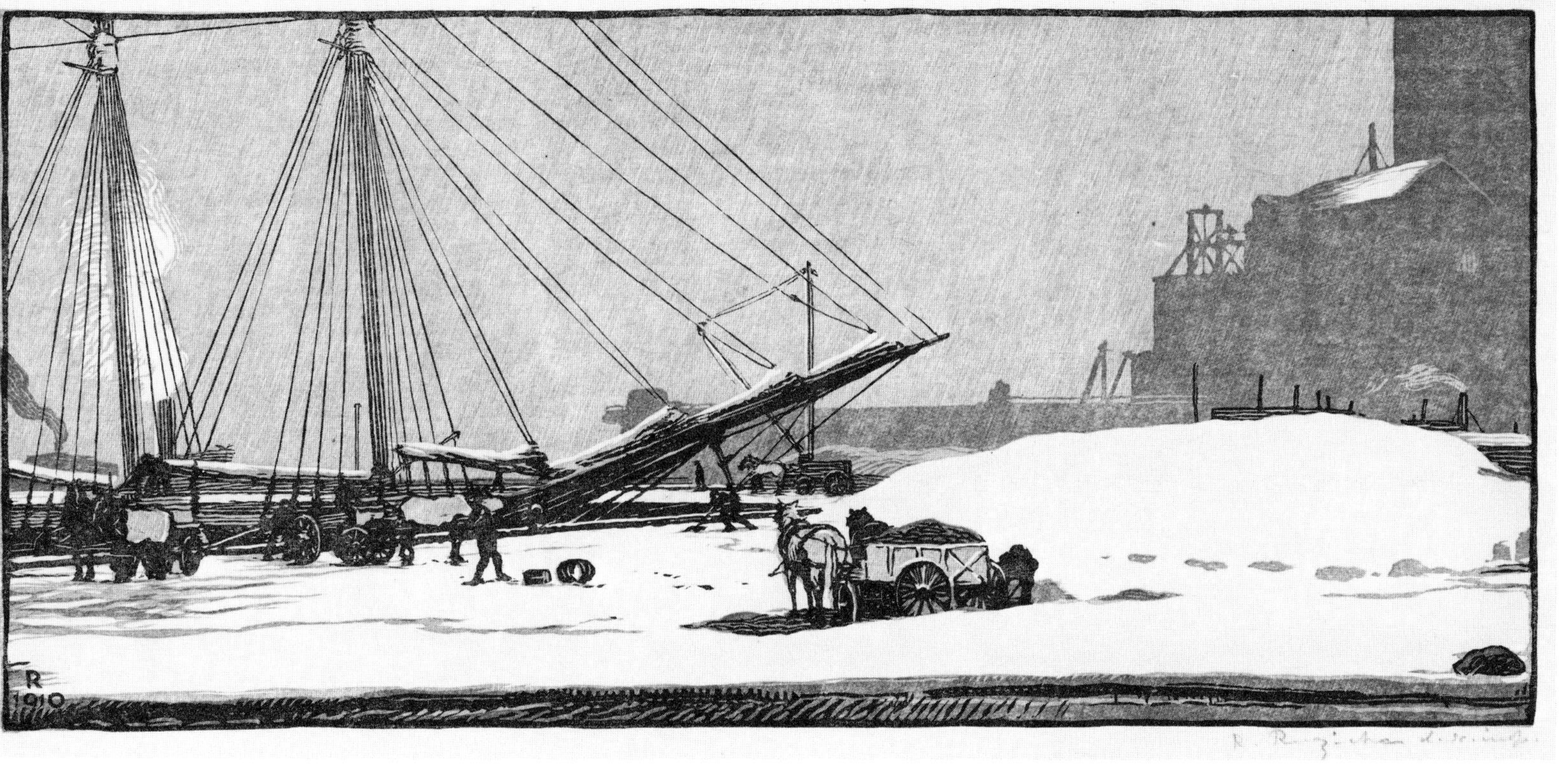

115. RUDOLPH RUZICKA. *East River, Winter* (New York City), 1910. Wood engraving printed in color. Edition 35. $3\frac{11}{16} \times 7\frac{15}{16}$. Grolier 17.

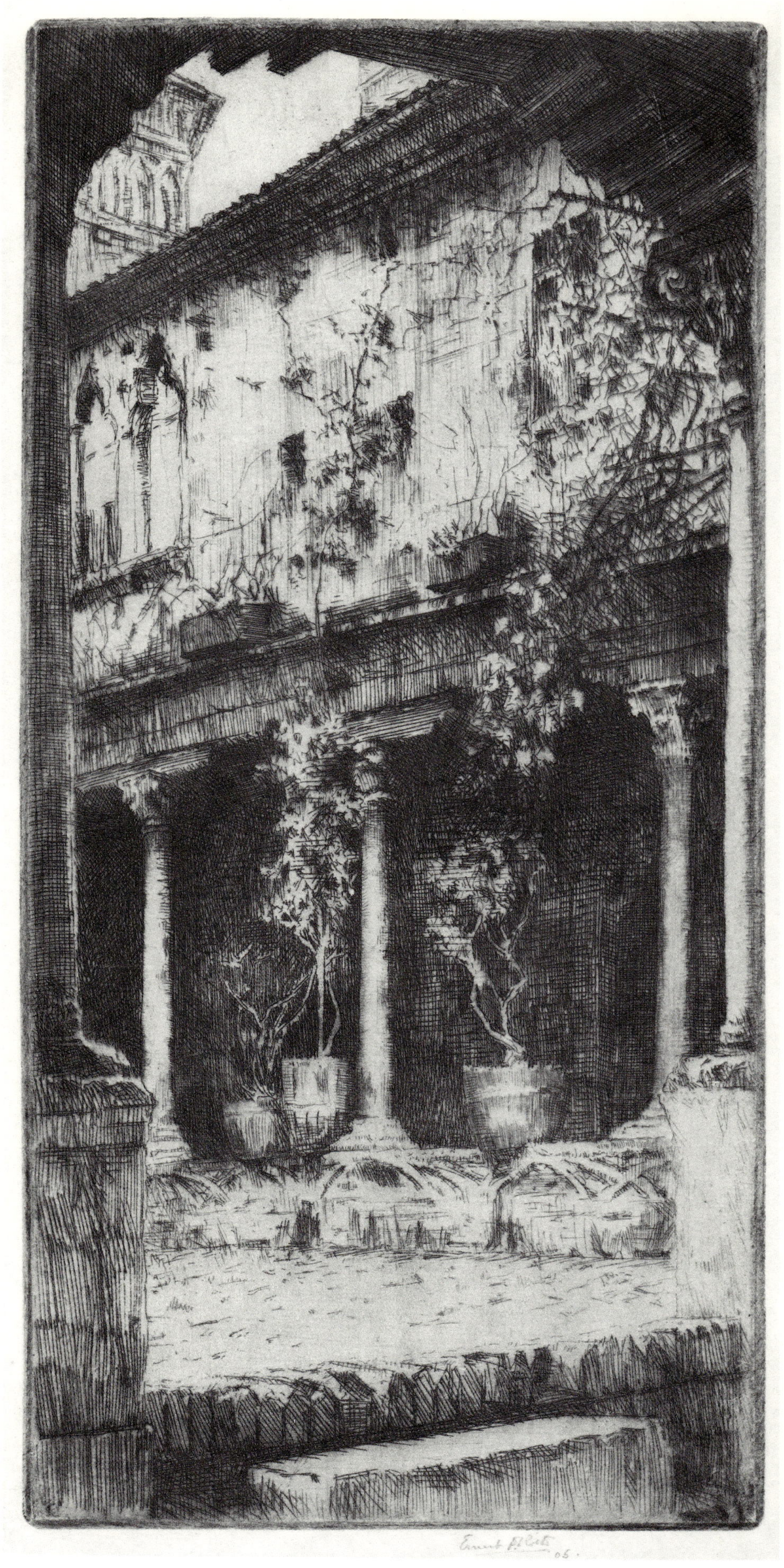

116. Ernest David Roth. *San Gregorio, Venice*, 1905. Etching. 9½ × 4¾.

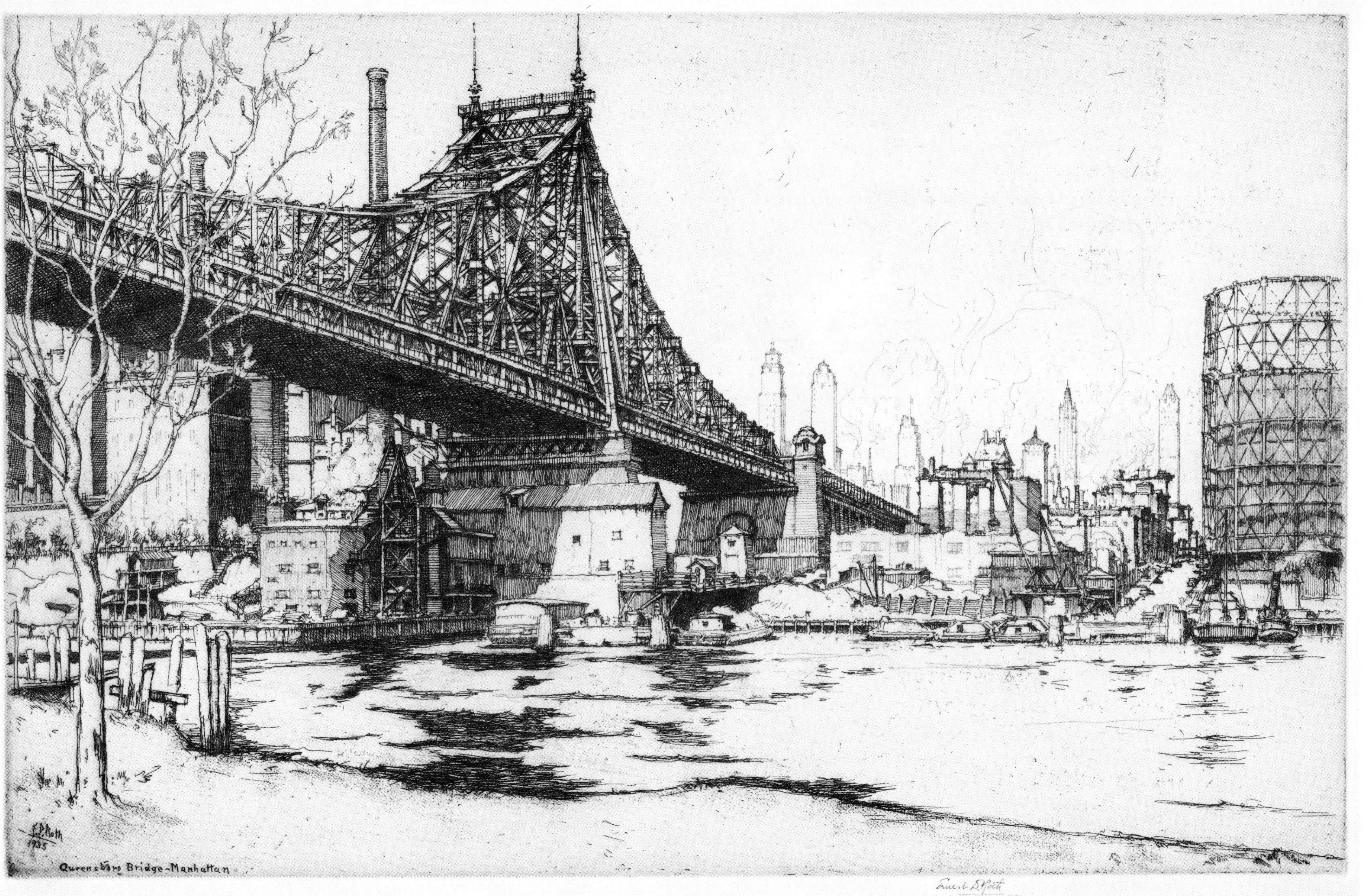

117. Ernest David Roth. *Queensboro Bridge* (New York City), 1935. Etching. 9⅝ × 14⅞.

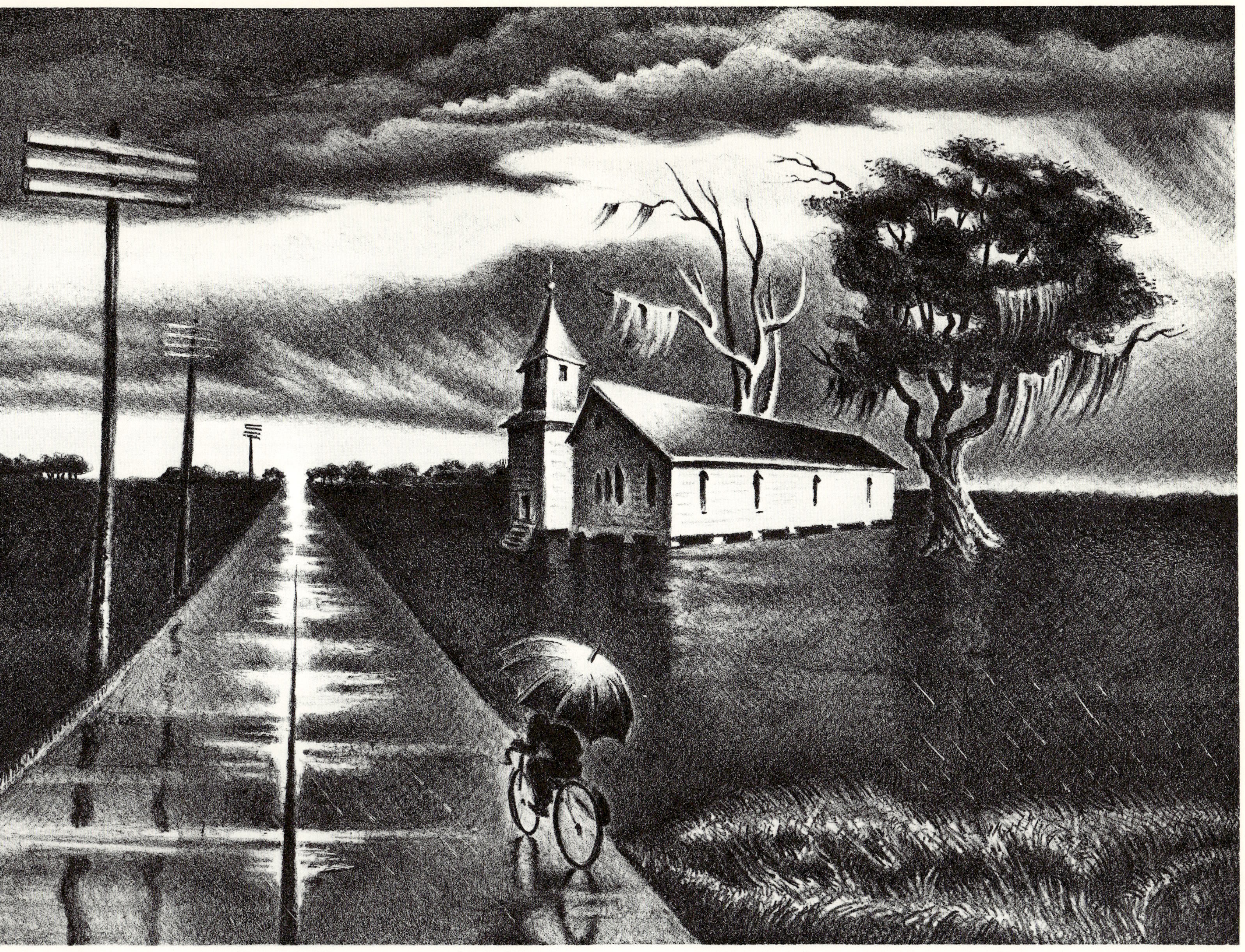

118. Georges Schreiber. *Rain,* mid-1940s. Lithograph. $9\frac{3}{4} \times 13$.

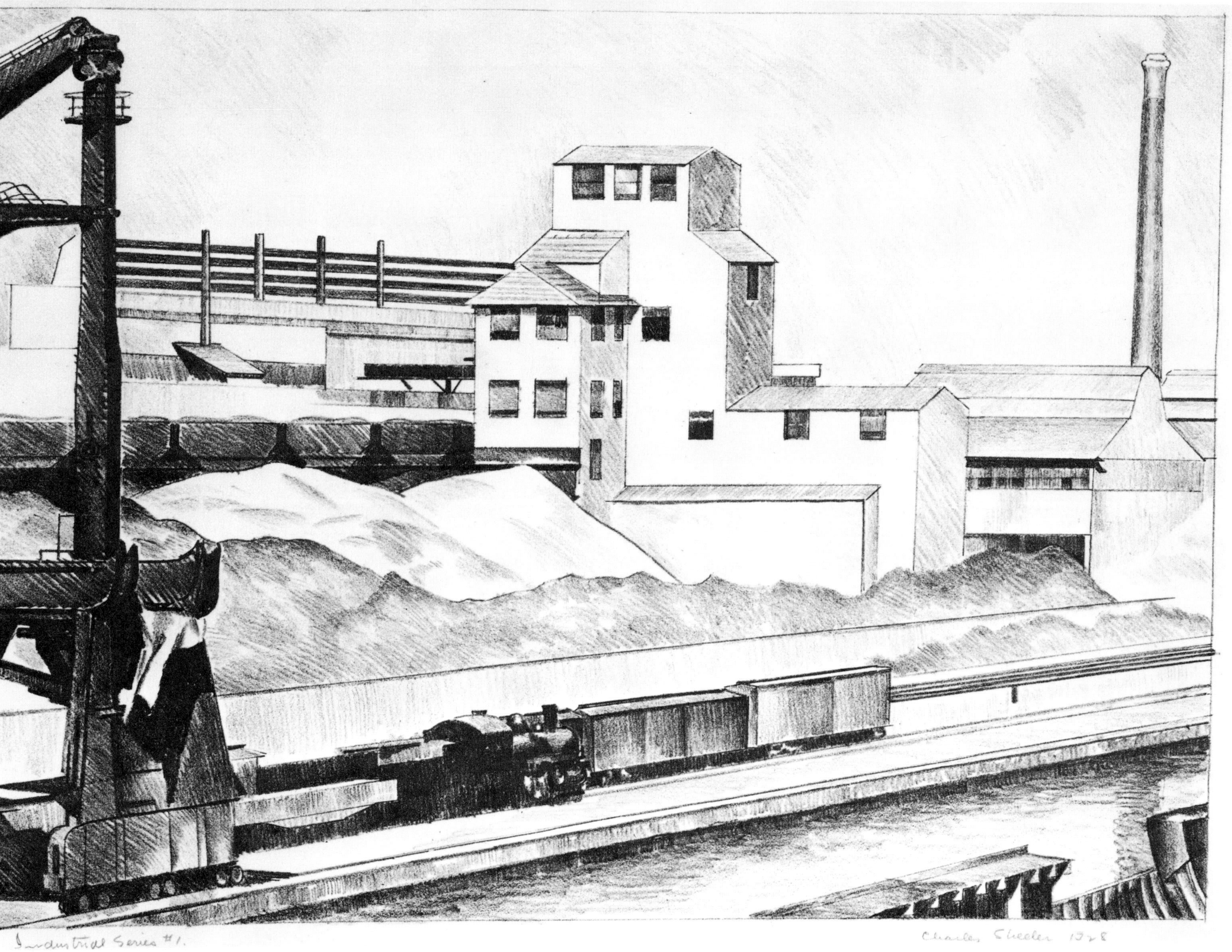

119. CHARLES SHEELER. *Industrial Series No. 1* (Detroit), 1928. Lithograph. 8¼ × 11⅛. Gordon 5.

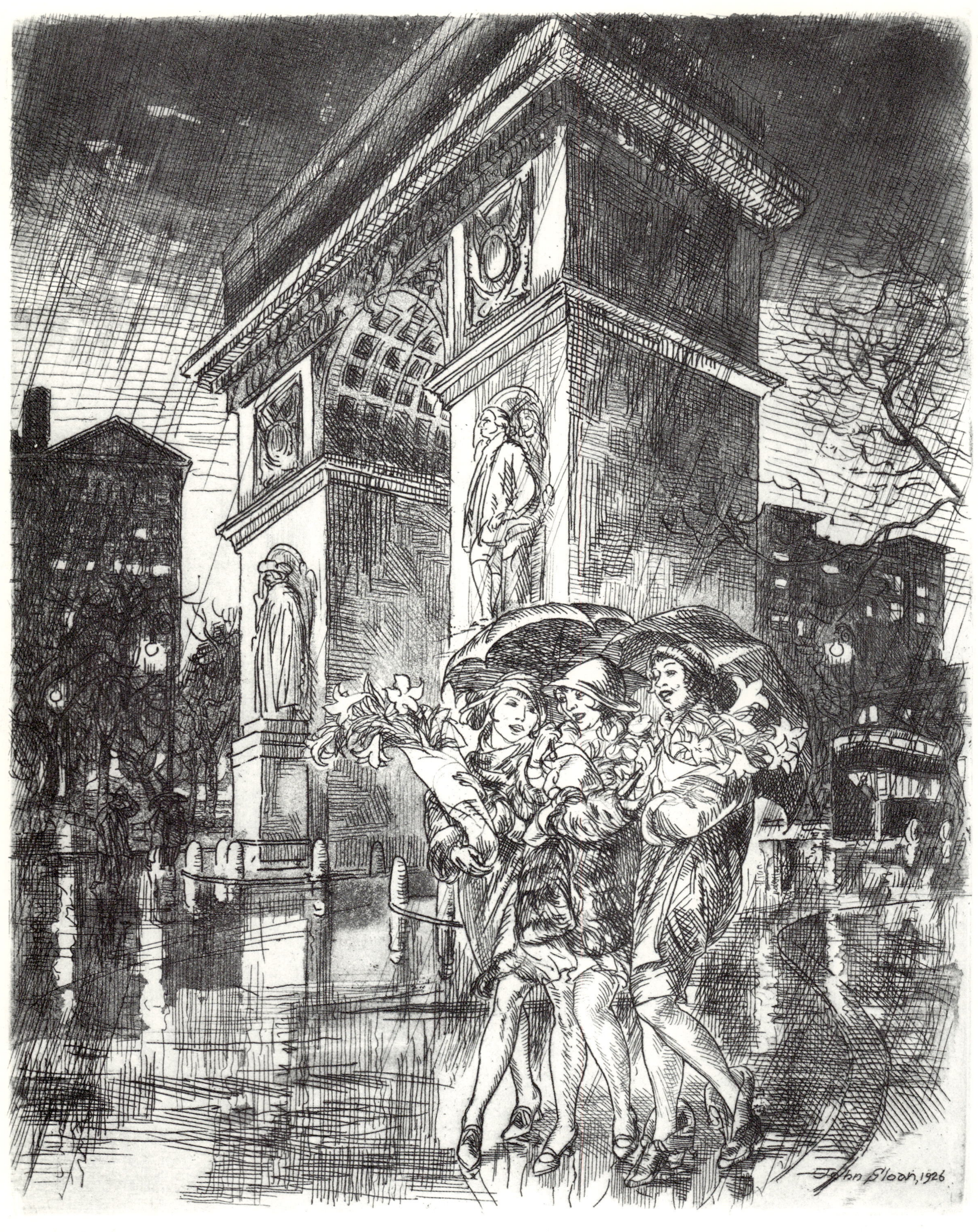

120. JOHN SLOAN. *Easter Eve, Washington Square* (New York City), 1926. Etching and aquatint. Edition 100, printing 60. 10 × 8. Morse 222.

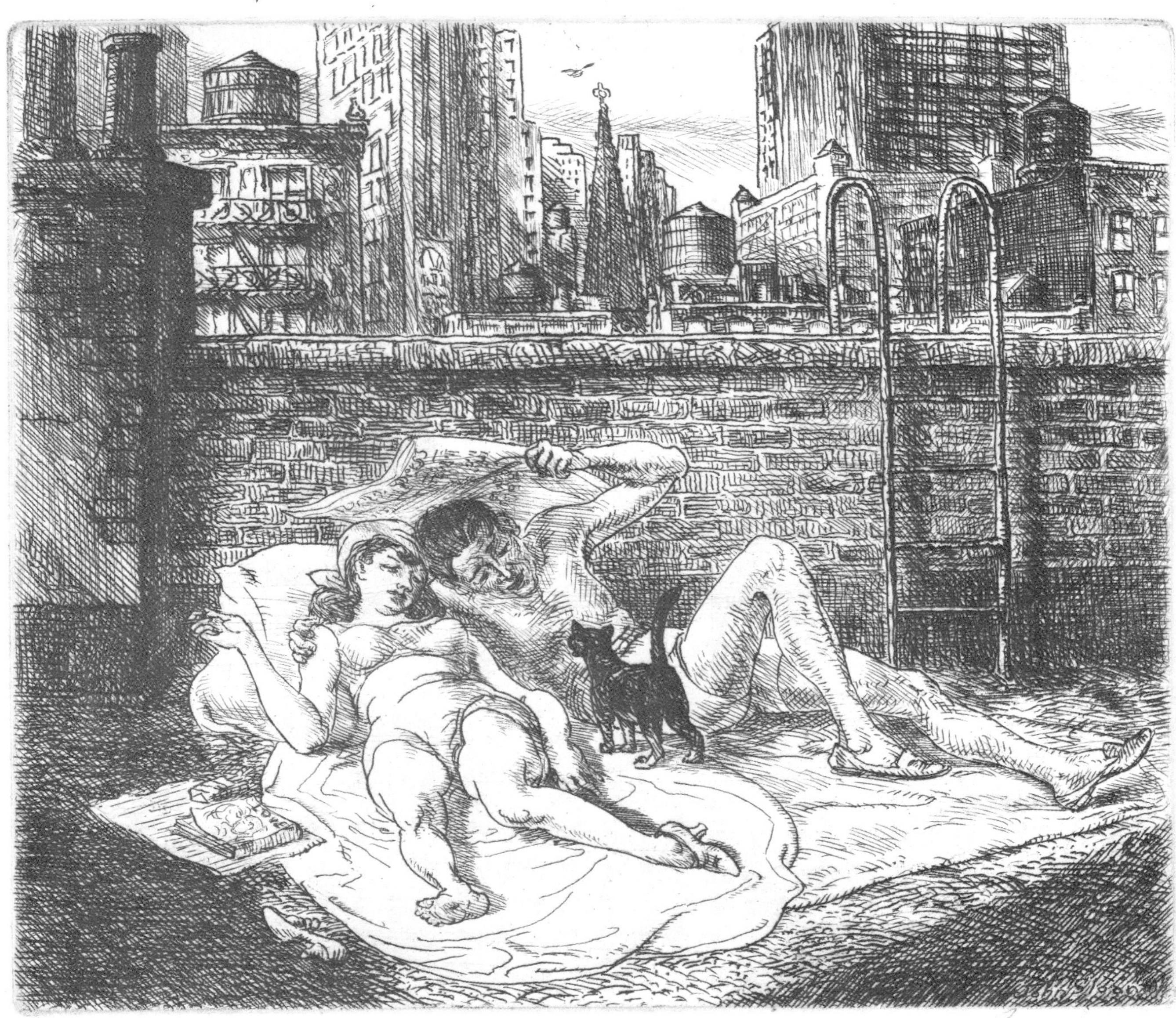

121. JOHN SLOAN. *Sunbathers on the Roof* (New York City), 1941. Etching. Edition 175, of which 125 were for the American College Society of Print Collectors. 6 × 7. Morse 307.

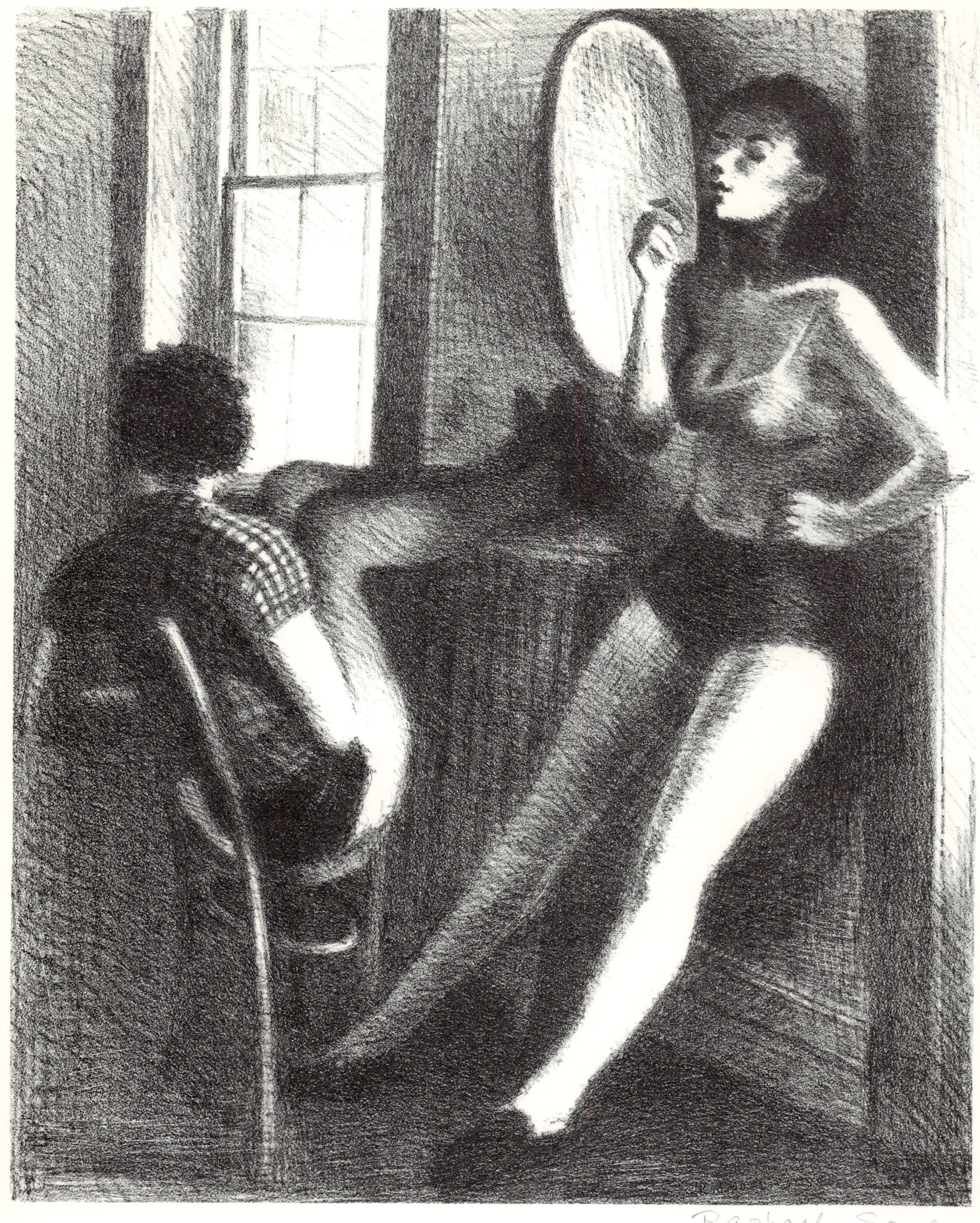

122. RAPHAEL SOYER. *Dancers Resting*, 1936. Lithograph. Edition 250, commissioned for the American Artists Group. $10\frac{3}{4} \times 8\frac{5}{8}$. Cole 42.

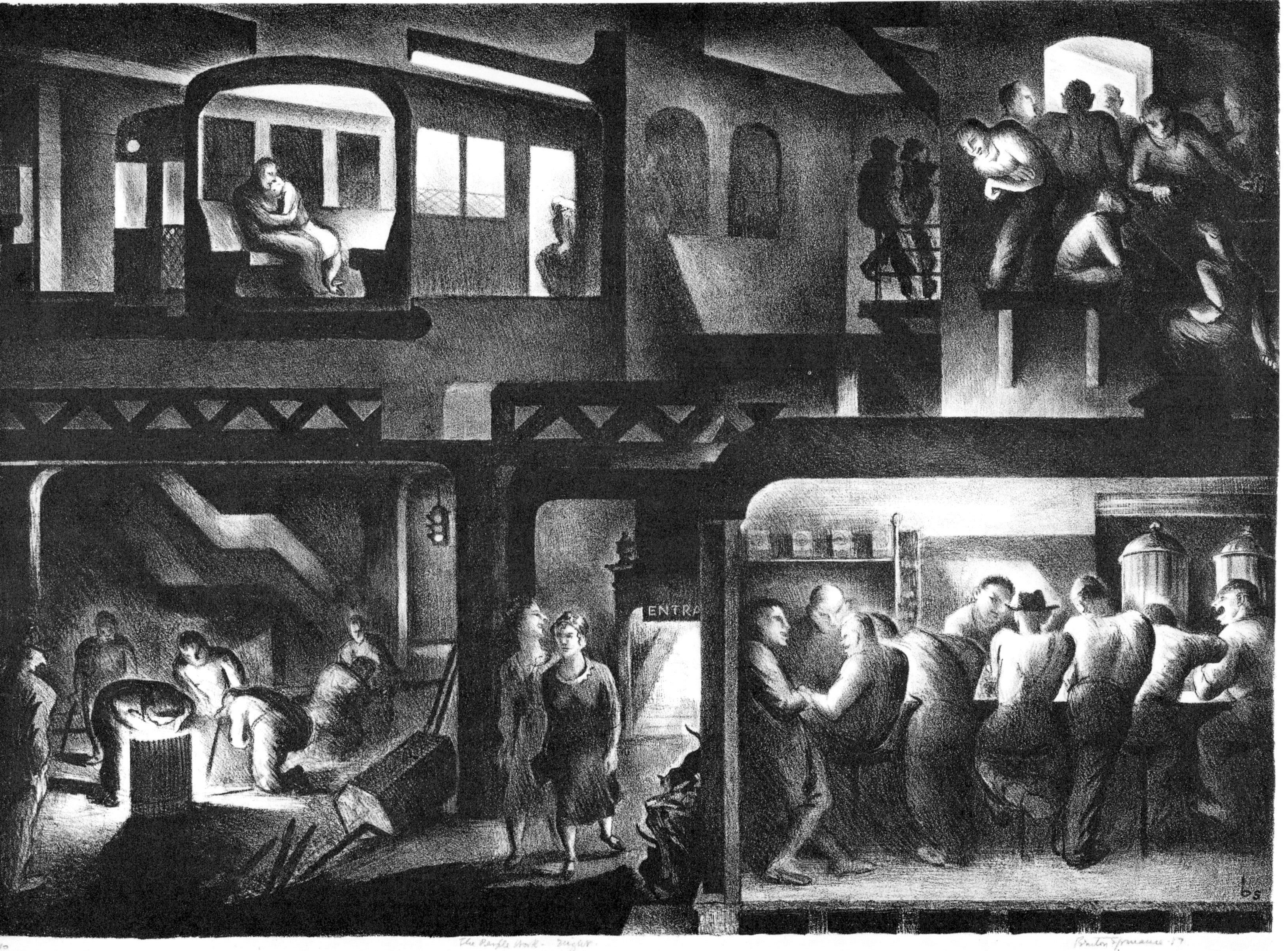

123. Benton Murdoch Spruance. *The People Work—Night* (Philadelphia), 1937. Lithograph. Edition 40. 13¾ × 19.

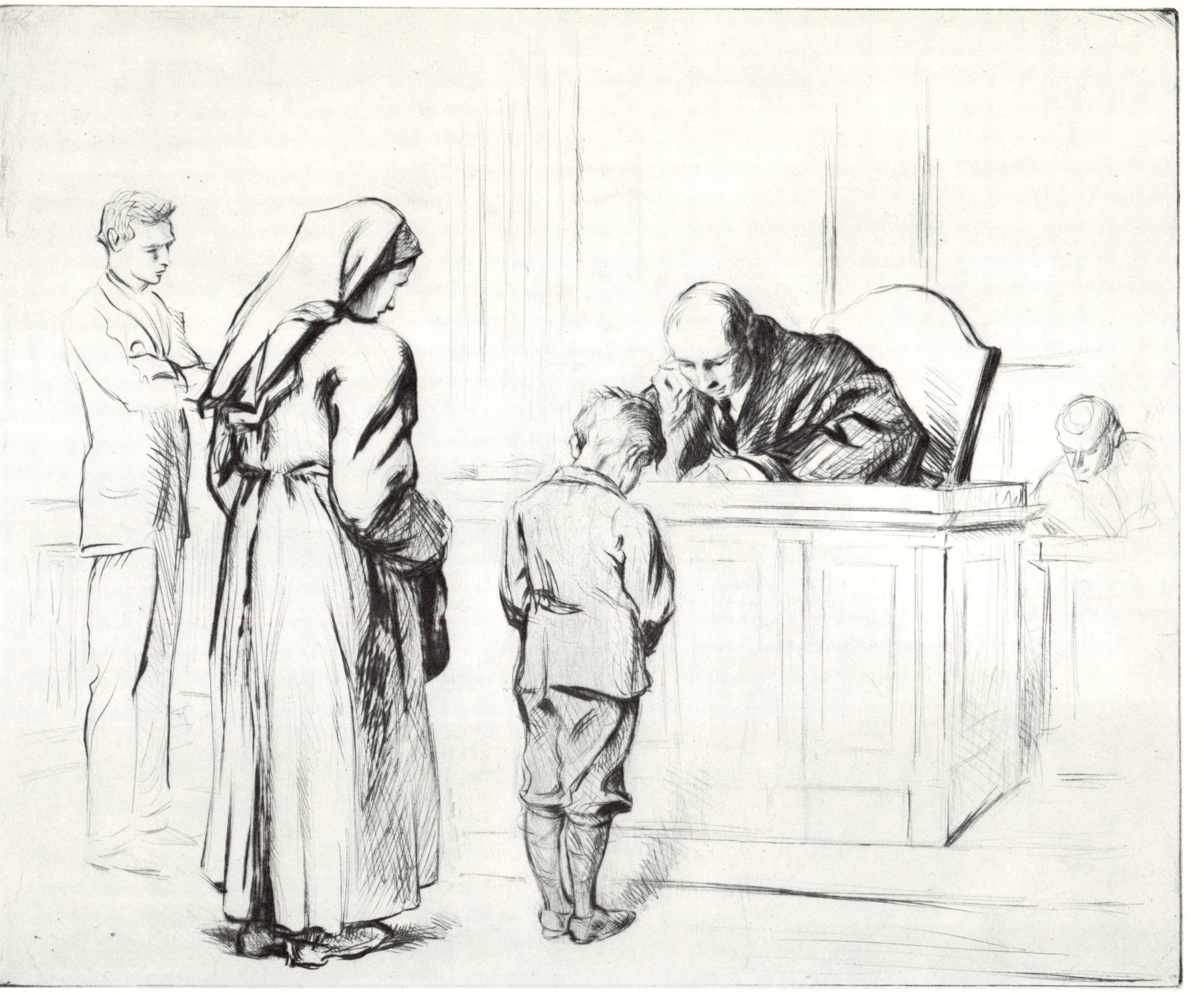

124. Albert Edward Sterner. *The Truant*, 1931. Drypoint. Edition 50. 9¾ × 11¾.

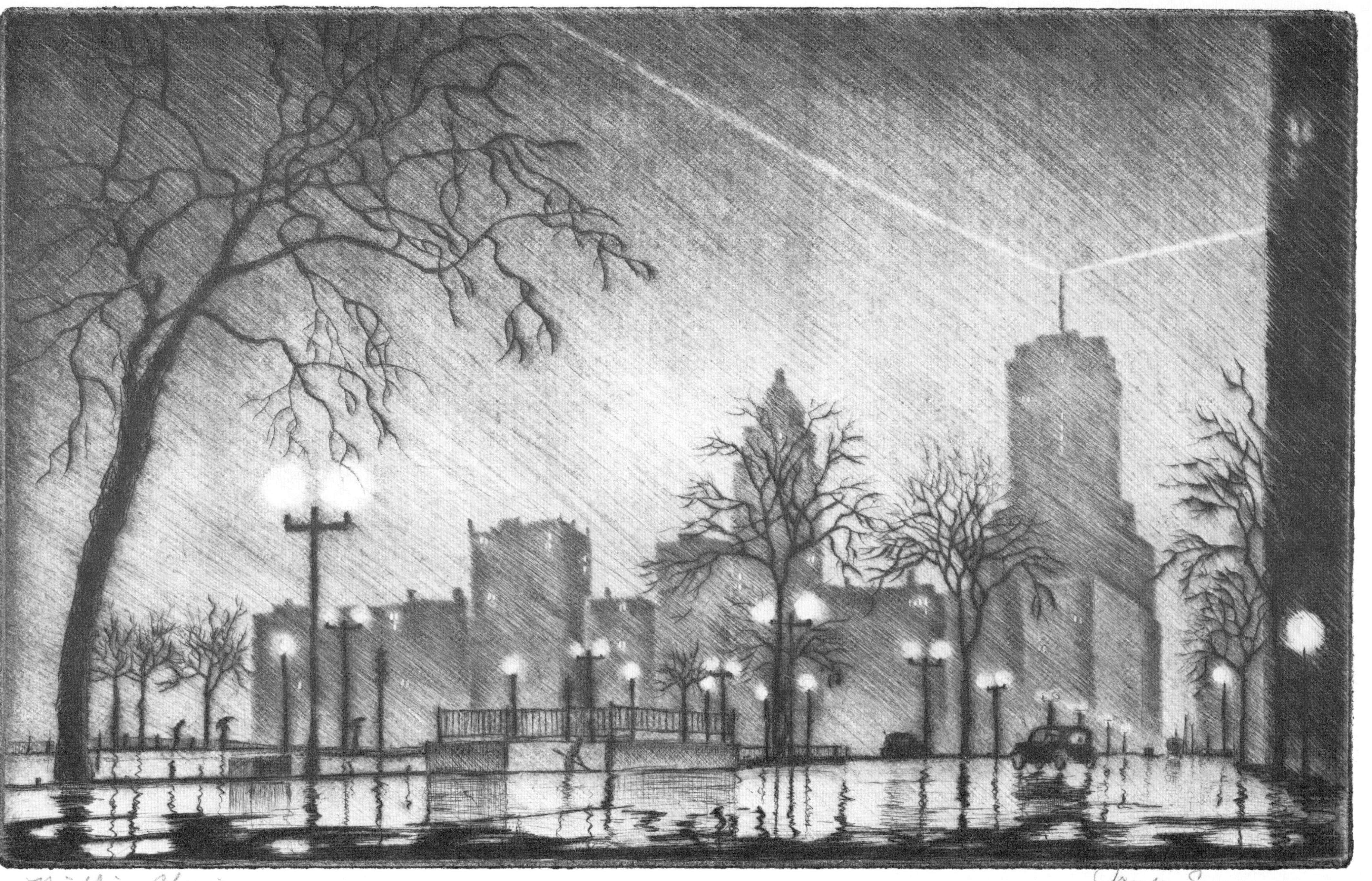

125. JAMES SWANN. *Night in Chicago*, 1940. Etching. Presentation print, Chicago Society of Etchers, 1940. 6⅞ × 10⅞.

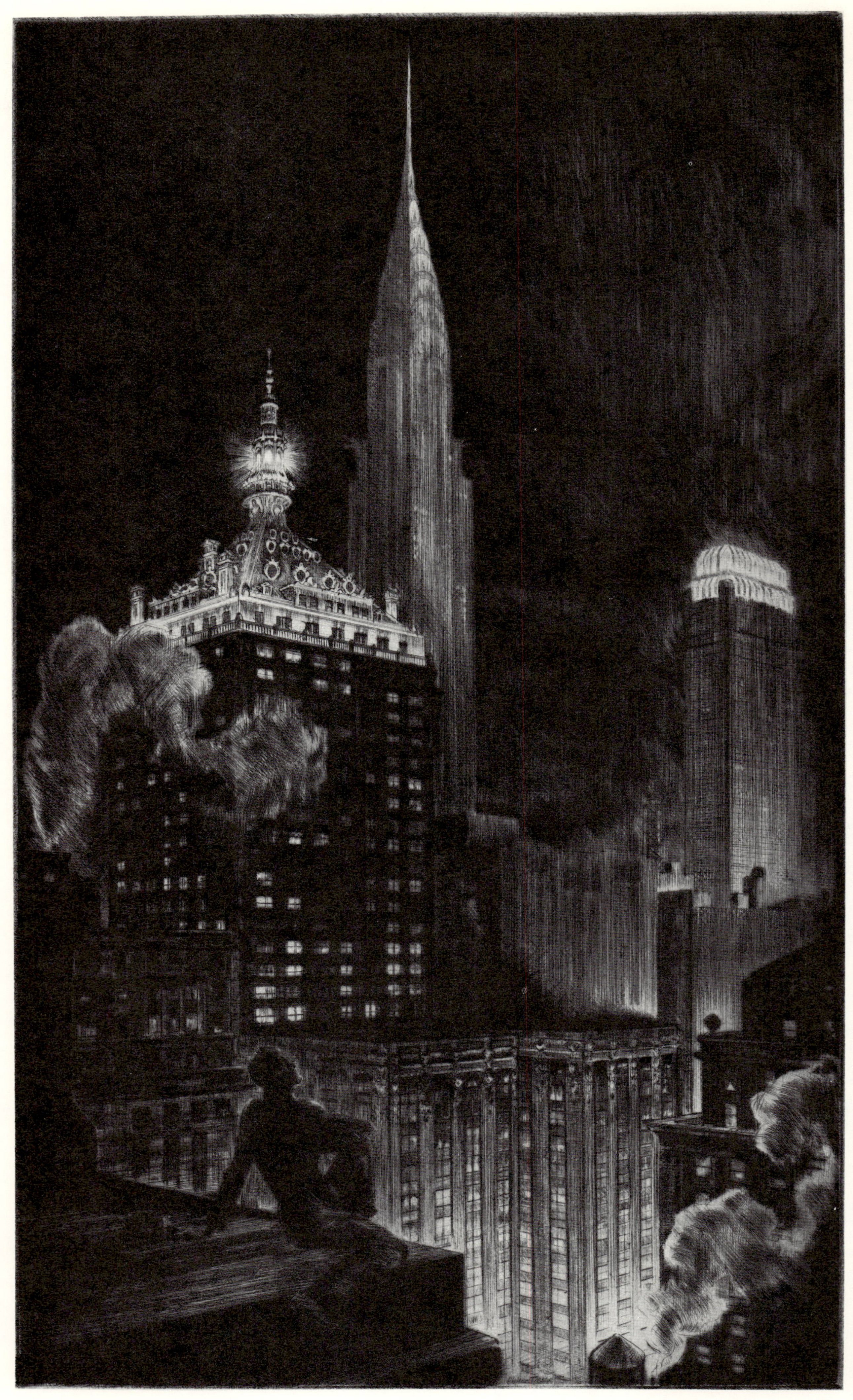

126. Walter Ernest Tittle. *Manhattan Minarets,* 1931–32. Drypoint. Edition 75. 14⅝ × 8⅞.

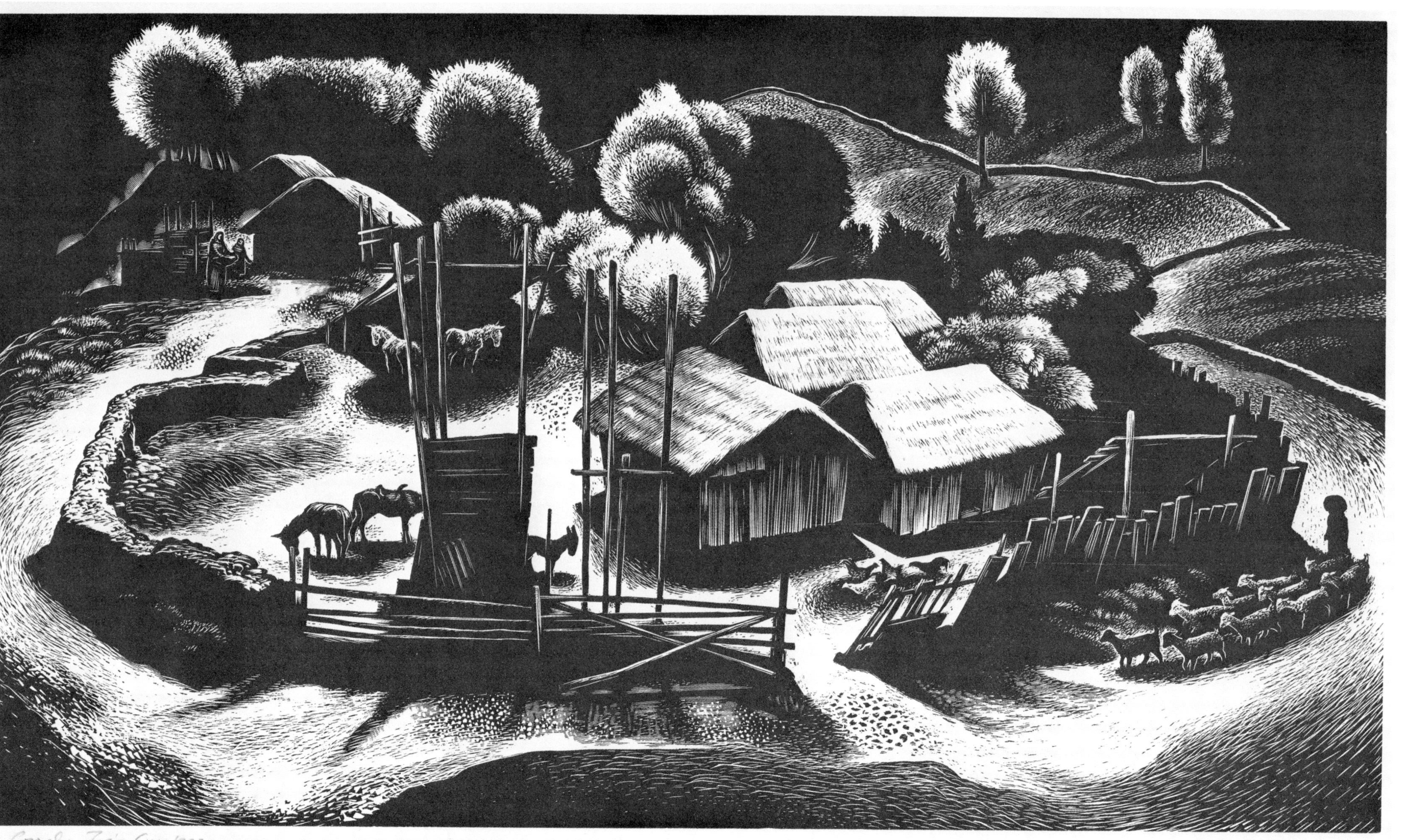

127. Lynd Kendall Ward. *Corral: Tres Cumbres,* 1953. Wood engraving. 7 × 11⅞.

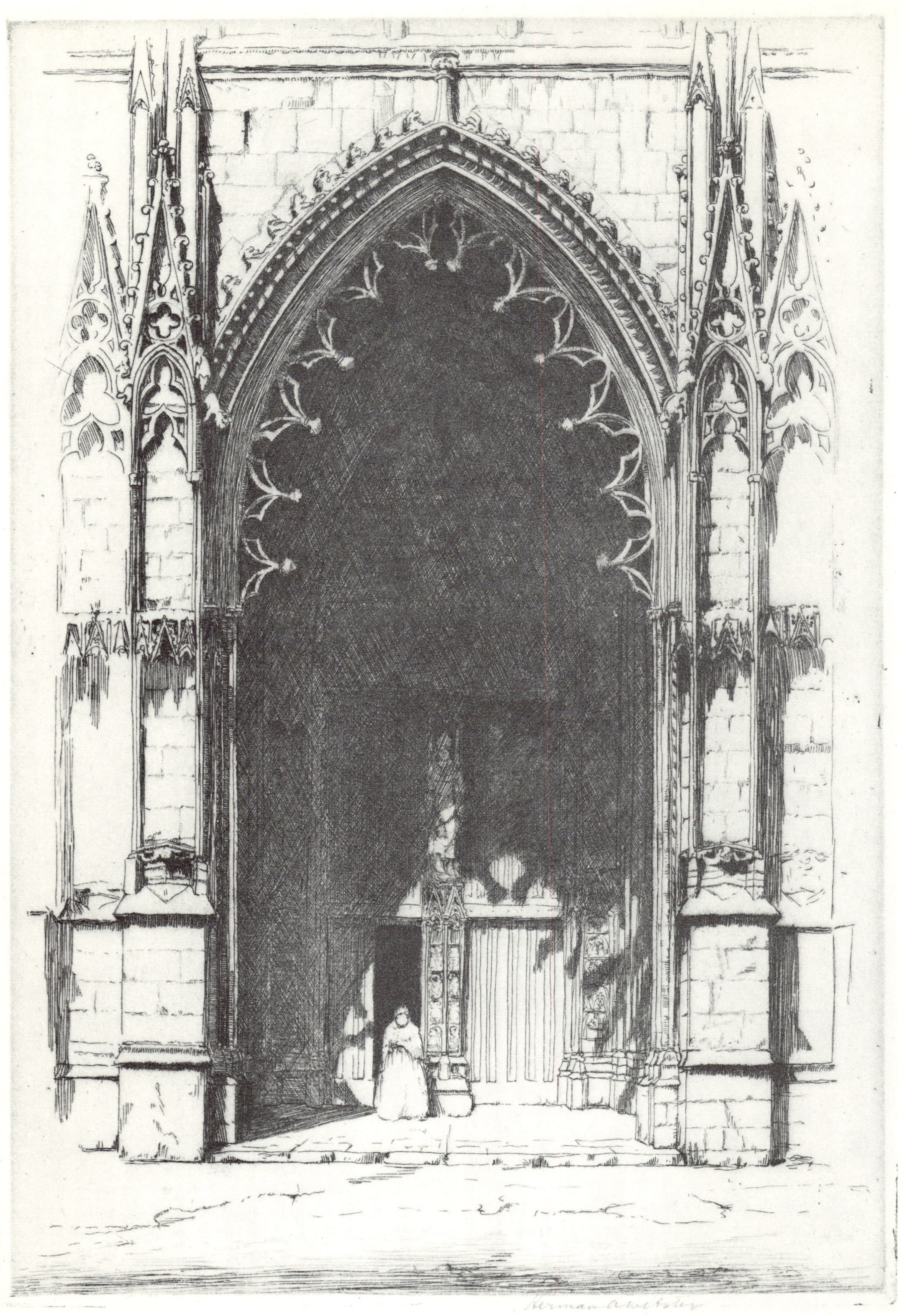

128. Herman Armour Webster. *Porte de Marmousets* (Paris). Etching. 10 × 6⅞.

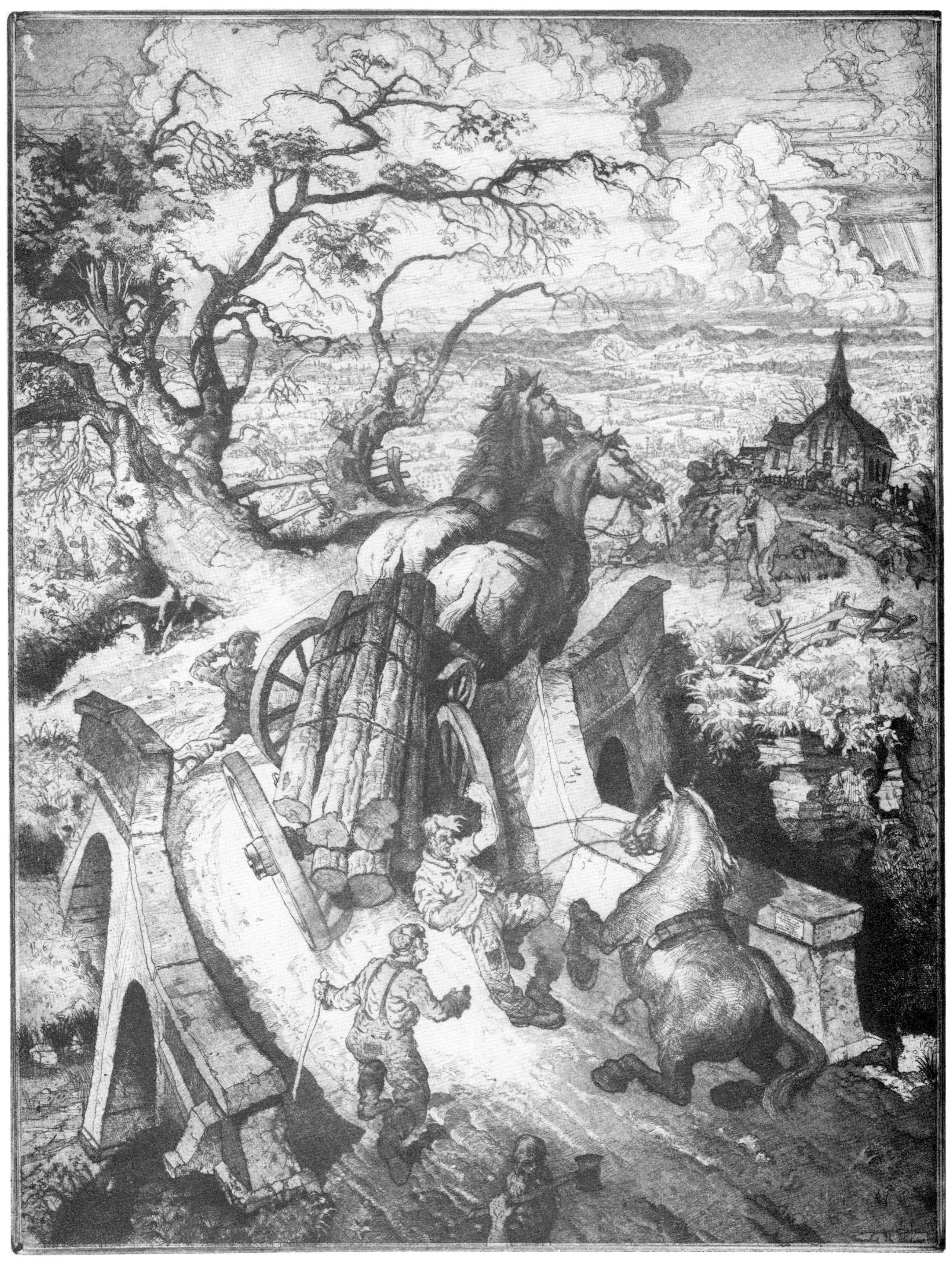

129. Reynold Henry Weidenaar. *Home from the Forest,* 1942. Etching with aquatint. Edition 100. 11⅞ × 9. Weidenaar 53.

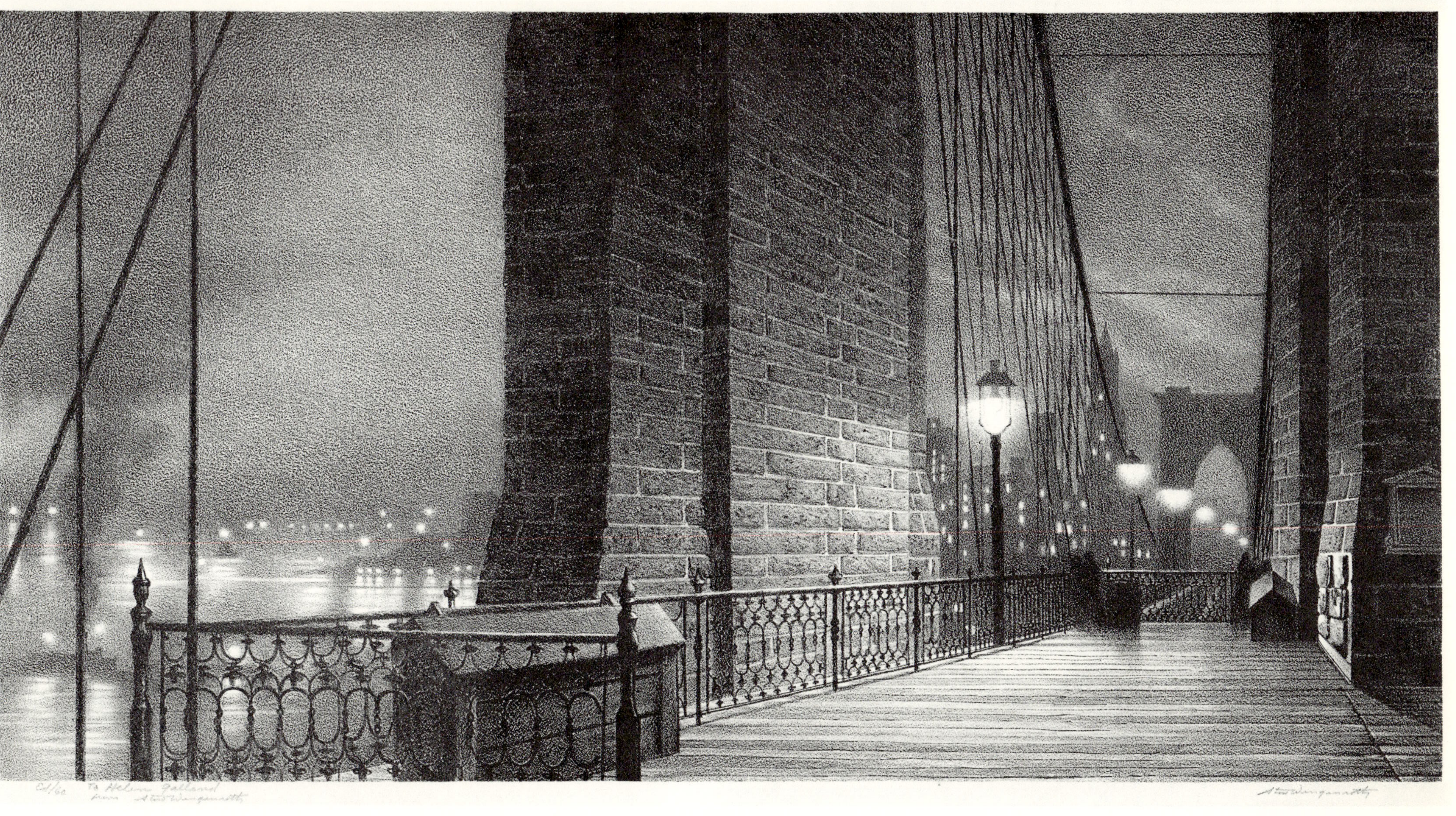

130. Stow Wengenroth. *Manhattan Gateway,* 1948. Lithograph. Edition 60. $9\frac{5}{8} \times 18$. Stuckey 176.

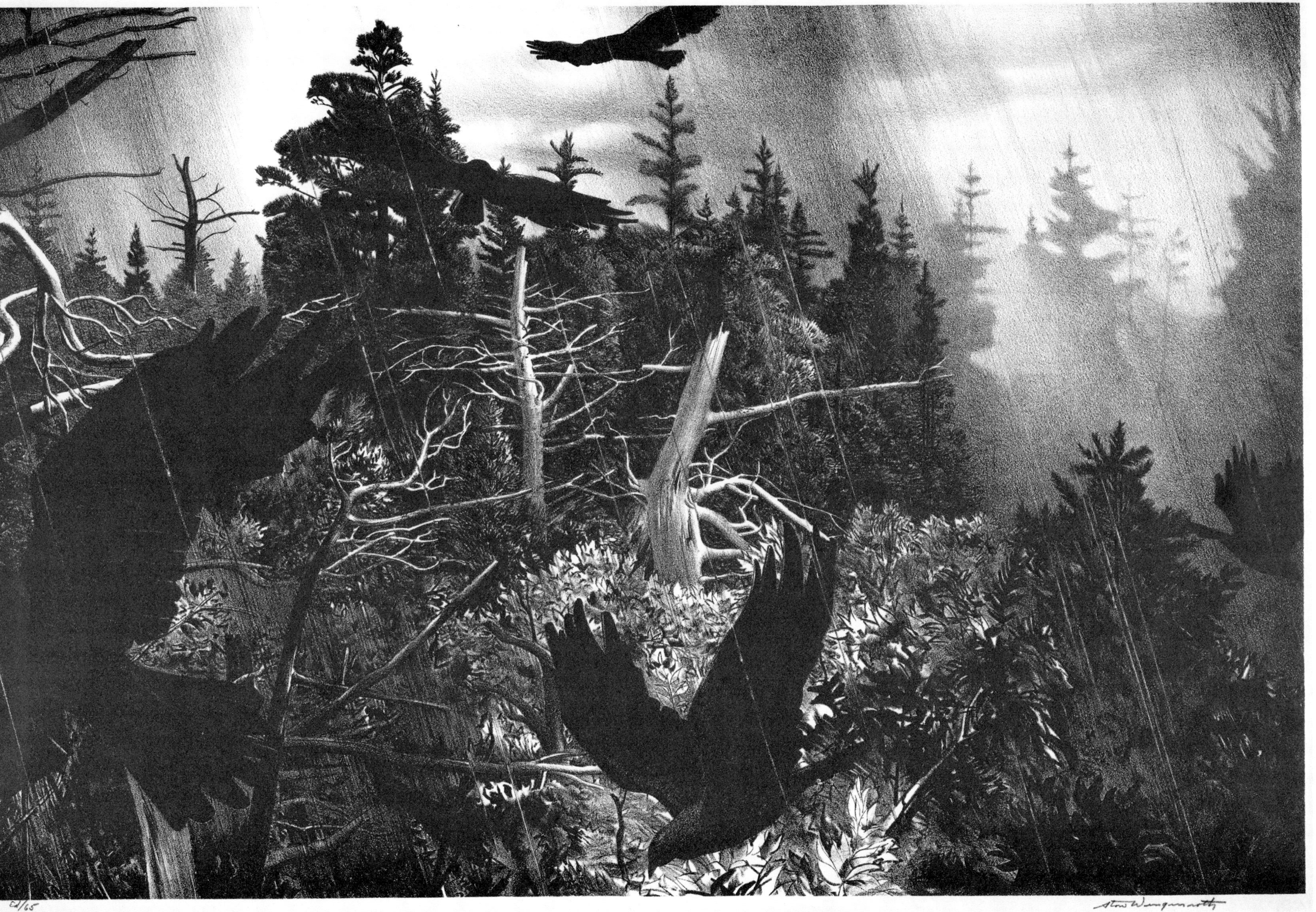

131. Stow Wengenroth. *Untamed*, 1946. Lithograph. Edition 65. $12\frac{5}{16} \times 18\frac{1}{16}$. Stuckey 159.

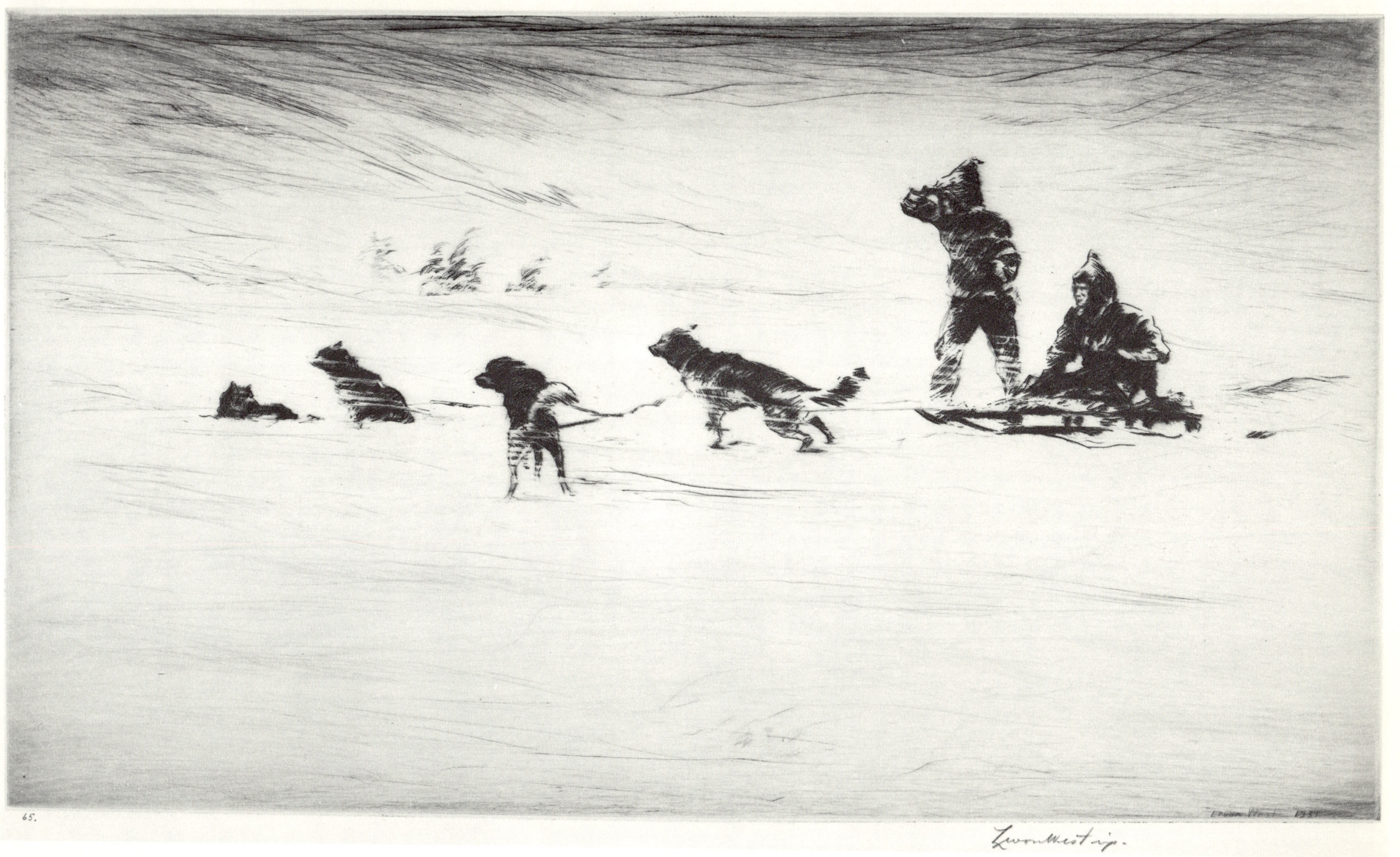

132. LEVON WEST. *Blizzard Coming*, 1931. Etching and drypoint. Edition 100. 8⅝ × 14¾.

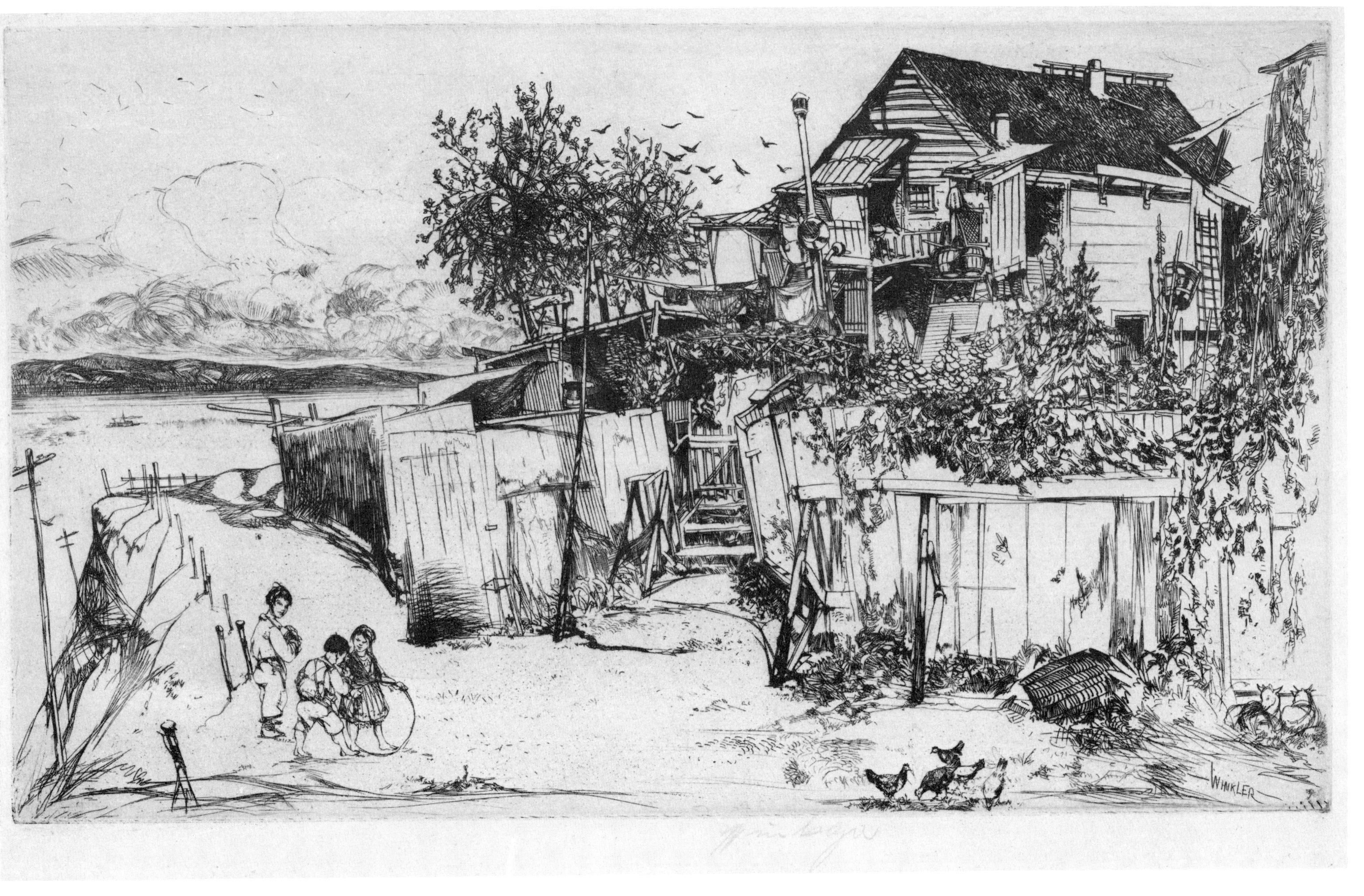

133. John William Joseph Winkler. *Fisherman's Home on Telegraph Hill* (San Francisco), 1921. Etching. 6 × 10.

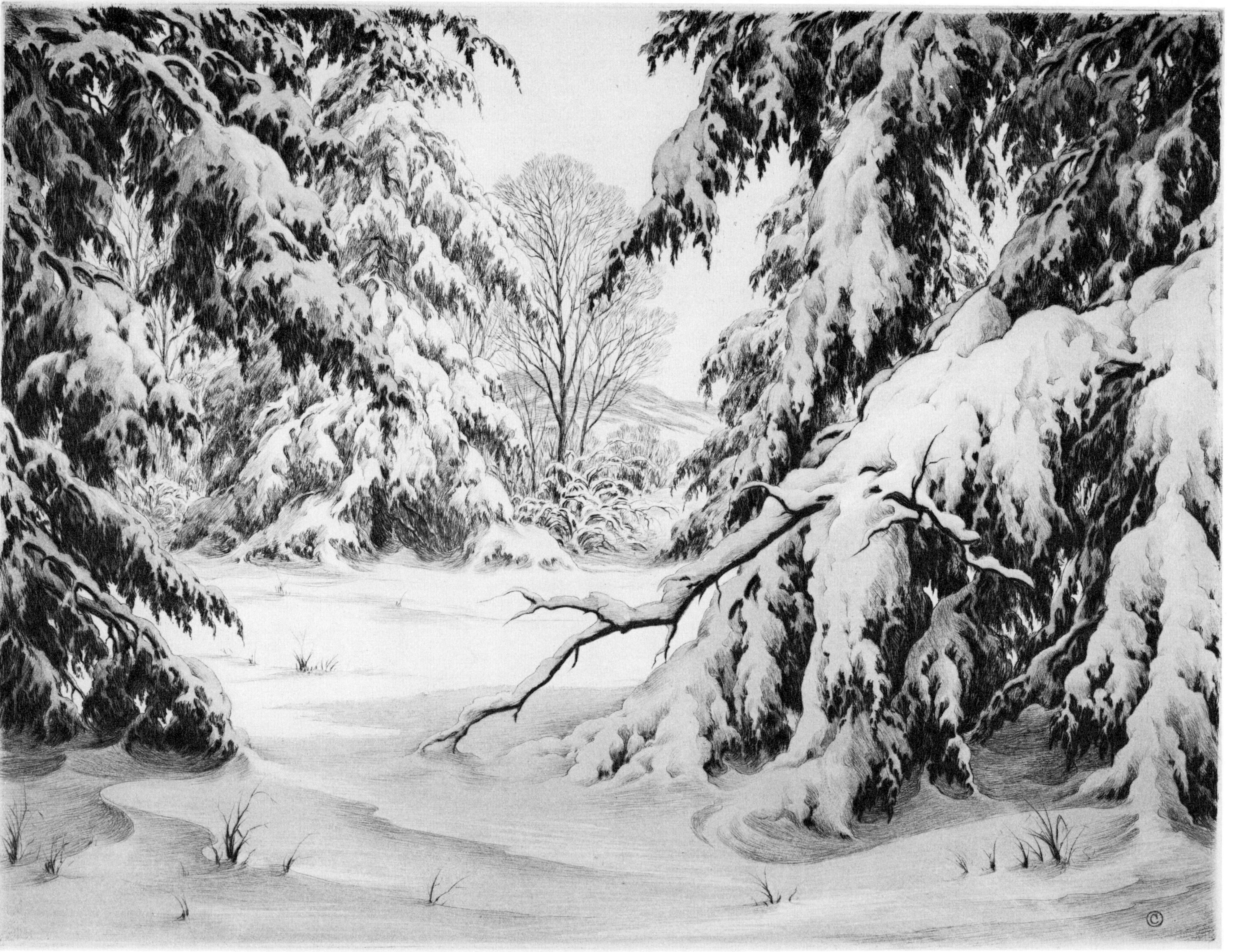

134. Ronau William Woiceske. *Winter Interlude,* 1945. Etching and drypoint. Edition 50, presentation print of Chicago Society of Etchers, 1948. 9⅞ × 12¾.

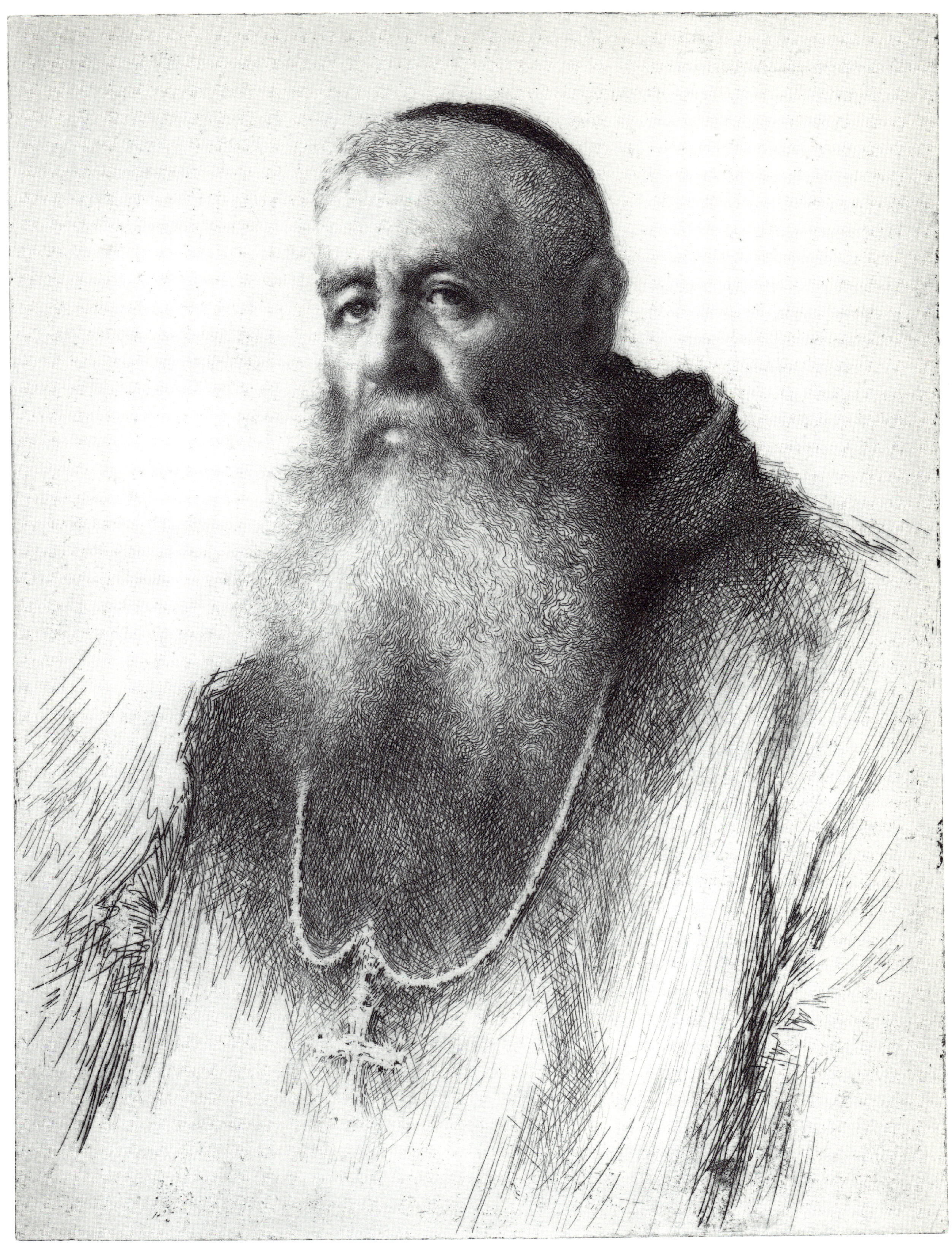

135. Franklin T. Wood. *Abbot of Grottaferrata.* Etching. 13 × 12. No. 64 in the list of Wood's plates in *The Print Connoisseur,* July 1925.

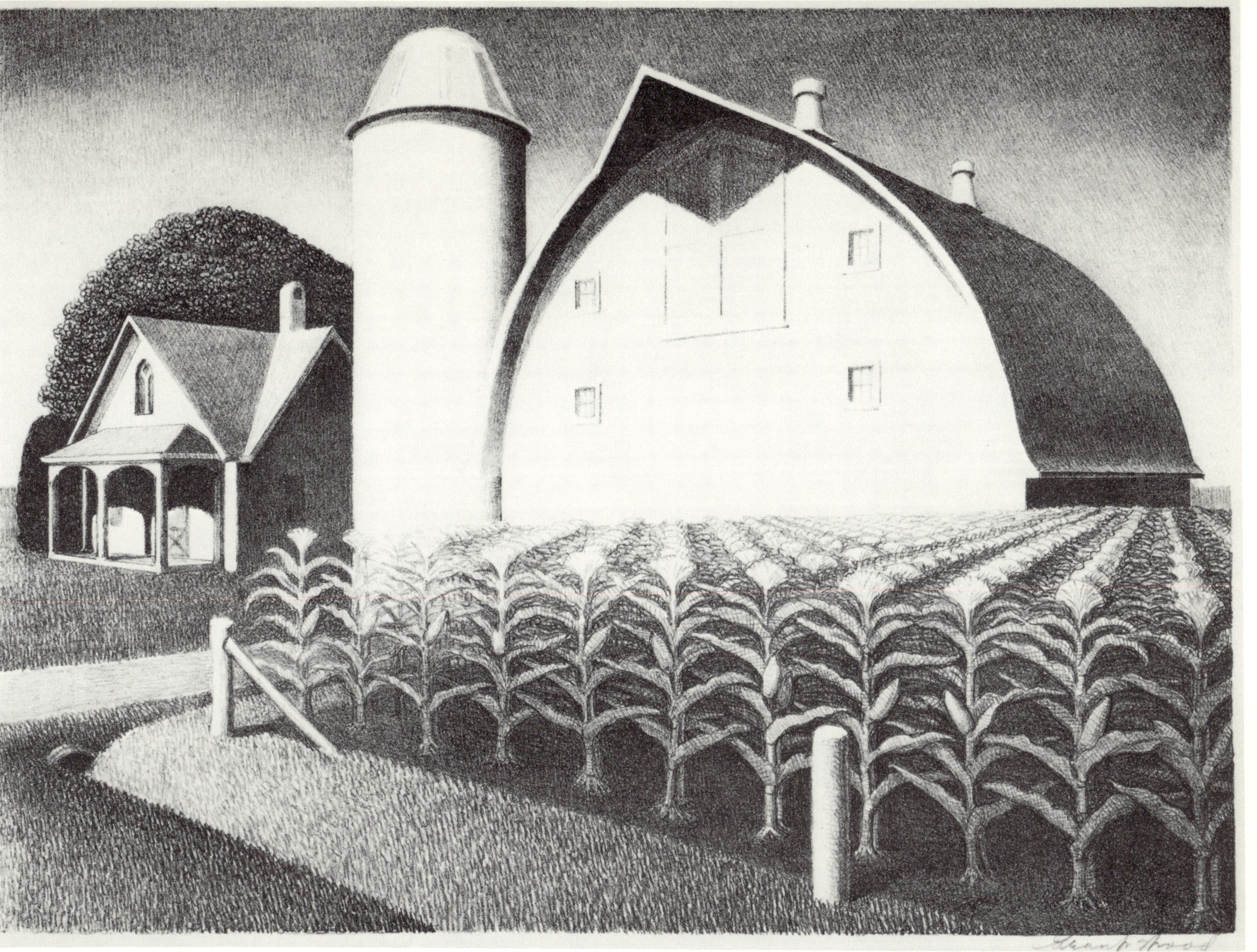

136. Grant DeVolson Wood. *Fertility*, 1939. Lithograph. Edition 250. 8⅞ × 11¾. Czestochowski W-12.

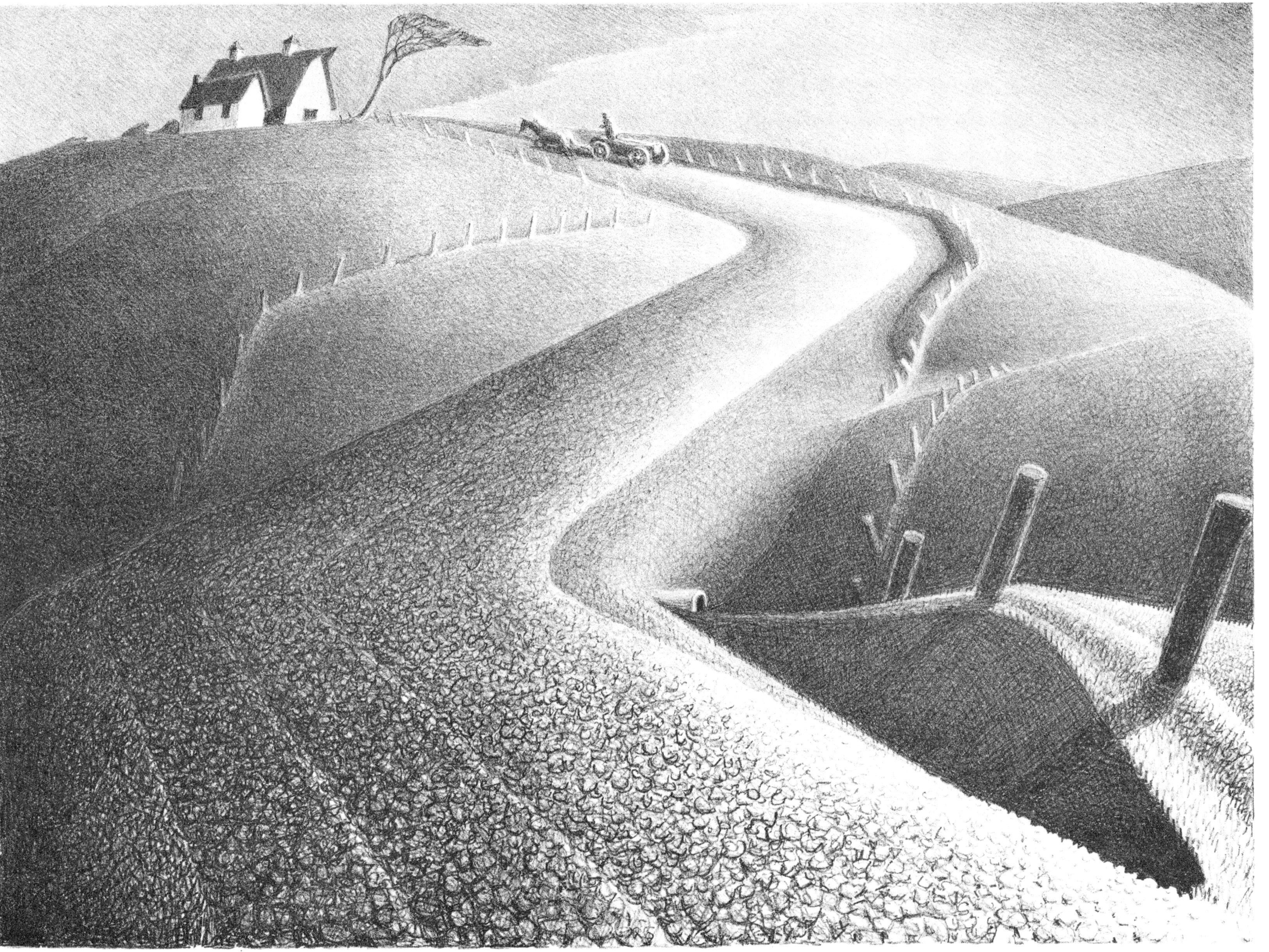

137. Grant Devolson Wood. *March,* 1941. Lithograph. Edition 250. 9 × 12. Czestochowski W-18.

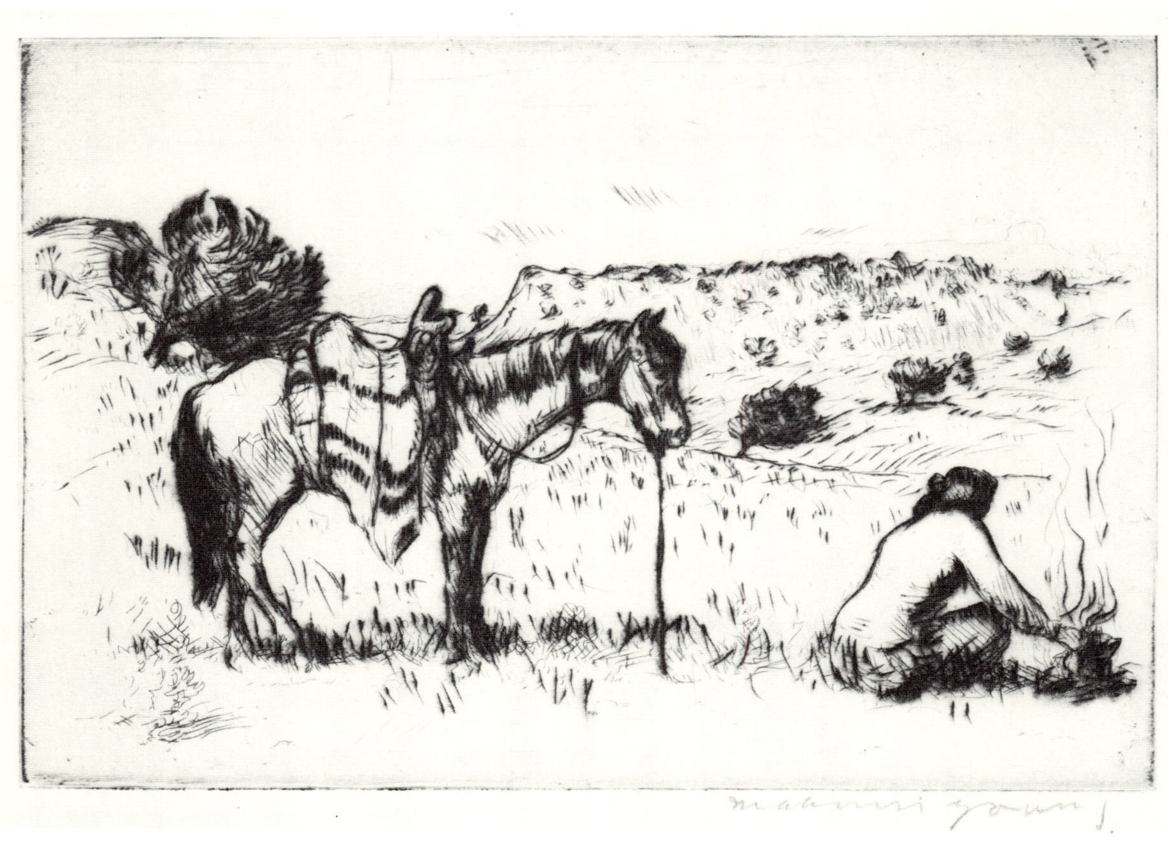

138. Mahonri Mackintosh Young. *Navajo Woman and Pony*, 1919. Drypoint. Edition 100. $3\frac{7}{8} \times 5\frac{7}{8}$.

BIOGRAPHIES OF THE ARTISTS

ALBEE, GRACE THURSTON ARNOLD (No. 1). Born Scituate, R.I., 1890. Resides in R.I. Wood engraver. Studied at Rhode Island School of Design; with Paul Bornet in Paris. Albee, who started wood engraving as a serious hobby, finding that it provided balance and distraction from the worries of life, favored rural themes and landscapes, particularly battered buildings and objects from the past.

ALBRIGHT, IVAN LE LORRAINE (No. 4). Born North Harvey, Ill., 1897. Died 1983. Lithographer, painter, etcher, teacher. Studied at Northwestern University, Ill.; Department of Architecture, University of Illinois (Urbana); Art Institute of Chicago; Pennsylvania Academy of the Fine Arts; Ecole des Beaux-Arts, Paris; National Academy of Design, N.Y. Participated in Federal Art Project, WPA. Regarded by some as the high priest of decadence in art, Albright utilized a distorted kind of realism to portray dissolution, decay and death in the world around him.

ARMS, JOHN TAYLOR (Nos. 2 & 3). Born Washington, D.C., 1887. Died 1953. Etcher, lithographer, illustrator, writer, lecturer. Studied at Princeton University, N.J.; M.I.T.; traveled abroad. "Architecture flowers into art with John Taylor Arms," noted Carl Zigrosser in *The Artist in America*. "The precision of his draftsmanship again demands superlatives: it once called forth Fitzroy Carrington's astounded exclamation: 'For God's sake, John, don't you ever make a mistake, get drunk or something!' "

AVERY, MILTON (No. 5). Born Altmar, N.Y., 1893. Died 1965. Etcher, wood engraver, lithographer, painter. Studied briefly at the Connecticut League of Art Students; was self-taught as a printmaker. Most of Avery's prints are stylized evocations of realistic images, even though many of his paintings are more impressionist, some tending toward the abstract.

BACON, PEGGY (Margaret Frances) (Nos. 6 & 7). Born Ridgefield, Conn., 1895. Married artist Alexander Brook. Resides in Cape Porpoise, Me. Etcher, lithographer, caricaturist, painter, author, illustrator, teacher. Studied at Art Students League with Kenneth Hayes Miller, George Bellows, John Sloan and Andrew Dasburg; briefly with George Bridgman and Max Weber; also with B.J.O. Nordfeldt in Provincetown, Mass.; received a Guggenheim Fellowship. "Her comments on humanity are nearly always sharp but seldom caustic," wrote Elizabeth Luther Cary in *Prints*, March 1931. "Occasionally, and these are the best moments, they are not much more than gleeful comedy. At best and worst, however, the comedy lies not so much in the situation as in the aspect of the individuals concerned in it."

BARKER, ALBERT WINSLOW (No. 8). Born Chicago, Ill., 1874. Died 1947. Lithographer, teacher. Studied at Pennsylvania Academy of the Fine Arts; Haverford College, Pa.; University of Pennsylvania. In the summer of 1927 Barker studied lithography with Bolton Brown, an experience that changed the course of his life, for Barker devoted the balance of his years to the creation and printing of stone lithographs, most depicting scenes near his home in rural Pennsylvania.

BELLOWS, GEORGE WESLEY (Nos. 10 & 11). Born Columbus, O., 1882. Died 1925. Lithographer, painter, illustrator, teacher. Studied at Ohio State University; New York School of Art, with William Merritt Chase; with his mentor Robert Henri and briefly with John Sloan; later with Kenneth Hayes Miller. Lithography was out of favor in 1916 when Bellows began to work on the stone, and he did a great deal to popularize the medium with his warm and beautiful lithographs of family, friends and childhood scenes, his rousing prints of sporting events and his strong pictorial statements against war, injustice and inhumanity.

BENSON, FRANK WESTON (No. 9). Born Salem, Mass., 1862. Died 1951. Etcher, lithographer, painter, muralist, teacher. Studied at Museum of Fine Arts, Boston; Académie Julian, Paris. Sportsman, ornithologist, artist, Benson found endless challenges in etching the habits and habitats of geese, ducks and feathered relatives; no other artist has approached him in the ability to capture the beauty of wild birds in flight.

BENTON, THOMAS HART (Nos. 12 & 13). Born Neosho, Mo., 1889. Died 1975. Lithographer, painter, muralist, writer, teacher, lecturer. Studied at Art Institute of Chicago; Académie Julian, Paris. "His friend Harry Truman called him 'the best damned painter in America.' And if you put it that way—proud, plain and just a bit defiantly anti-intellectual—Thomas Hart Benton . . . was probably the best damned painter around. He was, surely, if not the best painter in America, the best painter of it" (editorial in *The Washington Post*, Jan. 21, 1975).

BISHOP, ISABEL (No. 14). Born Cincinnati, O., 1902. Resides in New York City. Etcher, painter, muralist, teacher. Studied at Wicker Art School, Detroit, Mich.; New York School of Applied Design for Women; Art Students League with Kenneth Hayes Miller; also briefly with Max Weber and Guy Pène du Bois. Later she studied engraving with Stanley William Hayter. One of the so-called 14th Street School artists, Bishop lived and worked near Union Square in New York City. She etched the people and life-styles of that colorful area in prints that glow with poignant life.

BOHROD, AARON (No. 15). Born Chicago, Ill., 1907. Resides in Madison, Wis. Lithographer, etcher, painter, muralist, teacher, writer. Studied at Art Institute of Chicago; Art Students League with John Sloan, Boardman Robinson, Kenneth Hayes Miller, Charles Locke. Participated in Federal Art Project, WPA. Artist-in-residence at Southern Illinois University, Carbondale, and at University of Wisconsin, Madison. Bohrod was influenced by his teacher, John Sloan, to picture America as he found it, whether a Chicago auto junkyard, a solitary woman waiting for a train or a sagging Wisconsin barn.

BROWN, BOLTON COIT (No. 16). Born Dresden, N.Y., 1864. Died 1936. Lithographer, lithographic printer, etcher, painter, lecturer, writer, teacher. Studied at Syracuse University, N.Y. An interesting man on several counts, Brown was a master lithographic printer for Bellows and many other notable lithographers of that period; he was one of three founders of the famous art colony at Woodstock, N.Y. and was a superb artist on stone in his own right.

BURCHFIELD, CHARLES EPHRAIM (No. 17). Born Ashtabula, O., 1893. Died 1967. Lithographer, wood engraver, etcher, painter, teacher. Studied at The Cleveland School of Art (now the Cleveland Institute of Art) under Henry G. Keller and Frank N. Wilcox. Although known primarily for his breathtaking watercolors which reveal the beauty latent in familiar outdoor scenes, Burchfield also made three lithographs, ten etchings on zinc (all but one unpublished) and ten wood engravings, drawn on the block by Burchfield and cut by Julius J. Lankes.

BURR, GEORGE ELBERT (No. 18). Born Munroe Falls, O., 1859. Died 1939. Etcher, painter, illustrator. Studied at Art Institute of Chicago and for five years in Europe. Many of his more than 300 intaglio prints are of the Western desert, which he caught in all its manifestations on his copper plate.

BUTLER, ANDREW R. (No. 19). Born Yonkers, N.Y., 1896. Died ca. 1979. Etcher, painter. Studied at National Academy of Design; Art Students League under Eugene Speicher, F. Luis Mora and Joseph Pennell. The personality of a Butler etching is easy to identify, for his line is lean and spare, his treatment replete with New England frugality. There is much power and fulfillment with relatively few lines.

CADMUS, PAUL (No. 20). Born New York City, 1904. Resides in Conn. Etcher, lithographer, serigrapher, painter, muralist. Studied at National Academy of Design with William Auerbach-Levy; at Art Students League with Joseph Pennell and Charles Locke; also studied abroad. Participated in the Federal Art Project, WPA. In *American Prints and Printmakers*, Una Johnson wrote of Cadmus, "His meticulous rendering of the human figure in action or in relaxed abandonment has seldom been equaled in American prints. His glittering draftsmanship is reminiscent of a sixteenth century artist, but his statement bears the harsh impact of the twentieth century."

CASTELLÓN, FEDERICO (No. 21). Born Almería, Spain, 1914. Died 1971. Etcher, lithographer, painter, illustrator, teacher. Largely self-taught, he did credit high-school teachers with much assistance. In 1934, with Diego Rivera's help, he received a traveling fellowship from the government of Spain that enabled him to travel to European museums to study the works of the masters; also received two Guggenheim Fellowships. Super-realism or surrealism—either word can be used to describe different prints by Castellón, much of whose work has a strange, fascinating quality.

CHAMBERLAIN, SAMUEL (Nos. 22 & 23). Born Cresco, Ia., 1895. Died 1975. Etcher, lithographer, photographer, illustrator, writer, teacher, lecturer, gourmet cook. Studied at University of Washington; M.I.T.; Royal College of Art, London, with Malcolm Osborne; with Edouard Léon in Paris; traveled extensively and lived abroad. Chamberlain lost his heart to France and lived there for a number of years between the two world wars. Unlike the architectural prints of his friend John Taylor Arms, which focus only on the buildings themselves, Chamberlain's prints of monumental cathedrals and picturesque shops are frequently peopled by passersby, busy with their pursuits.

CHARLOT, JEAN (No. 24). Born Paris, France, 1898. Died 1978. Lithographer, painter, muralist, teacher, illustrator, writer, lecturer. Studied at Lycée Condorcet, Paris; received Guggenheim Fellowship. Although he was born in France and later became a U.S. citizen, Charlot's dynamic, almost sculptural style was influenced to a large degree by Mexican art and the Mexican artists with whom he worked for many years.

CHEFFETZ, ASA (No. 25). Born Buffalo, N.Y., 1896. Died 1965. Wood engraver, illustrator. Studied at Boston Museum of Fine Arts School; National Academy of Design. A master of wood engraving, Cheffetz achieved rich tones and textures in his prints of the scenes he saw in his adopted New England.

CIKOVSKY, NICOLAI (No. 26). Born Pinsk, Russia, 1894. Resides in Southampton, N.Y. Lithographer, painter, muralist, teacher. Studied at Vilna Art School; Penza Royal Art School; Moscow High Technical Art Institute. One of a number of Russian artists who emigrated to the U.S., Cikovsky ranged widely over representational subject matter in his lithographs and paintings.

CITRON, MINNA WRIGHT (No. 27). Born Newark, N.J., 1896. Resides in New York City. Lithographer, etcher, painter, muralist, writer. Studied at Brooklyn Institute of Arts and Sciences; New York School of Applied Design; Art Students League, with John Sloan, Kenneth Hayes Miller and Kimon Nicolaides; City College of New York; Atelier 17; and abroad. The art world is the richer for the 14th Street School and its artists such as Citron, who carried her sketch pads with her around Union Square and recorded an age in all its color, never losing track of the soul within it.

COLEMAN, GLENN O. (No. 30). Born Ohio, 1887. Died 1932. Lithographer, painter, illustrator. Studied with Robert Henri and Everett Shinn. Writing about Coleman in *Treasury of American Drawings*, Charles E. Slatkin and Regina Shoolman commented, "The many-faceted life of the metropolis [New York], especially its teeming East Side and Greenwich Village, fired his imagination. In a series of drawings, lithographs and paintings, sometimes purely descriptive, sometimes moody and full of overtones, he told the story of the city he loved and sought to express."

COOK, HOWARD NORTON (Nos. 28 & 29). Born Springfield, Mass., 1901. Died 1980. Etcher, wood engraver, lithographer, painter, muralist, teacher, lecturer, writer and illustrator. Studied at Art Students League; with George Bridgman, Joseph Pennell, Frank Dumond, others; also abroad; received two Guggenheim Fellowships. In the introduction to a Cook show held at the Weyhe Gallery in Feb. 1929, fellow artist Arnold Ronnebeck noted, "This knife sharp observation is already present in his early etchings and woodcuts of Southwestern pueblos and New England sailing ships, but New York seems to have developed it into something more generous and more independent. The unreality of its ever-changing veracities has added imagination to his feeling of organization, rhythm and solidity of design."

COSTIGAN, JOHN EDWARD (No. 31). Born Providence, R.I., 1888. Died 1972. Etcher, painter, muralist. Self-taught. Known for his prints of life on an American farm, Costigan actually farmed near Orangeburg, N.Y., dividing his time between farm chores and painting and etching the people of the soil at work and play.

COX, JOHN ROGERS (No. 34). Born Terre Haute, Ind., 1915. Resides in Wenatchee, Wash. Lithographer, painter, museum director. Studied at Pennsylvania Academy of the Fine Arts; University of Pennsylvania. Working in a style that would now be called photorealism, Cox contrasted fields of golden grain with varying kinds of weather in *Wheat Shocks*, his sole stone lithograph, and in paintings of similar subjects. During his tenure as director of the Sheldon Swope Art Gallery, Terre Haute, Ind., Cox acquired the major collection of American Scene paintings for which the museum is noted.

CURRY, JOHN STEUART (Nos. 32 & 33). Born Dunavant, Kan., 1897. Died 1946. Lithographer, painter, muralist, illustrator, teacher. Studied at Kansas City Art Institute; School of The Art Institute of Chicago; lithography with Charles Locke at Art Students League; also studied in Paris. Artist-in-residence at University of Wisconsin, Madison. "I learned that I belonged to the Regional School of Art long after I had done the work as I pleased, without once giving a thought as to what 'school' it might fit" (in Laurence Schmeckebier, *John Steuart Curry's Pageant of America*).

DAVIES, ARTHUR BOWEN (No. 35). Born Utica, N.Y., 1862. Died 1928. Etcher, lithographer, painter, illustrator, sculptor. Studied at Chicago Academy of Design; Art Institute of Chicago; abroad, including Mexico. Of Davies, William J. Glackens, fellow member of the Ashcan Eight, wrote, "He is the most important man in this country. But his art is not national, it is universal. He is a symbolist, a painter of ideas" (quoted in Michigan State Library's *Biographical Sketches of American Artists*).

DEHN, ADOLF (Nos. 36 & 37). Born Waterville, Minn., 1895. Died 1968. Lithographer, painter, writer, teacher. Studied at Minneapolis Art Institute; Art Students League; studied and traveled abroad extensively; awarded two Guggenheim Fellowships. Noted both for his landscapes and his satirical works, Dehn was a proficient and prolific artist whose art reflected the dominant passion of his life—to draw from nature and to depict human nature.

DEMARTELLY, JOHN STOCKTON (No. 38). Born Philadelphia, Pa., 1903. Died 1980. Lithographer, etcher, painter, illustrator, teacher, writer. Studied at Pennsylvania Academy of the Fine Arts; in Florence, Italy; Royal College of Art, London. Artist-in-residence, Michigan State College, East Lansing. While teaching at the Kansas City Art Institute, DeMartelly became a friend of Thomas Hart Benton, and DeMartelly's lithographs, like Benton's, mine the rich lode of the rural American scene.

DOHANOS, STEVAN (No. 39). Born Lorain, O., 1907. Resides in Westport, Conn. Wood engraver, lithographer, painter, illustrator, muralist, teacher. Studied at Cleveland School of Art; studied lithography with Stow Wengenroth. Served as Chairman and Design Coordinator of the Postmaster General's Citizen Stamp Advisory Committee for many years and has himself created more than 25 commemorative stamps. Perhaps best known for the 125 *Saturday Evening Post* covers he created between 1943 and 1959, Dohanos, who labels himself "an American realist," is equally impressive in his prints and paintings as he shows us the particular beauties and excitements in commonplace things we might otherwise never notice.

DURIEUX, CAROLINE WOGAN (No. 40). Born New Orleans, La., 1896. Resides in Baton Rouge, La. Lithographer, etcher, maker of electron and cliché-verre prints, teacher, illustrator. Studied at Newcomb College, New Orleans; Pennsylvania Academy of the Fine Arts; Louisiana State University. Consultant, Federal Art Project, WPA. When asked if her many bitingly satirical prints of the Old South gone to seed had antagonized her Southern neighbors, Durieux responded, "Oh, no, everyone thinks they are hilarious satires of someone else."

DWIGHT, MABEL (Nos. 42 & 43). Born Cincinnati, O., 1876. Died 1955. Lithographer, painter. Studied at Hopkins Art School, San Francisco. Unlike the often stinging satirical statements of her contemporaries Dehn and Durieux, Dwight practiced a more benign satire in her prints, mostly urban, of the human comedy.

EBY, KERR (Nos. 44 & 45). Born Tokyo, Japan, 1889. Died 1946. Etcher, lithographer, illustrator. Studied at Pratt Institute, Brooklyn; Art Students League. "Kerr Eby sees straight into the heart of his subject," wrote Dorothy Noyes Arms in vol. VIII of the "American Etchers" series, *Kerr Eby, A.N.A.* "With his sure skill, his uncompromising sincerity of purpose and his artistic vision, he contrives to give us the very essence of each experience in terms of lasting beauty."

EICHENBERG, FRITZ (No. 41). Born Cologne, Germany, 1901. Resides in Peace Dale, R.I. Illustrator, wood engraver, teacher, writer, lecturer. Studied at State Academy of Graphic Arts, Leipzig, Germany. Well known as both an illustrator and an early director of the Pratt Graphics Center in New York City, Eichenberg has created wood engravings to illustrate over 100 literary classics and children's books as well as independent engravings of both realistic and allegorical subjects.

EVERGOOD, PHILIP HOWARD FRANCIS (No. 46). Born New York City, 1901. Died 1973. Etcher, engraver, lithographer, painter, muralist, illustrator, lecturer, teacher, writer. Studied at Cambridge University; Slade School of Art, London; Art Students League with George Luks; Académie Julian, Paris. Member and supervisor, Federal Art Project, WPA. Resident artist, Kalamazoo College, Mich. Evergood frequently called himself a "social artist," and his prints mirror his concern with injustice as well as his willingness to use his art as a vehicle for bringing about reform.

FIENE, ERNEST (Nos. 48 & 49). Born Elberfeld, Germany, 1894. Died 1965. Lithographer, etcher, painter, muralist, illustrator, teacher, writer. Studied at National Academy of Design; Art Students League; in France, Germany, Italy; received Guggenheim Fellowship. Although born in Germany, Fiene, whose work reflects his interest in design and formal values, spent most of his life in the U.S., where he captured the rural scenes of New England, with an occasional detour to the city scene.

FREEMAN, DON (No. 47). Born San Diego, Calif., 1908. Died 1978. Lithographer, painter, illustrator, writer. Studied at Art Students League with John Sloan and Harry Wickey; received Guggenheim Fellowship. A master of caricature, Freeman is noted for his depictions of New York City "types," with emphasis on the theater and the political scene. He also wrote and illustrated a number of children's books.

GÁG, WANDA (No. 50). Born New Ulm, Minn., 1893. Died 1946. Lithographer, wood engraver, painter, illustrator, writer. Studied at Minneapolis Institute of Art; Art Students League. Millions of children have thrilled to Gág's *Millions of Cats* and other juvenile books she wrote and illustrated. The young at heart continue to treasure her prints of commonplace subjects made uncommon by her joyful, exuberant handling of them in her jaunty style.

GANSO, EMIL (No. 51). Born Halberstadt, Germany, 1895. Died 1941. Etcher, lithographer, wood engraver, painter, teacher. Studied at National Academy of Design; with Ronau Woiceske at Woodstock, N.Y.; received Guggenheim Fellowship. In 1939 became artist-in-residence at Lawrence College, Appleton, Wis. Having mastered all major print techniques, Ganso, one of the Woodstock artists, handled a wide range of subject matter with a virtuosity characterized by a subtle balancing of darks and lights.

GEERLINGS, GERALD KENNETH (No. 52). Born Milwaukee, Wis., 1897. Resides in New Canaan, Conn. Etcher, lithographer, illustrator, architect, writer, industrial designer. Studied at Milwaukee State Teachers College; University of Pennsylvania; Royal College of Art, London, with Malcolm Osborne; St. John's College, Cambridge University. Although he made fewer than 50 prints, most of them cityscapes, Geerlings will be remembered for his monumental portraits of Chicago and New York, in which the lights of the city punctuate his velvety aquatints of night.

GORSLINE, DOUGLAS WARNER (No. 53). Born Rochester, N.Y., 1913. Resides in Paris, France. Etcher, engraver, painter, illustrator, teacher. Studied at Yale University School of Fine Arts; Art Students League. An etcher who prefers the classic straight-line technique, Gorsline is at his best in the prints in which he captures city dwellers isolated in a bustling crowd.

GRANT, GORDON HOPE (No. 54). Born San Francisco, Calif., 1875. Died 1962. Lithographer, etcher, painter, illustrator, writer, muralist. Studied at Lambeth and Heatherley Art School, London. Ships, sailors and their home ports dominate the work of Grant, whose name is synonymous with marine prints of this period.

GROPPER, WILLIAM (No. 55). Born New York City, 1897. Died 1977. Lithographer, painter, illustrator, muralist. Studied at National Academy of Design; New York School of Fine and Applied Arts; with Robert Henri and George Bellows; received Guggenheim Fellowship. Like Daumier, Gropper was a powerful social commentator, attacking economic, political and social injustice where he found it—in sweatshops, courtrooms, Congress. In his prints he left us vivid reminders of the problems of his era, many of which are still with us today.

HART, GEORGE OVERBURY ("POP") (Nos. 56 & 57). Born Cairo, Ill., 1868. Died 1933. Etcher, lithographer, monotypist, painter. Largely self-taught, except for a few months' study at the

Art Institute of Chicago and three months at the Académie Julian, Paris. (Of the latter excursion into art instruction, Hart is quoted in Holger Cahill's *George O. "Pop" Hart* as saying, "That experience showed me that art schools are no places for an artist.") A vagabond artist, Hart roamed the world on a shoestring, capturing the humor, warmth and beauty of everyday life in prints that he created by experimenting with—and combining—intaglio techniques in ways new to the art of his day.

HASKELL, ERNEST (No. 58). Born Woodstock, Conn., 1876. Died 1925. Etcher, illustrator, painter. Studied independently in Paris. In a tribute to Haskell published in the catalogue raisonné of his prints, *Ernest Haskell: His Life and Work*, his close friend John Marin wrote: "Most of his working self was expressed through the medium of the etching needle handled by a master who knew his medium and whose medium knew him so that medium and man were welded together."

HASSAM, FREDERICK CHILDE (Nos. 60 & 61). Born Boston, Mass., 1859. Died 1935. Etcher, lithographer, painter, illustrator. Studied in Boston with I. M. Gaugengigl; at the Académie Julian, Paris; studied etching with Kerr Eby. One of the leading exponents of American Impressionism, or luminism, as it was called in this country, Hassam created elegant, fine-line etchings that capture the play of light and shadow on picturesque buildings, trees, streets and, not least, beautiful women. His achievements in lithography, though less well known, place him in the vanguard of the revival of lithography as an art medium in America.

HAUPERS, CLEMENT BERNARD (No. 59). Born St. Paul, Minn., 1900. Died 1982. Etcher, engraver, lithographer, painter, sculptor, teacher, lecturer. Studied at Minneapolis School of Art; various art schools in Paris. Served as State Director of the Federal Art Project, WPA; later regional director for seven Midwestern states before becoming assistant to the national director in Washington, D.C. "A talented artist with a Gallic wit, Clement Haupers is quick to seize upon the amusing, the incongruous side of human nature." So wrote Albert Reese in *American Prize Prints of the 20th Century*, and he continued, "People fascinate him, but he is not content to merely record the characteristic pose, the unconscious gesture; he insists on grouping his figures together so that they form an interesting and abstract pattern."

HEINTZELMAN, ARTHUR WILLIAM (No. 62). Born Newark, N.J., 1890. Died 1965. Etcher, writer, lecturer, museum curator. Studied at Rhode Island School of Design and abroad. A master of portraiture, Heintzelman is noted particularly for his sensitive portrayals of children and old people.

HIGGINS, EUGENE (No. 63). Born Kansas City, Mo., 1874. Died 1958. Etcher, painter. Studied at Ecole des Beaux-Arts, Académie Julian, Paris. Though friends characterized Higgins as a jolly fellow who told funny stories, he himself noted that "the sad side of life interests me." Indeed, his etchings frequently portrayed the lot of the underdog, the downtrodden, the wanderer—usually in the dark manner.

HIRSCH, JOSEPH (No. 64). Born Philadelphia, Pa., 1910. Died 1981. Lithographer, etcher, painter, muralist, teacher. Studied at Philadelphia Museum School; with George Luks. The big-city world of Hirsch was populated by slick lawyers whispering confidences, hecklers in the balconies of theaters, soup kitchens, sellers of apples, plus both tender and tough moments in the lives of urban dwellers.

HOFFMAN, IRWIN DAVID (No. 65). Born East Boston, Mass., 1901. Resides in New York City. Etcher, lithographer, painter, muralist, sculptor. Studied at School of the Museum of Fine Arts, Boston; also studied and traveled abroad. The artist of the working people, Hoffman descended into mines, the boiler rooms of ships, the villages and fields of Mexico and Puerto Rico to record the men, women and children at their work in his vital, animated style.

HOOVER, ELLISON (No. 66). Born Cleveland, O., 1888. Died 1955. Lithographer, painter, illustrator, cartoonist. Studied at Cleveland School of Art; Art Students League; traveled abroad. A versatile artist, Hoover was equally at home creating his lithographs—sometimes humorous, sometimes mysterious—as he was drawing the nationally syndicated cartoon feature *Mr. & Mrs.* in the N.Y. *Herald Tribune*.

HOPPER, EDWARD (Nos. 68 & 69). Born Nyack, N.Y., 1882. Died 1967. Etcher, painter, illustrator, writer. Studied at New York School of Art with William Merritt Chase, Robert Henri and Kenneth Hayes Miller; learned etching from Martin Lewis; traveled abroad. Like his friend Martin Lewis, Hopper rendered the effects of sunlight, moonlight, starlight and artificial light in his scenes of stark, moody realism, often reverberating with loneliness and austerity.

HORNBY, LESTER GEORGE (No. 67). Born Lowell, Mass., 1882. Died 1956. Etcher, lithographer, painter, illustrator, writer, lecturer. Studied at Rhode Island School of Design; Pape School, Boston; Académie Julian, Paris. Although he lived in France during his early working years and made many prints of French subjects in the traditional rather than the modern French manner, Hornby also left a legacy of fascinating prints and drawings of American cities and towns as they existed in the period 1910–23.

HORTER, EARL (No. 70). Born Philadelphia, Pa., 1881. Died 1940. Etcher, illustrator, painter. Self-taught. The particular mood and reality of the subject are captured by Horter, an accomplished practitioner of etching and aquatint, best known for his genre prints of New York and New Orleans.

HUNTLEY, VICTORIA EBBELS HUTSON (No. 71). Born Hasbrouck Heights, N.J., 1900. Died 1971. Lithographer, painter, muralist, lecturer. Studied at Art Students League with John Sloan, Max Weber, George Luks and Kenneth Hayes Miller; received Guggenheim Fellowship. Strong industrial and urban subjects are characteristic of her early lithography. Later she turned her attention to landscapes and floral and bird studies, such as the series she did in the Florida Everglades.

HURD, PETER (No. 72). Born Roswell, N.M., 1904. Died 1984. Lithographer, painter, muralist, writer. Studied at Pennsylvania Academy of the Fine Arts with N. C. Wyeth. One of the ablest of Southwestern painters, Hurd was led to lithography by the grim economy of the Depression.

HUTTY, ALFRED HEBER (No. 73). Born Grand Haven, Mich., 1877. Died 1954. Etcher, lithographer, painter. Studied at St. Louis School of Fine Arts; Art Students League; and with William Merritt Chase. Born in the North and trained as an architect, Hutty became well known for his lovingly detailed prints of street scenes in old Charleston and of the people and trees of the South.

KENT, ROCKWELL (Nos. 74 & 75). Born Tarrytown Heights, N.Y., 1882. Died 1971. Lithographer, wood engraver, painter, muralist, illustrator, writer, lecturer. Studied at Columbia University; Shinnecock Hills School with William Merritt Chase; Independent School with Robert Henri and Kenneth Hayes Miller. The prints of Rockwell Kent, a romantic realist preoccupied with symbolic and larger-than-life ideas and images, have been divided into three phases by Carl Zigrosser in his foreword to *The Prints of Rockwell Kent* by Dan Burne Jones: first, an intense mystical period born of lonely spells in Newfoundland and Alaska; second, a more-or-less documentary period, illustrating daily life in the Adirondacks or in Greenland; third, Kent's socially conscious period.

KINNEY, TROY (No. 76). Born Kansas City, Mo., 1871. Died 1938. Etcher, writer, lecturer. Studied at Yale University; Art Institute of Chicago. Unquestionably the outstanding etcher of the dance in this period, Kinney captured the grace and charm of dancers in motion not only because he was an accomplished etcher, but because he devoted most of his adult life to an intimate study of the dance, traveling with famous dancers when they went on tour.

KLOSS, GENE (No. 77). Born Oakland, Calif., 1903. Resides near Taos, N.M. Etcher, painter. Studied at University of California, Berkeley; California School of Fine Arts, San Francisco; Oakland

School of Arts and Crafts. Hailed by *Art News* magazine as "one of our most sensitive and sympathetic interpreters of the Southwest," Kloss has been particularly inspired by the rituals, habitat, life-style, art and music of the American Indians of that area.

KUNIYOSHI, YASUO (Nos. 78 & 79). Born Okayama, Japan, 1893. Died 1953. Lithographer, etcher, painter, teacher. Studied at Los Angeles School of Art and Design; National Academy of Design; Art Students League with Kenneth Hayes Miller; worked in Paris; received Guggenheim Fellowship. Having tried and discarded etching as a printmaking medium, Kuniyoshi found that in lithography he could achieve the subtle tones he was seeking for his portrayals of the female figure in many poses—seated at a table, on a circus highwire and clothed and unclothed.

KUPFERMAN, LAWRENCE EDWARD (No. 80). Born Boston, Mass., 1909. Died 1982. Etcher, painter, muralist, teacher. Studied at School of the Museum of Fine Arts, Boston; Massachusetts School of Art. In his etchings Kupferman lavished detailed attention on the gingerbread on old Victorian houses in his native Boston and elsewhere, thus preserving these elaborate monuments of that bygone era.

LANDACRE, PAUL HAMBLETON (No. 81). Born Columbus, O., 1893. Died 1963. Wood engraver, illustrator, teacher. Studied at Ohio State University. A highly skilled wood engraver, Landacre based his work on a close observation of nature. Never copying it, he achieved in his prints an almost subjective abstract quality in what remained an easily recognizable subject.

LANDECK, ARMIN (Nos. 82 & 83). Born Crandon, Wis., 1905. Resides in East Cornwall, Conn. Etcher, engraver, lithographer, painter, illustrator, teacher. Studied at University of Michigan, Ann Arbor; Columbia University; Art Students League; studied engraving with Stanley William Hayter; traveled abroad; received Guggenheim Fellowship. Like other architectural etchers of the period who cut their eyeteeth on European subjects, Landeck returned to New York City, was entranced with the bravura of the buildings that lined its streets and proceeded to translate them and the lonely aspects of the big city into superb art.

LANKES, JULIUS J. (No. 84). Born Buffalo, N.Y., 1884. Died 1960. Wood engraver, illustrator, teacher, writer. Studied at Art Students League; School of the Museum of Fine Arts, Boston. Known as "The Virginia woodcut man," Lankes made some 1,000 wood engravings, most of rural subjects. He also did much to popularize the woodblock print, not only through example, but in his teaching and writings, including his book, *A Woodcut Manual*, one of the twentieth century's classic treatises on the subject.

LEE, DORIS EMRICK (No. 85). Born Aledo, Ill., 1905. Died 1983. Lithographer, painter, illustrator, muralist, teacher. Studied at Rockford College, Ill.; Kansas City Art Institute, Mo.; California School of Fine Arts, San Francisco, with Arnold Blanch; also with André Lhote in Paris. A kissing cousin to the American primitive artists, Lee worked in a delightful, tongue-in-cheek manner to capture the picturesque charm of great and small moments in the lives of rural Americans.

LEIGHTON, CLARE VERONICA HOPE (No. 86). Born London, England, 1901. Resides in Woodbury, Conn. Wood engraver, illustrator, writer, designer of stained-glass windows. Studied at Brighton School of Art; Slade School of Fine Art, University of London; London County Council Central School of Arts and Crafts, where she learned wood engraving. A keen observer of nature and life in the country, Leighton has engraved almost 900 blocks, most of rural subjects.

LEWIS, ARTHUR ALLEN (Nos. 88 & 89). Born Mobile, Ala., 1873. Died 1957. Etcher, wood engraver, illustrator, teacher. Studied at Art Students League; Ecole des Beaux-Arts, Paris. At the time of the Allen Lewis exhibition staged by Alfred Stieglitz at his "291" Gallery in 1909, Paul Burty Haviland wrote in *Camera Work* (July 1909), "It is singularly refreshing to come across the work of a man who seems to have kept himself untouched by the modern spirit of indifference to the philosophy of life; and who combines a remarkable feeling for composition with a seriousness of purpose and a simple faith reminiscent of the spirit of the old German masters."

LEWIS, MARTIN (Nos. 90 & 91). Born Castlemaine, Australia, 1881. Died 1962. Etcher, lithographer, painter, teacher, illustrator. Studied briefly at the Julian Ashton Art School, Sydney, Australia; otherwise largely self-taught; worked in Japan 1920–22. Lewis is particularly noted for his achievements in depicting snow, rain, wind and the thousand and one nighttime lights across the city. He was a genius at capturing the spirit of New York at a particular moment and making it memorable.

LOCKE, CHARLES WHEELER (No. 87). Born Cincinnati, O., 1899. Died 1983. Lithographer, painter, illustrator, teacher. Studied at Ohio Mechanics' Institute; Cincinnati Art Academy; Art Students League with Joseph Pennell; also in Paris. Brought from Ohio to New York by Pennell to be his assistant and to teach the lithography class at the Art Students League, Locke was intrigued by the city and its colorful types. Both found their way into his lithographs, made between the early 1920s and the early 1940s.

LOZOWICK, LOUIS (Nos. 92 & 93). Born Ludvinovka, Ukraine, 1892. Died 1973. Lithographer, painter, muralist, illustrator, writer, lecturer, teacher. Studied at Kiev Art School; National Academy of Design; Ohio State University; traveled abroad extensively. Worked on Federal Art Project, WPA. A pioneer of precisionist art, Lozowick found his inspiration in the machines and factories of the industrial scene and in the geometry of the American city, particularly New York.

MARIN, JOHN (Nos. 94 & 95). Born Rutherford, N.J., 1870. Died 1953. Etcher, painter. Studied at Pennsylvania Academy of the Fine Arts with William Merritt Chase and Thomas Anschutz; Art Students League; traveled abroad. The etchings of Marin divide neatly into two periods: His early European prints (1905–10) are architectural in subject matter and traditional in manner, while his New York cityscapes from 1911 on, though still devoted to architectural structures, show more of an imaginative—even rollicking—flair.

MARSH, REGINALD (Nos. 96 & 97). Born Paris, France, 1898. Died 1954. Etcher, engraver, lithographer, painter, muralist, teacher, illustrator, writer, cartoonist. Studied at Yale University; Art Students League with John Sloan, George Luks and Kenneth Hayes Miller; studied engraving with Stanley William Hayter; traveled abroad. Included with Isabel Bishop, Minna Citron, Kenneth Hayes Miller and the Soyer brothers as printmakers in the 14th Street School, Marsh made earthy, realistic prints of New York City people on the streets and the el, at Coney Island and in the burlesque houses; he also created many wonderful railroad prints.

MASTRO-VALERIO, ALESSANDRO (No. 98). Born San Nicondre, Italy, 1887. Died 1953. Etcher, painter, teacher. Studied at Salvator Rosa Academy, Naples. A major exponent of the difficult medium of mezzotint, Mastro-Valerio achieved tone and mass in richly textured, velvety studies of nudes.

MATULKA, JAN (No. 99). Born Vlachovo Březi, South Bohemia (now Czechoslovakia), 1890. Died 1972. Lithographer, etcher, painter, teacher, illustrator. Studied in Prague; at the National Academy of Design; Art Students League with Eugene Fitsch; in Paris, France. Worked on the Federal Art Project, WPA. Merry A. Foresta, in the catalog for the 1980–81 Matulka exhibition organized by the Whitney Museum of American Art and the National Collection of Fine Arts, wrote: "Matulka maintained this duality between the coolly analytical and the expressive throughout his career . . . In the cityscapes he seems to be feeling his way toward a bold, simple abstraction with no strong desire to leave behind the structure of the city itself."

MESS, GEORGE JO (No. 100). Born Cincinnati, O., 1898. Died 1962. Etcher, painter, teacher, lecturer, designer, illustrator. Studied at John Herron Art Institute, Indianapolis; Tiffany Foundation, N.Y.C.; Butler University, Ind.; Columbia University; Institute of Modern Design, Chicago; and in France. The only print medium in which Mess worked was aquatint; it sufficed for the figure studies and rural inspirations that he brought to fruition beautifully.

MIELATZ, CHARLES FREDERICK WILLIAM (Nos. 102 & 103). Born Breddin, Germany, 1860 (or 1864). Died 1919. Etcher, teacher. An endless experimenter in the intaglio media, Mielatz was the first of his time in a long line of American etchers to portray the unending excitements and special beauties of New York City on the copper plate, leaving a legacy of history as well as of art.

MILLER, KENNETH HAYES (No. 101). Born Oneida, N.Y., 1876. Died 1952. Etcher, painter, teacher, lecturer. Studied at Art Students League; New York School of Art with William Merritt Chase. Miller taught painting to many, including all the members of the 14th Street School except the Soyer brothers. Most of his etchings and paintings are stylized versions of women shopping and nudes.

MYERS, JEROME (No. 104). Born Petersburg, Va., 1867. Died 1940. Etcher, lithographer, painter, writer. Studied at Cooper Union Art School; Art Students League. Myers noted in his autobiography, *Artist in Manhattan*, "Mine was the privilege to pencil the scenes [of the crowded East Side of New York City] . . . My love was my witness in recording these earnest, simple lives, these visions of the slums clothed in dignity, never to me mere slums but the habitations of a people who were rich in spirit and effort."

NASON, THOMAS WILLOUGHBY (No. 106 & 107). Born Dracut, Mass., 1889. Died 1971. Wood and copper engraver, illustrator, painter. Attended life classes in drawing in Boston, the only formal instruction in art he ever had. If Robert Frost was poet laureate to New England, Thomas Nason was its laureate of engraving. The comparison is not arbitrary, for Nason and Frost were friends, and their vision of New England differed only in their means of expression.

NICHOLS, DALE WILLIAM (No. 105). Born David City, Neb., 1904. Resides in Leucadia, Calif. Lithographer, painter, designer, illustrator, writer, lecturer, teacher. Studied at Chicago Academy of Fine Art; Art Institute of Chicago. Artist-in-residence, University of Illinois. Nichols captured in a stylized realism the contours of the rural Midwestern landscape.

PARTRIDGE, ROI (No. 108). Born Centralia, Wash., 1888. Died 1984. Etcher, teacher, writer, lecturer. Studied at National Academy of Design; traveled abroad. Partridge was a leading California printmaker during most of this century, detailing the trees, mountains, buildings and oil wells of the West in a style he made his own.

PENNELL, JOSEPH (Nos. 110 & 111). Born Philadelphia, Pa., 1857. Died 1926. Etcher, lithographer, illustrator, writer, teacher, lecturer. Studied at Pennsylvania School of Industrial Art; Pennsylvania Academy of the Fine Arts under Thomas Eakins; lived and traveled abroad extensively. This remarkable man, an iconoclast who earned the displeasure of many "true believers," created more than 800 etchings and more than 600 lithographs, at the same time completing thousands of illustrations for *Century*, *Harper's*, *Scribner's* and many other magazines on both sides of the Atlantic. He and his talented wife, Elizabeth Robins Pennell, wrote and/or illustrated over 70 books and, last but not least, Mr. Pennell left his fortune "to the nation" for the purchase of prints.

REED, DOEL (No. 109). Born Logansport, Ind., 1894. Resides in Taos, N.M. Etcher, painter, muralist, teacher. Studied at Cincinnati Art Academy. The undisputed master of aquatint in twentieth-century American art, finding his subject matter in the geography of the Southwest and of the female figure, Reed has said, "The landscape is, I believe, most sympathetic to creative work. I am afraid that some of the newcomers in the art world like the uninhibited life, but for the life of me I can't see why anyone should sit in a beautiful landscape and do completely non-objective work when the mountains themselves offer no end of abstract pattern" (quoted in the exhibition catalog *Doel Reed, N.A.*, Museum of Fine Arts, Museum of New Mexico, 1983).

REYNARD, GRANT TYSON (No. 112). Born Grand Island, Neb., 1887. Died 1968. Etcher, lithographer, painter, illustrator, lecturer, teacher, writer. Studied at Art Institute of Chicago; Chicago Academy of Art; with Harry Wickey and Mahonri Young; traveled abroad. Artist-in-residence, University of Wyoming. Deeply involved in music and literature as well as in art, Reynard recorded, in many of his prints, life as he experienced it in museums and concert halls.

RIGGS, ROBERT (No. 113). Born Decatur, Ill., 1896. Died 1970. Lithographer, illustrator. A skilled lithographer who liked to work in a large format, Riggs favored dramatic subjects such as circus acts, prizefights and hospital emergency wards.

ROSENBERG, LOUIS CONRAD (No. 114). Born Portland, Ore., 1890. Died 1983. Etcher, architect, illustrator. Studied at M.I.T.; American Academy in Rome with Robert Fulton Logan; Royal College of Art, London, with Malcolm Osborne; traveled extensively abroad. Of this brilliant American architectural etcher, Malcolm Salaman wrote, "He is yet another of that rare company of etchers who, having enjoyed the training of a practicing architect, divined that he would never build better than he knew, and that he would probably get more joyous excitement out of interpreting pictorially the spirit and design of earlier architects who had planned buildings to function through the centuries" (*Louis C. Rosenberg*, vol. X in the "Masters of Modern Etching" series).

ROTH, ERNEST DAVID (Nos. 116 & 117). Born Stuttgart, Germany, 1879. Died 1964. Etcher, painter, printer. Studied at National Academy of Design with James D. Smillie; New York School of Art with F. Luis Mora; lived and traveled extensively abroad. Roth spent his early years etching the hill towns, cathedrals and cities of Europe, later turning his attention and etching needle to the architecture of New York City and environs. He was also a master printer of etchings by others, including John Sloan.

RUZICKA, RUDOLPH (No. 115). Born Bohemia (Czechoslovakia), 1883. Died 1978. Woodblock printmaker, illustrator. Studied at Art Institute of Chicago; New York School of Art; traveled abroad. While Ruzicka and Allen Lewis continued the centuries-old tradition of creating their woodblock prints for magazine and book illustration, they also pioneered a tradition of woodblock prints as works of art independent of illustration.

SCHREIBER, GEORGES (No. 118). Born Brussels, Belgium, 1904. Died 1977. Lithographer, painter, designer, illustrator, author, teacher. Studied at Art Crafts School, Elberfeld, West Germany; Academy of Fine Arts, Düsseldorf and Berlin, Germany; also in London, Florence and Paris. Shortly after emigrating to the U.S. from Belgium, Schreiber undertook to visit all of the (then) 48 states, recording his impressions of each on the lithographic stone, leaving us an artistic record of rural life in this country during the 1930s and 1940s.

SHEELER, CHARLES (No. 119). Born Philadelphia, Pa., 1883. Died 1965. Lithographer, painter, photographer. Studied at Philadelphia Museum School of Industrial Art; Pennsylvania Academy of the Fine Arts with William Merritt Chase; studied abroad. Artist-in-residence, Phillips Academy, Andover, Mass. A precisionist artist and one of the first of the modern photographers, Sheeler discovered the industrial scene and made it his own, depicting bare and uncluttered factories and other works of man (including barns), usually devoid of human presence.

SLOAN, JOHN (Nos. 120 & 121). Born Lock Haven, Pa., 1871. Died 1951. Etcher, lithographer, painter, illustrator, muralist, teacher, writer, lecturer. Studied at Pennsylvania Academy of the Fine Arts; and with Thomas Anschutz and Robert Henri. We are indebted to Sloan not only for his brilliant etchings—realistic and often intimate renditions of life among the working people of New York City—but also for spearheading the drive in the early years of this century to free American art from the stifling restrictions imposed on it by the National Academy and other elements of the art establishment of that day.

SOYER, RAPHAEL (No. 122). Born Borisoglebsk, Tombov, Russia, 1899. Resides in New York City. Lithographer, etcher, painter, teacher, writer. Studied at Cooper Union, New York; National Academy of Design; Art Students League. Participated in Federal Art Project, WPA. In his book *Self-Revealment* Soyer wrote, "My art is representational by choice. In my opinion, if the art of painting is to survive, it must describe and express people, their lives and times. It must communicate." Soyer's paintings and prints have done that for over 60 years.

SPRUANCE, BENTON MURDOCH (No. 123). Born Philadelphia, Pa., 1904. Died 1967. Lithographer, painter, muralist, teacher. Studied at University of Pennsylvania School of Fine Art; Pennsylvania Academy of the Fine Arts; traveled abroad; received Guggenheim Fellowship. Spruance, who devoted most of his adult life to lithography and the teaching of art, created strong, realistic black-and-white lithographs during the 1920s and 1930s, later turning increasingly to color lithography, and themes of more mystical, mythological and metaphysical nature.

STERNER, ALBERT EDWARD (No. 124). Born London, England, 1863. Died 1946. Etcher, lithographer, painter, illustrator, lecturer, writer. Studied at Birmingham, England; Académie Julian, Paris; traveled abroad. Sterner was one of the pioneers in creating lithographs as a fine art in the early years of this century. The themes of many of his prints are, by present standards, out of date, yet they all have an unmistakable power.

SWANN, JAMES (No. 125). Born Merkel, Tex., 1905. Resides in Chicago, Ill. Etcher, illustrator, commercial artist, writer, lecturer. Studied at Sul Ross State College, Alpine, Tex.; in Dallas and Chicago; traveled abroad. A longtime leader of the Chicago Society of Etchers and Prairie Print Makers, as well as working with other print clubs and societies that were such an important part of the print scene of this period, Swann himself etched with deep feeling and obvious skill his native Texas and his adopted Chicago.

TITTLE, WALTER ERNEST (No. 126). Born Springfield, O., 1883. Died 1966. Etcher, lithographer, painter, illustrator, writer. Studied at New York School of Arts; and with William Merritt Chase, Robert Henri and F. Luis Mora; traveled abroad. Although the lion's share of his graphic work consists of brilliant portraits of the high and mighty of the world of his time, he also etched with a sure dexterity museum interiors and architectural exteriors, many of them night scenes of spectacular beauty.

WARD, LYND KENDALL (No. 127). Born Chicago, Ill., 1905. Resides in Reston, Va. Wood engraver, lithographer, illustrator, painter, lecturer, writer. Studied at Columbia University; State Academy for Graphic Arts, Leipzig, Germany, where he studied wood engraving with Hans Alexander Mueller. The first to introduce to America the novel in woodcuts, in which the pictures tell the entire story without help from a single word, Ward also has illustrated many books with words, and has executed an impressive body of independent wood engravings of widely varied subject matter.

WEBSTER, HERMAN ARMOUR (No. 128). Born New York City, 1878. Died 1970. Etcher, painter, draftsman. Studied at Yale University; Académie Julian, Paris; largely self-taught as an etcher. Webster, who lived in Paris for much of his adult life, etched and painted the things he loved best—medieval cities, serene landscapes, gnarled trees and ancient windmills, "expressed with a poetic sensibility in works of great charm" (Janet Flint, Curator of Prints and Drawings, National Collection of Fine Arts).

WEIDENAAR, REYNOLD HENRY (No. 129). Born Grand Rapids, Mich., 1915. Resides in Grand Rapids. Etcher, painter, muralist, illustrator, teacher, writer. Studied at Kendall School of Design, Grand Rapids; Kansas City Art Institute; received Guggenheim Fellowship. A master of all the intaglio techniques, particularly mezzotint, Weidenaar frequently combines several techniques in a single plate, which may be dramatic, whimsical, satirical, haunting, reminiscent of another age, but always realistic—and never dull.

WENGENROTH, STOW (Nos. 130 & 131). Born Brooklyn, N.Y., 1906. Died 1978. Lithographer, painter, illustrator, writer, teacher. Studied at Art Students League; Grand Central School of Art, N.Y.C.; summers at Woodstock, N.Y. and at Eastport, Me. Andrew Wyeth called him "the greatest black-and-white artist in America." Certainly, few artists have coaxed more from the lithographic stone. Whether portraying the magnificence of the Brooklyn Bridge; the particular truths of New England houses, churches and coastline; or the personalities of owls, gulls, chickadees and other birds, his mastery transcends the real, though he never departs from it.

WEST, LEVON (No. 132). Born Centerville, S.D., 1900. Died 1968. Etcher, illustrator, photographer, lecturer, writer. Studied at University of Minnesota; Art Students League with Joseph Pennell; traveled abroad. An etcher who later became a professional photographer under the name of Ivan Dmitri, West is best known for his impressive prints, filled with packhorses, dog teams, Indians and mountain rangers, which depict the rugged outdoor life in the Far West during the late 1920s.

WINKLER, JOHN WILLIAM JOSEPH (No. 133). Born Vienna, Austria, 1894. Died 1979. Etcher, painter. Studied at San Francisco Institute of Art; worked in England and France. San Francisco has undergone many changes since Winkler arrived there in the early years of this century and began to etch its scenic delights, but Telegraph Hill, Nob Hill, Chinatown, the bay, the wharves, the streets, as they existed then, have been memorialized in fine etchings that bespeak Winkler's loose, free-line drawing style.

WOICESKE, RONAU WILLIAM (No. 134). Born Bloomington, Ill., 1887. Died 1953. Etcher, painter, designer, teacher. Studied at St. Louis School of Fine Arts; at Woodstock, N.Y. with John Carlson; self-taught as an etcher. Participated in Federal Art Project, WPA. Woiceske is most famous for his brilliant depictions of snow scenes in and around Woodstock; he extracted from the copper plate definitive renditions of the beauty of snow.

WOOD, FRANKLIN T. (No. 135). Born Hyde Park, N.Y., 1887. Died 1945. Etcher, painter. Studied at Cowles Art School; Art Students League; abroad. T. H. Thomas in *The Print Connoisseur* (July 1925) noted of Wood's work, "there is always a delicately sympathetic human quality, wholly free from sentimentality." Wood's etched style probes untold depths of the subject portrayed and reveals it in etched lines that dance.

WOOD, GRANT DEVOLSON (Nos. 136 & 137). Born Anamosa, Ia., 1891. Died 1942. Lithographer, painter, muralist, illustrator, teacher, lecturer, writer, designer of stained-glass windows. Studied at Minneapolis School of Design and Handicraft and Normal Art; University of Iowa life-drawing classes; Art Institute of Chicago; Académie Julian, Paris. Director of Public Works of Art Project, WPA, for Iowa. Wood made only 19 lithographs in a lifetime cut short by cancer, but his American Scene prints of Iowa in both harsh and benevolent seasons, like his paintings, had a tremendous impact on the art world as well as on fellow artists, to whom he recommended a commonsense use of subject matter which they knew best.

YOUNG, MAHONRI MACKINTOSH (No. 138). Born Salt Lake City, Ut., 1877. Died 1957. Etcher, painter, sculptor, teacher, writer. Studied at Art Students League; Académie Julian, Paris. A grandson of Brigham Young, Mahonri spent much time in the Salt Lake City area etching American Indian life and landscapes of the West.

SELECTED BIBLIOGRAPHY

GENERAL REFERENCE WORKS

ADAMS, CLINTON, *American Lithographers 1900–1960: The Artists and Their Printers.* Albuquerque: The University of New Mexico Press, 1983. Full-dress treatment, not only of the artist-lithographers of the period, but of their printers—George Miller, Bolton Brown, and others—who contributed much to the final product.

American Art Today, Gallery of American Art Today: New York World's Fair, 1939. New York: National Art Society, 1939. Large sections on contemporary American painting, sculpture and graphic arts. 231 prints by as many artists.

America Today: A Book of 100 Prints Chosen and Exhibited by the American Artists' Congress. New York: Equinox Cooperative Press, 1936. With introductory articles by Henry Glintenkamp, Harry Sternberg, Louis Lozowick, others.

BEALL, KAREN F., *American Prints in the Library of Congress: A Catalog of the Collection.* Baltimore: The Johns Hopkins Press, 1970.

BENTON, THOMAS HART, *An American in Art: A Professional and Technical Autobiography.* Lawrence, Kansas: The University Press of Kansas, 1969. This book by Benton and the next contain extended discussions of Regionalism and American Scene art.

BENTON, THOMAS HART, *An Artist in America*, third, revised edition. Columbia, Missouri: University of Missouri Press, 1968. The first edition was published in 1937, but the third edition contains additional interesting chapters.

Biographical Sketches of American Artists, fifth edition, revised and enlarged. Lansing, Michigan: Michigan State Library, 1924.

BOSWELL, PEYTON, JR., *Modern American Painting.* New York: Dodd, Mead & Company, 1939. Biographical sketches and pictures of paintings by many of the printmakers featured in this work.

CAHILL, HOLGER, AND BARR, ALFRED H., JR., *Art in America: A Complete Survey.* New York: Reynal & Hitchcock, 1935. Prints of the 1930s are discussed on pages 92–108.

Contemporary American Etching. New York: American Art Dealers Association, 1930. Introduction by Ralph Flint. Illustrations of 100 fine American prints of that year.

Contemporary American Painting. New York: Duell, Sloan and Pearce, 1945. Written and edited by Grace Pagano; introduction by Donald Bear. For each of 116 artists, a biography, a portrait photograph and a picture of one of his paintings are given.

Contemporary American Prints, Etchings, Woodcuts, Lithographs, 1931. Introduction by Royal Cortissoz. New York: American Art Dealers Association, 1931. This volume pictures 100 fine prints of the year 1931.

CRAVEN, THOMAS, *A Treasury of American Prints: A Selection of 100 Etchings and Lithographs by the Foremost Living American Artists.* New York: Simon and Schuster, 1939.

GLACKENS, IRA, *William Glackens and the Ashcan Group: The Emergence of Realism in American Art.* New York: Crown Publishers, Inc., 1957.

JOHNSON, UNA E., *American Prints and Printmakers: A Chronicle of Over 400 Artists and Their Prints from 1900 to the Present.* Garden City, New York: Doubleday & Company, Inc., 1980.

KRAEFT, JUNE AND NORMAN, *American Architectural Etchers: The Traditionalists.* Bethlehem, Connecticut, June 1 Gallery, 1980. Catalog of an exhibition shown at a number of American museums.

LANKES, JULIUS J., *A Woodcut Manual.* New York: Crown Publishers, 1932.

LARKIN, OLIVER W., *Art and Life in America*, revised and enlarged edition. New York: Holt, Rinehart and Winston, 1960 (original edition 1949). One of the best-written histories of American art, it includes much on the printmakers featured in the present volume.

LAVER, JAMES, *A History of British and American Etching*, London: Ernest Benn Limited, 1929.

MASON, LAURIS, AND LUDMAN, JOAN, *Print Reference Sources: A Selected Bibliography; 18th–20th Centuries*, second edition, revised and enlarged. Millwood, New York: KTO Press, 1979.

MYERS, JEROME, *Artist in Manhattan.* New York: American Artists Group, Inc., 1940. With sketches of many of the American artist-printmakers Myers knew.

O'CONNOR, FRANCIS V., *Art for the Millions: Essays from the 1930s by Artists and Administrators of the WPA Federal Art Project.* Boston: New York Graphic Society, 1973. Seven printmakers contributed articles, pp. 139–157.

O'CONNOR, FRANCIS V., *The New Deal Art Projects: An Anthology of Memoirs.* Washington, D.C.: Smithsonian Institution Press, 1972. Jacob Kainen has a fascinating article, "The Graphic Arts Division of the WPA Federal Art Project," pp. 154–175.

REESE, ALBERT, *American Prize Prints of the 20th Century.* New York: American Artists Group, Inc., 1949. 230 prints pictured and described.

SCHMECKEBIER, LAURENCE E., *John Steuart Curry's Pageant of America.* New York: American Artists Group, 1943.

SLATKIN, CHARLES E., AND SHOOLMAN, REGINA, *Treasury of American Drawings.* New York: Oxford University Press, 1947.

John Sloan's New York Scene: From the Diaries, Notes and Correspondence, 1906–1913. New York: Harper & Row, 1965. Edited by Bruce St. John, with an introduction by Helen Farr Sloan.

SOYER, RAPHAEL, *Self-Revealment: A Memoir.* New York: Maecenas Press–Random House, 1967.

WATROUS, JAMES, *A Century of American Printmaking: 1880–1980.* Madison: The University of Wisconsin Press, 1984.

WEITENKAMPF, FRANK, *American Graphic Art.* New York: Henry Holt and Company, 1912. Weitenkampf was one of the earliest champions of American prints of the realist tradition.

Year Book of American Etching, 1914. New York: John Lane Company, 1914. Introduction by Forbes Watson. Illustrated with 100 reproductions of etchings shown at the annual exhibition of the Association of American Etchers.

ZIGROSSER, CARL, *The Artist in America: Twenty-Four Close-Ups of Contemporary Printmakers.* New York: Alfred A. Knopf, 1942.

ZIGROSSER, CARL, *The Book of Fine Prints.* New York: Crown

Publishers, 1948 (the original edition, titled *Six Centuries of Fine Prints*, was published in 1937). Interesting discussion of American realist prints, many of them pictured, on pp. 191–196.

SERIES

The following important reference works were each published in series:

The "American Etchers" series, consisting of 12 volumes. Each volume has an article on, or by, a given artist, a list of his prints to year of publication and pictures of 12 of his finest plates. Published by The Crafton Collection, New York. The series: I Ernest Roth, 1929; **II** Alfred Hutty, 1929; **III** Childe Hassam, 1929; **IV** Philip Kappel, 1929; **V** John Taylor Arms, 1930; **VI** Arthur Wm. Heintzelman, 1930; **VII** George Elbert Burr, 1930; **VIII** Kerr Eby, 1930; **IX** Troy Kinney, 1930; **X** Louis C. Rosenberg, 1930; **XI** Martin Lewis, 1931; **XII** Frank W. Benson, 1931.

Fifty Prints of the Year, published as follows: 1925/26, 1926, 1927, 1929/30, 1930/31, 1931/32, 1932/33, and finally in an issue titled *Fifty American Prints*, covering 1933–38, by the American Institute of Graphic Arts, N.Y.

Fine Prints of the Year, published annually from 1923 through 1938 by Halton & Company, Ltd., London, and usually containing pictures of 100 fine prints from various countries published during the preceding year. Generally, there are about 40 American prints in each volume.

The "Modern Masters of Etching" series, consisting of volumes similar to the "American Etchers" series above, except the "Modern Masters" series does not contain lists of the artists' prints. Most of the etchers considered in this series are British; there are five volumes devoted to Americans. Published by the Studio, Limited, London. The American "Modern Masters of Etching": **6** Frank W. Benson, 1925; **22** L. C. Rosenberg, 1929; **24** Levon West, 1930; **26** Martin Lewis, 1931; **28** Joseph Pennell, 1931.

PERIODICALS

Three journals which we have found particularly useful in our continuing research into American prints:

The Print Collector's Quarterly, probably the most useful single reference source on prints published in English in this century. Quarterly (with a few short lapses) from 1911 into 1942.

The Print Connoisseur, another outstanding reference source. Quarterly from 1921 through 1930.

Prints, a rich research source on American prints. Four or five times a year from November 1930 through February 1938.

CATALOGS OF THE ARTISTS' PRINTS

The catalogs below are arranged alphabetically by the names of the artists represented in this book. Unfortunately, there are as yet no catalogs for many of the artists whose work is included. However, we know that, at the present writing, catalogs are in progress for the prints of Adolf Dehn, Mabel Dwight, Wanda Gág, Robert Riggs, Ernest Roth and Benton Spruance.

[Albright, Ivan Le Lorraine.] Gael Grayson, *Graven Image: The Prints of Ivan Albright, 1931–1977*. Lake Forest, Illinois: Lake Forest College, 1978.

[Arms, John Taylor.] John Taylor Arms and Dorothy Noyes Arms, *A Complete Catalogue of the Etchings of John Taylor Arms*. Unpublished typescript in two volumes in the Print Department of the New York Public Library, 1962. This work is reproduced in the exhibition catalog *John Taylor Arms: American Etcher* (Madison, Wisconsin: Elvehjem Art Center, University of Wisconsin, 1975).

——. William Dolan Fletcher, *John Taylor Arms, A Man for all Time: The Artist and his Work*. Privately printed, 1982.

[Avery, Milton.] Harry H. Lunn, Jr., *Milton Avery: Prints 1933–1955*. Washington, D.C.: Graphics International Ltd., 1973.

[Bacon, Peggy.] *Peggy Bacon: Personalities and Places*. Washington, D.C.: Smithsonian Institution Press. Exhibition catalog published for the National Collection of Fine Arts, 1975. Checklist of 192 Peggy Bacon prints by Janet A. Flint on pp. 91–147.

[Barker, Albert W.] The Barker number—196—given for *The Fertile Earth*, pictured in this book, is the number given this print by the artist himself in an unpublished numbered list of all of his prints.

[Bellows, George.] Emma S. Bellows, *George Bellows: His Lithographs*. New York: Alfred A. Knopf, 1927.

——. Lauris Mason, assisted by Joan Ludman, *The Lithographs of George Bellows: A Catalogue Raisonné*. Millwood, N.Y.: KTO Press, 1977.

[Benson, Frank W.] Adam E. M. Paff, *Etchings and Drypoints by Frank W. Benson*. Boston and New York: Houghton Mifflin Company, 1917, 1919, 1923, 1929 and 1959. Five volumes published between 1917 and 1959 (volume 5 was edited by Arthur Wm. Heintzelman after Paff's death).

[Benton, Thomas Hart.] Creekmore Fath, *The Lithographs of Thomas Hart Benton*, new edition. Austin, Texas: University of Texas Press, 1979.

[Bishop, Isabel.] *Isabel Bishop*. Tucson, Arizona: The University of Arizona Museum of Art, 1974. Catalog of "The First Retrospective Exhibition Held in American Museums of Paintings, Drawings, Etchings and Aquatints by Isabel Bishop." Checklist of 65 Isabel Bishop prints done between 1925 and 1974.

[Burchfield, Charles.] *The Drawings of Charles E. Burchfield*. Cleveland: The Cleveland Museum of Art, 1953. Catalog of an exhibition sponsored by the Print Club of Cleveland and The Cleveland Museum of Art. On pp. 30–31 are listed Burchfield's etchings, wood engravings and lithographs.

[Burr, George Elbert.] Louise Combes Seeber, *George Elbert Burr: Catalogue Raisonné and Guide to the Etched Works with Biographical and Critical Notes*. Flagstaff, Arizona: Northland Press, 1971.

[Cadmus, Paul.] *Paul Cadmus: Prints and Drawings, 1922–1967*. Brooklyn, New York: Brooklyn Museum, 1968. Text by Una E. Johnson; research by Jo Miller.

[Castellón, Federico.] August L. Freundlich, *Federico Castellón: His Graphic Works, 1936–1971*. Syracuse, New York: Syracuse University, 1978.

[Chamberlain, Samuel.] Samuel Chamberlain, N.A., *Etched in Sunlight: Fifty Years in the Graphic Arts*. Boston, Massachusetts: Boston Public Library, 1968. Lists 199 published prints by Chamberlain on pp. 201–206.

——. Narcissa Gellatly Chamberlain and Jane Field Kingsland, *The Prints of Samuel Chamberlain N. A., Drypoints, Etchings, Lithographs*. Boston: Boston Public Library, 1984.

[Charlot, Jean.] Peter Morse, *Jean Charlot's Prints: A Catalogue Raisonné*. Honolulu, Hawaii: University Press of Hawaii, 1976.

[Cook, Howard.] *The Checkerboard: Cook Number*. New York: Weyhe Gallery, 1931. Lists 113 Cook prints done to time of publication.

——. Betty and Douglas Duffy, *The Graphic Work of Howard Cook: A Catalog Raisonné*. Bethesda, Maryland: Bethesda Art Gallery, 1984.

[Curry, John Steuart.] Sylvan Cole, Jr., *The Lithographs of John Steuart Curry: A Catalogue Raisonné*. New York: Associated American Artists, 1976.

[Davies, Arthur B.] Frederic Newlin Price, *The Etchings & Lithographs of Arthur B. Davies*. New York: Mitchell Kennerley, 1929.

[Durieux, Caroline.] Richard Cox, *Caroline Durieux: Lithographs of the Thirties and Forties*. Baton Rouge: Louisiana State University Press, 1977.

[Dwight, Mabel.] Carl Zigrosser, *Mabel Dwight: A Decade of Lithography, 1927–1937*. New York: The Weyhe Gallery, 1938. Exhibition catalogue; lists 93 prints of the period covered.

[Eby, Kerr.] "List of Prints Presented to the New York Public Library by Kerr Eby," unpublished typescript in the New York Public Library. A list of 145 prints made by Kerr Eby, supplemented with 14 more given in memory of Harry Katz by the latter's widow.

[Evergood, Philip.] Lucy Lippard, *The Graphic Work of Philip Evergood*. New York: Crown Publishers, Inc., 1966.

[Hart, George Overbury ("Pop").] *George Overbury "Pop" Hart, 1863–1933, Catalog of an Exhibition of Oils, Water Colors, Drawings and Prints*. Newark, New Jersey: The Newark Museum, 1935. Lists 83 prints by "Pop" Hart on pp. 48–60.

——. *George O. "Pop" Hart: Twenty-Four Selections from His Work*. New York: The Downtown Gallery, 1928. Edited and with an introduction by Holger Cahill; lists 82 prints by "Pop" Hart on pp. 19–25.

[Haskell, Ernest.] Nathaniel Pousette-Dart, *Ernest Haskell: His Life and Work*. New York: T. Spencer Hutson, 1931.

[Hassam, Childe.] Royal Cortissoz, *Catalogue of the Etchings and Drypoints of Childe Hassam, N.A.* New York: Charles Scribner's Sons, 1925.

——. *Handbook of the Complete Set of Etchings and Drypoints of Childe Hassam, N.A.* New York: The Leonard Clayton Gallery, Inc., 1933. Introduction by Paula Eliasoph.

——. Fuller Griffith, "The Lithographs of Childe Hassam: A Catalog," *Bulletin* 232. Washington, D.C.: The Smithsonian Institution, 1962.

[Hirsch, Joseph.] Sylvan Cole, Jr., *The Graphic Work of Joseph Hirsch*. New York: Associated American Artists, 1970.

[Hoffman, Irwin D.] *Irwin D. Hoffman*. New York: Associated American Artists, 1936. Lists 49 plates completed by Hoffman to the year of publication.

[Hopper, Edward.] Carl Zigrosser, *Prints*. New York: Holt, Rinehart and Winston, 1962. Chapter 8, "The Etchings of Edward Hopper," with checklist of 52 Hopper prints on pp. 155–173.

——. Gail Levin, *Edward Hopper: The Complete Prints*. New York: W. W. Norton & Company in association with the Whitney Museum of American Art, 1979.

[Hornby, Lester G.] Louis Arthur Holman, *Hornby's Etchings of the Great War, with a Complete, Authoritative List of All His Plates (1906–1920)*. Boston: C. E. Goodspeed & Co., 1921.

[Hurd, Peter.] John Meigs, *Peter Hurd: The Lithographs*. Lubbock, Texas: Baker Gallery Press, 1968.

[Kent, Rockwell.] Dan Burne Jones, *The Prints of Rockwell Kent: A Catalogue Raisonné*. Chicago: The University of Chicago Press, 1975.

[Kinney, Troy.] *The Etchings of Troy Kinney*. Garden City, New York: Doubleday, Doran and Company, Inc., 1929. Margaret West Kinney lists 50 Troy Kinney prints, to 1929.

[Kloss, Gene.] *Gene Kloss Etchings*, explanatory text by Phillips Kloss. Santa Fe, New Mexico: Sunstone Press, 1981. Lists 600 Kloss prints.

[Kuniyoshi, Yasuo.] *Journal of the Archives of American Art*, vol. 5, no. 3, July 1965, with a checklist of 47 etchings and 81 lithographs.

[Landacre, Paul Hambleton.] Anthony L. Lehman, *Paul Landacre: A Life and a Legacy*. Los Angeles: Dawson's Book Shop, 1983.

[Landeck, Armin.] June and Norman Kraeft, *Armin Landeck: The Catalog Raisonné of his Prints*. Bethlehem, Connecticut: June 1 Gallery, 1977.

[Lankes, Julius J.] "The Woodcut Record," unpublished manuscript catalog in collection of the Virginia State Library, Richmond, Virginia.

[Leighton, Clare.] . . . *American Sheaves, English Seed Corn* . . . . Boston: Boston Public Library, 1977. Exhibition catalog; more than 700 Leighton prints listed.

[Lewis, Martin.] Paul McCarron, *Martin Lewis: The Graphic Work*. New York: Kennedy Galleries, 1973. Exhibition catalog; lists 143 Lewis prints.

[Lozowick, Louis.] Janet Flint, *The Prints of Louis Lozowick: A Catalogue Raisonné*. New York: Hudson Hills Press, 1982.

[Marin, John.] Carl Zigrosser, *The Complete Etchings of John Marin*. Philadelphia: Philadelphia Museum of Art, 1969.

[Marsh, Reginald.] Norman Sasowsky, *The Prints of Reginald Marsh*. New York: Clarkson N. Potter, Inc., 1976.

[Matulka, Jan.] *Jan Matulka 1890–1972*. Washington, D.C.: Smithsonian Institution Press, 1980. Exhibition catalog published for the National Collection of Fine Arts and the Whitney Museum of American Art; with a checklist of 41 Matulka prints by Janet A. Flint, pp. 81–85.

[Nason, Thomas.] *The Work of Thomas W. Nason, N.A.*, edited by Sinclair Hitchings. Boston: Boston Public Library, 1977.

[Pennell, Joseph.] Louis A. Wuerth, *Catalogue of the Etchings of Joseph Pennell*. Boston: Little, Brown & Co., 1928.

——. Louis A. Wuerth, *Catalogue of the Lithographs of Joseph Pennell*. Boston: Little, Brown & Co., 1931.

[Reynard, Grant.] Harlan E. Knautz, *Grant Reynard, N.A.: An American Painter*. Berea, Ohio: Baldwin-Wallace College, 1974. Lists 105 prints by Reynard on pp. 114–117.

[Rosenberg, Louis Conrad.] Gail McMillan, *Catalog of the Louis Conrad Rosenberg Collection*. Eugene, Oregon: University of Oregon Library, 1978.

[Ruzicka, Rudolph.] *The Engraved and Typographic Work of Rudolph Ruzicka: An Exhibition*. New York: The Grolier Club, 1948. 182 Ruzicka prints listed on pp. 25–30.

[Sheeler, Charles.] Martin Gordon, "A Catalog of the Prints of Charles Sheeler," in *Photo/Print Bulletin*, vol. 1, no. 2, fall–winter 1976. New York: Martin Gordon, Inc.

[Sloan, John.] Peter Morse, *John Sloan's Prints: A Catalogue Raisonné of the Etchings, Lithographs and Posters*. New Haven, Connecticut: Yale University Press, 1969.

[Soyer, Raphael.] Sylvan Cole, Jr., *Raphael Soyer: Fifty Years of Printmaking 1917–1967*. New York: Da Capo Press, 1967.

[Ward, Lynd.] *Storyteller Without Words: The Wood Engravings of Lynd Ward*. New York: Harry N. Abrams, Inc., 1974.

[Weidenaar, Reynold.] The Weidenaar number—53—given for *Home from the Forest*, pictured in this book, is the number given this print by the artist himself in an unpublished numbered list of all of his prints.

[Wengenroth, Stow.] Ronald and Joan Stuckey, *The Lithographs of Stow Wengenroth, 1931–1972*. Boston, Massachusetts: Boston Public Library in cooperation with Barre Publishers, 1974.

——. Ronald and Joan Stuckey, *Stow Wengenroth's Lithographs: A Supplement*. Huntington, N.Y.: Black Oak Publishers, 1982.

[West, Levon.] Otto M. Torrington, *A Catalogue of the Etchings of Levon West*. New York: William Edwin Rudge, 1930.

[Winkler, John.] *Etchings, Drawings and Boxes by John W. Winkler*. San Francisco: The Achenbach Foundation for Graphic Arts, 1974. Exhibition catalog; lists 90 Winkler prints on pp. 8–24.

[Wood, Grant.] Joseph S. Czestochowski, *John Steuart Curry and Grant Wood: A Portrait of Rural America*. Columbia, Missouri: University of Missouri Press, with the Cedar Rapids Art Association, 1981. "Graphics of Grant Wood: A Catalogue Raisonné" on pp. 208–209.

ABOUT THE AUTHORS

June and Norman Kraeft are codirectors of the June 1 Gallery in Bethlehem, Connecticut, which specializes in American prints of the first half of the twentieth century. Noted researchers in the field, they have written *Armin Landeck; The Catalog Raisonné of his Prints* (1977) and a series of four articles on American prints for *Graphics* magazine (1979). They have cooperated in the preparation of museum exhibitions of the work of Samuel Chamberlain, Armin Landeck, Martin Lewis, Louis Lozowick, Doel Reed, the Regionalist Big Three (Benton, Curry and Wood) and other American printmakers. The Kraefts have lectured widely on American prints: at the Dallas Museum of Art, Georgia Museum of Art, Los Angeles County Museum of Art, Montgomery Museum of Fine Arts, Wichita Art Museum, and before the print clubs of Philadelphia and San Diego, among others.

At their June 1 Gallery the Kraefts mount five exhibitions featuring American prints and printmakers yearly, preparing and publishing an illustrated catalog for each show. They also write and publish *June 1 Jottings*, a newsletter devoted to American prints, six times yearly.

The Kraefts take special pleasure in rediscovering and putting forward the works of worthy printmakers of the first half of our century, feeling that too many fell into undeserved neglect during the decades when Abstract Expressionism rode high.